British town planning and urban design

About the author

Dr Eleanor Smith Morris completed an honours undergraduate degree in Architectural Sciences at Harvard University, a Civic Design Diploma at University College, London; a Master in City Planning degree at the University of Pennsylvania; a PhD at the University of Edinburgh, and is a member of the American Institute of Chartered Planners and the Royal Town Planning Institute. For many years in the former Department of Urban Design and Regional Planning, she is currently Faculty Lecturer in Environmental Planning in the Institute of Ecology and Resource Management and Academic Director, Centre for the Study of Environmental Change and Sustainability, University of Edinburgh. She has written for BBC television and numerous town planning and architectural publications and lectured extensively abroad; is a Past Chair of the Royal Town Planning Institute Scotland and currently on the Executive Committee, National Trust for Scotland.

British town planning and urban design

Principles and policies

Eleanor Smith Morris

LONGMAN

Addison Wesley Longman Limited
Edinburgh Gate, Harlow
Essex CM20 2JE
England

and Associated Companies throughout the world

© Addison Wesley Longman Limited 1997

First published 1997

ISBN 0-582-23496- 4

British Library Cataloguing-in-Publication Data
A catalogue record for this book is available
from the British Library

Library of Congress Cataloging-in-Publication Data
A catalog entry for this title is available from
the Library of Congress

Set by 4 in 9/11pt Times and Melior
Produced by Longman Singapore Publishers (Pte) Ltd
Printed in Singapore

To the memory
of
my cousin, Lucy Norton, OBE
and
my father, Lawrence Meredith Clemson Smith, MA (Oxon.), LLB (University of Pennsylvania),
OBE, Légion d'Honneur

Contents

Preface

This book is based on the lecture series which I gave from 1972 onwards at the University of Edinburgh, entitled the First and Second Ordinaries, traditional Scottish nomenclature for survey courses, for first- and second-year undergraduate students. The First Ordinary Urban Design and Regional Planning was attended by students from the Faculties of Arts, Science, and Social Science, while the Second Ordinary Urban Design and Landscape Studies was for architects, civil engineers, and geographers.

Readers may notice that even though I have spent over 30 years in Great Britain, there are moments of an 'offshore' vision. I have drawn on my architectural education at Harvard University and the Harvard Graduate School of Design, where I attended classes by Siegfried Giedion, Reginald Isaacs, Edward Sekler and Jose Luis Sert and studios with Serge Chermayeff and Jacqueline Tyrwhitt. Although Walter Gropius had long retired, he would occasionally tour the studios to teach us 'the Gropius method'. Following Harvard, I completed the Civic Design Diploma at University College London under Sir William Holford. Our 'ginger' group, which included John Ross and Michael Dower, persuaded Sir William to give us special seminars. During the day I joined Arthur Ling's planning department at the London County Council, working in the East End Reconstruction Area group (Stepney, Poplar, Hackney) under Percy Johnson-Marshall, which included Jim Amos and Walter Bor. On returning to the United States to complete my Master's degree at the University of Pennsylvania, Steen Eiler Rasmussen gave a memorable course to a group of us including my classmate, Denise Scott-Brown.

My first years at Edinburgh University were in the Department of Architecture, under Sir Robert Matthew, followed by the Department of Urban Design under Professor Percy Johnson-Marshall. My long association with the Royal Town Planning Institute (Scotland), culminating in the Chairmanship (1986–87), brought me into constant contact with everyday practice, while my PhD was subjected to Sir Robert Grieve's tough scrutiny.

'Pedestrian Streets and Spaces in Britain' was first given at an International Conference on Urban Design, University of Pennsylvania, Philadelphia, in 1979. The Association of European Schools of Planning provided the opportunity to present 'The Bêtes-Noires of Prince Charles', first given as a public lecture in the Department of Fine Art, Edinburgh University, then later in Tours, Aachen and Philadelphia. The discussion of 'London in Competition with Paris and Berlin' began in a joint Aesop–ACSP Conference lecture at Oxford, and was then presented at the 1992 Institute of British Geographers' Conference, Swansea, later being published in the book *Building a New Heritage: Tourism, Culture and Identity in the New Europe* (London: Routledge, 1994). All these strands are brought together in this book.

Eleanor Kenner Smith Morris
Academic Director, Centre for the Study of
Environmental Change and Sustainability,
Institute of Ecology and Resource Management,
University of Edinburgh, Edinburgh, 1997

Acknowledgements

A number of people were extremely helpful in discussing their ideas and giving support, and I would like to thank everyone whose interest and time helped me to complete this book. The individuals include Anthony Coon (Centre of Planning, University of Strathclyde), Hugh Crawford (Sir Frank Mears & Partners, architects), Professor Barry Dent (Institute of Ecology and Resource Management, Edinburgh University), Dr Ulrich Loening (Centre of Human Ecology, Edinburgh University), and Professor Colin Whittemore (Institute of Ecology and Resource Management, Edinburgh University). The two publishers, Vanessa Lawrence, publishing manager, and Sally Wilkinson, publisher, were very patient and the two editors, Tina Cadle and Sally Potter, very helpful.

One of my Master's students in the former Department of Urban Design and Regional Planning, Patrick Akindude, worked faithfully in the early stages and throughout gave unstinting help. The students and colleagues who did the drawings, including my son, Houston Morris (at the Architectural Association, London), are listed separately and have my great appreciation. My secretary, Margaret Bilsborough, was invaluable.

Finally my greatest appreciation goes to my husband, James Morris (Academician, Royal Scottish Academy; Morris and Steedman, architects), who gave me unfailing support and urged me on to the completion of the book.

Drawings and diagrams were drawn for this book by:

Ziad Alamedine	Chapter 2
Alison Grant	Chapters 1, 2, 3, 4, 5, 8, 9, 10, 11, 12 and 15
Houston Morris	Chapters 1, 2, 3, 4, 5, 6, 7, 8, 9, 10, 11, 13, 14 and 15
Amran Abdul Raman	Chapters 2, 3 and 4

We are grateful to the following for permission to reproduce copyright material:

Addison Wesley Longman for tables 2.1 and 2.2; Routledge for table 12.2; UCL Press Ltd for tables 15.4 and 15.5; the *Architect's Journal* for figures 1.29, 3.3, 13.3, 13.6, 13.10 and 13.11; *Country Life* for figure 2.9; Professor Curl for figure 2.20; the Architectural Press for figure 3.16; North Lanarkshire Council for figure 6.15; the Commission for New Towns for figures 7.9, 7.14 and 7.15; Colin Buchanan & Partners for figures 7.16 and 7.17; Architectural Review for figure 9.15; Venturi, Scott Brown & Associates Inc. for figure 13.9; the Academy Group Ltd for figure 15.6.

Sadly we were unable to trace the copyright holders of figures 2.3, 2.17, 2.19, 2.21, 7.1, 8.27, 12.2, 12.3, 13.2, 13.4, 13.5, 13.7, 13.12 and 13.13, and would like to take this opportunity to apologise to any copyright holders whose rights we may have infringed.

Introduction

This presentation of the evolution of British town planning takes the physical planning approach, as against a social, economic or policy planning approach. Historically, planning in Britain originated from within physical planning, from the organic creations of the medieval period through the brilliant manifestations of the eighteenth century to the development of the garden city. Mainly in the last 50 years, social, economic and policy planning have come to the fore, but always underpinned by physical planning implementation. The argument as to which approach should predominate will probably never be resolved. The physical planners will argue that a plan for an area is a predominantly physical process which, in its development, pays attention to but is not dominated by current economic and social forces. The policy planner will argue that a plan for an area should reflect economic and social forces and be contingent upon their correct interpretation. This presentation takes the former point of view.

Physical planning can be defined as the process for physically developing an area in terms of its three-dimensional form and physical functioning. The physical plan is influenced by the various social and economic determinants but the end results are physical entities on the ground. Latterly the physical plan has reflected the public interest, as against other interests, and indeed this reflection is one of the great contributions of British planning, but historically the public interest was quite often ignored in favour of the aristocratic, ecclesiastical, ruling class or entrepreneurial interest.

Policy planning emphasises the needs of preferences of the population using the place. Most often policy planning will attempt to redress social inequity by the systematic redistribution of resources, and again the British planning system is admired for its relatively successful policy planning within a physical planning system. In the last 50 years the impact of economic planning on Britain's planning system has seesawed with each different political party in government to such an extent that no clear pattern has emerged, although more economic planning has taken place than did before the Second World War.

A number of definitions of planning will help to illustrate how difficult it is to define planning. Sir William Holford wrote:

> 'The function of planning is the orderly drawing together of all the threads that determine the shape and colour and character of our physical environment, so as to create a pattern of design which is pleasing and effective and which corresponds to that inner sense of fitness and wholeness which has always been part of the spirit of progressive man.' (*Holford, 1950: V*)

A later definition, illustrating the changing perceptions of town planning, is that of E.A. Powdrill:

> 'Town and Country Planning … many definitions of this term … almost every thinking planner has his own ideas, and that is as it should be. To lay down a precise meaning for it is to limit in some way its scope for the individual.
>
> My own acceptance of the term is somewhere within the doctrine of utilitarianism, which holds that the sole end of public actions should be for the greatest good for the greatest number … this begs the question of 'What is the greatest good?' but since it is rarely defined one is never quite sure when one has reached it and so may keep on striving; and in my view that is as it should be.' (*Powdrill, 1975: 3–4*)

The professional attitude of the Royal Town

Planning Institute reinforced its concern with the physical environment of town and country but at the same time indicated that the process of physical planning should be related to the process of corporate planning. More recently the RTPI spoke of achieving an improved environment which enhances our day-to-day lives and quoted Sir Patrick Abercrombie's desire of achieving 'the maximum of health, safety, convenience, prosperity and enjoyment for everyone' (*RTPI, 1989*).

More technically, Bruton explained that 'The problem we face daily by the practising planner is that of integrating vertically oriented national sectorial policies with horizontally oriented land use and management programmes at the local level in an environment constrained by basic secular trends, conflicts of interests amongst groups, the values, attitudes and standards of the different interest groups, and the immediate circumstances' (*Bruton and Nicholson, 1987: 51*).

Physical town planning in Britain has evolved from historical bases over a period of approximately 2000 years of urban development, from the Roman period to the early medieval towns, progressing through the Elizabethan age of regulations and the rebuilding of London, to seventeenth and eighteenth century geometric planning. This long-range view is in direct contrast to those who believe that contemporary town planning came about primarily to cure the evils of the Industrial Revolution. Town planning is a term that belongs not only to the twentieth century but also to previous centuries. The methodical and visual placing of people and buildings on land is the art and science of town planning, and encompasses far more than mere town building.

Town planning in Britain has experienced several golden ages – those of the medieval towns and of the grand urban designs of Georgian London, Bath and Edinburgh, and most recently following the Second World War up to 1974. There is every likelihood that a new golden age of planning will occur with the advent of the third millennium. Viewing the evolution of town planning with an historical perspective allows one to retain the visionary aspects of planning as against documenting only the minutiae and legislative changes of the current planning world. The broad historical perspective also tends to underline the understanding the British people have of planning. Hence this book will open with a brief review of the historical ages of town planning in Britain before surveying the evolution of contemporary town planning.

Part I

Historical Background

1 Historical background

Roman inheritance and the founding of Romano-British towns

The Romans, coming to Britain first in 55 BC under Julius Caesar, were superb civil and military engineers, building systems of fortification, roads, bridges and water supply, of town planning and town building, of drainage and of central heating for cold climates which were not bettered until the nineteenth century. The colonising methods used by the Romans throughout their empire concentrated on three main aspects concerning physical changes to the environment (*Benevolo, 1980: 135–251*):

1 The creation of infrastructure, such as bridges, roads, lines of fortifications and aqueducts
2 The division of agricultural land into farmed units
3 The foundations of new towns.

The industrial and commercial life of Roman Britain depended not only on sea and river transport but also on the Roman roads, which were better aligned and better made than any that would traverse the island for another 1400 years. However, the economy of Roman life was based on slavery, and when Rome ceased to conquer, the slave population could not be maintained and the economy suffered. By the third century AD, there was commercial decline and the consequent decay of Romano-British towns. In the fourth century, the defensive dykes were threatened by the Anglo-Saxon invaders; by the fifth century the dykes were mostly destroyed and after 400 years the Romans left Britain in AD 410. Roman Britain had also become a Christian country.

Nevertheless the Romans in Britain had such a profound influence, particularly on certain cities, that it is important for the planner or urban designer to be conscious of the Roman inheritance in understanding the framework of certain cities. Further, since the Ancient Monuments and Archaeological Areas Acts 1979, there has been a wave of public enthusiasm for archaeological foundations which the planner ignores at his peril. In the Roman world, the concept of the town was synonymous with the city-state, in which cities ruled their hinterland, as a single constitutional unit. Thus, in the Roman Empire, the important towns were administrative centres as well as being trading towns. In Britain it was difficult for the Romans to impose such a pattern as the existing community did not generally have a tradition of living together in permanent towns and so the factors causing the Roman settlements in Britain were varied.

The main period of town building lasted from 55 BC to AD 150, and many towns took several generations before there appeared the recognisable features of a Roman town including forum, basilica and baths in a gridiron pattern (*de la Bédoyère, 1992*). Two main types of Roman town were built – the *coloniae* and the *civitates*. A first-class Roman provincial town was a *colonia*, a self-contained legal town created by colonies of retired soldiers settled on land. Colchester, Lincoln, Gloucester and York were the four coloniae (figure 1.1). (London was not a true colonia but was given honorary colonia status at a late period of the Roman occupation.) Each retired soldier was allocated a piece of land within and outside the town. The soldier would enjoy the benefits of Roman urban life and would support his family, and, at the same time, the government could rely on him as a trained resource who set a romanified example to the conquered barbarians.

The more common types of town were the *civitates*, a formalised development of the existing tribal groupings, consisting of 1000 to 2000 people (figure 1.2). The civitates were populated only by the native

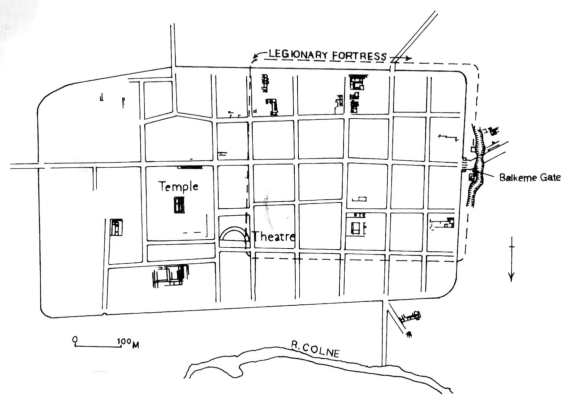

Figure 1.1   Plan of the developed colonia at Colchester (after de la Bédoyère)

population, who were hardly ever granted the status of Roman citizens. Examples of these second-class towns, or 'citivates', are Canterbury, Winchester, Chichester (indeed, all the towns ending in 'ester', such as Leicester, Alchester, Irchester, Dorchester), Aldborough, Caerwent, Bough on Humber, Caister St Edmund's, Ancaster, Mildenhall, Mancetter, Horncastle and Hardham. A *municipium* was a local centre of local people promoted to the rank of honorary colonia and given a regular municipal constitution. Only one municipium was allowed in Britain, Verulamium, now St Albans, Hertfordshire, although London eventually achieved municipal status.

Agricultural land was divided into a grid of main roads and secondary roads. The main roads (*documani*) ran parallel to the longest side of the territory while the secondary roads (*cardines*) were shorter and ran at right angles to the main roads. The two principal axes of the roads, the *documanus maximus* and the *cardo maximus*, were wider than the other documani and cardines and crossed at a point that was considered to be the ideal centre of the colony. It was particularly propitious when the two territorial axes coincided with the two axes of the town, so that roads leading out into

the country from the town were a continuation of those into the town. Examples of this are often found in Britain, as in Rochester.

Thus Roman towns, laid out in geometrical lines, are viewed as an urban application of the original agricultural grid and a standardised version of the Hippodamian gridiron system practised by the Greeks (*Benevolo, 1980*). The difference in scale between the urban and agricultural grids meant two distinct concepts, with the urban grid being more flexible and variable than the agricultural grid. In sloping sites, as at Lincoln, the major roads (documani) were arranged horizontally, and the lesser roads (cardines) followed the line of the steepest inclines (figure 1.3). In York, the two documani, the *via principalis* and the *via praetoria*, survive as the medieval streets of Stonegate and Petergate. In Chester, Eastgate Street is the Roman *via principalis* and Northgate the *via documana*. The grid consisted of a series of rectangular or square 'city-blocks' or 'islands', known as *insulae*. The blocks of buildings were square or rectangular and measured between 70×70 and 150×150 metres. Central blocks contained the forum and other public buildings.

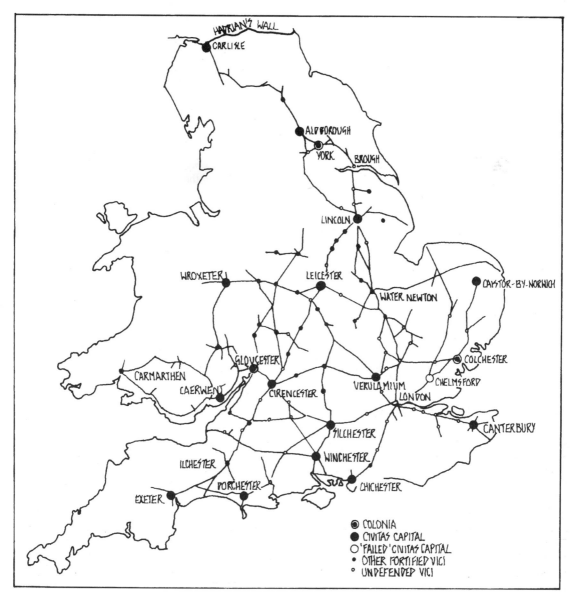

Figure 1.2 Map showing the distribution of towns in Roman Britain (after Carter)

The components of the town were (a) the forum with shops; (b) a basilica – the municipal centre placed at the highest point; (c) public baths; (d) a water supply for the baths and fountains, to supplement the private wells; (e) temples; and (f) a theatre (after AD 125), or (g) an amphitheatre outside the walls, with seats banked up from which thousands could watch the games. There was considerable unbuilt space – gardens; there were public buildings and some shops but little industry: the evidence points to administrative and residential towns. In the smaller towns, the insulae were not packed with urban housing, in the manner of the Romans, but were occupied by small country villas, with substantial gardens. Sir Patrick Abercrombie called these towns 'garden cities'. (*Bell and Bell, 1972*). This practice, despite the Romans, demonstrates one of the strongest themes in all British town planning. From the dispersed Romano-British *oppida* to the King's Green of Winchester, the allotments of Port Sunlight and the suburbs and garden cities of the twentieth century, the great passion of the British has been for gardens and parks.

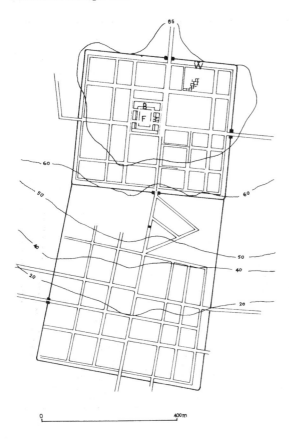

Figure 1.3 Lincoln town plan, showing two distinct parts of the settlement with the main centre at the top of the hill overlying the former legionary fortress. The basilica (B) sits in the forum (F); W marks the site of the water cistern which supplied the public baths. The Romans could only adapt to the steep gradient by using diagonal streets, as contoured streets were not their style. The contours show the steep slope upon which the inner town was built (after de la Bédoyère)

Unfortunately, no Roman public buildings in Britain remain totally intact. Excavations in London near Cannon Street have revealed traces of an enormous basilica and a monumental terraced complex, which included a garden with a park and a large hall (figure 1.4). At Lincoln and Caerwent, little survives except for the rear wall of a basilica. Triumphal arches too were used to make an architectural statement of power as well as symbolising the entry point into a town, as at the Balkerne Gate at Colchester (still standing), incorporated into the city walls as the west gate. Traces of theatres have been found in Colchester, Worcester, Silchester, Canterbury, Cirencester and London. Bath houses were entirely new to the British population. Although the Roman soldiers considered

bathing a necessary activity, the British were less enthusiastic. Leicester still contains one wall of its bath houses and remains of the drains. Likewise running water and drainage were regarded as important civic amenities of an organised Roman town. York's sewers are the best known and preserved, while the wells and fountains at York, Catterick and Corbridge still can be seen.

London, unlike Colchester (a colonia) or Verulamium (a municipium), had no official status at first but developed as a trade and communications centre, despite the official policy to found towns elsewhere, and consisted of 140 hectares, with some 200–500 people per hectare, or 50,000 inhabitants. It still bears traces of the grid system of documani and cardines in the City of London. The road network suggests a primary site suitable for development as a port with a bridge (now London Bridge) to the islands of Southwark.

Two roads were laid out parallel to the river on the northern side of the Thames connected by a road which went down to the bridge. At the centre of the grid was the site of the forum (AD 100–150). It had massive walls which enclosed over 300 acres, now mostly in the City of London, and was the hub of the road system. The perimeter, protected by defensive walls, was normally of rectangular shape and enveloped by a solid block of buildings. Fortification and four gates at each end of the main streets were normally important components. But in Britain, the defensive town walls mostly were built later. Only in the coloniae were the defensive walls part of the original town.

Urban decline in Roman Britain

By the third century AD, fewer public buildings were being built and the emphasis appears to have been on urban defences. Disorder in Rome and continual wars on all frontiers contributed to the economic decline. Although London had become the seat of government, Britain was divided into two provinces, each with a governor and a capital city. London remained capital of Britannia Superior while Britannia Inferior was ruled from York, which had become a superior colonia. Further divisions meant that Cirencester and Lincoln also became important minor capitals. The urban defences form the most conspicuous remains of Roman towns surviving today. The south wall and bastions of the third and fourth century defences at Caerwent are said to be the best preserved urban defences of any Roman town in Britain. Other examples exist at Aldborough, Gloucester, Lincoln,

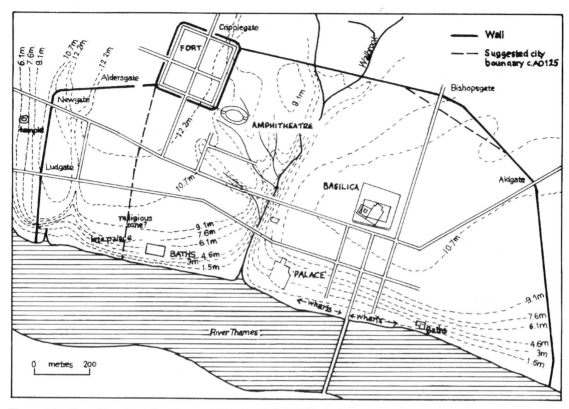

Figure 1.4   Plan of London (after Clout and Wood, and de la Bédoyère)

Winchester, Chichester, and the western gate of London (Newgate).

Roman town life more or less disappeared in the fifth century. Tribal incursions from northern Britain from the fourth century onwards hastened the disintegration. By the end of the fourth century the Romano-British were abandoned by Rome and had to fend for themselves. Many Romano-British town defences evaded wholesale demolition while the buildings did not, which suggests that the wall defences were needed. The rise of Christianity meant new buildings but very often the new churches were built on or out of temples of the Roman period. St Augustine established himself in the Roman St Pancras, Canterbury; in London, the church of St Peter on Cornhill lies in the middle of the Roman basilica. At York, the headquarters building of the fortress lies under the Cathedral Minster.

Present-day designers need to respect the possible Romano-British origins of Christian churches and other public buildings as the medieval Christians did themselves, as many Roman towns survived the Dark Ages and re-emerged as major settlements in the medieval period.

Effects of Roman Britain on current planning decisions

Very little of the original Roman Britain remains, save a wall here and a wall there. What does remain clearly in some large towns and many small towns is the framework of the Roman plan, which was reinforced in the medieval period and left in place by the Georgians. The Roman framework gave an ancient structure to the town and a sense of historical continuity. The question for all planners is: do they respect this framework by protecting it through Conservation Areas or do they obliterate it because the scale of the Roman/medieval framework is too small for modern-day buildings?

An example of such a dilemma is found in the city of Winchester (*Curl, 1983: 992—993*). The Roman walls of the civitates were constructed towards the end of the second century AD. In the medieval period, walls were superimposed on the Roman walls, and parts of the medieval wall survive almost intact. The medieval street patterns within the walls preserve very closely the Roman pattern with the single cross street and the rectangular grid.

Despite the designation of the whole of the medieval

area within the walls as a conservation area, a Local Plan (*Winchester City Council, 1983*) suggested that large sections be torn down to make way for parking, museum, hotel and office complexes, including the destruction of the Romano-medieval North Wall area for housing. In the opinion of many, this was a disastrous suggestion as large areas of the old city still preserved the scale and character of the historic Romano-medieval town centre. In the proposal, the North Wall was to become a four-lane highway, which would have involved the demolition of many houses of considerable character, obliterated the traces of the Roman and medieval city wall, destroyed the medieval city ditch, flattened the remains of the medieval North Gate bridge, and moved part of the Roman earth bank probably built by Vespasian.

The choice was clearly between maintaining the Romano-medieval Conservation Area or surrendering the city to the motor car. Road building, in this case widening the Roman street pattern, would have given short-term relief at best, but would have wrecked the town of Winchester in the process. Driving major roads through the centre of historic cities was a discredited solution, which luckily the townspeople rejected.

Another example of a Roman inheritance affecting current planning is Cirencester, where the original Roman plan of grid pattern streets, two roads crossing in the middle with the central space inhabited by the forum (figure 1.5), was overlaid with medieval, seventeenth and eighteenth century houses, and the forum by the Abbey (*Wright, 1977: 135*). The first stage of the Roman conquest of this part of Britain set up a frontier line along the military road, the Fosse Way, which to this day enters straight into the town. Cirencester became, during the period AD 70 into the fourth century, the second largest town in Roman Britain, five times larger than Gloucester, and under the Emperor Diocletian in the fourth century AD, the provincial capital of a subdivision of Britannia Superior. The town walls were strengthened and faced with stone to protect a population of 5000 people. Only the bare infrastructure of this once great Roman town remains, but what does remain should be preserved. Cirencester was more apposite by keeping excessive through traffic out of the centre with its 1976 by-pass.

Rochester, Kent, is a Roman and early medieval town whose High Street was part of the Roman Watling Street, which ran from Dover to North Wales (*Cornforth, 1985a: 1672–1675*). The city was a defensive site in Roman times and much of its history has been influenced by the layout of the Roman fortifications, thought to have been constructed in the third century AD. The Romans enclosed an area of 10 hectares (23 acres), with walls which were incorporated into the medieval defences, and developed Rochester as one of the principal stages on the main route to London, as Rochester provided one of the few river crossings that was defensible. Subsequently, the Augustinians built the cathedral and the castle within the Roman fortifications. Rochester, through town schemes and Conservation Areas, has been successful in preserving its character.

The City of London has probably been the most tortured Roman city site (*Cornforth, 1990: 50–52*). Comparing the map of Londinium's original fort with its gates and defensive walls built in AD 120 with the 1520 siting of the medieval walls, it can be seen that the medieval walls were directly imposed on the Roman walls, and that Silver Street and Wood Street are the central crossing roads of the original Roman plan. The unexpected discovery of the site of a Roman amphitheatre to the east of Guildhall helps to explain the curves of Old Castle Street and Aldermanbury and how it had determined the site of the fifteenth century Guildhall, which rests on the amphitheatre site. The shape of London was dictated for 1000 years by the great Roman wall of Kentish ragstone, built before AD 200, which protected the City of London area, from Blackfriars to the Tower of London and north-west up to the fort. In summary, Roman layout has dictated the framework of many English towns and it would be insensitive if an urban designer ignored the facts derived from the Roman influence.

Legislation to protect archaeology

Growing interest in the archaeological basis of towns culminated in the passing of the Ancient Monuments and Archaeological Areas Act in 1979, which consolidated all previous Acts, mainly the 1953 Historic Buildings and Ancient Monuments Act and the 1972 Field Monuments Act, and was a watershed for archaeology in Britain. Over 12,000 scheduled monuments in Britain were protected by this Act, which gave greater protection than before to the list of Scheduled Ancient Monuments, but more importantly allowed the Secretary of State or the local authority to designate Areas of Archaeological Importance, listed for the first time, with the idea of providing facilities for the investigation and recording of archaeological resources prior to development. The Secretary of State or local authority declares an area within, for example, York, Chester or Canterbury to be an area of archaeological importance. Development is then subject to detailed control and is allowed on the

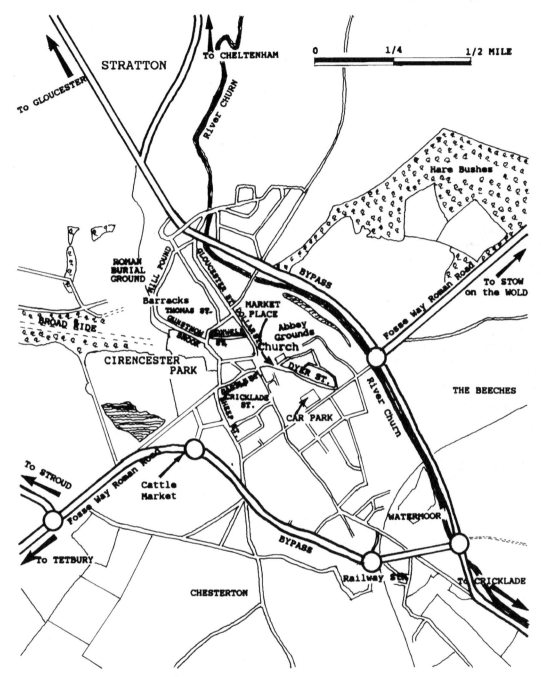

Figure 1.5 Plan of modern Cirencester showing by-pass around Roman town (after Wright)

approval of the local authority by an 'operations notice'.

Such areas are protected from development operations which either disturb the ground, cause flooding or involve tipping. The investigating authority can enter the threatened site and excavate it for a statutory period of several months. For example, under York there are many archaeological deposits, some of them 30 feet in depth, such as the Jorvik Viking village, discovered in excavations. Colchester, Lincoln and Gloucester are also particularly susceptible to archaeological designation.

The Ancient Monuments and Archaeological Areas Act was subsequently amended by the National Heritage Act 1983, which abolished the Historic Buildings Council for England and the Ancient Monuments Board for England, and established in its place the Historic Buildings and Ancient Monuments Commission (called English Heritage) and greatly increased its power. Similar mergers were made for Wales and Scotland.

A great many surveys have shown far more ancient monuments and sites than were suspected. With such information, planning authorities can incorporate archaeological constraints into the planning process. The conflicting demands of archaeological preservation versus central area development have to be carefully balanced in today's plans. Sites in agricultural areas are less threatened.

Medieval towns and village settlements

British medieval towns have similar social, economic and political contexts to those in most other European countries, which have been effectively explained elsewhere (*Morris, A.E.J., 1994: 92–156*). After the collapse of the Roman Empire in the fifth century, urban life virtually disappeared in Britain until the eleventh century, when political stability and trade allowed Roman-based towns to revive, boroughs to convert to market towns and small villages to become towns. Accordingly, there are five broad categories of European medieval towns, based on the classification of their origin from the eleventh century (Norman) to the sixteenth century (Tudor/Elizabethan) (*Morris, A.E.J., 1994*). The organic forms of towns which grew gradually over the centuries include:

1 Towns of Roman origin
2 Boroughs or bourgs, founded as fortified military bases and acquiring commercial functions
3 Towns that evolved through organic growth from village settlements.

The other two categories are of planned new towns which were established formally at a given moment in time, with full 'urban status' and a predetermined plan, built as a single undertaking over a period of five to ten years:

4 Bastide towns (Winchelsea, Kingston upon Hull)
5 Planted towns (Londonderry, Cullen).

Generally the building of the medieval town was organic, unplanned and without an aesthetic order. The towns grew as their functions demanded. Organic growth towns developed from their original village settlements, which numbered 13,000 English villages in existence on their present sites at the time of the Domesday Book survey of 1086 (figure 1.6). England had become a country of villages as a result of settlement by the Anglo-Saxons, who laid out their villages at regular intervals to suit agricultural needs. For example, in Northamptonshire 53 villages, recorded in the Domesday Book, give an average distance between villages of 1.2 miles. These villages were of two kinds – the enclosed village (i.e. surrounding a common) and the linear village along the roadside (*Sharp, 1968*). The enclosed village consisted of the common (triangular, rhomboid or irregular) surrounded by houses with gardens behind. A single church dominates the geographical high point. The linear village stretches on both sides of the road with housing.

The medieval village became a town when it acquired a commercial function – that of a market town. In Scotland, only towns designated by the King were allowed to become market towns (Edinburgh, Musselburgh, Aberdeen, etc.). Towns of Roman origin were large: York had 8000 people, Lincoln and Norwich each had 6000, and Ipswich had 3000 people (figure 1.7).

A thorough definition of the medieval town is 'the result of the interrelationship of the following six aspects: economic structure (market and trade); social structure (craftsmen, merchants, clergy, aristocracy); physical structure (town plan, public buildings, fortifications); legal aspects (constitution, legal organs, local government); situation (land, waterways, bridges, halting and reloading places), and political vitality. A medieval town should exhibit most of these characteristics'.

Bastide and planted towns

The Norman conquerors of Britain realised the usefulness of urban settlement in conquest and control, and therefore created 'plantations' to control the English. In the first decades after the Conquest 90 castles were built, generally with settlements built adjacent to the castle. Three-quarters of all the 40 towns begun between 1066 and 1140 were castle towns (*Bell and Bell, 1972*). Examples remaining today are Hastings, Windsor and Trematon (Cornwall), although hardly anything remains of these original plantations except the street pattern, as at Bury St Edmunds. Gradually the castle towns changed to commercial plantations, such as Dunstable and Stony Stratford located on the Roman road.

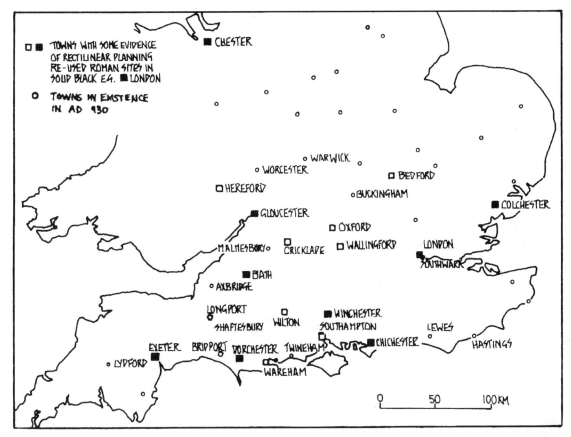

Figure 1.6   Towns in existence in AD 930 which became Domesday boroughs (after Biddle, in Carter)

Thereafter, for two centuries, mostly commercial plantations were created. Henry II contributed charters and liberties to existing foundations for cash. Kings Richard I and John created possibly a further 40 plantations, including Liverpool, Portsmouth, Stratford-on-Avon and Leeds. Cornwall ended with 38 new towns, of which 19 were new plantations. Cambridgeshire was ringed with 20 plantations, including Newmarket, King's Lynn, Chelmsford and Dunstable, but the county itself had no plantations but simply three organic towns.

Henry III's reign saw the founding of eleven Welsh bastides, founded in order to suppress the Welsh. None of them became important and few had any great plan. Their charm lies in their manifestations of a time warp, as they remained in use over the centuries without being overwhelmed by later growth. Edward I was a great town builder, in addition to being one of England's greatest kings. He built over 40 new plantations in England and Wales (and over 50 in France) in order to maximise his revenue to sustain all his campaigns. His French experience of building

bastides, or new towns, came to him before he ascended the throne. All of them were based on markets, tolls and taxes rather than on defence. He built only two completely new English foundations, Kingston upon Hull and Newton (Dorset); all the rest were reconstructions of existing foundations as in New Winchelsea and Berwick.

Edward's greatest legacy is also in Wales, where he built a chain of urban forts and 30 adjoining towns. All were designed to combine strategic defence and long-term anglicising dominance, as at Bangor and Caernarvon. Edward employed architects, masons and proper foremen, realising that town building was a civic art and needed expertise. None of the buildings survive, but, in terms of urban design, the layout in these towns remains essentially as they were originally. After Edward, at the end of the thirteenth century, there was a sharp reduction in the number of new towns, as Wales and France had been conquered. Coleraine and Londonderry (1610) were founded by James I, but the great royal town building era was over.

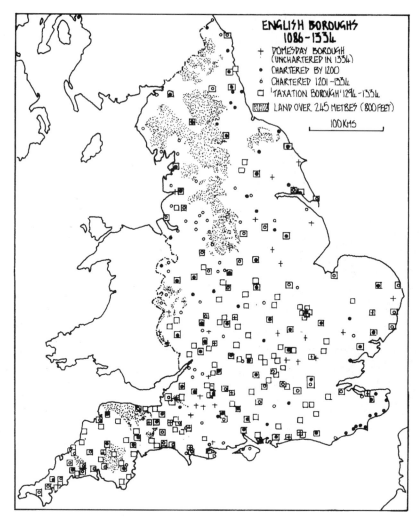

Figure 1.7   English boroughs, 1086–1334 (after Donkin, in Carter)

Design of the medieval town

British medieval towns tend to look alike as regards most visual details. Local vernacular architecture is the same in organic towns as in planned medieval towns. The component parts of medieval towns are normally the wall, with its towers and gates; the market place, possibly with a market hall; the church and its own public space; and the general mass of town buildings and related private spaces (figure 1.8).

The wall

The most complete medieval wall still to be seen in existence is the wall at York; yet pieces of wall remain in many British towns. As England became increasingly peaceful, the military necessity for protection by a wall was less necessary, and by the fourteenth century walls were being used as customs barriers protecting the tradespeople within and exacting a toll on those outside the wall, as at Norwich.

The street

Movement in medieval towns was largely by foot and transport of goods was by pack animal. Hence the street pattern was dictated by the quickest route from market place to the gate in the wall, and took routes which were most convenient to the pedestrian. The result was a complex pattern of little irregular lanes which united public and private spaces, cathedral and market place. There was no formal communication pattern, but rather a web of organically evolved lanes.

Figure 1.8   York, The Shambles, medieval street (by the author)

soon lost their functional usefulness with wheeled traffic, in many cases the market place was large and flexible enough to survive today. Several types of market place were created: first, where the market occupies a square to itself, normally located at or near the centre; secondly, where it occurs as the widening of the main street; thirdly, as lateral expansion of the main street; and fourthly as squares at the main gate (*Morris, A.E.J., 1994*) (figure 1.11). It was customary then to force the road to go through the market and hence enliven the trade of the townspeople, leaving today a legacy of bottlenecks in hundreds of villages because no medieval borough wished to be by-passed. It is an urban design feature that the market square is entered obliquely, i.e. no road enters or leaves in a straight line, forcing the shopper to hesitate and therefore conduct commerce (*Cullen, 1961*).

In planned towns, the market square was part of the gridiron structure in the centre, as at Monpazier, France, whose successful arcades were hardly repeated in Britain. Sometimes the market square included a market hall. In most cases the market square was of an irregular shape, many-sided, and seemed to be formed accidentally, because the function of the buildings surrounding the square took precedence and the open space was the residual space (*Zucker, 1959*). In the twentieth century, the medieval market square has enjoyed a revival with barrow stalls, flea markets and various promotions. Colourful stalls add marvellous urban variety and give great interest to the street scene, but can cater only to peripheral shopping interests.

The church square

The square in front of the medieval church was the place where worshippers gathered before and after the service and where processions were organised and mystery plays performed. In Britain, the church was also accompanied by its own burial ground, although in most minor city churches the burial ground has disappeared. English cathedrals created their own precincts, called closes, for the chapter house, the Bishop's palace and other ancillary functions, providing a green oasis of peace to this day (figure 1.12). Scottish cathedrals remained part of the urban parish.

Later, narrow passageways would form off the street, providing access to minor streets or courtyards. The City of London is a good example of these little passageways, as is Edinburgh's medieval town, whose closes (passageways) form a fishbone pattern from the spine of the medieval High Street, and St Andrews (figures 1.9 and 1.10).

There was also a tendency for buildings to encroach over the streets with bridges or upper floors projecting out over the street. The resulting medieval scene was informal, organic and full of surprises, which produces its charm. At the same time, some of the medieval towns were crowded and therefore insanitary, but surprisingly most still had gardens and orchards within the walls, as was the case in Edinburgh's medieval town.

The market place

The market place was the most important public space in the medieval town. Unlike the narrow streets, which

Housing

Generally, English medieval houses were of two or three storeys as at York and Lincoln (figure 1.14). In Scotland, housing followed the French pattern of flats in tenements, and in towns like Edinburgh, built on

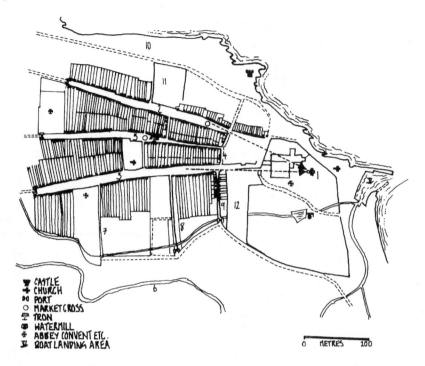

CASTLE
CHURCH
PORT
MARKET CROSS
TRON
WATERMILL
ABBEY CONVENT ETC.
BOAT LANDING AREA

0   METRES   100

Figure 1.9   Plan of St Andrews, twelfth century. 'The growth of the burgh was guided by a perfect sense of urban culture, one of the most distinguished medieval plans' (after Naismith: 28)

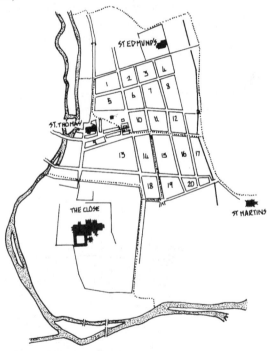

Figure 1.11   Plan of Salisbury, Wiltshire, founded 1209. The plan shows the 20 groups of buildings and the medieval city, the market place (M) and the four churches. The cathedral and close are to the left (after Benevolo)

Figure 1.10   St Andrews, Fife, Scotland (after Tibbalds)

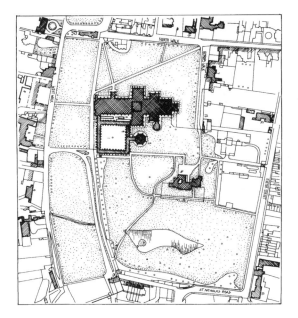

Figure 1.12 Detail of Salisbury Cathedral Close (after Benevolo)

slopes, the medieval tenements are mini-skyscrapers up to ten or twelve stories high. The size of the house plots in the planted towns was typically 24 × 72 feet, set in a gridiron pattern (*Burke, 1976*), whereas the shape of house plots in the organic towns was less regular and resembled the cultivated strips in the fields beyond: long and narrow with frontages barely 10 feet wide and depths of 100 feet or more. In Scotland, these strips were termed 'riggs', wide enough for a horse and plough to turn, as in Newlandrigg, Midlothian.

The medieval town today

To the urban designer, understanding the medieval origins of a town explains the context of many of the public spaces and thus gives a clue as to how they should be treated. From the conservationist point of view, the urban designer should conserve rigidly the original buildings in their entirety. In certain cities and towns such as York, Oxford, Cambridge, Windsor, Chester and Edinburgh, the medieval core is so well preserved and so powerful that the conservationists' view must prevail (figure 1.13). York, the most complete medieval town in Britain, had its Roman plan overlaid with an organic growth street pattern, although there is a remnant of the Roman cross axis. The Normans developed York, which by 1377 had a population of 11,000 people, as their northern capital.

York avoided the nineteenth century Industrial Revolution and the consequent commercial prosperity and industrial growth, and thus retained almost the full extent of the narrow historic streets and the complexity of a medieval town. York still has (1) its medieval walls, (2) its market place, (3) its cathedral and public space, (4) its lesser churches and their public spaces, (5) its organic street pattern and (6) its castle and many medieval buildings, all of which are conserved and enhanced in their medievality.

To the urban planner faced with modern demands, the issue is more of resolving the modern demands compatibly with restrictions of old buildings. The few concessions made to modern buildings should require infilling of buildings to the same scale, preservation of the street pattern, and priority to the pedestrian and amenity over the service vehicle and the car park, which should be kept at a distance.

Figure 1.13 Windsor, Berkshire: medieval skyline (after Tibbalds)

Figure 1.14   York: medieval housing (after Tibbalds)

Renaissance and Georgian towns

Britain was slow to adopt the new Renaissance style, so fervently espoused in Italy from 1419 onwards. Indeed in the fifteenth century, English builders were still creating Late Gothic Perpendicular masterpieces, such as King's College, Cambridge (1446), St George's Chapel, Windsor (1481) and Westminster Abbey, London (1503–19). The Renaissance in Britain in the visual arts, painting and sculpture was preceded by the creation of a new intellectual climate based on the growth of literacy and scientific humanisms. Sir Thomas More's *Utopia* came first, projecting an ideal city (*Hiorns, 1956*). More pictured hygienic and well-arranged cities, with open spaces, gardens, water supply, drainage, clean and pleasant streets in a predetermined form, set well apart from one another. In his Utopia, satellite towns were founded when they were needed.

Once the painters and sculptors from Italy had arrived in England, then the new architecture and urbanisation followed, although about 100 years later than in France. Scotland, on the periphery of Europe, embraced the Renaissance 50 years later still, with the building of Holyrood Palace (1671). In Britain, the first Renaissance building, the Banqueting Hall in Whitehall, was completed in 1621 by Inigo Jones, who went on to create the Queen's House at Greenwich (1635). Inigo Jones is considered to be the first English architect to understand the principles of Renaissance design and the originator of Renaissance urbanism in England (*Summerson, 1966*).

In the centuries since Roman rule, London's original grid plan, still visible in the layout of the City of London (figure 1.15), was gradually submerged and expanded by the organic growth pattern of the medieval centuries. By the eleventh century, the kings had moved their residence from Winchester to Westminster and it was only a matter of time before the land between Westminster and the original City of London was developed and the combined urban area became the London as we know it today. London grew not just by natural population growth but also by a continuous drift of population to the capital, causing urban overcrowding and decay, culminating in the plague of 1665, which killed an estimated 90,000 people. It was to prevent such a disaster that Queen Elizabeth I proclaimed in 1580, 'strictly command all manner of persons ... to desist and forebear from any new buildings of any house or tenement within three miles of any of the gates of the City of London' (*Rasmussen, 1937: 67–69*).

The first major urban development was at Covent Garden in 1630, by the architect Inigo Jones. Covent Garden was to be a total residential development with identical terraced houses surrounding a piazza which included the Church of St Paul (figure 1.16). Later a vegetable market opened in the piazza with permanent stalls eventually built in the early nineteenth century. As the district became unfashionable, parts of the terraced housing were demolished but enough remains to show the structure of the first Renaissance development, famous now as the home of the Royal Opera House. Further attempts to develop Renaissance squares occurred at Lincoln's Inn Fields, begun in 1613 and completed by 1657.

Wren's plan for London

The 1666 Fire of London, the second great disaster, occurred the year following the plague, destroying a total of 337 acres (about 80 percent of the city) and 84 churches, and making 80,000 people homeless (*Bell and Bell, 1972*). As it was necessary to rebuild London as quickly as possible, Charles II asked, principally, John Evelyn to prepare plans, but also others, including Christopher Wren. Evelyn and Wren produced similar plans for the rebuilding of London (although Evelyn's were less grand), as they had similar ideals on town planning (*Sekler, 1956*) (figure 1.17).

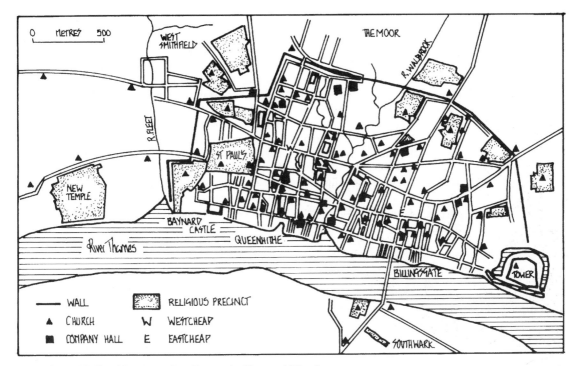

Figure 1.15   Medieval London (after Clayton, in Clout and Wood)

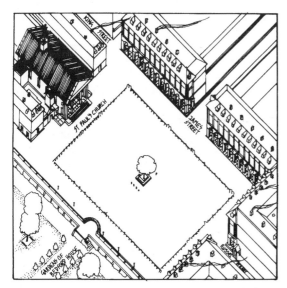

Figure 1.16   Covent Garden, St Paul's Church and Piazza (after Summerson)

Both Evelyn's and Wren's plans spoke the language of Renaissance design – piazzas, triumphal avenues, interlocking urban spaces, tensions created by magnificence and resolved by dramatic punctuation, all following the rules of Rome as explained by

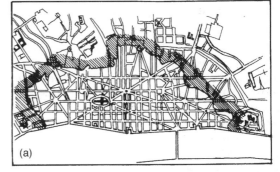

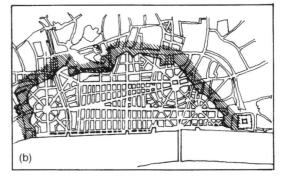

Figure 1.17   London: plans for rebuilding the city centre after the Great Fire, as proposed by (a) Evelyn and (b) Wren (after Benevolo)

Vitruvius, the Roman architect-engineer in the time of Caesar and Augustus, whose *Ten Books on Architecture* influenced architects for 2000 years (*Vitruvius, 27 BC; Bell and Bell, 1972; McKay, 1978*). Wren's plan particularly exhibits Renaissance objectives: '(1) The entrances to the town were its gates and bridges; (2) that a town is composed of rectangular houses; (3) that all street corners should preferably be rectangular; (4) that the entrances should give easy access to the different parts of the town (by broad avenues); and (5) that the centre of commerce, the Stock Exchange, and the religious centre, St Paul's, should have a dominating position' (*Rasmussen, 1937: 74*).

The most imposing piazza was sited in Fleet Street, completing a vista which began on the steps of St Paul's Cathedral, and set itself in a triangular space, united by an axial avenue to the Stock Exchange with small streets opening into other squares. Although in parts of the plan the grid still remains, in the areas to be rebuilt the plan is totally Renaissance. In those areas, Wren attempted self-contained vistas of many streets and intersections, focusing on the many churches, which Wren himself designed and rebuilt. Evelyn's plan had far more piazzas (18) while Wren's plan had six. The merits of Wren's plan were based on the initial connection of important points, the broad streets and the generous spaces allowing for building space, and the removal of the tiny medieval streets, which encouraged disease.

However, Wren's plan was rejected in favour of rebuilding exactly on the street lines as before. Some consider Wren's brilliant plan for London as one of the greatest missed opportunities in urban history: 'the opportunity for generous roads and spaces and much hygienic gain was neglected' (*Hiorns, 1956: 287*).

Mumford attributes the failure of Wren's plans to jealous property rights and the unsuitability of the plan for the trading merchants of the City (*Mumford, 1961*). In the eyes of mostly foreigners, if the plan had been adopted, London would have ranked as one of the great town planning examples, along with Paris, Washington, DC, and parts of St Petersburg and Helsinki (*Hiorns, 1956: 287; Sekler, 1956*). It would have been an international architectural masterpiece and a place of pilgrimage. In the British view, neither the climate nor the British temperament favours piazza life: the warm pub is more favoured than the pavement cafe (*Bell and Bell, 1972; Morris, A.E.J., 1994*). The piazzas would eventually have been deserted and the City would have become dehumanised. The British favour the intimacy of the neighbourhood and Wren's plan was too grand and might have suffocated the ordinary man in the street.

In the event, neither Wren's nor Evelyn's plans were accepted. London was rebuilt according to the Rebuilding Acts of 1667 and 1670, as a restatement of the old streets with a few new routes, standardised street widths and building regulations concerning the height (no more than four storeys), thickness of walls and the controlled size of floor and roof timbers (figure 1.18). The elevations were to be of either brick or stone, with most of the housing in brick and the public buildings in stone.

The greatest legacy of the 1665 plague and 1666 fire towards creating beautiful urban development, in addition to St Paul's, was not the rebuilding of London, but the impetus it gave for the nobility and the wealthy to leave London and develop new housing estates to the west. Here was created the English square, defined as 'a green park formed by architecture' (*Zucker, 1959*),

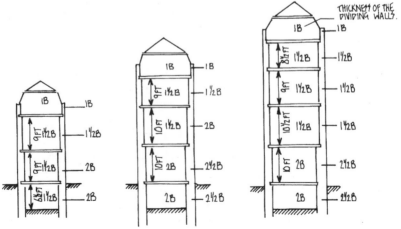

Figure 1.18 London: regulations governing the reconstruction of houses, as laid down by the law of 1667 (after Benevolo)

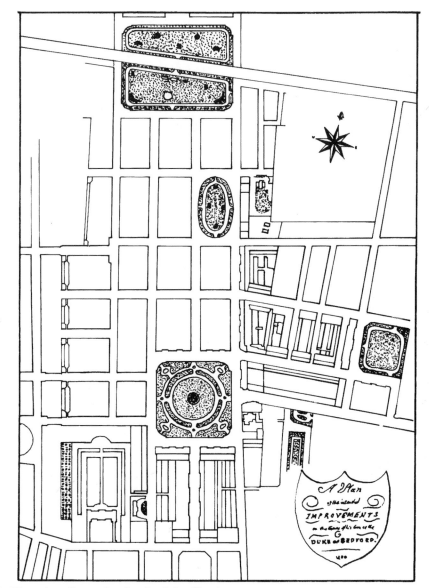

Figure 1.19   Bloomsbury Estate plan, London (after Olsen)

creating that feeling of '*rus in urbis*' the countryside in the city, allowing its inhabitants to enjoy one of the most civilised ways of living in a high-density city. The development of the London square with its architectural character of unity, with dignified houses and surrounding a green oasis of peace, was based on three principles, according to Sir John Summerson (*Summerson, 1946*): (1) the principle that the aristocratic landowner had his own house in the square; (2) the principle of a complete unit of development, comprising square, secondary streets, market and sometimes a church; and (3) the principle of the speculative builder, building the houses.

Thus were developed the great estates to the west of London for the upper and middle classes. Originally the squares and their surrounding streets had simple layouts, on the gridiron principle. Gradually the figure of the square gave way to circles ('circuses') and ovals (crescents) in the late eighteenth and early nineteenth centuries. These squares (discussed in minute detail elsewhere) include Bloomsbury Square, St James's Square, Soho Square, Red Lion Square, the Mayfair Square, the squares north of Oxford Street (Portman, Cavendish, Fitzroy, Portland Place) and countless lesser examples (*Olsen, 1982*) (figure 1.19).

Significantly, all these private developments represented piecemeal additions to the growth of London. The overall effect had been to add new neighbourhoods to the city, without losing the continuity of the city feeling. The only negative aspect to the building of the great squares was that there were not the grand avenues to connect the squares or the new sections of the city. Thus true town planning on the larger scale had not been implemented, only the market forces and, luckily, beautiful taste to accompany it. However, all these squares were the precursor to the later Georgian work of John Nash (1752–1835) and his development of Regent's Park and Regent Street.

Bath and Edinburgh

The three major cities of Renaissance urbanism are London, Bath and Edinburgh. But many other cities contained fragments of Georgian Renaissance development, such as Bristol, Buxton, Brighton and Newcastle. Bath began as a Roman spa and retains today various Roman legacies including the Roman Baths, where one may still bathe! However, Bath's greatest architectural period was during its eighteenth century entertainment heyday. Beau Nash (1704) made Bath into a social centre, enforcing rules of etiquette and elegance which attracted the eighteenth century aristocrats for whom the buildings were created. The two most famous architects were John Wood the Elder (1700–54) and John Wood the Younger (1727–81), both sponsored by Ralph Allen, owner of large stone quarries and Bath's richest citizen. The Woods created a series of designed spaces which together provide some of the most elegant urban developments in Britain (figure 1.20). Starting with Queen Square, John Wood was lucky enough to be architect, contractor and estate agent all in one. Queen Square is dominated by the palatial composition of the northern elevation, with the eastern and western sides stepping down in conformity to the sloping ground, creating a forecourt to the composition of the northern side. The houses are of different sizes within an overall composition whose single elevations hold the disparate houses together. He gave complete freedom to the designs of the interiors but demanded strict adherence to his exterior design (*Ison, 1948*).

The sequence of spaces followed from Queen Square up Gay Street into the (King's) Circus (figure 1.22). Here a total of 33 houses form three equal-length segmented elevations of 11, 12 and 10 houses respectively (*Morris, A.E.J., 1994*). Pevsner describes the King's Circus as Wood's most monumental urban

Figure 1.20   Plan of Bath (1810) with buildings remaining shown in black (after Tibbalds)

space (*Pevsner, 1995: 129*).

John Wood the Younger continued his father's work with another street linking to the equally famous Royal Crescent (1765–67). Here the one-sided crescent sits on the undulating land, looking out over the park with such beauty that it is considered also one of the most beautiful urban designed spaces. But, unlike Queen Square, which is totally urban, Royal Crescent makes that statement of the '*rus in urbis*', the countryside in the city, which is the unique British approach to urban design (figures 1.21 and 1.22). The houses, which make up the Crescent, are behind the strictly controlled elevational design. Lansdowne Crescent followed, in a still more baroque form, with the elliptical form undulating to suit the contours of the land (figure 1.23).

Queen Square and the Circus marked the Palladian Georgian style, which Bath helped to spread all over Britain for the next 80 years (figures 1.24–1.27). The principles on which Bath was built were principles of grandeur and beauty for the visitor, but not for the residents' convenience. The inhabitants had to conform to the demands of elevational control. But the Woods' work turned Bath into a definitive statement as to how cities should be built. The beauty and the resultant publicity all helped to make Bath successful – both at the entertainment level of Assembly Rooms, Pump Rooms, hotels and lodging

Figure 1.21   Royal Crescent, Bath (by the author)

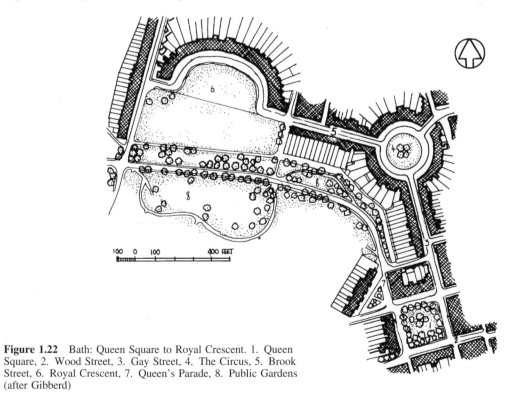

Figure 1.22   Bath: Queen Square to Royal Crescent. 1. Queen Square, 2. Wood Street, 3. Gay Street, 4. The Circus, 5. Brook Street, 6. Royal Crescent, 7. Queen's Parade, 8. Public Gardens (after Gibberd)

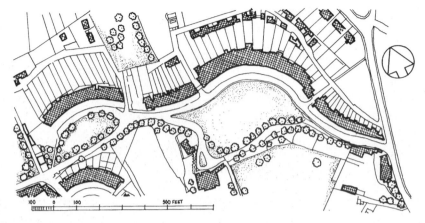

Figure 1.23   Bath, Landsdowne Crescent (after Gibberd)

Figure 1.24   Terraced housing in Bath in Georgian era (after Summerson)

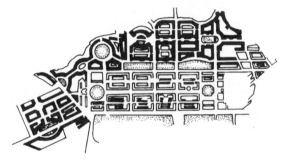

Figure 1.25   Edinburgh New Town showing (in black) the later extensions planned under the influence of Woods' work in Bath (after Summerson)

houses, and also at the highest artistic level. Bath provided an example of urban style which was later emulated in London, Edinburgh and the lesser resorts of Brighton, Buxton and Weymouth (*Bell and Bell, 1972*).

Edinburgh's New Town, consisting of at least five Georgian developments, stands miraculously intact and is a major reason why Edinburgh is considered to be one of the most beautiful towns in Europe (figure 1.25). In 1766, Edinburgh Town Council organised a competition for the layout of their New Town to be developed across the loch away from the crowded and dirty medieval town (*Youngson, 1966*). The competition was won by a young architect, James Craig, whose scheme consisted of three parallel major streets (Queen, George and Princes Streets) with the principal middle street, George Street, closed at each

end by a square (St Andrews and Charlotte Squares) (figure 1.26). The scheme was designed as a self-contained residential suburb, and not envisaged as the business centre that it is now.

Since further development was not foreseen, neither of these squares was provided with direct east or west access to the surrounding countryside. This has proved a blessing in terms of the preservation of the New Town but a present-day nightmare in terms of traffic. The two other principal streets were designed as terraces with Princes Street looking south to the Castle and the Old Town, and Queen Street looking north over the fields to the Firth of Forth. Although attempts were made from time to time to build on the south side of Princes Street, luckily these were stopped, thus preserving one of the most famous urban promenades protected from the northern winds, basking in the sun, overlooking the gardens of the drained loch, with the miniature Castle and jagged outline of the medieval skyline laid out before one's eyes. It is one of

Figure 1.26   Edinburgh's Georgian New Town, Charlotte Square (by the author)

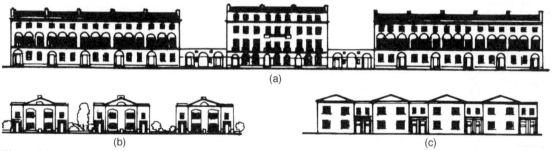

Figure 1.27   Three types of Georgian housing development: (a) linked terraces, (b) semi-detached houses, (c) quasi-semi-detached houses (after Summerson)

Scotland's touristic jewels and the threat in the 1990s is that it may be relegated to Disneyland status for the benefit of the tourists.

None of this was in the minds of the eighteenth century developers who built houses in conformity to the plan. Designs for Charlotte Square were prepared by Robert Adam and the north side was built conforming to them, but following his death, the church, which closed the New Town vista, was completed by Robert Reid in 1814. A second New Town was created with the layout of the ground immediately to the north of Queen Street Gardens by Reid and Sibbald in 1802. Its design is similar to the first New Town – a principal central street (Great King Street) with open spaces at either end with narrower streets and mews in between. Although the houses still had to conform, one great difference from the first New Town is that each block was treated as a single

architectural composition, as was done in Bath (*Lindsay, 1948*).

A third development was the layout of Calton Hill by Playfair in 1819. A fourth New Town was developed at the west end of Princes Street, although it was not completed until the end of the nineteenth century. The fifth and final magnificent scheme was the layout of the estate of the Earl of Moray. The design was no longer gridiron squares but in the baroque manner, consisting of an octagonal circus (Moray Place), an oval (Ainslie Place) and a crescent (Randolph Crescent), giving a magnificent kaleidoscopic experience as one progresses from one to the other. The impressive elevations are heavier than those of the earlier New Town, but as they were to be houses of Edinburgh's leading citizens (and have so remained), the grandeur of the elevations was considered appropriate. Many individual public

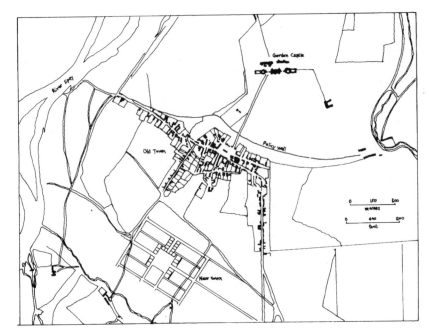

Figure 1.28 The lost town of Fochabers and its planned successor (after Adams)

buildings (churches, monuments, academies, galleries, etc.) were also built, all adding to the magnificence of Georgian Edinburgh (*Lindsay, 1948; McWilliam, 1984*). Luckily, when Edinburgh was attacked in the 1960s by office developers, the ever-watchful citizens fought vigorously and saved Georgian Edinburgh for posterity.

Planted and tied towns

One small segment of British Renaissance urban design, before the coming of the Industrial Revolution, was the development of the eighteenth century planted town or town tied to its landowner, such as Harewood, belonging to the Earl of Harewood. Town building history in the eighteenth century is full of aristocrats enriching their estates by planting tied towns in places which suited them. Well described elsewhere (*Bell and Bell, 1972; Naismith, 1989*), these tied towns included projects such as those of the Marquis of Stafford at Helmsdale and of the Earl of Elgin at Charlestown, Lowther in Westmorland, Blanchland in Northumberland, Harewood in Yorkshire and Milton Abbas in Dorset. The highlands of Scotland are full of these tied towns, built on Georgian urban design lines, such as Inveraray, Argyll, rebuilt by the Duke of Argyll; Fochabers in Morayshire by the Duke of Gordon (figure 1.28); Dufftown by the Earl of Fife, and many

others. Altogether there were over 150 new planted towns in Scotland in the Georgian period, 1745–1845 (*Adams, 1978*). Many further English tied towns were created in the nineteenth century such as the Blaise hamlet, designed by John Nash. Wales had so many planted towns that some argue that there are practically no modern Welsh towns which are not plantations in origin (*Bell and Bell, 1972*). These include the castle towns, the ports, the resorts, and the great market towns down to the New Towns of the twentieth century.

Thus, when the reformers of the Industrial Revolution created new towns for their workers, they were simply following a well-established tradition of creating tied towns. This tradition expanded into the Garden City movement, which in turn led to the New Town movement, when the concept was adopted by government and the local authorities with the creation of New Towns following the Second World War. When the post-war New Towns came to an end in the 1990s, almost immediately there sprang up counter-proposals for the creation of over 200 new urban villages.

Although the type of builder changes from century to century – from the King (medieval) to aristocrat (eighteenth century) to industrialist (nineteenth century) to high-minded citizens (early twentieth century) to government-appointed development

Figure 1.29 Patronage (from Hellman, reproduced by kind permission of the *Architect's Journal*)

corporations (mid-twentieth century) to entrepreneurial developers (twenty-first century) – the tradition of new town building ever continues (figure 1.29).

Summary

Britain is blessed with a long history of town planning from the Romans to the Georgians. Much of each historical period, Roman, medieval, Renaissance and Georgian, remains to give infinite variety and beauty. Although, in one's youth, one is apt to think there are too many historic buildings preventing the creation of exciting new forms, as one matures the collective power of so many beautiful buildings juxtaposed and still being used as part of daily life is thrilling and very reassuring. The continuity of town planning history becomes a mainstay of a civilised life.

2 The industrial slum and model industrial towns

The Industrial Revolution and its effect on urban conditions

Modern town planning in Britain began as part of the reform movements concerned with health and sanitation measures to overcome the adverse effects of the Industrial Revolution. Historically, town planning in Britain had other origins such as the social organisation roots of the medieval towns and the architectural roots of the Georgian town. But, although contemporary town planning in Britain also developed social and architectural roots, its origins lie with the health reforms considered necessary to overcome the evils of the Industrial Revolution.

In Britain, the Industrial Revolution has been defined as that period of events happening between 1770 and 1840 (*Kitson, 1965*), whose manifestations can be summarised in four categories (*Briggs, 1968*). Firstly, the development of inventions caused a change in industry from a hand-powered domestic decentralised manufacturing process to an industrial process which developed mechanical power for centralised manufacturing. Secondly, manufacturing towns emerged at the locations of the new centralised manufacturing processes with the consequent growth in population as people moved from country to town. Thirdly, appalling social conditions occurred from the side-effects of the new manufacturing processes and the tremendous growth in population. Thus, the Industrial Revolution was a great catalyst for social and economic change. With the emergence of new inventions and new machines, the existing way of life was completely changed, and major cities became the exciting yet problem-ridden conurbations whose problems are still being experienced today. Fourthly and finally, continual

reforms were required to overcome the legacy of the Industrial Revolution. The effects of these four categories of the Industrial Revolution were not restricted to the period from 1770 to 1840. For instance, many of the inventions and changes in manufacturing processes had started before 1770 and many of the results of the Industrial Revolution remained long after 1840, indeed to the present day. But the main impact of the social and economic changes occurred in that period.

The industrial reasons for the cause of the Industrial Revolution in Britain are considered to be the development of new powered machines for the manufacture of goods and their application to transport and communication. The first of the new inventions was the steam engine; this was followed by the railway train, then by the horse car, the electric tram car, the underground railway, and finally the automobile.

In 1765, Watt developed the steam engine so that mechanical power could replace hand operation. The early Georgian mills in Manchester, for example, had depended on water power, but the later mills depended on steam power, which worked best in large concentrated units, with the manufacturing plant no further than one-quarter of a mile away from the steam plant. The more units there were, the more efficiently the steam power worked. In place of a single small mill beside a little river providing water power, the new steam plant could provide power for larger mills and, even better, several mills working off the same steam plant. The single mill by the river might employ 100–200 people. A dozen mills off a steam plant meant the beginning of a small town. Thus the spiral began: production power was increased, the number of goods produced multiplied, the number of workers increased, and the factory town was born. The steam engine itself was not complicated; rather complications arose from the use of the steam engine as a prime generator for production. The steam engine changed the scale of operation and made it possible to concentrate large numbers of workers and industries in a location. As a secondary consequence, the worker was removed from his rural setting.

The causes and effects of the Industrial Revolution were more pronounced in Britain than elsewhere. Many historians agree that the reasons for this pronounced effect are as follows (*Briggs, 1968*):

1 the great political and financial stability within Britain;
2 the freedom from invasion and warfare which, for instance, France and Germany never had;
3 the greater mobility of labour: for example, the agricultural population were not serfs as in Russia or 'tied' peasants as in France;
4 the accessibility of capital for investment in the new industries;
5 the physical advantage of Britain as an island, which gave an easy communication system plus the availability of many navigable rivers;
6 the availability of iron and coal, which provided the vital resources for the industrial expansion;
7 the marvellous inventiveness of certain Scottish engineers, which created the machinery.

In contrast, industrialisation in France was delayed until the mid-nineteenth century, due to her participation in military campaigns, major wars and her crippling internal tax system.

The inventions produced the machines. Consequently, the factories in which the machines were used attracted workers away from rural areas and rural industries, encouraging urban population growth in cities. Once the worker was removed from his rural background, the machine started to dominate the worker, his job, his house, his home, his children. The factory became the magnet and all life was subordinated to the hungry machines.

There is some discussion as to whether the first result of the Industrial Revolution, that of the change in manufacturing processes, caused the growth of population or whether the growth of population stimulated the expansion of industry. The population, growing as rapidly as the industrial output, has increased faster in the last 200 years than it ever has before in all history (figure 2.1). For example, England and Wales experienced enormous increases in their population between 1750 and 1900 (tables 2.1 and 2.2).

Major cities showed substantial population increases in the first half of the nineteenth century. For instance, Bradford in the ten-year period 1821–31 had an 81 percent increase in population, from about 37,000 to 67,000, while Manchester and Birmingham had 273 percent and 348 percent, respectively, population growth between 1801 and 1851 (table 2.2).

On the one hand, the growth of industry generated an improvement in the standard of wealth and health of a great many people, causing a lowering of the death rate and thus an increase in population. On the other hand, countries in Western Europe were also noted to have substantial population growth but without the dramatic Industrial Revolution which occurred in Britain. The impact of the two major factors of the Industrial Revolution, expanding population and industrial growth, provided an intertwined cause-and-effect relationship throughout the period on Britain's towns and countryside.

Table 2.1 Population of England and Wales, 1801–1901 (millions) (from Greed, 1993. Reprinted by permission of Addison Wesley Longman Ltd)

Year	Total population
1801	8.9
1851	17.9
1901	32.5

Table 2.2 Urban growth, 1801–1901 (from Greed, 1993. Reprinted by permission of Addison Wesley Longman Ltd)

Year	Population		
	Birmingham	Manchester	Leeds
1801	71 000	75 000	53 000
1851	265 000	336 000	172 000
1901	765 000	645 000	429 000

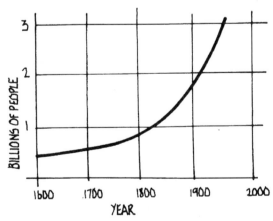

Figure 2.1 World population growth, 1600–1950 (after Spreigregen)

Transport

The greatest inventions were in the field of transport. The steam engine was developed into the railway engine and railway trains followed. Within a short period of time the railways spread a thick network of railway lines, railway sidings, duplicating stations, water towers and signal boxes, providing a better communication system. After the development of the railway, the horse-car was introduced into London in 1829, having been invented in Paris in 1818. By 1885, the electric tram car replaced the horse-car and became the principal means of urban transportation. The tram car persisted, as in Glasgow, where trams remained in use until the early 1960s.

Each new method of communication – the railway, the horse-car, the tram car – increased traffic congestion in town centres, adding another dimension to the problem of congestion and overconcentration of population. On the positive side, in the late nineteenth century, the railways promoted the growth of suburbs, allowing some people to escape the congestion of the central city. Tram cars also extended into the suburbs, relieving some population congestion, but not enough to solve the total city congestion problem. With the railway came more smog and soot in the cities, leaving British cities with an air pollution problem.

The ingenuity of the Victorian engineers made them create further inventions to better the previous ones. When the railways and the tram cars were seen as insufficient to cope with traffic problems, the underground railway, first built in 1863, was introduced into London in an attempt to solve the traffic problems. But the underground railways attracted even more people. As population increased (figure 2.2), the physical extent of cities spread, and improvements in transport intensified concentration in the urban centres.

Daimler first applied the internal combustion engine to a motor vehicle in 1884, and Benz built the first automobile in the following year. Thus the Victorians contributed a great benefit to city development by inventing the automobile, but one which, at the same time, acted as a catalyst for population decentralisation from cities.

Social and economic conditions: the industrial slum

The factory town produced the industrial slum. The factory appeared, the railway line spread its network of tracks to the factory, and the houses were built on the left-over land. All urban life was sacrificed to the

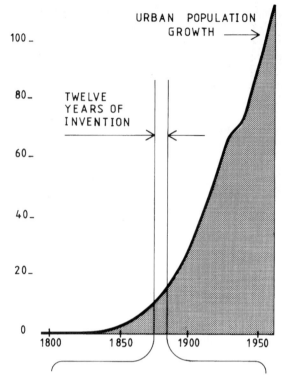

Figure 2.2 Urban population growth and inventions (after Malt)

requirements of industrial production. The workers were poorly paid, and accompanying this urban poverty came the slum (*Mumford, 1938*).

The typical slum of the factory town in England was the two-storey terraced house with a small backyard, or the two-storey back-to-back with no yard and with narrow alleyways in between. The homes were small, with no sanitation or only outdoor sanitation, no ventilation, no heating, little light and the air polluted from the smoke and grime of the factory chimneys (figure 2.3). It is no coincidence that Karl Marx developed his thesis on the exploitation of the poor in 1847, after living in industrial Manchester. A description of the development of slums is found in Friedrich Engels' important study, *The Condition of the Working Class in England in 1844*, where he said (*Engels, 1971*):

> 'cottages were run up hastily in confined spaces with little or no access to light and air, in alleys, in rows, placed back to back, in folds and folds within folds, in the backyards of existing houses or what had been their garden.'

These urban cottages were tightly packed against the

Figure 2.3 A poor district in London situated amongst railway viaducts, from an engraving by Gustave Doré (1872) (from Benevolo, 1980)

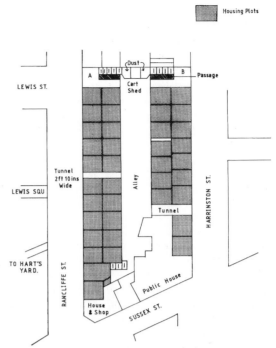

Figure 2.5 Slum layout (after Benevolo)

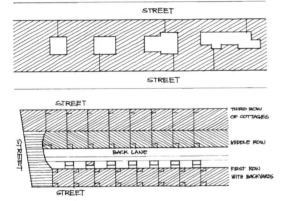

Figure 2.4 Details of new housing in Manchester, from sketches in Engels' book (after Benevolo)

factory. The need for a water supply for the factory sometimes meant placing these urban cottages on less useful land, at low ground level insalubrious for housing. The workers' cottages were built in large numbers, a dozen to sixty at a time. Behind the back wall of these cottages was a narrow alley called a back lane, which was enclosed at both ends. In this manner the back-to-back type of workers' cottages developed. The middle row of cottages was poorly ventilated without proper sanitation, attracting the lowest rent, and was considerably neglected (figures 2.4 and 2.5).

Stockport's Medical Officer described the conditions in Chadwick's 1842 *Report on the Sanitary Conditions of the Labouring Population of Great Britain*:

'Two houses placed back to back. There are no yards or outdoor conveniences; the privies are in the centre of each row, about a yard wide – over these there is a sleeping room. There is no ventilation in the bedrooms; each house contains two rooms – viz., a house place and sleeping room above. Each room is about three yards wide and four yards long. In one of these houses there are nine persons belonging to one family. There are 44 houses in two rows and 22 cellars, all the same size. The cellars are let off as separate dwellings; these are dark, damp and very low, not more than six feet between the ceiling and the floor. The street between the two rows is seven yards wide, in the centre of which is the common gutter into which all refuse is thrown; it is a foot in depth. Thus there is always a quantity of putrefying matters contaminating the air. At the end of the rows there is a pool of water very shallow and very stagnant, and a few yards further, a part of the town's gas works. In many of these dwellings there are four persons in one bed.' (*Chadwick, 1965*)

Though the effects of the Industrial Revolution were more pronounced in Britain than on the Continent, the slums on the Continent were often even more dense and more crowded. In Vienna the tenement blocks were four and five storeys high, with no sanitation and only narrow interior courts. Sadly, Scotland followed the custom on the Continent of five-storey tenements,

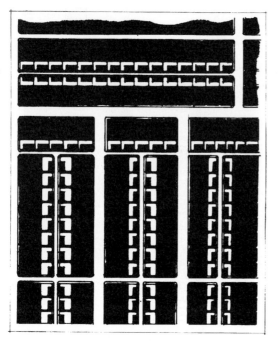

Figure 2.6 The Mechanical Slum built in accordance with the 1875 regulations; 'a desire to stretch the legal limits to their maximums led to an obsessive uniformity' (after Benevolo: 770)

such as Edinburgh's Arthur Street tenements, demolished in the 1960s, while most of the slums in Glasgow were also of this type. As Lewis Mumford explained in his famous description of Coketown, 'The seventeenth century European slum had been a picturesque slum – but the nineteenth century slum was a mechanical slum' (*Mumford, 1938*). Row upon row of monotonous slum dwellings occurred (figure 2.6).

All tenements had the common fault of excessive density. In 1870, the density of population in London was 265 persons per acre. Tenements, like the Peabody Trust Dwellings (1862), covered at least 90 percent of the land, and were highly profitable to the money-spinning Victorian entrepreneurs. By the mid-twentieth century, to replace any of these high-density Victorian dwellings was costly and difficult.

Great population growth need not necessarily have caused population congestion and the industrial slum. It was the combined effects of enormous population growth, the lack of adequate local administrative structure, such as local government, and the intense speed of development which combined to produce the urban environment of the industrial city (*Benevolo, 1970*). Nearly all the manufacturing centres of the

early nineteenth century developed from villages. Even Manchester and Birmingham, with populations in 1801 of 75,000 and 71,000 respectively, remained feudal villages administratively until 1838. A few towns, such as Liverpool, Leeds, Newcastle and Bristol, did have ancient city charters. But, on the whole, there was a lack of municipal government, and with it a lack of clear planning considerations. There was no thought given to the interrelationship of land uses, and consequently, unpleasant mixtures of land use occurred. Land uses lacked adequate planning and detailed layout, as the main desire was to obtain the highest densities.

The ad hoc mixture of land uses and high densities might not have been so disastrous if they had occurred slowly over a period of time. What caused the appalling situation in towns was the tremendous rate of growth of urban areas. At the same time it was not really clear from the census statistics whether the whole of Britain suffered from overcrowding because of this rapid urbanisation. It was thought that the overcrowding occurred only in the newly created slums (figure 2.7).

Results of overcrowding, poor housing and sanitation; legislation for public health

The main result from so much overcrowding, poor housing and lack of sanitation was an appalling high death rate in the cities from disease, though the average national death rate was decreasing. The deaths occurring from typhoid alone by 1848, the year of the Public Health Act, were as high as 564,681. The death rate was higher for the cities than for the countryside. For example, death rates were twice as high in the city of Manchester than in the country. But because of the relatively low death rate and less pronounced disease in the countryside, the ruling classes, who lived in the country, did not see the need for improving the health of the inhabitants of the manufacturing towns.

Up until the population explosion of the nineteenth century, cities had functioned on rather simple systems of drainage and sewerage. Natural draining effectively kept the streets clean, water was pumped and sewage disposed of. But the population explosion and the intensity of land use which occurred in the factory towns resulted in the need for whole new drainage systems. With each new problem, the Victorian entrepreneurs invented remedies, some of which were the building of public baths, the construction of new reservoirs and the laying of new sewers.

Artificial gas lighting was established in London in 1812 and by 1840 most of London's streets were lit.

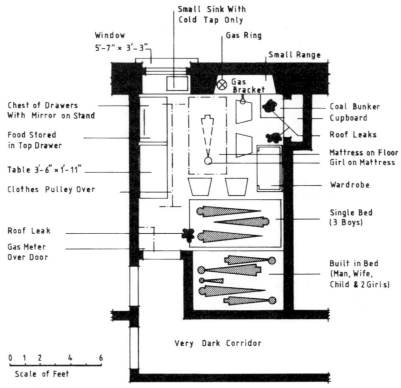

Figure 2.7 Glasgow – example of one of the many one-room dwellings, in this case 9 ft 6 in wide by 10 ft long, plus bed-recess, used for a family of nine (discovered in Glasgow, 1948). Such dwellings still existed in Dalry, Edinburgh, in the 1970s (after *RIBA Journal*, in Benevolo)

The first generating plant for London's electricity was built in 1882, and from then on electricity replaced gas for street lighting. In fact, utility services advanced further in the nineteenth century than in all past history. But at the same time the actual working and living conditions of the people sunk to a very low standard.

It was left to a few socially conscious people, such as Sir Edwin Chadwick, Secretary of a Government Committee, to initiate reforms. Chadwick argued that the cost of preventing disease would be lower than the price society paid for disease. His famous *Report on the Sanitary Condition of the Labouring Population of Great Britain* in 1842 led to the setting up of the Royal Commission on the Conditions of Towns (1844), which led to the Public Health Act of 1848, the first Public Health legislation, and to later legislation controlling by-law housing. In the first Sanitary Report, Chadwick wanted to create a desire for change by showing the appalling nature of the existing situation, the inadequacy of the existing legislation, and the need for new administrative measures to deal with the sanitation problem, including the creation of a special governmental department. Despite opposition against government interference, there were further reports with a final one in 1845 in which Chadwick was the author cum secretary, while the other reformers made up the commission. The second report included in its recommendations (*Chadwick, 1865*):

1 minimum sanitary requirements for all dwellings making efficient sanitation obligatory;
2 delegating the power to insist on adequate ventilation to local government;
3 delegating sanitary control to local authorities;
4 setting up regular panels of Medical Officers of Health;
5 giving funds to open public parks for industrial cities which did not have them;
6 the main recommendation was that 'the Crown should have the power to inspect and supervise the execution of all general measures for the sanitary regulations of large towns and popular districts.'

The first Public Health Act in 1848 was full of compromises. Many of the regulations were permissive or optional, but the new Act did require and enforce that no new dwellings could be built without adequate provisions for sewage disposal. To oversee this regulation, a General Board of Health was created and thus began the first steps towards Britain's present-day National Health Service. The Public Health Act was the first recognition by the Victorian entrepreneur that the conditions which they had created in towns were not advantageous to the bulk of the population and that something needed to be done. With the Public Health Act began real reforms.

The swan song of the Baroque city: London's Regent's Park and Regent Street

Two major urban design attempts to overcome the squalor of the industrial city were made in the nineteenth century. Both attempts were grandiose and yet extremely beautiful. The first was the creation of Regent's Park by John Nash in London. The second was the redevelopment of Paris by Napoleon III and Haussmann in the grand Baroque manner, which unfortunately had little influence in Britain.

The swan song of well-balanced and well-controlled eighteenth century urban planning in Britain was the development of Marylebone Park into Regent's Park and the redevelopment of the area to the south into Regent Street – both by the architect John Nash (1752–1835). Regent Street and Regent's Park could be considered the last breath of the Baroque City, and although John Nash designed his plan for Regent Street and Regent's Park in 1812, his concepts and design had little to do with the rising industrial monotony and squalor of the major cities (*Nash, 1811*).

The development of Regent's Park began when the then Prince of Wales became Regent in 1811 and continued until he succeeded to the throne as George IV. Marylebone Park belonged to the Crown as part of the old hunting grounds of Henry VIII, and was available for development. The Regent commissioned John Nash to design buildings and gardens for residential purposes, and particularly to include a large park which would be available to all the people living in the nearby housing.

Nash's first plan showed not only a magnificent scheme but also a financially viable real estate venture (figure 2.8). Although Nash designed his final plan for Regent's Park in 1812, the work was not carried out until the 1820s (*Nash, 1812*). Not much is known of the full role of the Regent, but the Regent is quoted as saying that he was 'so pleased with this magnificent plan (which) will quite eclipse Napoleon' (*Summerson, 1949a*). Nash's intentions were first, to make as much

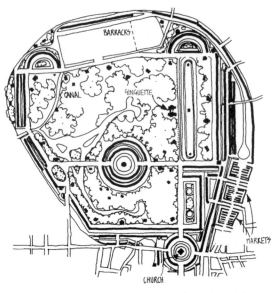

Figure 2.8   Plan for Marylebone Park, 1811 (after Nash, in Davis)

money as possible for the Regent (in that respect he was like all the Victorians), secondly, to add to the beauty of the Metropolis, and thirdly, to better the health and convenience of the public. The original plan for Regent's Park, according to Sir John Summerson, was to be more than pleasant eighteenth century housing. It was to form a kind of 'independent urban unit' as there were to be places for all members of society – a palace for the king, barracks for the army, a church, villas for the nobility, terraced houses for the middle classes and a market for the working classes (*Giedion, 1967*).

Nash wanted villas, a canal through the park, a central double-circus building and nearby accommodation for workers and tradesmen. In his first plan, Nash attempted a freer disposition of building than was actually built, by suggesting that the proposed semi-circular buildings should be built in the centre of the park. Fortunately, these were never built, as it was argued they would have destroyed the rural illusion of the park. Rather, around the edge of the park, designed as picturesque landscape, terraces of houses were designed as crescents (Park Crescent) and squares (York Square) in a manner similar to Wood's design for Bath. Eight villas and the canal around the park survived into the final plan (*Mumford, 1961; Davis, 1973; Bacon, 1979*).

Nash created a beautiful *'rus in urbe'*, bringing the feeling of a country estate right to the flat window. Georgian terraces in Bath and Edinburgh had already given the illusion that everyone could live as in a great mansion, that is by living in a part of a mansion terrace at the edge of a park. Already, Georgian houses had shared common pediments, porticos and columns. But what was so different about Nash's scheme was that the illusory mansion could now overlook a supposedly private parkland filled with lawns, specimen trees and lakes, including a view of the Regent's Canal. Nash's idea was to create free-flowing forms of large buildings facing a natural English park.

In this he was helped by his long partnership with Humphry Repton, who used the familiar landscape techniques of borrowing the landscape and detailing water basins which reflected the buildings and doubled their image.

Thus Nash's idea was to build grandiose houses for the new rich, and although the houses are grand in themselves, yet they are part of a larger unit and the park itself is so vast that the houses cannot dominate it. For example, Cumberland Terrace is one of Nash's most dramatic compositions, consisting of five blocks of houses divided by arches, behind which are pairs of smaller houses (figure 2.9). The whole composition is capped by a great central pediment supported by ten link columns, and includes alternating recesses and protrusions of form. Luckily, Nash had particular ideas of circulation separating services access from entry access and from the main road, so these sensitive circulation aspects have allowed the Nash terraces to adapt easily to present-day traffic.

Park Crescent, meant to be a proper Georgian circus, was not completed and, in its crescent form, serves as the entrance to Regent's Park. The great curve of the Ionic columns transfers the eye from the stability of Regent Street to the naturalness of Regent's Park. The composition appears pure and domestic and is a gentle opening to the very grandiose compositions, like Cumberland Terrace, which face onto the park.

Nash next connected his Regent's Park design to the business centre of Piccadilly by redeveloping a new avenue from Portland Place (which had been built by the Adam brothers in 1774) to Piccadilly, to be connected on an axial basis to Pall Mall. From the viewpoint of the town planner, what mattered was Nash's sustained vision of the new spine he planned for London. Regent Street, the link between the proposed Waterloo Place (now the forecourt of Carlton House) and Portland Place (to become the final broad entry to what was to have been Park Circus, and is now Park Crescent), was not to be driven through existing property in one straight line but to follow the natural curve of the division between Soho and Mayfair.

The avenue, named Regent Street, is the English

Figure 2.9   Cumberland Terrace (from *Country Life*, November 11 1971, reproduced by permission)

counterpart of Napoleon I's Rue de Rivoli in Paris. In Nash's own words, 'the new Regent Street should constitute a boundary and complete separation between the Streets and Squares occupied by the Nobility and the Gentry and the narrow Streets and meaner Houses occupied by mechanics and the trading part of the community' (*Summerson, 1949a*). He foresaw it becoming an extended piazza, where 'those who have nothing to do but walk about and amuse themselves may do so.' Even with the present-day disturbing intrusion of endless streams of crawling motor cars, his placement of the street remains successful. It does provide a satisfying approach to the quieter splendour of Portland Place; it is one of London's streets for idle promenading, and it does delineate the natural border of the two districts, Soho and Mayfair, with strong personalities of their own. His own buildings have been demolished, except the quadrant at the foot of the street, but its shape, and the grandeur of the Regency Parade, have survived (figures 2.10 and 2.11).

Since Regent Street crossed Oxford Street at right angles, he obscured this problem by creating the circular form of Oxford Circus. Langham Place occurred because property interests refused to be redeveloped and forced a kink in the straight line of Regent Street. The property-minded landlords of Cavendish Square pushed the new Regent Street to the east, but Nash concealed the problem of the kink in the road by cleverly designing the circular church of All Souls. Nash also designed a series of compositions for Regent Street itself for shops and offices, but little

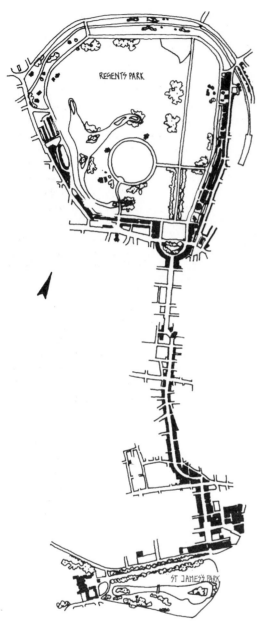

Figure 2.10   Plan of Regent's Park and Regent Street development (after Davis)

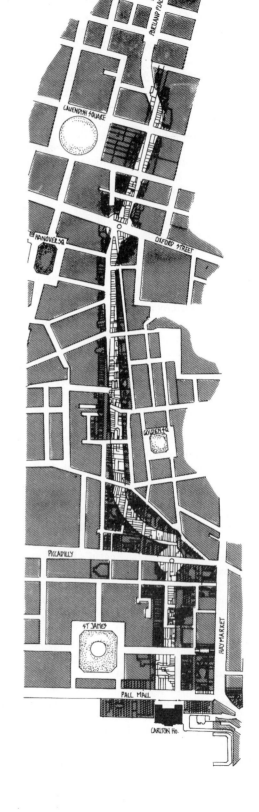

Figure 2.11   Plan showing redevelopment required to build Regent Street (after Bacon)

remains of their design as the buildings have long since been changed or destroyed.

Regent Street was meant to end in the south with a focus on a dramatic building – Carlton House, the then home of the Regent. Nash meant to achieve this with a formal avenue and a square on the axis of Carlton House. He therefore swung Regent Street around in a circle to cut the axis of Carlton House. Ironically though, the Regent, now George IV, decided to leave Carlton House, and instead extended Buckingham Palace. Carlton House was torn down and thus there was no terminus to the great Regent Street project. In its place Nash designed the Duke of York's Steps flanked by the two Carlton House Terraces.

Piccadilly Circus literally was to be the circus pivoting between the northern and southern parts of Regent Street, as a much smaller space than the amorphous space it became. Unfortunately, the change in the Regent's plans left a design problem at Piccadilly Circus which has remained unresolved. The end of Regent Street now forms one grand sweep of colonnades to Piccadilly Circus, in a grandiose quadrant, which, as a quarter of a double circus, is very reminiscent of earlier work at Bath. Interestingly, Nash personally became the developer of the quadrant so that he could develop the whole site and build a continuous curve without being forced by multiple ownership to alter his own composition. For decades, later architects were forbidden to be their own developers, for professional reasons, causing possibly one of the reasons why there have not been similar monumental urban planning schemes after Nash.

Nash's Regent Street scheme shows three influences: firstly, that of Bath and Edinburgh, and the late eighteenth century planning traditions; secondly, that of Paris and Versailles under Louis XIV, Louis XV and Napoleon I; and thirdly, that of the Picturesque Tradition. Beautiful as it was, it had no effect on the urban problems created by the Industrial Revolution (*Rasmussen, 1951*).

First reform movements and Utopian communities

The nineteenth century industrial city glorified the machine and the factory which resulted from it. The factory town bred a kind of mediocrity into every facet of daily life. People and machines were rigidly organised; a monotonous order regulated life. Environmental conditions were appalling; smoke hung over factory towns; sewers were few and sometimes non-existent.

Cultural progress was drained by the devouring greed of industrial development. Victorian life even at its best was routine and dull. The machine was perfected and man was proud of his achievements. A few architect/designers, such as John Ruskin and William Morris, and the housing reformers Octavia Hill and Jane Addams, spoke out against the industrial squalor and the cultural monotony (*Ruskin, 1853; Morris, 1883; Addams, 1910; Darley, 1990*). Octavia Hill, although underrated by later male bureaucrats, and yet a co-founder of the National Trust for England and Wales, was one of the most important Victorian pioneers for public housing, emphasising the need for careful and diligent housing management. Thus, there emerged philanthropic social reformers and Utopian thinkers who protested against the filth of the industrial slums. Other reformers who produced ideas for several Utopian communities included the Frenchman, Le Doux, and James Silk Buckingham, Pemberton and Robert Owen. Except for Owen's New Lanark, none of the other ideas for Utopian communities was built.

Claude-Nicolas Le Doux (1736–1806) had considerable influence on the British Utopian dreamers looking for an ideal city and his 'Chaux' ideal town is really the precursor of the later Garden Cities (figure 2.12). Until the French Revolution, Le Doux had been Building Inspector, Architect, and Surveyor of the Royal Saltworks, where he was required to design and build offices, factory buildings and housing (*Binney, 1980*). But Le Doux considered that the architect should concern himself with all aspects of the community, from work, morals and education to legislation, culture and government. Le Doux turned into a Utopian architect, by designing an ideal city called 'Chaux', for an ideal community but designed for an actual rather than a mythical site (*Rosenau, 1983*). Loosely linked to the overall plans are many designs for particular buildings to suit the inhabitants of a new age. Instead of palaces for princes, princesses and aristocrats, Le Doux designed houses for lumbermen, engineers, writers, brokers, art dealers, surveyors and charcoal burners. In place of the aggrandisement of royalty, he projected a heroic context for the newly liberated citizens. Temples are dedicated to Justice and Happiness, and a Union House, designed as a meeting place and club house, expresses the ideal of fraternity. The House of Passion, or Temple of Immorality, is an educational building in which young people were to be exposed to the concentrations of vice so that they would be repelled in the direction of virtue!

Le Doux, a typical architectural Utopian, explored few of the social implications of his symbols. Inspired by Rousseau and his recommendations of rural life, Le

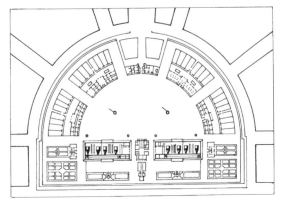

Figure 2.12   Le Doux: plan for Chaux (after Rosenau)

Doux's other projects showed country communes. In the sheltered retreats, people could escape the sophistication and corruptions of the city and live 'natural' lives surrounded by orchids, vineyards and fields, a later Garden City ideal.

The social reformer-architect, James Silk Buckingham, proposed a Utopian temperance community called 'Victoria', as a model association, in a book which dealt with 'existing evils of society' and contained the author's views, amongst others, on ignorance, intemperance, and the condition of the poorer classes (*Buckingham, 1849*). Buckingham expressed his solutions, such as financial reform, emigration and colonisation, electoral reform and the regeneration of Ireland, and explained his proposal for the model town of Victoria, to combine within itself every advantage of beauty, security, healthfulness and convenience that the latest discoveries in architecture and science could confer upon it.

The nature of his ideal town was part social regeneration, a moral theme which held the imagination of the Victorian urban reformer. Victoria was a carefully detailed plan for 10,000 people; the design was built up in a series of concentric squares, with a focal point being a central tower for electric light, with clock and gallery, 92 metres high (figure 2.13). The area, about one kilometre square, was divided by eight main radial avenues, named Justice, Unity, Peace, Concord, Fortitude, Charity, Hope and Faith!

Manufacturing trades were to be established near the outer edge of the town and the inner areas reserved for houses and offices; working-class houses were on the outside. All dwellings were to have flush toilets; there were to be houses of many different sizes, and each was to accommodate the appropriate size of household. Public baths were to be provided at convenient distance in each quarter of the town. All more unsavoury buildings, such as abattoirs, were to

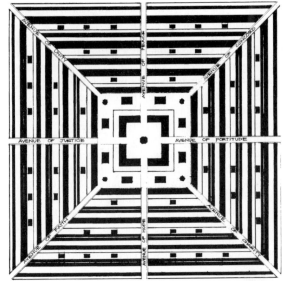

Figure 2.13   Plan of Victoria (after Rosenau)

be located away from residences and workshops. Thus, Buckingham recognised the importance of separating houses from industry. The most obnoxious industries were to be outside the town, while the workshops were to be in the centre, with the houses on the perimeter of the land. All the land was to be owned by the company, and buildings occupied for rent. To reduce the pollution problem, Buckingham proposed a most perfect apparatus to be applied for consuming smoke.

Beyond the town were to be 4000 hectares of farmland where there would also be a public promenade or park. He suggested a green belt of 4000 hectares of agricultural land, an idea that Ebenezer Howard was to adopt in his Garden City. Indeed Buckingham's plans for a model town gave Howard most of the main features for his diagram of the Garden City, such as the concentric plan, the radial avenues, and the peripheral industries. The publication of the plan for Victoria was one of the first examples in Victorian Britain of a town plan being sketched in such detail. As a design it was rigid, romantic and idealistic. But in containing every improvement and convenience it pointed to the limitations of existing towns and incorporated all the main objectives of the health and environmental reformers.

Forming these Utopian communities, the ideal remained the village (*Tod and Wheeler, 1978*). Blake's Dark Satanic Mills illustrated the dislike of the reformers for the city who searched for names to illustrate their ideals, such as Pemberton's plans for a 'Happy Colony' and Owen's Villages of Cooperations (figures 2.14 and 2.16).

Figure 2.14 Pemberton's plan for a model town, Victoria, on a Pacific island, influenced Ebenezer Howard in his Garden City plan, particularly the circular town centre (Pemberton, 1854) (after Rosenau)

Figure 2.15 New Lanark restored in the 1990s (after New Lanark Conservation Trust)

One of the most complex of these Utopian reformers was Robert Owen (1771–1858), a mill owner who married his boss's daughter and subsequently took over reputedly the largest and best-equipped spinning mills in Scotland, at New Lanark, in Lanarkshire. The community experiment at New Lanark by Robert Owen during the first two decades of the nineteenth century attracted considerable attention (figure 2.15). His ideas for the building of a township were described in his *Report to the County of Lanark* in which, in an attempt to meet the problem of unemployment, he conceived the creation of what he termed agricultural and manufacturing villages of unity and mutual cooperation, with housing populations of between 1000 and 1500 persons (*Owen, 1817*). The concept of towns with limited population came from Le Doux, Buckingham, Pemberton and Owen and finally appeared definitively in Howard's Garden City.

In his spinning mill, Robert Owen paid better wages, required shorter working hours and gave better conditions than other mill owners. He developed his special kind of cooperative community providing many social innovations. For example, he refused to employ children under the age of 10 years, and provided the community with its own school, which he called 'An institution for the Formation of Character', operating as a day school for children and a night school for adults. He established bulk-buying for all household necessities and thus helped to start the Cooperative movement.

New Lanark was a cotton manufacturing village built at the Falls of Clyde in 1784, taken over by Owen in 1799 and subsequently governed as a community on

paternalist lines where his measures for social reform were advanced. The physical plan of New Lanark is not exceptional, but at the time it was more advanced in concept than other factory towns. The dwellings and gardens were grouped around a large open space and were separated by the roadway from the workshops and factories (*Butt, 1971*).

By 1816, Owen proposed a special plan for a 'Village of Cooperation'. Failing to get financial backing in Britain, he decided to sell New Lanark, and in 1824 took his family, 800 followers and his plans for villages of cooperation and, with the New Lanark money, bought 30,000 acres in Indiana in the United States. There he attempted to superimpose a village of cooperation on an existing religious community called New Harmony (*Harrison, 1969*) (figure 2.16). It did not work and Robert Owen eventually returned to Britain with great financial losses. New Lanark is one of the few built idealistic communities and has now been completely restored as a Cooperative Housing Association and Conservation Trust (the New Lanark Conservation Trust).

Model towns

The model towns followed the Utopian communities, as reforming zeal continued. One of the most influential and ambitious model towns was Saltaire, the model industrial town near Bradford built by Sir

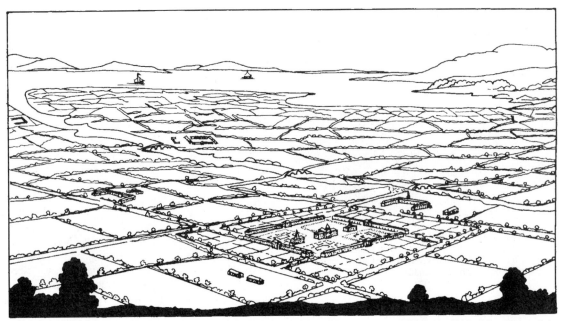

Figure 2.16   A 'Village of Harmony and Cooperation' as envisaged by Owen in a drawing from 1817   (after Benevolo)

Figure 2.17   Saltaire (from Powell, 1984)

Titus Salt during 1848/49–63 in partnership with his architects, Lockwood and Manson. Saltaire appropriately began with the mill, a massive building of six floors capable of employing 3000 to 4000 people. Adjoining the mill was the railway line, south of which sits the town in a mundane grid-iron pattern of terraced houses (figure 2.17). The quality of the housing was high.

The main contribution of Saltaire is not so much its physical layout as its underlying policies and in the transition from the cramped conditions in the city to a newly built town in the countryside (figure 2.18). Salt provided better conditions than elsewhere and exhibited true Victorian paternalism. For example, he introduced a 'no washing in public' policy and made certain it was observed by a permanent patrol. Perhaps

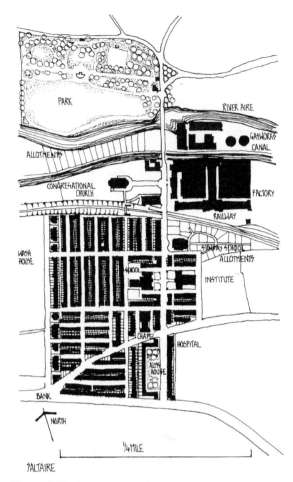

Figure 2.18   Layout of Saltaire (after Benevolo)

Few houses had gardens, although the managerial houses in Albert Road had quite reasonable front gardens. Bathing, like washing clothes, was expected to take place communally, and Salt provided 24 Baths and a Turkish Bath in Amelia Street. Salt's greatest benefactions were the number of community buildings and parks which he provided in the order that he thought beneficial: first, the churches; second, baths and work houses; third, factory schools; fourth, an infirmary; fifth, the Saltaire Club and Institute; and finally, a Sunday School building, which was provided just before he died.

Saltaire, today, seems to provide minimal housing standards with its houses without gardens. The town has been preserved in respectability, not just by conservationists (it is a Conservation Area) but also by ordinary working people wanting to live there, in a quiet grey-stoned limbo, as the mill has closed (*Powell, 1984*). On the other hand, Saltaire, seen in its Victorian context, was a vast improvement over the slums in the city centre.

The model town of Bournville, built by the Cadbury Brothers in 1894, is special compared with Saltaire. The Cadbury Brothers transferred their factory from the city centre to the south-west of Birmingham to a green field site on the outskirts and built a number of workers' houses close to the works. There the Cadbury Brothers showed that it was possible to create decent housing in a self-supporting industrial town. Unlike Saltaire or Port Sunlight, Bournville was not meant to be a 'company town' but was meant for all workers of all classes, no matter where they worked. Their goal was expressed in a later Trust Deed of 'alleviating the evils which arise from the insanitary and insufficient accommodation supplied to large numbers of the lower classes, and of securing to the workers in factories some of the advantages of outdoor village life.'

In Bournville, great attention was paid to house design, the provision of open space, sunlight and environmental conditions as a whole. The earlier houses were well spaced, with large gardens and adapted from the 'tunnel backs' of the Public Health Act of 1875, which required an air space on two sides of a house (figure 2.19). Later homes included variations of cottage styles. In blocks of twos, threes and fours, they were spaced 20 feet apart along the road frontage, with large back gardens, and normally contained a parlour, living room and kitchen on the ground floor with three bedrooms above. Few had separate bathrooms, largely because the rents were too low to allow such luxuries.

Suitably sized gardens, tree-lined roads, parks and recreation grounds gave the workers living conditions

the most remarkable piece of philanthropy on Salt's part was to conduct a survey of the workers' actual housing needs. Saltaire had a great distinction, over not only most Victorian working-class houses but over many modern council estates, of offering different units of accommodation. The number of desired rooms was seen by Salt to be a function of family size as well as of social class. Therefore, there are a mixture of two-, three- and four-bedroomed houses designed for workers, as well as the more usual choice open to the managers and overseers. The different house sizes, coupled with minor variations of style and decoration, enabled the architects to lay out inexorably regular streets without too much monotony; at least the houses do not look identical row by row.

Internally, the houses were of good standard; each had a living room, a parlour, a kitchen, pantry and cellar in addition to the bedrooms, and most had a small yard, with coal, ash pits and outside lavatory.

Figure 2.19   Bournville – workers housing, 1890 (source untraceable)

quite different from elsewhere. Cadbury completed the estate with a village institute and a hall for the Adult Education Movement. By 1900, 313 houses had been built and the estate covered 330 acres. By 1960, the estate covered rather more than 1000 acres, of which 750 acres were developed, with 4000 dwellings, with a population of 13,000. The Trust had its own architects, direct labour and housing managers.

One of the village's best aspects is its landscaping of roads along existing features, and the varying settings of the housing groups in relation to the road. Even quite mundane houses are improved by being set in large gardens and in irregular street patterns. Bournville developed the cul-de-sac and the crescent, the minor elements of planning arrangements that make up the garden suburbs. None of the principal thoroughfares is completely straight, and there are a number of open spaces in addition to the generous gardens and pavement borders.

The Bournville Estate was always independent of the firm and, on average, only about 40 percent of the householders were (and subsequently have been) connected with the factory. George Cadbury, having founded the village and imposed upon it his own vision of seemingly permanent garden suburbanism, handed it over in 1900 to a non-profit Bournville Village Trust, with twelve trustees answerable only to the Charity Commissioners originally, and since including trustees from the Corporation of Birmingham, the Society of Friends and the University of Birmingham. The estate expanded and continues to develop, largely through Housing Association schemes. However, when the Cadbury family sold out to the Schweppes Company, one of the stipulations was that the philanthropic aspects were to be dropped, and thus the public buildings are no longer supported by the company.

In 1888, the Lever Brothers built Port Sunlight, more significant architecturally than Bournville, which was based more on Quaker social ideals than design (*Unilever, 1976*). The objective was similar to that of Saltaire: improved business results along with a model housing development for the workers of their factory, as part of an expansion scheme of their soap business, Unilever, with the same emphasis on social facilities. The keynotes were good housing and generous amenities, and by 1904 two schools, social clubs, a church, technical institute, theatre and swimming baths had been provided.

The Levers' social impulse was primarily an extension of their faith in profit sharing. They acknowledged that part of their success derived from the surplus value produced by their employees, but they had no confidence in the capacity of the lucky workers to use their dividends wisely. They chose instead to convert the workers' share of profits into improved housing. They loathed the tenements built by Samuel Peabody, saying that 'flats were for crowding a maximum amount of humanity in a minimum amount of ground space', and so built low-density housing (ten dwellings to the acre) (*Port Sunlight, 1990*).

Port Sunlight was substantially more baronial in concept, and the plan is suggestive of Versailles, particularly after it was reorganised in 1910. The planned Beaux-Arts layout was quite uncommon in Britain and was not dictated by conditions of terrain. Port Sunlight has vistas, perspectives, formal gardens and public buildings on the consciously grand scale; ravines have been filled in and contours scraped down. Some claim that its character became more City Beautiful and Beaux-Arts due to the American connections of the architect, Sir Charles Reilly (*Tarn, 1980*).

Thus Port Sunlight developed under the same enlightened Victorian paternalism as Saltaire. But although the layout was French-inspired, the English Village concept dominated the housing design (figure 2.20). The 'Anne Hathaway' cottage look was applied

Figure 2.20   Port Sunlight, 1892 (copyright James Stevens Curl. Reproduced by kind permission)

to all the dwellings. Each house-dweller had his own garden and, in addition, generous allotment areas. Interestingly, the front gardens were undivided and present a continuous frontage along the streets. Port Sunlight is a large and complete museum piece, indicative of the thoughts and ideals of those fin-de-siècle architects working under the influence of the pre-Raphaelites. Nearly every traditional European house-style has been plundered for inspiration. There are Cheshire black and white Tudor groups next to Dutch colonial, set on sweeping French loops, with gables and crenellations.

Port Sunlight has not survived as well as Bournville. The presence of the manufacturing buildings, the soap factories and the tanneries, produces pollution and smells which no amount of good housing can overcome. The Unilever company eventually sold to Birkenhead District Council, which has built houses on the allotments and garages in the gardens, so the open spaciousness has disappeared. But the way of life remains, as a reminder of a gentler Britain, where crime is rare and the 3000 residents are untroubled by juvenile offenders, drug barons or joyriding (*Pendry, 1993*).

By 1905, Sir Joseph Rowntree, the cocoa industrialist, built Earswick near York and employed Barry Parker and Raymond Unwin. These few model villages only demonstrated more clearly how it was possible to provide good living standards and how terrible it was that all factory workers did not have the same equally good conditions. The actual number of

model villages was so few that, in terms of solving the overall housing and sanitation problems, they were a drop in the bucket. The model village contributed little to the quantitative problems of the vast factory slums in the cities.

The retreat of urban design in the nineteenth century

In Newcastle is a late Georgian development of merit built in the early nineteenth century by the enterprising entrepreneur Grainger and his architect Dobson (*Wilkes and Dodds, 1964*). Of grey stone in the classical manner, the houses on Grey Street curve up the hill and structured Newcastle's urban form as Regent Street structured London's. Edinburgh also continued to build in the Georgian discipline well into the middle of the nineteenth century. Victorian architects concentrated either on public health issues (as did their fellow industrialists) or on building magnificent public buildings for civic pride. Many a town hall appeared as a Venetian palace, or as a medieval hall as in Leeds, Manchester and Birmingham, with a St George's Hall in Liverpool.

Newcastle's Georgian Grey Street and Edinburgh's Crescents were the last gasps before a retreat from urban design which lasted for almost 75 years. Georgian classical design did not provide a convenient solution to the organisational problems of the industrial town and after 1840 it ceased to be emulated almost everywhere. When urban planning came to be regarded as a special skill in the early twentieth century, it was the medieval town which provided the inspiration for garden city planners like Raymond Unwin (*Tarn, 1980: 77*).

Other architects were inspired by a fashionable Renaissance revival led by the architectural genius of Sir Edwin Lutyens, who set the example with his three-dimensional development in the Renaissance manner for the new imperial city of New Delhi. Other minor urban improvements, such as Kingsway in London and the Headrow in Leeds, employed the Renaissance approach following closely that of Nash in Regent Street (*Johnson-Marshall, 1965: 19*). With these few exceptions, the classical town was abandoned as a design ideal until, in the mid-twentieth century, the aesthetic thinking of urban designers realised that a fundamentally new approach was required.

Public Health Act 1875 and population explosion

More to the point of solving the quantitative problems of slum housing was the new Public Health Act of 1875. A Royal Sanitary Commission, appointed in 1868, issued its report in 1871, criticising the permissive character of the provisions of the existing sanitary code, the lack of adequate inspection, the friction caused by the presence of numerous ad hoc bodies, and the absence of a strong system of central control. Immediate reforms came with the creation of the Local Government Board of 1871, the passing of the Public Health Act 1872, and the Sanitary Amendment Law Act 1874.

Both these Acts and others were repealed and consolidated by the Public Health Act 1875, which formed an essential foundation for public health legislation for over 60 years, and a public health service for the first time all over the country (*Cherry, 1972*). It gave power to the local authorities to purchase land and build dwellings for the working class, divided the country up into Urban Sanitary and Rural Sanitary Districts, and required their Commissions to make and enforce by-laws regulating the dwellings. The Sanitary Districts lasted until local government reorganisation in 1973.

The first national legislation concerned with the removal of slum housing came with the Torrens Act (Artisans' and Labourers' Dwellings Act 1868) and Cross Act (Artisans' and Labourers' Dwellings Improvement Act 1875). The Torrens Act permitted local authorities to require clearance of individual slum properties, but without the requirement to replace the

houses with good new dwellings. In consequence, Medical Officers decided that an unfit dwelling was better than no dwelling at all. The second Cross Act improved the situation by requiring that local authorities clear insanitary areas, draw up schemes and lease the land to others who would rebuild. These two Acts were legislative landmarks but their actual effect was minimal.

The General Board of Health devised a set of model by-laws. Some cities already had their own by-laws, limiting street widths and such matters as the heights of the buildings, but it was not until the 1875 Act that general permission to make building by-laws was extended over the whole country. But even with later legislation – the Public Health Acts Amendment Act 1890 – it still did not become compulsory for all local authorities to make building by-laws, and the situation, because of local laxity, was far from perfect.

Nevertheless, the 1875 legislation did have an important impact on the urban scene by standardising appearances, and creating for most of the period 1875–1900 vast areas of industrial cities covered with a monotonous grid of dull and unimaginative by-law housing, comparatively and physically the healthiest housing in Europe, but desperately depressing. Germany, the Netherlands and Sweden followed Britain's example and developed public utility housing societies and thus brought about the beginning of public housing in Western Europe.

By-law housing (figure 2.21) could not keep up with the ever-expanding need for more and more houses. Because of the continuous population explosion, the real problem of the slums and the congestion of the population remained. Between 1800 and 1900 the urban population of Europe grew by between 300 and 400 percent. For example, London had a population of one million in 1800, and by 1900 it was seven million (*Cherry, 1974*).

Into the twentieth century

By 1901, Britain was decidedly an urban country. Twenty-five million people lived in towns; only 7.5 million lived outside the urban areas. Population concentrated on certain urban magnets such as London, Manchester, Liverpool/Merseyside, Tyneside, West Yorkshire, the West Midlands and Central Scotland. As late as 1913, Birmingham City Council's Inquiry into Housing Conditions showed that 200,000 people lived in 43,366 back-to-back dwellings, resulting in unimaginable overcrowding since most dwellings contained only three rooms; 42,020 dwellings had no separate water supply, no sinks, no

Figure 2.21   Birmingham housing: by-law housing (left) and housing in Bournville (right) (source untraceable)

drains, and 58,028 people still had to use communal lavatories situated in exposed courts (*Birmingham City Council, 1913*). The Public Health Act of 1875 was inadequate for solving the housing problem. The nineteenth century ended with its focus on the plight of the underprivileged and badly housed in the big cities. The success of a handful of benefactors in providing better conditions for their workers was well known but the problem, particularly in London, seemed to be getting worse and more radical solutions were necessary.

3 The beginning of contemporary town planning

The outcry against the deteriorated and rotten environment of the industrial city was not limited to a few conscience-stricken businessmen. Literary men, writers like Charles Dickens and Thomas Carlyle, also spoke out against the terrible conditions of the city in the nineteenth century. These writers gave birth to the social issue novel. Previously the novel had been a vehicle for plot, description and repartee, but after Dickens in Britain and Emile Zola in France, the novel became yet another tool for expressing the social conscience and proposals for social reform, and has since remained so. The descriptions by Zola and Dickens helped to stimulate the public into action.

Patrick Geddes

One of the most famous of those who decried the industrial city was the Scottish town planner, Patrick Geddes (1854–1932), who began his professional life as a zoologist, but because of serious eye trouble had to redirect his energies away from the microscope (*Boardman, 1978; Mellor, 1990*). He was appointed as a professor of Botany at Dundee University, but the appointment only required one term in residence so that for the rest of the year Patrick Geddes was free to write and travel. He held this appointment from 1888 to 1919, during which time he organised many of his great planning projects including a series of international summer meetings, the forerunners of 'summer schools'.

Living in a poor part of Edinburgh, Geddes developed various urban renewal projects, converting several medieval buildings in the High Street, helping to preserve parts of the Dean Village and regenerating Ramsay Gardens, near Edinburgh Castle, where he first converted three Georgian houses and then built the picturesque Ramsay Gardens in the manner of Camille Sitte (figure 3.1). Geddes was an admirer of Sitte's aesthetics and saw him as having accomplished for historic city conservation what the Gothic Revivalists had achieved for cathedrals and town houses.

Not only did Geddes regenerate worn-out parts of Edinburgh and Dunfermline (*Geddes, 1904*), he also expressed his evolving ideas of town planning through the medium of exhibitions held within the Outlook Tower, and sponsored by the Outlook Tower Association, which he founded in Edinburgh in 1892. Through the exhibitions, Geddes presented the whole complex range of urban life. His constant theme was the principle of integration of physical planning with social and economic improvements, which is accepted today but then was entirely new.

Geddes' concept of physical, social and economic integration was at variance with the conventional and all too successful neo-Baroque method of planning executed by Nash in London and by Haussman in Paris. In the late nineteenth century, town planning was an assortment of a mixture of a 'Parisian Boulevard à la Haussman', the English Garden Village, and a German Town extension plan, which produced a mechanical mixture (figure 3.2). But Geddes had unearthed the basic problem of the industrial city – the need to consider the social and economic problems together with the physical problems. Geddes demonstrated this integration through different exhibitions on each level of the Outlook Tower. At the top of the tower was and still is the Camera Obscura, a device with mirrors, which enables the observer to see the entire panorama of Edinburgh and the region. This was in line with Geddes' view about the planning process, which starts with understanding the city region, the geographical and topographical features of the regional site. Below

Figure 3.1   Ramsay Gardens, Edinburgh (by Rahman)

the Camera Obscura, standing outside on the terrace is the panorama of Edinburgh. Here Geddes would talk about Edinburgh's contexts: astronomical, anthropological, archaeological, historical and economic aspects. Geddes, as a botanist and biologist, was interested in the whole science of environment and based his philosophy of urban civics on an understanding of the total environment.

Below, one floor held exhibitions of relief model maps, mostly geological painting, drawings, photographs, etc., showing the city of Edinburgh from its prehistoric origins through its medieval and Renaissance period up to a complete survey of the present day. Other floors held exhibition materials about Scotland and the relation of Edinburgh to the Clyde and the Forth river basins, the Highlands, Glasgow and the other main towns; and its relation to European civilisation, where the exhibition included a comparison of three European towns whose plans were similar. Finally, the ground floor Geddes allocated to the Oriental civilisations and to the general study of man. Along with the exhibition, Geddes organised lectures, clubs, citizenship days and occasional talks for businessmen and the general public, all illustrated by diagrams and models.

The civic survey and the planning process

Geddes' great contribution to planning was the concept of the 'planning process', his emphasis on civic surveys, the idea of 'survey before plan' and 'diagnosis before treatment' (*Geddes, 1915*). Even in 1915, the preparation of surveys was not actually specified in the 1909 Housing Act when considering the preparation of a town planning scheme. The statutory need for survey was only first included in the 1947 Town and Country Planning Act, after a time lag of almost 40 years.

Geddes advised that planning surveys were needed on two accounts, firstly to provide sufficient knowledge of past development and present conditions of the town and secondly to ensure that planning designs were based upon an adequate knowledge of comparative good and bad town planning schemes. The Town Council, the Street and Buildings Committee, the City Architect and the City Engineer knew very little of important and successful projects done elsewhere; they were usually narrowly educated on planning, and did not possess any preparation in understanding the geographical, economic and design problems of the town, nor at that time did the training of architects involve town planning.

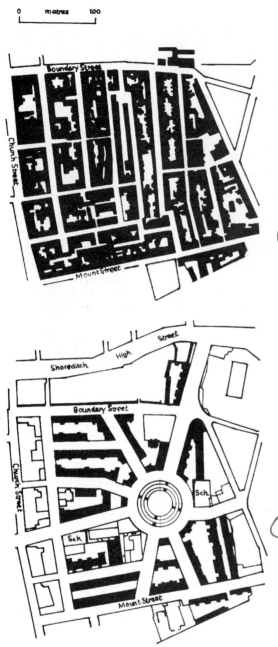

Figure 3.2 Redevelopment of the Boundary Street Estate, Bethnal Green, London, 1895 (after Clout and Wood)

The civic survey and planning process concepts were published in Geddes' famous book *Cities in Evolution* – which has profoundly influenced all succeeding generations of urbanists (*Geddes, 1915*). *Cities in Evolution* concerns the education of the citizen towards his or her understanding of the

planning process and his or her active participation in urban development. Geddes has been credited by many as the creator of the basic planning process of survey–analysis–plan, underlying planning after the 1947 Act (*McLoughlin, 1969; Hall, 1974*). Geddes was certainly in favour of an explicit and scientifically based planning process, but he only partially created the concept of 'survey–analysis–plan' (*Breheny, 1989*). Geddes' original ideas of civic survey and diagnosis were expanded by others, most notably in the 1940s and 1950s, by inserting analysis into the Geddesian planning process, creating an orderly process of thinking in the following steps: (1) Survey; (2) Analysis/Diagnosis; (3) Design synthesis; (4) Plan implementation (*Tyrwhitt, 1945; McCallum, 1945*).

The first step in the preparation of a plan should be the 'Civic Survey', beginning with the topography of the town, understanding its historical development both geologically and geographically – soil, climate, rainfall, winds, with contour maps, plans and relief models. Secondly, he considered it important to map graphically comparative historical periods and the development of the town, as such maps often revealed how different the actual progress of the town has been from the plans proposed or forecast. An analysis of examples from other towns, British and foreign, was preliminary to the actual design problems. Thirdly, the means of communication in the past, present and future needed graphic mapping. Fourthly, population maps gave an understanding of the social basis of the town. The civic survey included first-hand visual experience, in the manner advocated by Sitte. Decades later, a scientific method of visual survey was to be promoted by the Townscape School of the Architectural Review and Civic Trust adherents.

The second step in the planning process is analysis of the survey information, and the needs and activities proposed as goals for the development of the town. This is the stage where survey factors are reviewed and given a priority value. Goals (quantitative) are suggested and modified, and principles (qualitative) defined. This second step of analysis depends for its success on the total understanding of the philosophical and social aims of the community for which the plan is being made. Geddes combined the analysis and diagnosis stages into one, calling it the Diagnostic Survey, concentrating on the diagnostic aspects, or the defining of goals, without the analysis.

In the plan stage, intuitive action takes place and goals become three-dimensional concepts. The synthesising of stated goals and principles becomes physical designs and possibilities. Geddes, not being a physical designer, suggested the design process itself only in outline, covering possibilities for small areas, town expansions and city development schemes. Geddes' weakness was a failure to explain how to move past survey to policy. Geddes found the three-dimensional aspects difficult and beyond his personal talents, yet he proposed that civic surveys should be permanently exhibited in a city museum. This goal is only occasionally achieved in a few British cities, but should be a requirement of all municipalities.

Geddes might be called one of Britain's first ecological planners. He pursued an understanding of the city based on biological, psychological and sociological knowledge. These concepts he transferred from the civic survey to the concept of Regional Survey. In contrast, living at the same time, Charles and Mary Booth in London approached industrial conditions from the other end of the scale. In Booths' detailed house-to-house survey of industrial conditions in London (*Booth, 1892*) they drew attention to the detailed problems of the city. But Geddes was broader-minded and examined the overall synthesis of the problem.

In his *Cities in Evolution*, Geddes speaks in simple terms of Greater London and the appearance of Greater Liverpool. He shows how these large city groups were forming new social groupings, needing new government administration. He described this new social form thus: ' "Constellations" we cannot call them; conglomeration, alas, nearer the mark at present, but it may sound unappreciative. What of "Conurbation"? – the expression of a new form of population grouping' (*Geddes, 1949: 14–15*). Thus evolved for the first time the concept of 'conurbation'.

Despite the simplistic approach, the regional survey was an important step towards the concept of regional planning. Although anticipated by Haussmann in his proposal for creating a large Seine-et-Oise administrative department upon the incorporation of the suburbs of Paris, it was Geddes who first proposed regional planning.

Geddes' main opportunity for practising town planning occurred in India, where he published Town Planning Reports on Madras, Lucknow, Indore, Patiala and other Indian cities between 1916 and 1919 (*Geddes, 1917; Tyrwhitt, 1947*) (figure 3.3). At that time, rather than large-scale redevelopment, which was the principal process known and accepted in India, Geddes preached the need for diagnostic survey and developed his planning technique of 'Conservative Surgery' (figures 3.4 and 3.5), conserving the best of the existing fabric of the city while renewing the worst elements. Conservative Surgery tackled the planning problem in a slow and patient way. Streets were individually widened; a few houses removed here; a

Figure 3.3 Patrick Geddes with Indian planner (from Tyrwhitt, reproduced by kind permission of the *Architect's Journal*)

vacant lot made into a playground there. Improvements were done on a small individual scale where the need particularly arose. No great roads were allowed to slash through with sweeping clearance of buildings. Instead Geddes urged the painstaking enhancement of what already existed. An entirely new concept, 'Conservation Surgery', was incorporated by Patrick Geddes into the planning concepts of Conservation and Rehabilitation, that is infill housing rather than mass clearance, and careful piece-meal development rather than sweeping redevelopment. He thus had great influence on later planners like Patrick Abercrombie and eventually the Conservation Movement of the 1970s to 1990s.

The legacy of Geddes lies in his philosophy of synthesising civics and town planning. Civics, for Geddes, was an amalgam of social, economic, historical, geographical, ecological and cultural studies, and most importantly, a science. Town planning could never be a science; it was aesthetic and physical, but coupled with the science of civics, it could produce the best environment on a regional basis. Geddes and those later system analysts of the 1960s failed to make planning scientific and to create a truly scientific methodology. But Geddes would not regard this as a failure, because he considered that statistics were not enough for planning to be considered a science. Social and cultural relationships were more important, and the only way to control the process of evolution was through nurturing, i.e., public education. Geddes succeeded in exposing the need for

PUCCA PRIVATE HOUSES TO BE ACQUIRED   [hatched box]

HOUSES NOT TO BE ACQUIRED   [light hatched box]

KUTCHA PRIVATE HOUSES   [hatched box]

MUNICIPAL LANES   [empty box]

BOUNDARY OF THE PROPOSED ROADS.   [solid line]

Figure 3.4   Madura: Uppukara Block: part of the Municipal Council's proposals (after Tyrwhitt)

HOUSES   [solid black box]

NEW HOUSE SITE   [hatched box]

KUTCHA BUILDINGS   [hatched box]

OPEN SPACE AND MUNICIPAL LAND   [empty box]

Figure 3.5   Madura: Uppukara Block: the same corner as it would appear after the application of 'Conservative Surgery' (after Tyrwhitt)

public education about town planning. He could be considered the propagator of public participation, which resulted in the Skeffington Report on Public Participation a half century later (*Skeffington Report, 1969*).

Geddes' main contributions to town planning are (1) his emphasis on place, (2) his emphasis on civics and the cross-fertilisation of disciplinary boundaries, (3) synthesising aesthetic action and rational thought, and (4) the excitement in understanding and directing the evolution of cities and regions. Geddes continued to lecture and propagandise for planning until his death in 1932, leaving behind a golden legacy of planning inspiration. His greatest work is contained in his marvellous *Cities in Evolution*, still read as a planning bible today.

The Garden City movement

The reform movement with the greatest positive physical effect on British town planning was the Garden City movement, which was based on a combination of planning ideas brought together by Ebenezer Howard with the publication in 1899 of *Tomorrow: A Peaceful Path to Real Reform*, better

known as *Garden Cities of Tomorrow* (*Howard, 1902*). The special significance of Howard's proposals was the possibility of converting them to workable examples for actually creating a new environment. In this respect he upheld the traditions of the model villages of the Victorian industrialists in contrast to the more theoretically Utopian concepts of the social thinkers who influenced his ideas. Lewis Mumford distinguished the important components of Howard's proposals (*Howard, 1976*), which included: (a) the permanent ownership of land by the municipality with leasing to private concerns; (b) the resultant recouping of unearned increment by the municipality rather than private land holders; (c) a sufficient diversity of activities, including social institutions; (d) industry; (e) agriculture to make the Garden City fairly independent; (f) the use of a Green Belt for agriculture and to restrict the physical growth of the city; (g) a limit on population to a planned size; and (h) further growth in new communities arranged as a 'Social City'. Howard was able to see his proposals realised in the Garden Cities of Letchworth and Welwyn Garden City but the development of a regional Garden City never happened.

Howard's philosophy arose from a simple practical

heart. He viewed town life as offering economic and social opportunities and country life as offering all the human benefits. In his famous drawing of the three Magnets – town, country and his third Equaliser, town–country – Howard showed that neither the town nor the country fulfilled all the needs of people. His third Magnet would fill the vacuum by being both town and country. He would create a community which offered the best of town life and the best of country life, to be called a Garden City. Thus Howard's objectives were: (a) for the industrial population, to find work at wages of higher purchasing power; (b) to secure healthier surroundings; (c) to provide more regular employment; and (d) to raise the standard of health and comfort of the workers of whatever grade. The means by which these objects were to be achieved was a healthy, natural and economic combination of town and country life, and this on land owned by the municipality (*Osborn and Whittick, 1977*) (figure 3.6).

Municipal control of the land was the key to Howard's scheme. Initially this was to be accomplished by means of a private corporation acquiring an agricultural site and holding it in trust for both the stock and debenture holders and the future residents, with trustees acting on their behalf. The town's revenue was to be used for the benefit of the townspeople. Dividends would be paid from rents, but the percentage of the dividend would be strictly limited. Both Letchworth and Welwyn were initiated in this way, Letchworth with a 5 percent and Welwyn with a 7 percent limit on share interest. Once the interest rates and fees were paid, the accrued money was to be used for the creation and maintenance of all public works, such as schools, parks, roads, etc. Howard used a considerable portion of his book outlining the financial and administrative details and it is thought that this was one major reason why the Garden City Movement has been so successful.

Arranging ownership of land in this way permitted the implementation of a comprehensive plan for the development of the new Garden City. The capital was to originate from two sources: investment by other interests given use of land, or funds, primarily for infrastructure, of the land-holding corporation. Letchworth and Welwyn both had difficulties stemming from inadequate capital under their immediate control. Welwyn Garden City eventually had to be financially reorganised in 1934.

Wythenshawe, a later Garden City, benefited from being under the ownership of Manchester, which had the resources to develop the site at a more rapid rate, making it larger than Letchworth or Welwyn by 1935

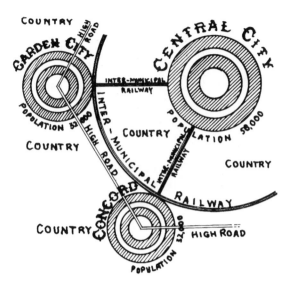

Figure 3.6 Howard's diagram of the central city and satellite cities (after Creese)

(*Creese, 1966a*). Despite the difficulties stemming from lack of capital, ownership of land was important to controlling successfully the pattern, if not the pace, of development.

Howard had a second reason for municipal land ownership, which was just as important as planning control. The essence of the plan was that all profits through increase in the value of the land should be returned to the community in order to discourage speculation of any sort (*Giedion, 1967*). Increase in land values arose from planned population movements to new sites and were collected in the form of rents. In practice, it proved very difficult to draw off anywhere near the total increment in land value, because the original leases had to be extended for long periods (99 years in Letchworth) to attract outside investment, such that the rents could not be adjusted to current land values. At Welwyn Garden City earlier commercial investment was forgone in favour of shorter leases, but leases for major factories were still as long as 99 years. Thus Howard's concept on which he concentrated was one of the less successful in practice, due to the technical difficulties of adjusting rents while still attracting outside investment.

Howard felt that municipal control of land was sufficient for the reforms he desired and hastened to point out that he differed on this point from several social experiments that had failed, such as the Victorian model villages, which were generally operated entirely under the auspices of the patron. The two Garden Cities gave private enterprise a certain

importance of ownership of land

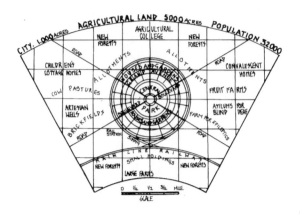

Figure 3.7   Diagram of Garden City (after Howard)

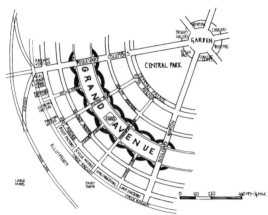

Figure 3.8   Diagram of ward and centre of Garden City (after Howard)

freedom; indeed, in Letchworth and Welwyn Garden City, limited capital made this a practical necessity.

The plan of the ideal Garden City was laid out as a circular diagram (figures 3.7 and 3.8). Six magnificent boulevards, cutting across the city from centre to circumference, divided the city into six equal wards. In the centre was a circular space, containing about five and a half acres, laid out as beautiful gardens, surrounded by the large public buildings – town hall, principal court, lecture hall, theatre, library, museum and hospital. The second green space, encircled by a Crystal Palace, was a public park of 145 acres, which included recreational grounds within easy access of all the people. The unique Crystal Palace concept, influenced by Joseph Paxton's designs, was a larger than usual glass house to be a sheltered area in wet weather, to be used partly for shopping, partly for exhibitions and partly as a Winter Garden. The Garden City was planned for a population of 30,000 people to live in housing areas surrounded by a permanent green belt, beyond which were to be the factories and warehouses, indicating early zoning. The reserved open space fostered agriculture by protecting it from competition of uses able to pay higher rents.

The encouragement of private industry and commercial activity was an aspect of Howard's goal of a balanced community for his Garden City. Other desired activities included community facilities and charitable institutions, which were offered inexpensive sites. The lack of balance between industry and housing on one hand and diversity of activities on the other had been one of the weaknesses of the early model villages. But in Letchworth and Welwyn Garden City, a large number of varied commercial and industrial enterprises and a fair number of social institutions developed and have continued to contribute to the success of the social life of the communities.

Howard's most striking and realistic physical proposal was the Green Belt, a band of open land around the Garden City, under the ownership of the municipality. This served many functions in Howard's system. Firstly, it could be a source of large-scale open space easily accessible from anywhere in the Garden City. Secondly, it could serve as a location for agriculture and other space-consuming activities. Thirdly, the green belt could act as a device for planning control made possible by municipal ownership of land. In particular, it could be used to limit the physical growth of the city to the desired size of 30,000 people.

The model villages of the nineteenth century industrialists generally did not encompass this idea, perhaps from an assumption that no-one but farmers would have an interest in the bordering land. On the other hand, the idea of a green belt had previously appeared in some theoretical proposals to improve cities. An example of this was James Buckingham's plan for a model city, of which Howard was aware. Each of the built Garden Cities had green belts, but they tended to be smaller than the proposed rule of thumb, that is, five times the built-up area.

Hand in hand with the limit on physical growth provided by the green belt was the complementary limit on population of 30,000 people. Although the number was not sacrosanct, it was important to maintain a balance between the ability to support a diversity of opportunities and yet remain in close harmony with the surrounding countryside. As with green belts, the concept of limiting population to an ideal size was much stronger in the theoretical tradition, going back at least to Aristotle, than in the practical tradition of the industrialists. Letchworth and Welwyn reached roughly the scale prescribed in Howard's Garden Cities, but Wythenshawe was planned to be considerably larger, because Manchester needed housing for 80,000 to 100,000 overspill population.

Howard's solution to growth beyond the limited population was to envisage a group of Garden Cities, called 'Social Cities', grouped around the 'Central City' (figure 3.9). Unlike other aspects of the concept, the idea of the group of social cities does not appear to come from any previous source. Howard visualised colonisation and combined it with the realisation 'that no small city, no matter how well-balanced could be wholly self-contained: there were many specialised functions, easily performed in a big city because of its immense reservoir of varied occupations, its diversity of human interests, and the accumulation of capital resources that no smaller unit could encompass' (*Howard, 1976*).

This led Howard to a cluster of cities near enough to have ties and including a central city of somewhat larger size (58,000 population). Each 'Social City' would be governed by the principle of growth, always preserving a green belt around each city, in a way that the city was relieved of congestion but the residents of the Garden Cities still enjoyed some of the cultural advantages of the main city, yet, through the series of green belts, had all the advantages of living in the country. Rapid transit would provide the communication.

The 'Social City' idea was never applied, although the later notion of satellite cities developed from the Social City concept, and eventually reappeared in the concept of New Towns. With perspicacity, Howard recommended his clusters of Garden Cities as a way of solving London's problems of housing and employment, approximately 50 years before Abercrombie's 1944 Greater London Plan, which proposed siting eight to ten new satellite towns surrounded by green belts. The eventual New Towns around London and Glasgow fulfilled Howard's vision of the 'Social City'.

Letchworth and Welwyn Garden City

The Garden City idea took hold when a Garden City Association was formed in 1899. By 1903, Garden City Limited established the first Garden City on a site at Letchworth, totalling 1529 hectares (3822 acres), 30 miles from London. Two unknown architects, Raymond Unwin (1863–1940) and Barry Parker (1867–1947), were chosen to develop the town and it was here that Raymond Unwin first came to prominence (*Miller, 1992*). Unwin and Parker adopted Howard's social concepts and designed Letchworth to be a complete Garden City for 35,000 people. The principle of the limited dividend society was to create a town for the benefit of all the inhabitants. Therefore the rights of the shareholders were limited to a maximum of a 5 percent dividend, and any profits above 5 percent were used for the benefit of the whole community.

Letchworth remains a faithful fulfilment of Howard's ideas, with (1) a wide range of industries and local employment; (2) spirited community life; (3) houses with gardens and large open spaces; (4) a green belt; and (5) single ownership, with excess profit for the benefit of the town (figures 3.10 and 3.11).

Cottages for the workers were one of the leading features of the town built by private enterprise until after the First World War. These attractive, but cheap, dwellings set an example all over the world. Public buildings were also properly provided – school buildings first and then town halls, churches, then a golf club, cricket ground and football fields, in that order.

The plan of Letchworth resembles a group of connected villages around a civic centre, with the factory area outside the town. Each of these 'villages' or neighbourhoods had its own minor centre. This concept, which followed Howard's idea of the self-contained wards, was Unwin's early version of the neighbourhood concept, later developed by Clarence Perry as a major town planning concept. In fact, there

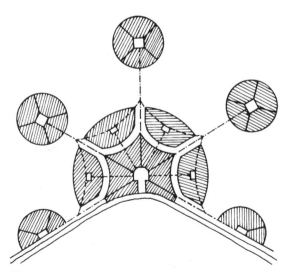

Figure 3.9 City with defined suburbs and satellite towns (after Unwin)

Figure 3.10   Letchworth (by the author)

Figure 3.11   Letchworth (by the author)

was no attempt to impose any geometric pattern and when the first experiment at Letchworth was undertaken, the designers' creativity was shaped by the physical conditions of the site. Of the original 1500 hectares, 500 hectares were included in the town, and 1000 hectares became the green belt. Since then Letchworth has purchased more land, although the density is still approximately 62 persons per hectare. In the first 30 years the town grew to a population of 15,000 people, with more than 150 shops and 60 industries.

The most characteristic feature of Letchworth is the very open layout of the roads and houses, such that the whole town looks like a garden. Where Letchworth may be regarded to have failed or to be mundane is in its architectural character. There is a lack of consistent architectural control and no large buildings which form a particular focus. Unwin was unable to keep architectural control, and concentrated his talent on effects such as cosmetic façades, picturesque gables and hand-made tiles. Nevertheless Letchworth was probably the first English expression of a New Town on a large scale.

Welwyn Garden City was established after the First World War on Howard's personal initiative as part of the response to the need for new housing. It was not part of a governmental plan or Act. Welwyn Garden City was designed in 1919 on a site of 1000 hectares for an ultimate population of 50,000 people. But in its first 15 years it achieved a population of only 10,000. Welwyn, like Letchworth, followed Howard's ideas of (1) zoned land use; (2) permanent green belt; and (3) saving the profits from the town and applying them to public building. Although Welwyn is closer to London than Letchworth, 85 percent of the people still work in the town and it has managed to keep its own identity.

The town plan provided for a definitely fixed urban

area surrounded by a green belt. It was not an ideal plan, but one which directly related to the natural features of the site. The architect-planner Louis de Soissons attempted to give the town a strong civic character and greater architectural cohesion than was shown in Letchworth. The plan was circular in form, with a central civic centre, but, when built, the position of the civic centre became distorted. The residential areas are divided into neighbourhoods, and feature the early use of cul-de-sacs.

Two features emerge from the synthesis of ideals that propelled the Garden City movement. The first is the brilliant meshing of different ideas – green belts, land ownership, cottage housing and many other ideas – in a practical concept. Secondly, the proposals and concepts were developed with an eye to actually applying them. Although Howard himself was unable to produce the physical form of his idea, Unwin and Parker not only understood but put his ideas into their plans. Considering the complexity of the ideas, Letchworth and Welwyn Garden City were surprisingly successful. The examples of Letchworth and Welwyn continued to have their impact not only in Britain but also abroad.

The original Garden City Association advocated town planning legal reform. Following the 1909 Housing Act, the association changed its name to the Garden Cities and Town Planning Association. Then in 1941 it became the Town and Country Planning Association, and remains an influential leader in planning. Howard lived first in Letchworth and then in Welwyn, becoming President of the International Housing and Town Planning Federation before his death in 1928. In 1940, the Town and Country Planning Association had its share in promoting the Barlow Report and then, following the Second World War, the New Towns Act, which legally accepted Howard's

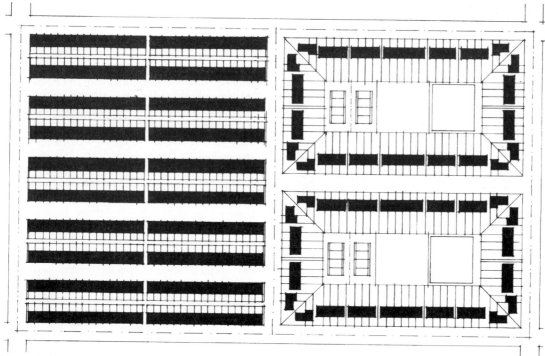

Figure 3.12 Two systems of land development contrasted, from *Nothing Gained from Overcrowding* by Unwin (1912). On the left is the plan of the old by-law street and on the right is a plan of a superblock. By reducing the number and length of streets, Unwin showed that development costs could be cut and more green space provided (after Miller)

concept of decongesting the large cities by dispersing population and industry to complete New Towns, where population size would be limited and where physical size would be contained by the green belt.

Hampstead Garden Suburb

Unwin went on to plan Hampstead Garden Suburb in 1907 and the village of Gretna in 1915. Raymond Unwin was unusual for his time, in that as an architect/town planner he also had strong social ideas and a sense of public duty. The contribution of Unwin and Parker to the Garden City movement consisted of (a) advocating the social importance of beauty, clothed in a naturalistic attitude; (b) limiting density and internal open spaces, including a concern for health; and (c) classifying roads, including the use of cul-de-sacs.

Originally Unwin advocated his ideas in his *Town Planning in Practice* (1909) and then in a pamphlet entitled *Nothing Gained from Overcrowding* (*Unwin, 1909*) (see figure 3.12). Unwin popularised the vernacular cottage traditions in low-density schemes, but he also interpreted Camille Sitte's three main principles, i.e. (1) that towns should be deliberately informal and irregular in building; (2) that groupings

of buildings should also be irregular and that one should understand the relationship between buildings; and (3) the recognition of the parts of the town as units (*Collins and Collins, 1965*) (figure 3.13).

Raymond Unwin is credited with bringing to Britain the design ideas of Camille Sitte, who preached that human and artistic ideals were equally as important as the technical accomplishments of urban development (*Sitte, 1889; Collins and Collins, 1965*). He applied Aristotle's philosophy that towns should be built to protect their inhabitants and at the same time make them happy by advocating that urban design must overcome the rigidity and monotony of the mechanical industrial town. However, Sitte's method of accomplishing his artistic goals was by the simplistic means of suggesting building squares, or placing monuments in open spaces, or creating green spaces in city centres. These were urban design goals and to those who understood the real horrors of the industrial slum, his reforms were thought to be weak and merely window-dressing, a kind of cosmetic surgery to cover up the real problems which festered underneath. His methods were thought to be superficial reforms and did not attack the real problems of overcrowding, lack of mobility, and lack of sanitation.

Sitter principle s

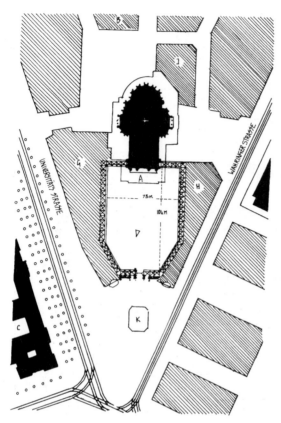

Figure 3.13   Vienna: Sitte's proposed square for the church, indicating the form of new buildings (G, H, L, B) to create urban spaces (after Sitte, in Collins and Collins)

However, Sitte's cosmetic approach can be applied immediately and is easily understood. Its attractiveness produced a loyal following. For example, following Sitte's rules, urban designers would design closed vistas and curved roads, and create little urban spaces. The Townscape advocates in Britain, the Civic Trust movement, and many of the amenity societies are descendants of Sitte's approach and have received popular support.

Unwin became familiar with the work of Sitte after designing Letchworth, but even in Letchworth the integration with nature and absence of rigid geometry in street layouts showed a similar attitude to planning to that of Sitte. Unwin, though, did not understand how to cope with traffic or population pressure, or any of the mechanics of cities, and allowed the principles of informality to carry too much weight. His was an intellectual approach without understanding the real workings of a town.

To Unwin and Parker the village was an 'animate symbol' of society, and consequently it was important to make it beautiful and stylistically cohesive – in short, the physical aspects of Garden City planning to go with the more socially oriented ideas of Howard. Beauty was to be introduced for two reasons: to slow down change to the point where it would have an enduring rather than a transitory effect (unlike a style) and to demonstrate, visibly and externally, once and for all, that an internal order of society was possible. While Howard's and Unwin's ideas are not conceptually dependent, Unwin himself pointed to the complementary nature of the ideas. But, as in the larger scale, the Garden City movement defined the proper relation and proportion between urban and rural and between residential, industrial and recreational areas, so within these areas it defined in detail the relation and proportion between the buildings themselves and the ground surrounding them. Unwin's other important contribution was a differentiated road network, which reduced paving costs, separated residential areas from through traffic, and enhanced the psychological values of important locations. The cul-de-sacs and superblocks, appearing in Letchworth and Hampstead Garden Suburb, became the popular physical features of their planning which were adopted by so many suburban developers. Unwin wrote and spoke well and thus was able to express his architectural concepts to numerous people.

Hampstead Suburb grew from the aim of the reformist, Dame Henrietta Barnett, to save some of the landscape and tops of the hills around London. Very much influenced by the famous slum social worker, Octavia Hill, Dame Henrietta determined to save Hampstead Heath by turning it into a village green surrounded by domestic English houses (*Barnett, 1918*).

Eton College owned a 128-hectare (320-acre) estate immediately to the north of Hampstead Heath. Following the extension of the underground railway to Hampstead Heath, 96 hectares (240 acres) were laid out as a garden suburb according to the designs of Sir Raymond Unwin, with the important buildings by Sir Edwin Lutyens. Influenced by Letchworth, Dame Henrietta's idea was to produce a naturalistic layout in the form of a traditional village, with plenty of open space and private gardens (figure 3.14). In 1905 Unwin, as resident architect, developed the variety of residential 'closes', admired today. To help Unwin achieve the effect he desired, the Hampstead Garden Suburb Act was passed by Parliament in 1906, allowing him to act within the building regulations. The most beautiful and artistic of Garden Cities is thought to be Hampstead Garden Suburb.

Three main principles formed the basis for the

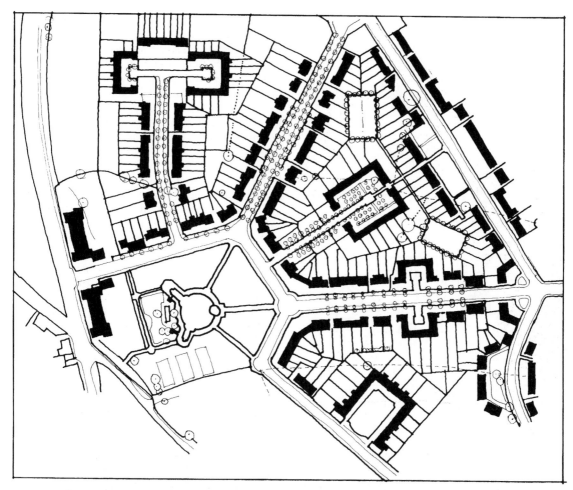

Figure 3.14 Plan of Hampstead Garden Suburb (after Gibberd)

planning of Hampstead Garden Suburb. The first was harmony with nature; the second was to create a communal effect of all the houses; and the third was to provide extensive greenswards and open spaces. The chief controlling factors of the road pattern were the irregularities in the shape of the site and the contours; the provision of private gardens to the majority of the dwellings; the location of the two centres; and the grouping of dwellings round short lengths of comparatively narrow roads. Most of the long roads were developed in depth by the use of cul-de-sacs and closes – a form of clustering houses around a street, thereby resulting in a dead-end street. The street junctions were designed as architectural spaces.

The rectangular closes are perhaps the most successfully designed aspect. A close is formed by a U-shaped block of buildings with the open end screened by trees, shrubs or flowers and small houses

(figure 3.15). The built-up corners and continuous walls of the 'U' give the space definition and the walls are in proportion to the floor plan. Access to the dwellings is by a single carriageway quite close to the façades and separated from them only by grass and informal planting. Access to the gardens behind the end houses is through alleys and those at the sides by back lanes at right angles to the main road. The buildings adjacent to the main road are turned round the corner to start off the return frontage and, together with sheds, screen the back gardens. Unwin tried (1) to enclose space; (2) partially close and define the view with his streets; and (3) create street pictures in the areas of vision. In the end the architectural result is picturesque, with the emphasis on the enclosed space and the rural peace of the village.

In contrast, Lutyens designed the famous Central Square with its two churches to achieve

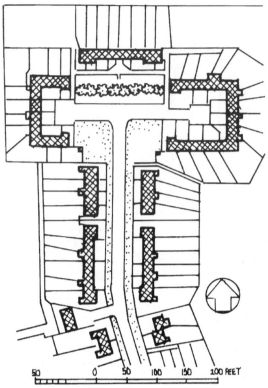

Figure 3.15 Plan of a typical close, Hampstead Garden Suburb (after Gibberd)

monumentality. But Dame Henrietta desired the cosiness of the village atmosphere, and in the end Lutyens had to modify his monumentality and preserve the domestic nature of the suburb: a common enough debate between the popular view wanting cosiness and the architect wishing to exhibit his talents in monuments. Lutyens' composition consists of one large space subdivided by two churches into a central square (with one side open to a view), and two end squares in which there is a greater sense of enclosure (figures 3.16 and 3.17).

The spaces are far too large and open for the buildings surrounding them, and the appearance generally is of one vast, ill-defined area dotted with two churches. But the Central Square is more architectural in character than the other areas and those parts of the design that have been built have a fine scale and robust character far removed from the usual idea of 'Garden City' development.

The Central Square, being divorced from shopping and lacking variety in its communal facilities, does not function as a true neighbourhood centre for the community. Shopping for the suburb is confined to the peripheral roads. As a Garden City, Hampstead Garden Suburb did not fulfil one of Howard's major objectives, as the suburb itself did not contain any industry, but relied on people finding employment in London. But, as a Garden Suburb, it did recreate the

Figure 3.16 Central Square, Hampstead Garden Suburb (from Gibberd, 1953, by kind permission of the Architectural Press)

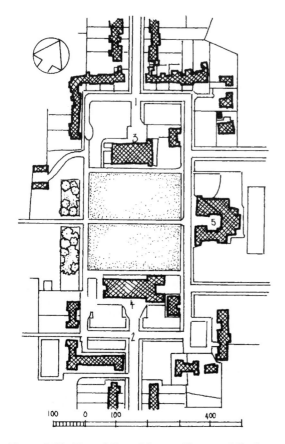

100 0 100 400

Figure 3.17 Plan of Central Square, Hampstead Garden Suburb (after Gibberd). The Central Square has the opposite flank walls of the churches (3) and (4) as its sides, and the Institute (5) is placed centrally on the the other side facing the open space and the view. The other flank walls of the churches terminate the view from the approach roads at either end, and from one side of the two smaller squares

democratic ideas of village life, where all types of people could gather on the village green. So Hampstead is seen not only as a technical and artistic achievement but also as a social achievement.

Raymond Unwin exercised great influence on both town design and the town planning movement up to his death in 1940 while Parker, in his turn, continued building Letchworth until his death in 1943 (*Jackson, 1985*).

Summary

The early model villages, the development of the Garden City and the ideas of Raymond Unwin all point to a particularly British concept of planning which emphasised a desirable quality of life. This quality was obtained through 'cottage' house design, and cottage furnishings with a craft approach. The English remained a nation who lived in houses rather than flats, and loved their houses and gardens. The English concept of town design in the first part of the twentieth century was neither the French Beaux Arts approach, nor the American City Beautiful. Rather the natural indigenous idea of town planning then in Britain was the idea of the garden suburb, until the Futurist City of the linear town planners overturned this approach in the mid-twentieth century.

4 Urban design approaches: the linear city

The linear city idealists

Reacting to Sitte, there were architects and engineers who thought otherwise, that the 'Linear City' held the answer to controlling the growing city. These people included Soria Y Mata, Antonio Sant'Elia, Anthony Garnier, and the greatest linearist of them all, Le Corbusier. Particularly, Le Corbusier scorned Sitte's approach, in that the latter's solution was simply cosmetic and did not solve the basic problems. Indeed it was thought that the earliest linearist was Leonardo da Vinci who, in sketches only, first proposed the multi-level city form. Linear city ideas were later incorporated in the Adams' eighteenth century proposals (figure 4.1).

La Ciudad Linea was the earliest linear city, designed by the engineer Soria Y Mata in 1882 (figure 4.2). His linear city is based on central linear transport and utility systems, which supplied water and electricity to the houses and buildings set alongside the central communications system. In 1922 Soria Y Mata built, on the outskirts of Madrid, a speculative linear suburb based on the tram car as the central transportation system for a few thousand residents, who lived in villas laid out in superblocks. Later, an addition to Leningrad was planned as a linear city in 1930 following the example of Soria Y Mata.

The development of the cast iron and later the steel framework coupled with the invention of the Otis lift in Chicago in the 1880s and 1890s gave architects and planners the opportunity to build skyscrapers of heights vastly greater than had been possible with stone and brick supporting walls. The new vision showed skyscraper flats of thrilling magnificence.

From a totally different viewpoint, various Futurist Italian architects were fascinated by the interaction between vehicular and pedestrian movement in the new city and proposed a metropolis with architectural elements implying either horizontal or vertical circulation (figure 4.3). One of the Italian futurist architects, Antonio Sant' Elia, incorporated in his La Città Nuova concepts of traffic circulation as an

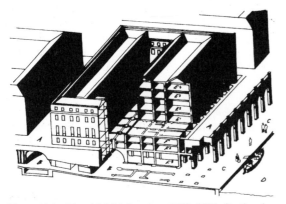

Figure 4.1 The Adelphi, London, 1768–1774. Sectional drawing of speculative venture by the Adam brothers showing multi-level communications 150 years before the linear city. The inner levels were designed as wharfs and storage vaults, while terraced houses were built on the main street level (after Johnson-Marshall)

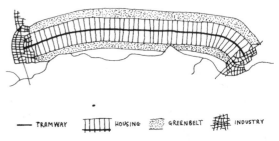

Figure 4.2 The Linear City of Soria Y Mata, 1882 (after Gallion)

Figure 4.3 La Città Nuova by Sant' Elia (after Johnson-Marshall)

integral element of city building (*Caramel, 1973*). Due to his early death in the First World War, Sant' Elia's ideas remained merely passionate sketches, but they show skyscrapers with underground railways, pedestrian walkways connected to lift shafts and roads on different levels, supposedly inspired by the plans for the Grand Central Station area of New York City (*da Costa Meyer, 1995*).

At the same time that Ebenezer Howard developed his Garden City concept, the Frenchman, Anthony Garnier, proposed his concept of a Cité Industrielle while a student holder of the Grand Prix de Rome. Eventually Garnier published his ideas and caused a tremendous stir through Europe (*Garnier, 1917*) (figure 4.4).

Garnier, in his plan for the Cité Industrielle, synthesised all the functions of the town into a comprehensive architectural concept. In this synthesis of functions and in his attempt to express this synthesis at the scale of the house, room by room, he was imaginative and ahead of his time. There is a clear differentiation of city-wide functions – work, homes, recreation space, and entertainment – into distinct, separate zones. The form is linear and designed for 35,000 people (*Wiebenson, 1969*). The plan consists of long, narrow lots running from east to west, placed at right angles to the main traffic roads. At the time Garnier published his plan, it was quite revolutionary to depart from a centralised Renaissance grid and suggest an elongated linear form. The centre of the linear town contains the civic centre, an educational zone and the administrative centre, containing the main railway station, with its tracks underground. The playing fields lead into the green belt of open country, which separates the residential areas from the industry, as in Howard's Garden City.

Garnier also designed the individual houses, keeping them low in height but high in density by relying on communal garden space between the houses. He also suggested rooftop gardens long before Le Corbusier suggested them in his Ville Radieuse. Garnier carefully designed all the public buildings for

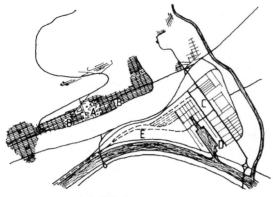

A   Civic Centre
B   Residential District
C   Industrial District
D   Port
E   Railroad

Figure 4.4   Cité Industrielle (after Garnier, in Gallion)

each of the land use zones: hospitals for the hospital zone; schools for the educational zone; offices, museum and libraries for the administration zone. He was the first to design all public buildings in reinforced concrete, which lent itself to a rigid square aspect with whitewashed walls. Probably his most advanced architectural statement in reinforced concrete, steel and glass was the railway station.

Garnier's Cité Industrielle is outstanding for its integration of high-density housing and open space, its concept of the separation of functions, yet providing in its linear pattern space for the expansion of schools, open spaces, and civic space. This allowance for expansion is altogether absent from Howard's Garden City idea, which followed the more traditional myth that cities stayed a static size. Garnier's centrally placed town centre and administrative zone with a spectacular railway terminus and hotel buildings was an exceptionally modern design concept thought out in the later stages of the nineteenth century and drawn up before the First World War.

Garnier's Cité Industrielle and Soria Y Mata's Linear City were probably the two most important influences on Le Corbusier. Additionally, the Frenchman, Eugene Hénard, published *Les Villes de l'Avenir* in which he proposed buildings on stilts with underpasses, roundabouts going under buildings and airplanes landing on rooftops, and it is thought that he too influenced Le Corbusier (*Wolf, 1968*).

Le Corbusier's dominance on city form

Another great single-minded influence on British town

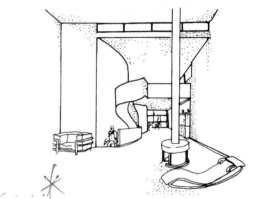

Figure 4.5   Citrohan House (after Dennis)

planning, for better or for worse, was the giant architect/town planner, Le Corbusier (1887–1968). While the English were trying to solve their mammoth housing problem with country cottages, Le Corbusier in Paris projected one tall block after the other. To Le Corbusier, architecture in the twentieth century could no longer be the single building, when the city as a whole was architecture. Le Corbusier took from Garnier's Cité Industrielle the idea of a network of transport arteries, providing for each type of transport separately. He also adapted the idea of separate zoning as against mixed zoning, providing separate areas for a civic centre, industry, education and other functions. Le Corbusier's town planning ideas originated with the basic element of the individual dwelling, a specific house type; unlike Garnier's, which were imposed one on top of the other. The concept of the 'cellular house unit' was first developed in his Citrohan house as the prototype for his city, La Ville Contemporaire (*Blake, 1960*).

The Citrohan house was the first expression of a major spatial change in house design, with its concept of interlocking spaces of different but related heights

Figure 4.6   Villa Stein, Garches, Paris (by the author)

(figure 4.5). The house was two storeys high, two levels on one side, with the kitchen and dining area on the lower level, and the bedrooms above; and on the other side, the living area was a double-storey room with a spiral staircase leading to the bedrooms above. Each flat unit contained a tall two-storey living area contrasted with single-storey service rooms. The flat roof was treated as a garden.

Le Corbusier had conceived the Citrohan House form of plastic expression through earlier studies of the cube, which he tested in several private houses. He was searching for the answer to the continual problem of achieving an open plan that is sympathetic to the movements of people yet still satisfies an accepted architectural order. In 1927, his Villa Stein at Garches, outside Paris, utilised the cube, where the form and proportion were strictly determined by the proportions of the golden section (figure 4.6). Later, one of Le Corbusier's most brilliant expressions of the open plan within the cube was that of the 1930 Villa Savoye, Poissy, where the frame enclosed an open plan, and then, projected in three dimensions, produced a single, clean architectural statement in Cubist form (figure 4.7). Portrayed originally in his single houses, the uncompromising geometry of Le Corbusier's open and closed cubes controlled the expression of his later tall blocks. He had to wait 20 years to build his apartment blocks, but the Villa Savoye and the Villa Stein are consistent with the house types proposed in La Ville Contemporaire.

La Ville Contemporaire, 'The City for Three Million People' by Le Corbusier, was the urban plan

Figure 4.7   Villa Savoye, Poissy, France (by the author)

which attempted to create order, convenience and efficiency – the exactly opposite approach to Camille Sitte's attempt to bring charm to the city. Le Corbusier's 1922 scheme laid out the principles of town planning that he followed in all his subsequent projects (*Le Corbusier and Jeanneret, 1929*). In the centre of the city was a group of skyscrapers cruciform in plan, 50 or 60 storeys in height and spread apart to allow a generous park (figure 4.8). Around the centre were arranged a series of concentric rings of zoning, containing blocks of flats and garden flats.

The First Ring contained blocks of flats – six 'double' storeys high, in the form of long continuous walls, changing direction and creating parks for the dweller. The Second Ring contained garden flats, an area of 'superimposed' villas (figure 4.9) placing one cellular unit on top of another, and providing each of the two-storey houses with a two-storey garden terrace

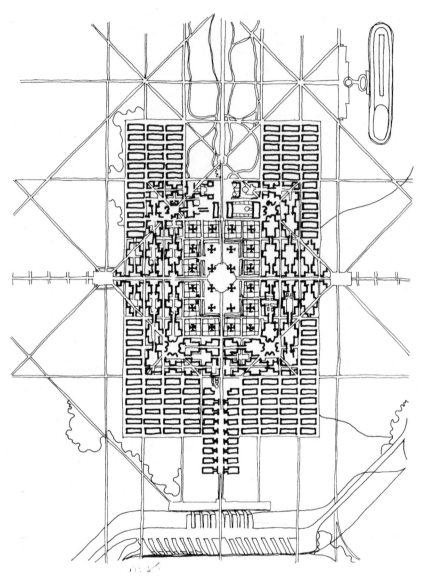

Figure 4.8   The City for Three Million People by Le Corbusier. In the centre are the cruciform office blocks. Surrounding the office blocks are the blocks of flats, then the garden flats, surrounded by the green belt. Beyond (bottom of drawing) are an industrial district, suburb and stadium (after Le Corbusier)

punched out of the building at regular intervals, grouped around inner courts laid out as recreation areas. The Third Ring was a green belt, the only idea Le Corbusier borrowed from the Garden City. The Fourth Ring was an industrial district, a sports area and a suburb.

The traffic plan was the most efficient part of the plan. A hierarchy of roads was determined by the scale of the speed of the vehicles. All urban grids (figure 4.8) were surrounded by one-way elevated roads operating on the figure-of-eight principle, either specific routes for high-speed mass transport, or specific motorways for lorries. A peripheral highway by-passed the city. Finally the pedestrian was to be 'liberated' by keeping all the area within the grid free of vehicles. Pedestrians on normal ground level meandered through parks and gardens, as the buildings were elevated on stilts or 'pilotis' (an idea inherited from Garnier), to enable pedestrians freedom to walk everywhere. The street pattern combined the American gridiron system, which he had admired in Chicago, with the radial plan of his native Paris.

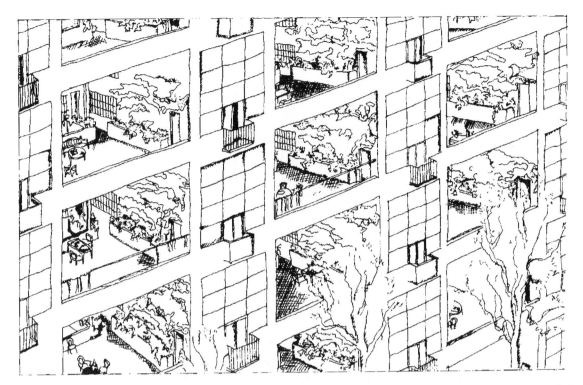

Figure 4.9 'Superimposed' villas showing double-height balconies off the double-height living areas (after Le Corbusier)

Le Corbusier was highly impressed with the mechanics of the automobile, designing a circulation system of straight roads subordinating the human being to the mechanical functioning of the city. Anxious to reduce the journey to work from home to office, he proposed a high-density skyscraper centre. Around this central district ran residential zones which provided only two classes of dwellings, one for the middle class and one for the rich. The workers had to live outside the city centre. Although Le Corbusier claimed he was building for 'the people', he was in fact building for a well-off group.

The 'City for Three Million People' is really the ideal city for business. It does not turn its back on the industrial city, but accepts the high densities of the future megalopolis, and in that regard Le Corbusier's ideas provided a solution for the increasingly large industrial/business city, unlike Camille Sitte or the Garden City adherents such as Ebenezer Howard and Raymond Unwin. Le Corbusier always stated that the huge city was a wonderful place to be. However, Le Corbusier never understood the social consequences of such high density and such concentration of activities. This was his 'Achilles heel' and was to be the downfall of all those many disciples who slavishly followed his concepts at enormous social cost.

As an urban renewal scheme for Paris, the Plan Voisin (1925) was an extension of Le Corbusier's ideas, proposed just after the First World War, and applied to that area of Paris north-east of the Louvre, the Marais (*Le Corbusier and Jeanneret, 1929*) (figure 4.10). He thought of redeveloping Paris in much the same density and height level as that of Chicago skyscrapers in the 1880s and although he chastised American civilisation, nevertheless he adopted its attitudes of ignoring the existing historic urban fabric in favour of total redevelopment (*Le Corbusier, 1947b*).

In the Plan Voisin de Paris, he proposed 15 twenty-storey apartment dwellings at a density of 320 persons per acre, rather like densities on Park Avenue, New York. These skyscrapers are shown rising in a green park, and standing on 'pilotis' to make the ground free for pedestrian use (figure 4.11). Land saved by the use of high density is used for playgrounds, nurseries and sports fields; even the 12 percent of the ground which was used by building gives its roof space to playgrounds for nurseries. In this scheme, the traditional street is turned up on its end, the street becoming a vertical circulation shaft (lifts, fire stairs, etc.).

Le Corbusier reiterated his ideas for the skyscraper city in his summary, La Ville Radieuse. There he

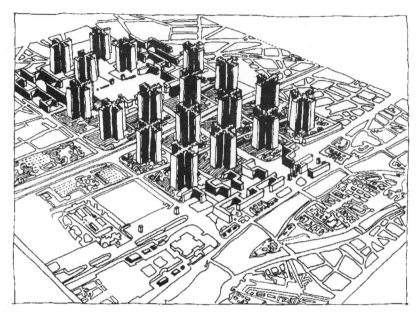

Figure 4.10   Plan Voisin, Paris (after Le Corbusier)

Figure 4.11   Skyscrapers in a green (after Le Corbusier)

argued against Howard's Garden City, as follows:

'The Garden City leads to individualism, in reality to an enslaved individualism – a sterile isolation of the individual. For the sake of one per cent of society or one tenth of one per cent – for the sake of the people who are well off and whose needs it can satisfy – the Garden City plunges the rest of society into a precarious existence. ... Instantly, events of urban life are organized: traffic problems, communal services eliminate waste, residential neighbourhood in the Radiant City. If one eliminates the corridor-street, entire ground surface of the city is allotted to the pedestrian. The earth is occupied by lawns, trees, sports and playgrounds' (*Le Corbusier, 1933*).

Le Corbusier argued strongly for his flats in skyscrapers, later hated by thousands of hapless tenants. He argued for high density, that the vertical solution had all the answers. The size of each grid was scaled to the supposed distance that people are willing to walk, linked to an underground station at each street location. The resulting superblock scale was a

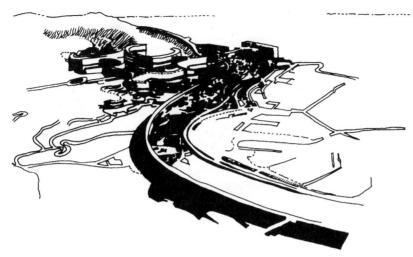

Figure 4.12   A plan for the city of Algiers (after Le Corbusier)

rectangular grid of 200 m × 400 m blocks, surrounded by clover leaves and underpasses. The population for the whole scheme was three million and each superblock housed 3000–4000 people, with a high density of 150 dwelling units per residential acre (375 persons per hectare).

In the office area, the densities were raised to 1200 workers per acre (almost 3000 per hectare). Compared with a British national average of 30 workers per acre (75 workers per hectare), Le Corbusier's concentrated zones are very dense. He also proposed 'garden cities' for two million workers on the outskirts, adjacent to the factories. Le Corbusier's plans placed great emphasis on the mechanical functions of the central office and business areas and in this he was extremely far-sighted and revolutionary. Le Corbusier realised that in order to preserve any kind of decent-size park space he had to build high. The result was a detached attitude to nature – detached physically because of the high densities and detached spiritually as a consequence of the physical plan. The approach is the opposite to that of other contemporary architectural giants, such as Frank Lloyd Wright who, for example, attempted to get closer to nature by building inside a waterfall as at the Kaufman House, Falling Water, Pennsylvania.

The roof gardens of the 'villas superimposés' became a communal roof garden – an elevated piazza for everyone, as in the later Unités at Marseilles, and Nantes. In terms of plastic expression, the physical units of terraced houses were regularly divided within the slab block – but the plaza on the roof was allowed to be freer in form. The concept, that every family in a skyscraper could have its own private garden in the sky, was one of the most radical ideas of urban living.

In the late 1920s and 1930s, Le Corbusier created plan after plan, for rebuilding Rio de Janeiro, São Paulo, Antwerp, Stockholm, and a final scheme for Paris (1937), all carefully worked out according to the principles described in La Ville Radieuse, but none of them built (*Le Corbusier and Jeanneret, 1934, 1938*). The Algiers plan (1930–34) contains some of his most brilliant conceptions of the continuous terraced house, and multi-level highways that separated traffic (figure 4.12). The buildings became integrated with the continuous highways, as earlier conceived by Sant' Elia. His famous hillside apartment house was proposed in a continuous strip and entered on the uphill side of a floor half-way up the building. This entrance floor was open to allow all pedestrians a view of the Mediterranean, along with the continuous highway and parking below. Years later, the concept reappeared in the multi-storey high-rise blocks of Park Hill and Hyde Park in Sheffield.

Following the Second World War, Le Corbusier made proposals for the reconstruction of St Dié (figure 4.13). In the 1945 plan, which incorporated many of the theories embraced in La Ville Radieuse, he replanned the central part of the city, as the civic, cultural and residential section (*Le Corbusier and Jeanneret, 1946*). Eight tall apartment buildings were to surround the civic centre, each building being about 150 feet high and housing 1500 persons. The initial development presupposed the building of four tall buildings – a 'vertical garden city' – to accommodate 6000 people, while the single-family district to the north was to house about 4000 persons. The large open space throughout the town plan permitted the retention

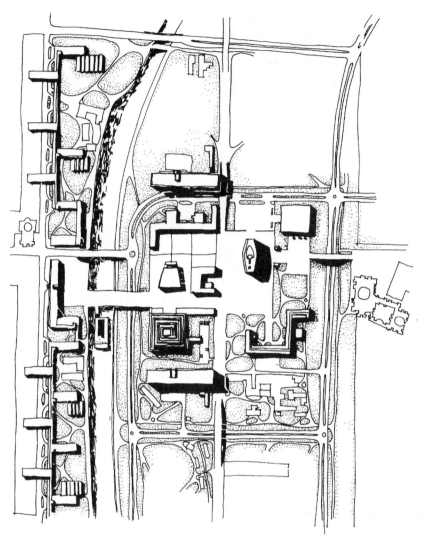

Figure 4.13   A plan for the town of St Dié, 1945 (after Le Corbusier)

of historic old buildings which survived the devastation of the war. The large cells created by the major traffic arteries were to be developed as landscaped parks and informal circulation. The St Dié scheme was important as it influenced the designs for many British town centres in the 1950s and 1960s.

Le Corbusier's completed projects and CIAM

Le Corbusier finally achieved recognition in his own country with the building of several vertical skyscrapers, which he christened Unités d'Habitation. The first Unité was built at Marseilles and others followed at Nantes, Berlin and Briey-en-Forêt (*Le Corbusier and Jeanneret, 1952, 1957*) (figure 4.14).

They contained flats with double-height living rooms, superimposed on each other, until they reached 20 storeys. Disastrously, the municipalities would not pay for 'gardens in the air', reducing the gardens to tiny balconies, harbingers of the social malaise which was to appear decades later, particularly in Britain. Le Corbusier's only other built planning achievement was the creation of Chandigarh, the new capital city for the Punjab, India (*Evenson, 1966; Le Corbusier/Gans, 1987*). There, he built magnificent monuments in the Court of Justice, the Secretariat and the Assembly buildings (figure 4.15). Some insist that he was the last of the City Beautiful planners, wishing only to create monuments (*Hall, 1988*).

In Britain, one of the few schemes influenced by Le

Figure 4.14   Unité, Nantes, France (by the author)

Corbusier before the war was that at Highpoint, London, built by Tecton. Otherwise there were no built examples in Britain of Le Corbusier's ideas until after the Second World War, 25 years after he first suggested La Ville Radieuse, though generations of British architects have been and still are hypnotised by the brilliance of his architectural drawings. Particularly after the Second World War, architects from the British architectural schools were determined to create a brave new world of 'mini-Le Corbusiers', utilising the technology and socialist principles to build in the International style of the Modern Movement, intermingling the Corbusian approach to building with the Gropius and Mies Van der Rohe approach to comprehensive urban redevelopment. Examples of Le Corbusier's influence can be found everywhere. They include the Roehampton II Estate, designed by Sir Robert Matthew and Sir Leslie Martin, and probably the most extensive and lavishly built example, a true realisation of La Ville Radieuse (chapter 9). Sadly most of the other examples, some 384 towers built in Britain between 1954 and 1974, were cheap partial imitations of Le Corbusier's ideas, with devastating consequences.

Le Corbusier also influenced British town planning by helping to organise, with Siegfried Giedion, founder in 1928, the Congrès Internationale d'Architecture Moderne (International Congress for Modern Architecture), which greatly influenced planners and architects over the world. In the Athens Charter of 1931, CIAM proposed systems for the study of the development of urban planning on a major scale (*Sert, 1942*). At the time, there was considerable disagreement between the old important centres of academicism and decorative classicism in the USSR and the École des Beaux Arts in Paris, which gradually changed their position to the new positions of the CIAM members. For CIAM adherents, the concept of the modern movement was reinforced by the philosophy of logic, economy and reliability and, most importantly, grew from a functional approach to the programme, connected with poetic and plastic values. Aesthetic values *per se* did not exist in isolation from the functional issues. The CIAM group were influential until the late 1950s, when it became clear

Figure 4.15   High Court, Chandigarh, India (by the author)

that the members' interests were no longer directed only at the development of modern architecture as they had been in Le Corbusier's day, but more towards the development of the total human habitat (*Tyrwhitt, Sert and Rogers, 1952*). In the 1930s, the aim of Le Corbusier, Gropius and others had been to establish 'modern architecture'. Now established in all its forms, CIAM was no longer needed.

The Mars Plan for London

Greatly influenced by Le Corbusier, the Mars Plan for London was produced by a committee in December 1937 under the chairmanship of Arthur Korn (figure 4.16). At that time, London had a population of 8.4 million, half of whom worked in the City, the West End, the port or the industrial area of the west and north-west. The Mars Plan tried to coordinate housing and work, to give maximum amenities and to link housing and work with a planned traffic system. Korn considered that the most important contribution was the articulation of the vast housing areas into a concept of a sequence of units starting from the smallest unit, the family, and proceeding through graded stages to the city as a whole (*Korn, 1953: 89–90*). Each unit was to be part of a larger unit and each had a centre about which its life revolved. Seven different units were proposed: (1) the family; (2) the dwelling block; (3) the residential unit of 500 people; (4) the neighbourhood unit of 5000 people; (5) the borough unit of 50,000 people; (6) the district unit of 500,000 people; and (7) the city as a whole. Each unit was to be expressed architecturally and thus give visual articulation to the vast urban area. In addition, each of the larger units (500 or more) was to be given its own set of health, educational and cultural facilities.

Post-war, neighbourhoods and reconstruction areas were designated, but not the larger units, and it was important that these larger units were articulated. Each of these larger units (of 50,000) had a width of half a mile with an unspecified length so that both transport and recreational facilities would be available within walking distance. In the Mars Plan, the arterial road is on one side and open green space on the other. The Civic Centre of each borough unit opened out on the green with its public buildings. The Mars Plan was a more detailed version of the linear plan, with the main artery along the work area.

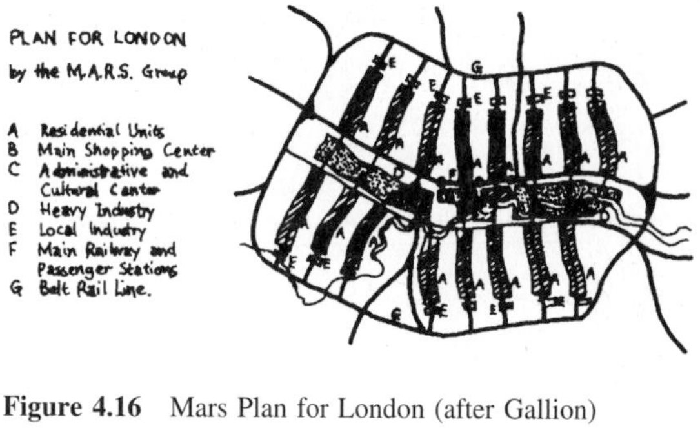

Walter Gropius and the Bauhaus movement

Great opprobrium is directed towards Le Corbusier for the stark multi-storey blocks of the 1950s and 1960s, but what is less well understood is that some of the responsibility for the layout design is due to the theories of town planning of Walter Gropius (1883–1969) and the Bauhaus movement. So penetrating and lasting an influence has been the Gropius approach to physical planning that, even in the post-modern 1990s, one can still see perfect Bauhaus layouts in the latest New Towns, such as Almere in the Netherlands. Thus Gropius and the Bauhaus method of town planning can be said to have influenced town planning for over 70 years.

In 1908, Gropius initially worked for Peter Behrens, where he met Adolph Meyer, who together with Mies Van der Rohe, Karl Feger and even, for a limited time, Le Corbusier, made up Behrens' professional staff. Gropius became obsessed by the conviction that modern constructional techniques would not be denied expression in architecture and that expression demanded the use of unprecedented forms. His first commission, with Meyer, was the Fagus Factory of 1911, which stood as a manifesto of the new architecture.

Following the First World War in 1919, Gropius became simultaneously head of the Weimar School of Arts and Crafts and head of the Weimar Academy of Fine Art, which he combined into the Bauhaus School for Design (Das Staatlich Bauhaus Weimar). Gropius and his colleagues set out to revolutionise the approach to design. As Gropius stated, 'The Bauhaus sought to establish the common root of all the arts not only by studying a wide range of design activity, but by a study of aesthetic fundamentals, such fundamentals as line, space, movement and proportion, in an effort to define a common language of communications between the artist and the community' (*Herbert, 1959: 4*). These goals were taught in its inspiring preparatory course developed first by Gropius, then by Moholy-Nagy and subsequently by Gyorgy Kepes (*Kepes, 1944; Moholy-Nagy, 1961*). The revolutionary method of teaching incorporated both training in imaginative design and

PLAN FOR LONDON
by the M.A.R.S. Group

A Residential Units
B Main Shopping Center
C Administrative and
   Cultural Center
D Heavy Industry
E Local Industry
F Main Railway and
   Passenger Stations
G Belt Rail Line.

Figure 4.16 Mars Plan for London (after Gallion)

great technical proficiency. Manual instruction in the famous workshops was 'mandatory as providing good all-round training for the hand and eye and being a practical first step in mastering industrial processes' (*Gropius, 1935: 63*). The emphasis was on evolving good designs for mass-production. So successful was this aspect of the Bauhaus training that its products in chairs, furniture, kitchen equipment and china are featured in every Museum of Modern Art in the Western world.

Likewise there was a revolutionary approach to a new architecture, which derived its architectural significance solely from its own organic requirements, devoid of all trivialities. New principles of construction meant new designs, such as (*Gropius, 1935: 23, 24*):

(1) The liberation of architecture from ornament
(2) Emphasis on structural functions
(3) Concentration of concise and economic solutions
(4) A new spatial vision of design
(5) The abolition of the separating function of the wall. With the new steel or concrete framework, the wall became a screen and could be made of lightweight material
(6) Technical improvements in steel and cement reduced the area required by supporting members, allowing rooms to open up
(7) The old-fashioned window could become a continuous horizontal casement window, subdivided by thin steel mullions. Thus glass began to assume tremendous importance in the design of the new architecture
(8) The flat roof superseded the gable roof.

It was then but a small step to apply the new architecture to town planning. Gropius recognised that most people wanted a separate house with a garden, but as this was not possible to provide for the masses, he considered that the tenement should be redesigned and that 8–12 storey blocks of flats could satisfy all requirements in regard to light, air, tranquillity and egress. High blocks did away with the sunless courtyards of the old tenements and the spaces in between could be developed as parks for children.

The slab block of high-rise housing, the linear multi-storey building with flats opening onto both façades, was Gropius' contribution to urban design in the 1930s. Maximum light and air and landscaped public space combined with a minimum allocation of surface areas for the walkways, connecting the buildings, resulting in a reduction in the cost of layout and maintenance. Gropius' logical proposals, developed in numerous competitions, met with

objections between 1929 and 1932 concerning mainly (a) technical suitability and cost of installing lifts in low-cost housing; (b) psychological adjustment (adapting to living in small flats high above the ground); and (c) urbanisation – the loss of urban quality. Gropius saw the high-rise flat building as providing the necessary standards of space, sun, light and heat and the possibility of connected parks and play areas between buildings, and also technically being able to incorporate the ideas of the centralised master household with centralisation of the domestic work of the individual small family and/or single person. Thus would housing be provided for the masses.

> 'The slab block was an extreme development of the dwelling as a minimal space for people to rest in while devoting the greater part of their time to social living. The high-rise building became the central ideological figure in the modern architecture culture and the coherent representation of both its ideals and its limitations' (*Berdini, 1983: 14*).

Gropius further thought that a garden city of nothing but detached houses would destroy the concept of a town. His aim was to combine a mixture of high-rise (vertical) and low-rise (horizontal) housing. The low-rise should be restricted to outer suburban areas and the high-rise to the popular central areas. Blocks of

Figure 4.17 Dammerstock housing, Karlsruhe, 1927–28: 4–5 storey flat blocks with $2\frac{1}{2} - 4\frac{1}{2}$ flats (after Gropius, in Giedion)

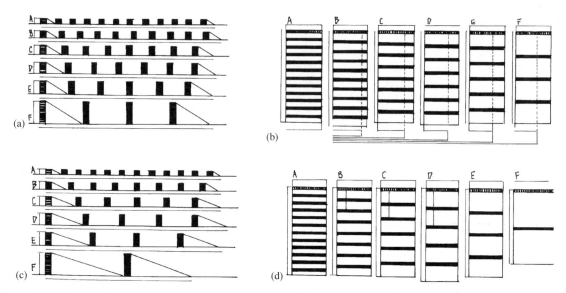

Figure 4.18   Diagrams illustrating the development of a rectangular building site with parallel rows of dwellings of different heights, from the one-storey terrace house to the ten-storey flat blocks. On the same site, slablike ten-storey buildings result in greater green space than between terraced houses. (a, b) If the size of the ground and the angle of sunlighting remain the same, the number of rooms increases with the number of storeys. (b) If the sunlighting angle and the number of rooms remain the same, the size of the ground diminishes as the number of storeys increases. (c, d) If the size of the ground and number of rooms remain the same, the sunlighting angle diminishes and the sun exposure improves (after Gropius, in Giedion)

flats in between these two heights had the advantages neither of houses nor of multi-storey flats and so should be abandoned. His diagrams show that, with the same angle of light between buildings, one achieved higher densities with four ten-storey blocks than with three-storey blocks (figure 4.18). He therefore advocated restricting the density of population in terms of the maximum amount of floor space per acre of building land, but abolishing limitations on the height of buildings, thus freeing more ground space per inhabitant. He was most concerned with improving light and ventilation for overcrowded slum dwellers.

He praised parallel rows of apartment blocks, which 'have the great advantage over the old peripheral blocks that all apartments can have equally favourable orientation to the sun, that the ventilation of blocks is not obstructed by transverse blocks and that the corner apartments are eliminated' (*Gropius, 1935*) (figure 4.18). This was how miles of parallel housing slabs were born, which can be seen in Czechoslovakia, France, Britain, the Netherlands, etc.

Resigning from the Bauhaus for internal reasons, he moved his architectural practice to Berlin. With the advent of Hitler and Nazism, the Bauhaus was closed in 1932 and its many members scattered to safety throughout the Western world, including Gropius, who came to Britain. The culture of the Modern Movement filtered very slowly through to the British professions

so when Gropius arrived in Britain in 1934, associated with Maxwell Fry, he immediately attempted to transfer the new continental architecture to Britain, and free the rationalist theory from the social developments of Weimar Germany. Having built some private houses and schools, he published *The New Architecture and the Bauhaus* in 1935. However, too much scepticism underlay British culture's superficial interest in modern architecture and instead Gropius, in 1937, left Britain for the United States, accepting an invitation to become head of the Graduate School of Design at Harvard University and teach architecture and town planning (*Isaacs, 1991*).

His module in planning was the basic minimum dwelling required for urban industrial populations. He quoted German sociologists who foresaw deep-rooted changes in the social structure of the nation, i.e. the decline of the family unit, and, with the emancipation of women, the growth of centralised households of co-living units which lightened the double burden of employed women with families (*Gropius, 1943*). Thus Gropius, a half-century ago, anticipated a social pattern requiring new housing types which, by 1990, was the majority pattern of all households in Nordic countries and an increasing pattern in Britain.

Gropius argued for the compact city, for settling large numbers of working people around a concentrated city core, making for short commuting distances, which implied the use of multi-storey skyscraper blocks to reduce the commuting distance. The single family house was against this trend; and for the average low-income population, suburban life was uneconomic. He also felt that the high-rise dwelling was better adapted to the needs of a mobile working class, little realising that in the years to come the working class would become stuck in their high-rise buildings with little or no occupational mobility. The costs of road building and utilities would be less. The effectiveness of land use becomes extremely functional, resulting in improved conditions of hygiene, economy and traffic.

Gropius acknowledged that the prejudice against high-rise buildings lay in the difficulty of supervising children. He solved this by placing supervised kindergartens in the landscaped areas between the blocks and supervised nurseries for babies on the rooftops. Ultimately, when the high-rise blocks were built in Britain, the politicians refused to pay for the kindergartens and the nurseries, and so the disadvantages, which Gropius predicted, occurred.

Gropius considered that the building of 'community centres is of even greater urgency than housing itself, for these centres represent a cultural breeding ground which enables the individual to attain his full stature within the community' (Gropius, 1935: 146). If only the politicians had listened, instead of building acres of housing for thousands of people without community facilities as at Easterhouse, Glasgow; Southwark, London, and many other examples.

The geometric rigidity which is so evident in most of Gropius' town planning work began to disappear in the last years of his life. With experience, Gropius' approach to planning became freer, as he was influenced by the work of the Americans Clarence Stein, Henry Wright and Lewis Mumford, who contributed to a more organic concept of planning (Isaacs, 1991).

The last surprising fact about Walter Gropius is that he was an early 'green' advocate. He wrote that the greatest responsibility of the planner and architect was the protection and development of our habitat: 'Until we love and respect the land almost religiously its fatal deterioration will go' (Gropius, 1935: 184). He termed designing within the natural habitat of the Earth his 'total architecture'. He was wrong about high-rise flats being the panacea of town planning but in his other planning strictures he was right.

Summary

Lewis Mumford, Raymond Unwin and the Camille Sitte school were critical of Le Corbusier for planning cities in which there was no place for the human being to express his personality and for the human scale to survive (Fishman, 1977). On the other hand, Mumford's regional approach was similar to Le Corbusier's regional approach and concept of linear cities for the whole of Western Europe. The greatness of Le Corbusier lies in his acceptance of the megalopolis. Thus his architectural solutions are always in keeping with the complex technological, overpopulated scale that the megalopolis represents. His solutions require vast sums of money to be executed properly, whereas in Britain, the housing estate trauma of the 1950s and 1960s resulted partially in his ideas being cheaply half-built and thus contributed to the destruction of the social fabric. In contrast, the Garden City idea can be built lavishly or cheaply, and still works either way.

Both Le Corbusier and Gropius were as prolific with their writings as with their drawings. Both were the prophets of the Modern Movement, but emotionally totally different. Le Corbusier was magisterial and dogmatic, whereas Gropius appealed to the intellect rather than to the emotions, seeking to explain and to sow understanding of the new architecture (Giedion, 1954). Le Corbusier was the most imaginative of European architects, whereas Gropius was the great teacher and communicator. Of Gropius' many contributions to contemporary architecture, it is his contribution to architectural education that is most widely acclaimed. Gropius's theories and teachings spawned many of the most famous of the original modern architects – Marcel Breuer, Mies van der Rohe, Serge Chermayeff, Maxwell Fry, and the members of the Architects' Collaborative. Gropius and the Bauhaus ideas are inseparable, and together, through all the generations of students, they constitute a decisive influence on the shape of the architecture and town planning of the twentieth century.

i) Mixed use — why should it be better then separation of functions ?
ii) Short commuting distances by use of multi storey blocks

does it not say that community is dead ?

Part II

Planning Principles

5 The development of planning principles

Early town planning legislation and tinkering reforms in the thirties

Britain had seen the Utopian experiments at Saltaire (1853), Bournville (1878) and Port Sunlight (1887). The Garden City movement produced Letchworth and Welwyn Garden City in 1903 and 1919 respectively. The Public Health Acts had made some impact on the condition of housing. Nevertheless large numbers of people lived in slum conditions, in overcrowded houses lacking basic amenities, and in very high densities. Then government bodies and professional associations alike started movements for the extension of sanitary and health measures into town planning. These various movements culminated in the first piece of legislation which actually bore the name town planning – the Housing, Town Planning, Act 1909.

The Act did not provide a definition of town planning and was generally vague, due partly to the lack of experience with legislation of this nature. Instead it emphasised solely raising the standard of new development. The preliminary parliamentary debates best describe its purpose as follows: 'The object of the Bill is to provide a domestic condition for the people in which their physical health, their morals, their character and their whole social condition can be improved by what we hope to secure in the Bill. The Bill aims in broad outline at, and hopes to secure, the home healthy, the house beautiful, the town pleasant, the city dignified and the suburb salubrious' (*Parliamentary Debates, 1908*).

The new powers of this Act authorised the preparation of schemes by local authorities for controlling the development of new housing areas. The Act permitted local authorities to prepare town planning schemes with the object of 'securing proper sanitary conditions, amenity and convenience'; this was 'only for land which was being developed or appeared likely to be developed' (*Cherry, 1972*). The layout of Garden Cities and green suburbs required that new schemes dealt with streets, roads, buildings, sewerage, lighting, water supply, and ancillary works. Thus the acceptance of town planning came through public health and housing measures. The new town planning measures provided for large areas of new housing. By 1915, 74 local authorities were authorised to prepare a total of 105 schemes, but many were never completed, partly due to the advent of the First World War (*Hall, 1988*).

In London, the London County Council was allowed by Parliament to build estates for working-class tenements. Between 1900 and 1914, the LCC provided approximately 4000 dwellings in tenement schemes on clearance sites and some 3000 houses on peripheral and county estates (a total of 18,000 local authority houses had been built by 1914) (*Hall, 1988*).

During the First World War, a reconstruction committee, under the chairmanship of Sir Tudor Walters, proposed a new standard for working-class housing and thereby laid down the pattern for local authority housing which was to be built during the inter-war years (*Tudor Walters Report, 1918*). The Tudor Walters ideal was a development of houses built at a density of not more than 30 houses per hectare (12 houses per acre), each standing in its own garden, in a well laid-out estate. There was to be a minimum distance of 70 feet between houses to guarantee winter sunshine, and houses were to be built in short terraces and cul-de-sacs. A large living room with a sunny aspect was laid down as essential and every house was to be fitted with a bath in a separate room, a WC approached under cover, a larder of reasonable size and a coal store (*Cherry, 1972*). These new standards evoked the ideas of Unwin.

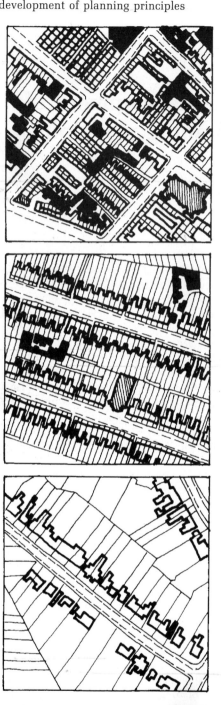

COMMUNITY USE   RESIDENTIAL   INDUSTRIAL

Figure 5.1 Birmingham: pre-1914 housing. Top: pre-by-law back-to-back housing. Middle: post-by-law tunnel-back houses. Bottom: detached and semi-detached villas (after Gibson and Langstaff)

The Tudor Walters report proved to be one of the most potent influences on the development of the twentieth century British city (*Hall, 1988: 68–71*). After the First World War, the housing shortage became the major crisis in many European countries, and the need to adequately house the returning soldiers became the battle-cry of conscience-stricken nations. In Britain, with an estimated deficiency of 600,000 dwellings, the house became the primary element of town planning. Neither the private sector nor the well-intentioned reform idealists could make up this shortage, particularly at rents which people would be able to pay.

The British soldiers came back from the war to a 'Homes Fit for Heroes' campaign which helped bring in the Housing and Town Planning Act of 1919 (the Addison Act) (*Stewarton, 1981*). In the 1919 Act, town planning was made obligatory on local authorities above a certain size, i.e. all boroughs and urban districts having a population of 20,000 or more had to prepare schemes under a time limit, until 1932 when the time limit was abolished. The 1919 Housing and Town Planning Act accomplished more for housing than it did for planning. For the first time, the 1919 Act accepted the principle of state subsidies to local authorities for the clearance of slums and the building of low-cost housing. Thus it was this Act which started the nationwide growth of council housing estates. This Act adopted the Tudor Walters standards of dwelling to be provided, such as the three-bedroomed house, at not more than 30 houses per hectare (12 houses per acre). Development generally took place on virgin land on the edge of the town, with the resulting paradox that vast municipal estates grew alongside private suburbs, which were also growing rapidly, accelerated by equally rapid development in transport. Between 1919 and 1933/34, local authorities in Britain built 763,000 houses (*Burnett, 1978*).

After the First World War, Raymond Unwin became Chief Architect at the Ministry of Health and thus many of the elements of the Garden City were transferred into a garden suburb housing estate. Relatively low density set in individual gardens, a romantic style of cottage architecture and street layout, and landscaping in sympathy with natural form were some of the features that came to characterise not only inter-war municipal estates but also, less often, suburban private house builders (*Hall, 1988*) (figure 5.2). Some of these estates were planned around extensions to the growing suburban railway. A good number of these dwellings were designed in the manner of William Morris and the Arts and Crafts Movement, and still have a lingering charm which

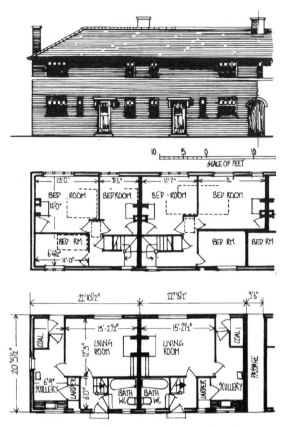

Figure 5.2 Cottage homes: Unwin's plans from the Ministry of Health Manual (1920), following the Tudor Walters Report (after Hall)

Figure 5.3 Inter-war housing (by the author)

later, more efficient tenements lacked (*Donnison and Soto, 1980*).

A few local authority cottage estates were built in the 1920s, providing excellent but more expensive housing for former slum dwellers. These charming cottage estates are prized even today. Unfortunately most of the other houses are dull and monotonous, reflecting the financial constraints and lack of social concern of the period. Seventy years later they blight the urban landscape, requiring rehabilitation techniques to reface them (figure 5.3).

The largest of the vast council estates was probably Becontree Estate, a 'cottage' estate built by the London County Council in Essex on the outskirts of London. Virtually a new settlement of over 100,000 persons was built over a long period from 1921 to 1934. Although originally it served as a model for other towns to copy, it later became the prime example of what not to do. The most serious criticism was that Becontree, like the other municipal estates of this period, was simply a dormitory, devoid of community facilities, industries and other employment opportunities.

A better example was Wythenshawe (1928) in Manchester, more properly developed as a satellite garden town, 'which would have industries of its own and be partly self-contained, but which would nevertheless be a part of Manchester and provide accommodation for Manchester workers' (*Simon and Inman, 1935*). The land on which it was built was bought by Manchester Corporation in 1926, and developed throughout the 1930s, but community facilities such as the shopping centre were built only in the 1960s (*Deakin, 1989*).

Later the Housing and Town Planning Act 1919 became the more comprehensive Town and Country Planning Act of 1932, containing many innovations. It was the first planning legislation to include the word 'country' and therefore introduced concern about the need to protect Britain's countryside from unplanned and sporadic development. The Act required local authorities to prepare and enforce plans for urban

T+CP 1932
1st mention of country

areas. The general objectives were to control development; to secure proper statutory conditions (amenity and convenience); to preserve existing buildings or other objects of architectural or historic interest and places of natural interest or beauty; and generally to protect existing amenities (*Cherry, 1972: 150*). There was an important extension of powers, additional to legislation, namely, that land might be zoned for building, temporarily reserved from such development, or subject to compensation, permanently so reserved. Thus, for the first time, land might be kept permanently free from building on account of certain planning criteria. This was a major step forward in obtaining some development control over what was previously haphazard development. However, the compensation provisions were not easy. In order to avoid payment of compensation, local authorities zoned vast areas of land for building purposes, but often held the land temporarily in reserve, thus helping create early forms of planning blight. In addition, the procedure of preparing and passing a planning scheme through all the stages took about three years. Developers took advantage of a legislative loophole, when they did not have to apply for planning permission, giving them a great deal of leeway. Another deficiency was the weakness of the administrative structure of local authority. Thus the solution to the slum problem, finally implemented in the 1930s, was not to replace slums with cottage estates but to replace slums with walk-up tenement flats. The cleared inner-city sites and some overspill cottage estates on the fringe were built to lower standards than the cottage housing of the 1920s.

The Town and Country Planning Act 1932 became coupled with the Housing Act of 1936, which brought the issue of housing, slums and town planning even closer together. In blighted areas the local authority for the first time was given the power to prepare a redevelopment plan, compulsorily purchase the land, and rebuild either privately or by a local authority. Unfortunately the 1932 Town Planning Act and the 1936 Housing Act were weakened by continued administrative difficulties and the fear of having to pay excessive compensation.

The effect of transport and the spread of suburbia

At the same time that Ebenezer Howard and others were developing the Garden City, prompted by their deep concern for the social and environmental welfare of the people, there were land planners stimulated by the competitive spirit and profit motive. These speculators took advantage of the dissatisfied and crowded city dweller of the industrial city. High land costs squeezed the single-family household further and further away from the centre. Suburbs were laid out in the country, miles from existing community facilities, and 'house-hungry' families grabbed them. Thus suburbia was born.

Suburbia expanded along railway lines, electric tram lines, main radial routes, and eventually all along the ever-expanding underground railway system, gobbling up existing villages and pressing on into the country. The growing city forced the suburban dweller further and further out, until he was beyond the community facilities which served the populations. Then, when facilities were developed in the suburbs, the suburbs became satellite communities or dormitory areas. It was the development of the underground rail systems which prompted an explosion of speculative housing and an extension of local authority housing estates in satellite communities, providing mainly housing without community facilities (figure 5.4).

One result of the suburban expansion was ribbon development, the exploitation of the frontage of main roads leading out of towns for housing purposes. Long narrow plots 25–35 feet wide were built in endless rows following the long routes out of the city. Building followed the endless roads of the bus services. Each house had an individual feature, like a bay window or a stained-glass window, designed to set it off from the council housing. Mock Tudor, gabled details or modified Elizabethan were favourite architectural idioms in the tradition of the Arts and Crafts Movement (figure 5.5).

There were some exceptions, such as one of the earliest planned railway suburbs, Bedford Park in West London, built in 1876 by the architects Norman Shaw and Phillip Webb, who finely detailed their houses in the Gothic or Elizabethan manner (*Creese, 1966b; Bolsterli, 1977*) (figure 5.6). Architects were prohibited by their professional institute from engaging directly in speculative building, to the misfortune of Britain's landscape. But in any case, in the 1930s, most architects were designing either in pseudo-Georgian or in a revolutionary Bauhaus Modern, neither of which appealed to the white collar worker.

In an attempt to control a situation that was already out of hand, in 1935 new legislation, the Restriction of Ribbon Development Act, required all development within 68 metres of the middle of a classified road to have the approval of the highway authority. By the outbreak of the Second World War in 1939, private ownership had increased so much that nearly one-third

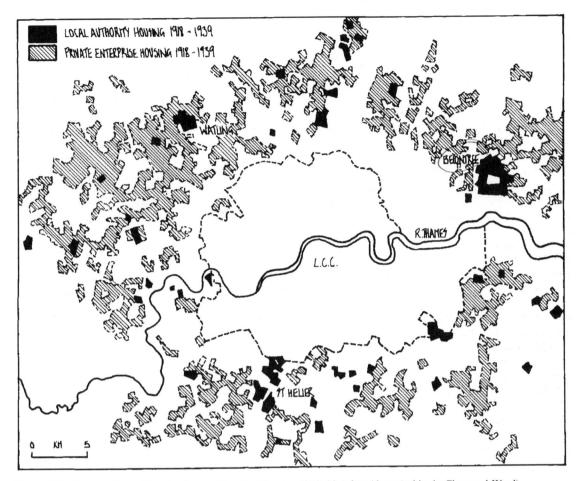

Figure 5.4   Construction of housing beyond London County, 1919–39 (after Abercrombie, in Clout and Ward)

Figure 5.5   The new suburbs: Osbert Lancaster's drawing of the new suburban house (after Hall)

of all dwellings, out of a total of 12.7 million dwellings, were owner-occupied, while 10 percent of these had been built by local authorities since the First World War (*Cherry, 1972: 133*).

The Depression: social and economic problems

The Depression hit Britain in the early 1930s causing widespread unemployment and consequent misery and hardship. One of the few lasting solutions to come from the tinkering of the 1930s was the concept of trading estates. The Special Areas Act of 1934, which made £2 million available for creating employment in depressed areas, included a provision for the setting-up of trading estates as a means of providing local employment to stop the steady drain of out-migration from areas of high unemployment, such as Central Scotland, the North East, and South Wales. Little effect was made by monetary inducements to

Figure 5.6   Design for terraced houses by Norman Shaw (after Bolsterli)

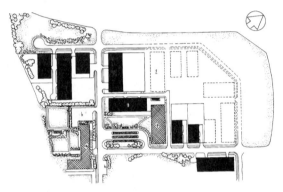

Figure 5.7   North Tees Trading Estate, designed by William Holford (after Gibberd)

industrialists but one of the success stories was the ability of new trading estates to attract new industry. The trading estate was and still is a separate area for medium- and small-scale industries in a specially provided zone, with its own infrastructure, parking and services. The most famous of these estates were the Team Valley Estate in Gateshead, the Hillington Estate in Glasgow, and Treforest near Pontypridd, which were models of advanced planning layouts, providing more suitable industrial opportunities for economically depressed parts of the country (figure 5.7). By 1939, about 12,000 people were employed in factories in special areas owned by the state, many of them on these trading estates, which successfully operate to this day.

In summary, in the 1930s the city had growing pains. Traditional life was engulfed by the impersonal life of the industrial city. Suburbia attempted to recreate a village atmosphere, but without the community facilities and employment. The jobs were still in the city centre, forcing the family to become mobile, to go to the city to work, and return to the suburb to live. For the suburbanites the city thus became a place in which to work or visit, but not a place in which to live.

The major housing evil remained, and slums still abounded, although most towns could point to a slum clearance programme, however modest. The limited slum clearance programme meant that a very large number of old and unfit dwellings, where sanitary conditions were primitive and amenities rare, were still inhabited. In the late 1930s, perhaps one-third of working-class dwellings in London were in poor condition and due for demolition. For example, just before the Second World War, Manchester had 68,000 dwellings (one-third of the total in the city) unfit for human habitation (*Cherry, 1972: 135*).

In Birmingham, a survey suggested that 20 percent of housing should be condemned immediately. Conditions on Tyneside and in Scotland were even worse. In Great Britain as a whole, 550,000 dwellings were ready for immediate demolition and a further 350,000 had a life of not more than six years. More effort needed to be expended on slum clearance and new housing construction but political events with the occurrence of the Second World War caused a delay in such efforts.

The green belt principle

A green belt, defined by the then Ministry of Housing and Local Government, was an 'area of land, near to and sometimes surrounding a town, which is kept open by a permanent and severe restriction on building. The form it takes depends on the purposes it is to serve' (*MHLG , 1962a: 1*). The ancient idea of an agricultural belt around communities is mentioned in the Book of Numbers and can be traced back to the days of Moses (Book of Leviticus). As a formula for town planning, green belts appeared even in Plato's Utopia (*Ginsberg, 1955*). Thus, since ancient times, communities have had open areas around them, serving a variety of purposes, for growing crops, grazing animals, festivals and other public activities; serving as a barrier to the spread of epidemics and providing an open field of fire against an advancing enemy.

By the medieval period, when Sir Thomas More wrote *Utopia* (*More, 1516*), the pattern of green belts emerged closer to modern trends (*Osborn, 1956*). In More's *Utopia*, towns were surrounded by country belts which made a permanent boundary preventing the town from extending over the green belt. Population shifted from town to town in a way that a town lacking people would take the overspill population from other towns till all towns were filled. Once this stage was reached, a new town would be built beyond the existing green belt. The green belt around each town provided a field for adults to walk about and a safe area for children to play. Thus the emphasis of the green belt shifted from economic reasoning to that of pleasure and close proximity to fresh country air.

The first planned attempt at establishing a green belt in Britain was Queen Elizabeth I's Royal Proclamation of 1580 (*Rasmussen, 1937*). Elizabeth I felt that London was too populous and needed regulation to prevent crowded housing and the consequent poverty, although the stated aims of her Proclamation were to ensure an abundance of cheap food and to minimise the effects of an outbreak of plague. Thus to limit growth, her Proclamation forbade any new building on new sites within three miles of the London City Gates. James I made a similar Proclamation, and later the Cromwellian Parliament in 1657 passed an Act to limit the growth of London. Under Cromwell all new houses within a ten-mile radius of London were required to have at least four acres of land. These regulations, however, failed to curtail the growth of London.

In the nineteenth century, many of the Utopian new town schemes proposed a type of green belt. The linear city theorists, although dramatically opposing the Garden City concept in every other aspect, also proposed green belts. Sir Ebenezer Howard, in his Garden City, proposed a green belt of some 5000 acres, outside the city, separating houses from industry. Further uses for the green belt, such as separating communities and permanently restricting the growth of communities, appear at Letchworth and Welwyn. Thus Howard was amongst the first to build the green belt as a permanent and inviolate limit on growth.

After Howard's proposal for green belts in the Garden City, other proposals were discussed in the 1920s, but were not implemented. At the same time, the growth of suburbia mushroomed in the inter-war period, encroaching on proposed green belt land. Thus, the green belt concept sharpened up the planning process by focusing people's attention on urban growth and land use planning on the fringe of the big cities, and the need for a clear demarcation between town and country.

Implementation of the green belt

It was left to the London County Council to implement the green belt for the contemporary city. Sir Raymond Unwin in the 1931 Report of the Greater London Regional Planning Committee (1929–33) reviewed the planning of building development coupled with a green belt. Control of the green space would ensure the orderly distribution of urban development, reserve recreation land on the edges of large urban areas to compensate for the lack of space within the city boundaries, and provide land for expansion (*GLRPC, 1931*). However, Unwin recommended that the green belt be only a temporary reservation of land, but later recommended that land be purchased by the local authorities to form a 'green girdle', a continuous tract of land three or four kilometres wide around London (*Elson, 1986: 5*).

The essence of green belt provision was that landowners be compensated for the loss of the development value of their home parks and farms, and that other green belt land be purchased for permanent retention. Several years of lobbying and jockeying followed, with conferences, reports and recommendations, until a crisis point came in 1934 when Neville Chamberlain, the Minister of Health, stopped compensation for green belt land from Exchequer funds. Without funds the scheme was impossible.

However, the London County Council (LCC) adopted Unwin's Parks Committee recommendations 'to establish a green belt "girdle" of open space lands, not necessarily continuous but as readily accessible from the completely urbanised area of London as practicable' (*MHLG, 1962a: 2*) (figure 5.8). The scheme, which came into effect on 1 April 1935, covered the counties of Buckinghamshire, Essex, Hertfordshire, Kent, Middlesex and Surrey, and the

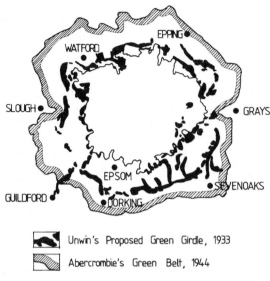

Figure 5.8   Unwin's Green Girdle (after Elson)

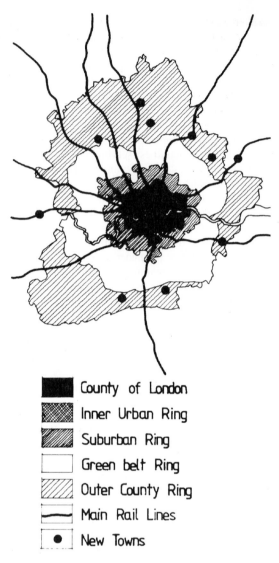

Figure 5.9   London's Green Belt *after Abercrombie* (in white)

then county boroughs of Croydon, East Ham and West Ham. In July 1937, the Parks Committee proposed that the LCC should promote parliamentary legislation to give protection to the green belt, and, within one year, the Green Belt (London and Home Counties) Act 1938 was passed, which allowed local authorities to enter into covenants with landowners, which were restrictive of the use of land, to pay compensation, and to buy land for the green belt. The Act conversely restricted the right of local authorities to dispose of green belt land, but did not rule out disposal.

Thus the 1938 Act viewed the green belt idea as limited open space against a background of development. The open space was for the health and amenities of the people living near the green belt. True to Howard's original concept, the Act required the permanent sterilisation of open land against building use. Although eventually the Act proved inadequate because of the high acquisition costs of land, yet large amounts of land were bought before World War II which were to become extremely important (figure 5.9).

The Scott Report on Land Utilisation in Rural Areas (*Scott Report, 1942*) further aided the implementation of green belts in Britain, by viewing the green belt as a tract of ordinary country of varying width around the town and as 'a tract where the normal occupations of farming and forestry could be continued so that here, as elsewhere in rural land, the farmer is the normal custodian of the land – it is then the reverse of sterilisation and could include golf courses and open land' (*Skinner, 1976: 7*).

In 1943, the Clyde Committee recommended a green belt for Edinburgh in its report *The Future of Edinburgh*, which stated: 'We realise that the day will undoubtedly come when the present boundary will not contain sufficient available land for all the needs of Edinburgh's growing population, but the solution appears to us not to be in completely building up the area within the boundary nor in the spreading out over the adjoining agricultural land immediately outside, but in decanting the surplus into growing communities in the adjoining country areas to the south and east of

emphasis on agricultural nature of greenbelt.

the agricultural belt' (*Skinner, 1976: 9*). The green belt was not immediately designated around Edinburgh, but was eventually implemented in the 1960s.

The last major events in the evolution of the green belt before the 1947 Town and Country Planning Act were the 1944 Greater London Plan (*Abercrombie, 1945*) and the 1946 Clyde Valley Regional Plan (*Abercrombie and Matthew, 1949*), both of which proposed green belts. In the Greater London Plan, Abercrombie adopted the agricultural basis put forward in the Scott Report, while the green belt policy aided the policy of population and industrial dispersion throughout Britain, outlined in the Barlow Report (*Barlow Report, 1940*). As Abercrombie's primary objective was the relief of the congestion in London, the green belt provided within its inner boundary a limit on future expansion, and with its outer boundary a definition of the distance where building could begin again. Though Abercrombie superimposed the idea that the agricultural belt would also support the recreational needs of London, no explanation was offered on how to reconcile the agricultural and recreational objectives. Even so, Abercrombie proposed that 125,000 people move into the green belt from London and Croydon, and some 4000 acres of green belt land were eventually taken up for housing.

Interrupted by the Second World War, London's green belt was not officially incorporated into plans until 1947, by which time the London County Council had acquired 23,118 acres for the green belt, was liable to pay for 1577 acres, and had provisional arrangements for 48,746 acres (LCC progress report 1947). Altogether approximately 55 square miles of land were purchased.

The Clyde Valley's green belt needs were seen by Abercrombie and Matthew to be different from that of London. For London, Abercrombie had conceived the green belt to be largely serving as an 'impact zone' between London and the satellite communities. The Clyde Valley was seen as 'a great agricultural zone which contains not only the conurbation itself, but also the proposed new towns' (*Skinner, 1976: 24*). After allowing for future foreseen development, the green belt was to occupy all the land between the urban edge and the moorland edge, including all the developed farmland surrounding the urban areas. The moors were to provide recreation, such as hill walking at the time.

The green belt policy led to the concept of urban growth also being controlled by the decentralisation of industry and its population to areas beyond the green belt. Thus the 1938 Green Belt Act and the Distribution of Industrial Population Report (*Barlow Report, 1940*) were a conceptual pair. Having halted growth in the green belt, the growth had to go somewhere, and thus an overspill policy was required.

The decentralisation of industry and people: the Barlow, Scott and Uthwatt reports

Despite the increasing amount of legislation, the growth of the metropolis of London had not been halted, while the dire effects of the Depression continued to be felt. Increasing unemployment, publicised by hunger marches, forced the government to designate 'special areas' where the main objective was to attract new industries. Secondary aims were to provide new public and social services and to provide for the clearance of derelict sites. Although the new trading estates, such as Team Valley near Gateshead, and Hillington near Glasgow, managed to attract new industry, most of the concentration of new industry occurred in the London area, leaving high numbers of unemployed in the depressed areas.

In response, the government set up the Barlow Commission to investigate the 'Distribution of Industrial Population'. The Barlow Report, published in 1940, just after the beginning of the Second World War, was a milestone in planning thought and contained a wealth of material. Most of its major policy recommendations were accepted by all post-war governments as basic planning policy.

The Barlow Commission was appointed:

1 to investigate 'causes of the present distribution of the industrial population and the probable direction of any change in that distribution in the future';
2 to investigate 'social, economic or strategic disadvantages of concentration'; and
3 to recommend remedial measures, if any, to be taken in the national interest (*Barlow Report, 1940: 5*).

After examining the nature of the chief industrial areas, industrial development around London and the depressed industries, the report concluded there was no reason for supposing that the trend of industrial movement to the South East would be permanently checked, although it was not inevitable. The Commission regarded the trend as undesirable and recommended measures to stop it. These measures included:

1 'continued and further redevelopment of congested urban areas, where necessary, with due regard being paid to the attention of such advantages as a well planned town can provide, of the cultural and

physical attributes of the country;

2 decentralisation and dispersal of both industry and industrial population from such congested areas;

3 provision of checks, as far as possible, to further growth of London' (*Barlow Report, 1940: 86*).

The term 'decentralisation' implied a spread of industry or population over a limited area; dispersal implied a spread over a far wider area. Thus, for the first time, decentralisation and dispersal appeared as government policy. The Barlow Report considered that the economic advantages of concentration to industry consisted of proximity to the market, reduction of transport costs, and the availability of a supply of suitable labour. The disadvantages included high taxes on high site values, loss of time because of traffic congestion, and loss of efficiency due to fatigue because workers had to make long journeys to work. The Commission considered that Garden Cities, satellite towns and trading estates made the most useful contributions to the problems of relieving congested urban areas, but considered that such development could not be left to private enterprise because of the enormous financial commitment involved, and therefore, government finance was required. London was the major problem, but the planning of London was bound to the existing multi-tiered system of local government. Hence, the Barlow Commission followed its examination of London by advocating the development of a new local government system along regional lines, incorporating Regional Councils, which would become the principal planning authority for the region. With adequate financing, decentralisation could be encouraged.

The Commission's conclusion contains most of the major planning principles of the period 1935–75, that the problems of location of industry were national in character, therefore national action was necessary and a central authority, national in size and character, was required (*Barlow Report, 1940: 201–207*). The activities of this authority should be beyond those of existing departments. The objectives of national action should be: (a) continued and further redevelopment of congested urban areas; (b) decentralisation or dispersal of both industries and industrial population from such areas; and (c) encouragement of a reasonable balance of industrial development throughout the regions of Great Britain. The continued drift to London and the Home Counties constituted a social and economic problem which demanded immediate attention. The dispersal of people could be achieved by developing Garden Cities and garden suburbs, satellite towns, trading estates or the expansion of existing small towns

and regional centres.

The Barlow Report began the trend towards comprehensive planning. The exceptional part of the report was that it emphasised the economic drawbacks of continued urban growth. The idea that it might be better from an economic standpoint to control the national growth of urban areas was completely new. The Second World War changed the unemployment problems and 'depressed areas' were the first to receive munitions factories. The war also provided the opportunity to test many of the recommendations of the Barlow Report. The bombing of Britain created a fervent desire to rebuild anew and this was a tremendous stimulus to town planning. Everywhere people were enthusiastic and determined to rebuild new cities in the bombed areas. By the end of the Second World War, the ideas of curbing industrial development around London and pumping new industries to the still depressed areas had been accepted. The coalition government in 1945 implemented some of the recommendations of the Barlow Report in the Distribution of Industry Act of 1945, and inducements were offered to industrialists who established in the Development (Special) Areas. The government was given permanent powers to limit industry in the London area with powers that lasted through the 1970s. It was not until the 1980s that industry and new office building were once again permitted in London. The Barlow Report also recommended a central authority with responsibility for industrial location.

In this same optimistic atmosphere of rebuilding and establishing industries, in 1941 the government set up a series of committees to report on other post-war reconstruction problems, including (a) the Uthwatt Committee on Compensation and Betterment (*Uthwatt Report, 1941*); (b) the Scott Committee on Land Utilisation in Rural Areas (*Scott Report, 1942*); and (c) the Beveridge Committee on Social Insurance and Allied Services (*Beveridge Report, 1942*).

The Uthwatt Report concentrated on the vexing question of betterment, the taxing of unearned profits from land resulting from planning decisions. This became a contentious issue throughout the post-war period with three separate attempts to implement a betterment policy, under the 1947 Town and Country Planning Act, the 1967 Land Commission Act, and the 1975 Community Land Act, all repealed by subsequent governments.

The Uthwatt Report saw planning controls as part of a much larger and more comprehensive scheme for the nationalisation of all development land and that public authorities would carry out the development. In the

1947 Town and Country Planning Act, all development rights were vested in the state via a central land board set up to acquire land for development and to levy a 100 percent tax on private development land gains.

This attempt to nationalise development failed, as adequate funds were never available. The Uthwatt provisions of the 1947 Act were repealed in 1953. The attempts of subsequent Labour governments to resurrect the scheme came to nothing, although Wilson tried twice. In 1967 he set up a Land Commission to undertake development on behalf of the public but the Conservatives abolished the Act in 1971. Wilson tried again with the 1975 Community Land Act and the 1976 Development Land Tax Act, both of which were later repealed by Mrs Thatcher.

The Scott Report on Land Utilisation in Rural Areas expressed grave concern about the rate of loss of the countryside under urban sprawl, and recommended that there should be no automatic right to develop and that there should be a comprehensive planning system of schemes which were in the public interest. This approach supported the notions of urban containment and high-density urban development to save precious agricultural land. The implications of the four reports – Barlow, Scott, Uthwatt and Beveridge – were that town planning could no longer be considered in terms of development schemes, but needed to address numerous economic and social problems as well.

The County of London Plan, 1943, and the Greater London Plan, 1944

The 1943 County of London Plan (*Abercrombie and Forshaw, 1943*) and the Greater London Plan, 1944 (*Abercrombie, 1945*) were the first town planning schemes to embrace the recommendations of the Barlow Report, and both were conceived during the struggles of the Second World War and promoted by Lord Reith, then Minister of Works, who was also later to promote New Towns. The County of London Plan was based on expected new legislation and financial assistance. The authors agreed to present a moderate, comprehensive plan, where all attempts would be made to retain the old structure and make it workable under modern conditions. Yet the plan's great strength was the breadth and boldness of its proposals. Abercrombie wrote of a living and organic structure which had persisted despite overgrowth, decay and the Blitz. He realised that London was a collection of communities fused together physically with a strong local emotional loyalty. It was to be one of the main objectives of the plan to 'disengage these

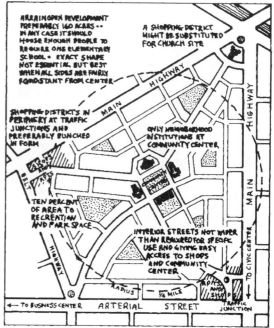

Figure 5.10   Neighbourhood diagram by Clarence Perry in the New York Regional Plan (1929) (after Creese)

communities, to mark more clearly their idealities, to preserve them from disturbing intrusions' such as traffic, and to restore the London communities. 'The planning of an existing town should stimulate and correct its natural evolution trends' (*Abercrombie and Forshaw, 1943: 1–20*). London's four major defects were traffic congestion, depressed housing, inadequate and maldistributed open spaces, and the 'jumble of houses and industries', generally termed indeterminate zoning. The fifth defect, urban sprawl, became the subject of the Greater London Plan, 1944. A further defect was the lack of coherent architectural development in recent buildings.

In the Geddesian tradition, a detailed extensive survey was the basis of the plan. The suggested remedies covered not only physical defects but also the legal and financial machinery. Foremost in the plan was the reconstruction and decentralisation of the congested areas. With the wholesale rebuilding of the bombed areas, new communities were to be created, such as the redevelopment of 1500 acres of Stepney and Poplar. Another proposal was to provide adequate open space, which meant a further increase in the number of people to be decentralised, estimated between 500,000 and 600,000 people. Secondly, the County of London Plan attempted to relocate industries from the congested areas, but these proposals were less successful than the

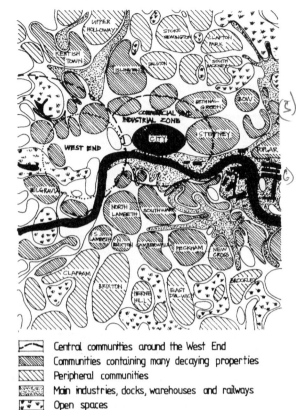

Central communities around the West End
Communities containing many decaying properties
Peripheral communities
Main industries, docks, warehouses and railways
Open spaces
Waterways

Figure 5.11   Neighbourhood diagram, County of London Plan, 1943 (after Abercrombie)

decentralisation of people.

Thirdly, the County of London Plan advocated the conservation or creation of communities which would divide into smaller 'neighbourhood' units of between 6000 and 10,000 people required to service a primary school, a concept which had been proposed years before by Clarence Perry in the New York Regional Plan as the planning unit for the creation of new communities and the retention of old ones (*Perry, 1929: 88*) (figure 5.10). Abercrombie incorporated Perry's basic neighbourhood unit concept into the County of London Plan as one of the means of retaining London's cellular structure. The purpose of the neighbourhood unit was to create a physical unit within which family life would be lived, with physical bonds to the primary school and the neighbourhood centre, which together form the focus of the neighbourhood (figure 5.11).

Fourthly, the special features of any new development, such as rebuilding the areas along the Thames and creating beautiful open spaces, were to be enhanced. Great emphasis was placed on new open space standards, and, as most of London was woefully deficient in open space, new open spaces were to be provided first in areas in which they were deficient. The open space plan aimed at providing a coordinated system of open spaces for whole areas, linked up with the existing parts. Fifthly, higher densities of population were to be housed without discrimination between flats and houses, so as to provide more flexibility. Flats were proposed in high blocks to keep the ground space free, being consistent with Le Corbusier's philosophy. Sixthly, Central London was to be designed with many pedestrian precincts, with traffic by-passing the precincts. The transport plan was minimal and perhaps the worst part of the whole plan. The road plan proposed outer ring roads (North and South Circular), two corresponding inner ring roads, fast traffic ring roads (elevated or sunk), and sub-arterial roads from ring(s) around the precincts. The radial roads and the sub-arterial roads were to be designed as parkways. The surface and railway plan was shown in conjunction with the roads. The underground railway system fared better than the surface rail and extensions were made to it. The docks were to be rebuilt, but that great scheme never actually occurred until the London Docklands development in the 1980s, when the docks were developed for housing and offices and not for shipping purposes. Public utilities and markets were to be rebuilt, as were schools and hospitals, all in accordance with revised planning standards.

In order to achieve the plan, the authors proposed stricter zoning, statutory development plans, and the detailed relocation of industry. The County of London Plan was based on new and greater planning controls which later appeared in the 1947 Town and Country Planning Act. The plan also hinted at programming, incorporating financial considerations. The proposal for the decentralisation of the population was perhaps the most important policy, and was to be achieved in five ways (*Abercrombie and Forshaw, 1943: 35*).

1   'In-filling of gaps in incomplete housing schemes within the County;
2   creating close-in housing groups attached to areas of industry ... metropolitan satellites;
3   satellite communities located within the Metropolitan traffic area;
4   outer satellites, usually developing towns in the fifty mile radius; and
5   dispersal of population remote from the Metropolitan influence.'

The method of achieving the decentralisation of

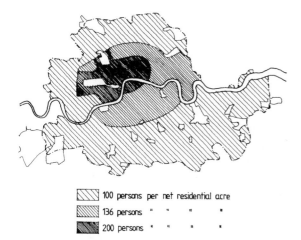

100 persons per net residential acre

136 persons   "   "   "   "

200 persons   "   "   "   "

Figure 5.12   Diagram of proposed population densities, Greater London Plan, 1944 (after Abercrombie)

people was outlined in the subsequent Greater London Plan, 1944, which concerned the regional area of about 30 miles radius from the centre, where there existed a blighting jumble of houses and industry, which had developed sporadically, coupled with inadequate transport facilities (figure 5.12). The development of Outer London had been hasty and ad hoc, and contained only pockets of planned communities, like Hampstead Garden Suburb, and the settled areas near the green belt.

Finding the concept of the London region rather nebulous, Abercrombie based the plan on the following assumptions (*Abercrombie, 1945: 5*):

1 In line with the Barlow Report, no new industry was to be admitted to London or the Home Counties (this was not put into effect).

Table 5.1   Decentralisation

1.	Immediate post-war housing programs within the County – quasi-satellite	125,000 people
2.	Additional to existing towns within the Greater London region – the Outer County Ring	260,000 people
3.	Additional to existing towns outside the Greater London region mostly 40–50 miles from the centre of London	163,750 people
4.	Eight new satellite towns outside the Green Belt Ring	100,000 people
5.	Dispersed wholly outside the Metropolitan influence	100,000 people
Total		1,033,000 people

Greater London Plan Abercrombie, 1944: 32–38

2 Decentralisation of the people and industry from the congested centre (table 5.1). The County of London Plan had recommended an inner city maximum density of 136 persons per acre. This figure was difficult to realise, as densities in the blitzed areas and nearby had been between 300 and 500 persons per acre. Abercrombie would have preferred a density of 100 persons per acre (which was still higher than Garden City standards of 36.5 persons per acre), but it was considered too expensive and difficult for so much industry to move out from the city to allow such a reduction in density. Abercrombie assumed that if a density of 100 persons were achieved, 818,000 people would have to be decentralised from the County of London. By adopting the higher figure of 136 persons in the inner city, Abercrombie calculated that only 616,000 people would need to be decentralised from the County. In addition to the decentralisation of people within the County, Abercrombie proposed that 415,000 people be dispersed from the region outside the County area, making a total of 1,033,000 persons to be decentralised. The two factors of people and industry were to be decentralised together, creating a rearrangement of population and industry within the region. The relocation of over one million people was an incredible concept.

3 The net hope of the first two objectives was that the overall population would decrease, on the basis that population and industry would go beyond the regional area.

4 The Port of London was to remain an international port.

5 New planning powers were to be created to help control land values.

The structure of the 1944 plan was based on zoning in four rings (figure 5.13). The Inner Ring contained the congested areas requiring decentralisation. The Suburban Ring was a static zone in regard to housing and industry. The Green Belt Ring would allow limited expansion of existing communities but with no new centres. In the Outer County Ring beyond the green belt was the proposed expansion of existing centre sites for new satellite communities. The Outer County Ring was to be the chief reception area for London's overspill.

The plan detailed how decentralisation could be accomplished, with further chapters on community planning standards, industrial decentralisation and a discussion of the new legal machinery required.

Other valuable plans included the West Midlands

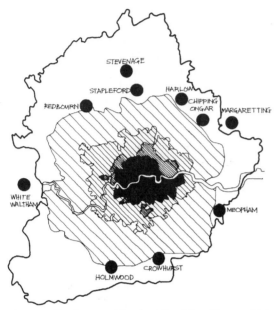

Figure 5.13   County of London Plan (after Abercrombie)

Figure 5.14   Clyde Valley Plan, 1946 (after Abercrombie and Matthew)

Plan (*Abercrombie and Jackson, 1948*) and the Clyde Valley Regional Plan (*Abercrombie and Matthew, 1949; Grieve, 1991*). The West Midlands Plan dealt with the three counties of Warwickshire, Worcestershire and Staffordshire, including Birmingham and its 2½ million people. Since this conurbation had at its centre a large area of derelict and waste land, it was thought that reclamation of this land would suffice to house the overspill of Birmingham and Wolverhampton, and together with the development of secondary centres within a 50-mile radius in the region would act as counter-magnets to the attraction of the conurbations (*Cherry, 1988*).

The Clyde Valley Regional Plan area was a narrow congested plain, hemmed in by moors and hills, thus limiting development, which was further limited by the liability of much land to either flooding or mining subsidence. After preserving a green belt, as discussed, three New Towns were proposed as part of a goal of sending half a million people from the slums of Glasgow to suburban extensions, New Towns and other towns beyond the region, a considerable measure of decentralisation (figure 5.14). Other advisory regional plans to establish a framework for urban dispersal were made towards the end of the war. Most were less effective and comprehensive (*Self, 1957*).

Summary

Abercrombie's two London plans and Matthew and Abercrombie's Clyde Valley Plan became the philosophical expression of physical planning thought well into the 1960s, and continue to be not only a pleasure to read but stirring in their imaginative percepts. The Barlow Report's conclusions formed the basis for planning for the next half-century, while the green belt principle remains the most tenaciously held of all planning principles.

6 Land use planning, new towns and town development

The 1947 Town and Country Planning Act

The Second World War created a great and enthusiastic desire to build a new and better Britain. The old system was to be replaced by a new system, and the old social and economic problems were to be corrected. Everywhere, the new spirit dominated people's thoughts. A number of concepts arose from the London plans. Most people agreed that the growth of the large cities had to be restricted by large-scale overspill to New Towns and expanded towns. In addition, the plans for the reconstruction of blighted areas and distribution of industry needed new planning machinery to effect the new planning approach as provided by the 1944 Town and Country Planning Act, an interim Act to the final 1947 Town and Country Planning Act.

Historically the three Acts created immediately after the Second World War – the 1946 New Towns Act, the 1947 Town and Country Planning Act, and the 1952 Town Development Act – were the most drastic and far-reaching planning legislation ever proposed. After the 1947 Act, the concept of the ownership of land was completely changed, as an owner no longer had the right to develop land, and no right even to change its use, without permission. From that point onwards, ownership of land has meant nothing more than the bare right to go on using the land for its existing purposes. The 1947 Town and Country Planning Act was not the work of one political party, but was accepted by both of the parties as a major piece of legislation passed with a consensus view. For the first time the state was placed in the position of having an absolute right to give or to withhold its permission to changes in the use of land. The Act accomplished six major objectives:

1 It devised a new system of land use control by means of development plans subject to regular review.
2 It prohibited (with certain exceptions) the carrying out of any kind of development without the consent of a local planning authority.
3 It provided for the levying by the Central Land Board of development charges payable on the carrying out of any kind of development.
4 It expropriated the development value of all land. Initially, compensation for the loss of the development value was to be paid out of a £300 million fund, which accepted compensation based on the existing use value only. There was no compensation required, however, for the refusal of planning permission.
5 It conferred upon local authorities wide powers to undertake developments themselves, and together with these powers, the acquisition of land.
6 It provided financial assistance to local authorities to enable them to acquire land, and to develop or redevelop.

Compensation and betterment clauses have changed radically over the years. The 1947 Act provided a compensation fund, which was reviewed in the 1950s and then changed again so that the development value of private property and compensation for compulsory purchase was paid on a market value basis. But in the 1960s, the rapid rise of land values made planning more complex and fears of heavy compensation stopped timid planning authorities from enforcing development plans. Eventually, a Land Bank was established to overcome the problem of rising land value. The Land Tribunal had a large sum of money offset to loan for compulsory purchases in major cities. Even so the Land Bank did not have enough money to provide for all the development needed. Both the original £300 million fund and, later, the Land Bank were disbanded.

The development plan and planning permission

The instrument of land use control was the development plan, a two-dimensional plan indicating (a) the manner in which the land covered by the plan was to be used, and (b) the temporal stages by which the development was to be carried out. The 1947 Act defined a development plan as 'a plan indicating the manner in which a local planning authority propose that land in their area should be used'. It was intended to show, for example, 'the direction in which a city will expand; the area to be preserved as an agricultural green belt, and the area to be allocated to industry and to housing' (*MTCP, 1947b*). The range of maps of the development plan, along with other maps which the authority thought appropriate, included a statutory Development Map showing all land uses; a statutory Programme Map showing the time periods in five-year intervals by which the proposals were to be implemented; a statutory Designation Map showing land designated as liable to compulsory purchase; a statutory Comprehensive Development Area Map showing areas to be totally redeveloped; and Survey Maps (land use and condition of buildings particularly, but including others).

The development plan had to be approved by the Minister, but first was advertised in the local press, and the public was allowed to view it for six weeks. People sent in their written objections to the Minister, who decided whether or not to hold a Public Inquiry. Then each objector had a right to a private hearing before one of the Minister's Inspectors. The Minister then approved, disapproved, or suggested modifications to the plan. Modifications were given in a modification drawing and had to be incorporated into a new submission. A development plan was supposed to be reviewed by a new survey and analysis at least every five years. In fact so much work was involved that very few authorities actually achieved the timetable, and most major cities ran 3–5 years late.

The new and long-lasting effect of the development plan lay in the definition of the term 'development' for which planning permission was required. Development meant:

(1) the carrying out of building operations, mining operations in, on, or under land; and
(2) the making of any material change in the use of any buildings or land.

In addition, development included:

(1) the use of a single dwelling for the purpose of two or more dwellings;
(2) the deposit of refuse on an extension of a dump;
(3) the display of advertisements on the external part of a building.

Those items which did not constitute development and for which no planning permission was required were:

(1) internal or external improvements to a building which did not constitute a material change;
(2) the use of land for agriculture or forestry and the use of any building occupied with such land;
(3) the repair, renewal or inspection of sewers, mains, pipes or cables.

Permitted development, that is, development which did not require permission, was listed under a new General Development Order of 1950 and included 24 classes of use. Exemptions included development by government departments and 'statutory undertakers' (rail, road, transport, utilities, etc.), who had special planning procedures. They needed only to consult but not to apply for planning permission. This was and has remained one of the major development loop-holes, causing, in the view of the conservationists, considerable damage to the nation's heritage. It was originally accepted as a necessary legacy from wartime 'Emergency Powers'.

Planning permission from a local authority came and still comes in three forms: unconditional permission, permission 'subject to such conditions' or refusal. There was and still is the right of appeal. The 1947 Town and Country Planning Act also brought in a new enforcement procedure where, if an owner was caught developing his land without permission, he could be compelled to undo the development and, if need be, to revert the land to its original form, demolish the building or pay a fine.

One of the defects of the 1947 Town and Country Planning Act was its clumsy administration. Although the Act managed to shift the responsibility of town and country planning from the smaller authorities to the counties, the counties proved inadequate to the task in the dense urban areas, and to the areas outside the city where most of the growth took place. Hence the need for local government reform, which eventually came in the 1970s.

The 1947 Town and Country Planning Act transferred responsibility for planning to the major authorities – the counties and county boroughs – without any stipulation for regional authorities. Instead the Ministry of Town and Country Planning, set up in

1943, appointed regional planning officers, who became regional controllers, presiding over regional planning committees, which advised the local authorities. Later, when the Ministry of Town and Country Planning was subsumed into the Ministry of Housing and Local Government, the regional planning officers were disbanded.

The 1946 New Towns Act: first-generation New Towns

The New Towns movement in Britain was one of the most extraordinary phenomena of the post-war period. Whatever an individual's opinion is towards New Towns in detail, that perspective is irrelevant to the brilliant feat of creating 15 New Towns, following the Second World War. Internationally, Britain achieved a spectacular standard which other countries, including China, Israel and the United States, continue to imitate.

No-one will deny the enormous debt which the British New Town movement owes to Ebenezer Howard and his Garden City movement. The early experimental New Towns of Letchworth in 1903 and Welwyn Garden City in 1920 provided tangible evidence that New Towns could achieve the purpose for which they were created. Between the wars, comment on New Towns continued, but no practical work occurred until the effects of the devastation of the Second World War were felt. The Addison Committee, appointed to deal with unhealthy areas, recommended the establishment of self-contained Garden Cities for London, but no action followed this recommendation (*Addison Report, 1920*). In 1927, the then Minister of Health, Neville Chamberlain, requested the Greater London Regional Planning Committee to consider the establishment of New Towns. Although Raymond Unwin was the committee's technical adviser, the local authorities gave no support to the idea (*GLRPC, 1929*). Interest in the creation of New Towns was given further stimulus by the publication of Abercrombie's Greater London Plan in 1944 in which he made the historic proposal that 1.25 million people should be decentralised beyond the county boundaries.

After the Second World War, the government requested the ubiquitous Lord Reith, who also created the British Broadcasting Corporation, to set up a committee to establish a New Town policy. The New Towns Committee recommended the parameters of New Towns: that the government should decide (a) the siting of the New Towns; (b) that each New Town should have its own development agency for the purpose of planning and developing the New Town; and (c) that the Treasury should provide the finance

through a separate government corporation (*Reith Reports, 1946*).

The new Labour government possessed a dynamism and sympathy towards the town planners' objectives of New Towns, particularly as they were consistent with the newly elected Socialist government's belief that the state should take a larger initiative in production and development. Furthermore, emergency war powers, including the control of building licences and materials, still existed, which could make development easier. This, coupled with the efficient Civil Service, argued well for the New Towns. The particular circumstances conspired to make New Towns a definite possibility, and, unusually, the New Town concept was transformed into legislation in the New Towns Act of 1946 in little over a year from the inception of Reith's committee.

New Towns policy was implemented, not by a central ministry or by existing local authorities, but by new individual and separate development agencies, the New Town Corporations, specifically for the purpose of building New Towns, giving the New Town Corporations a degree of independence which local authorities did not have. New Town Development Corporations, appointed and financed by the Ministry to plan and create New Towns, were given the power to

> 'acquire, hold, manage and dispose of land and other property, to carry out building and other operations, to provide water, electricity, gas, sewerage and other services, to carry on any business or undertaking in or for the purpose of the new town, and generally to do anything necessary or expedient for the purpose of the new town or for the purpose incidental thereof.' (*Reith Reports, 1946*)

Each New Town had its own separate agency – justified on the basis that each New Town needed to develop a balanced community enjoying a full social, industrial and commercial life. The Development Corporation consisted of a Chairman, a Deputy Chairman and not more than seven members, appointed by the then Ministry of Housing and Local Government, and later by the Department of the Environment and by the Department of Development in Scotland. The technical staff, responsible to the Corporation, consisted of the General Manager, as the Chief Executive Officer; the Chief Architect; the Finance Officer; the Engineer; and the Estate Officer. Administratively, however, the various community services within the boundaries of the New Town were still managed by the local authorities. New schools, new hospitals, water, sewerage, gas and electricity were the responsibility of the local authorities. Therefore, the New Town Corporations and the local authorities had continually to work together, and in some cases considerable friction occurred.

The Corporations were financed entirely by central government, by means of loans payable over 60 years at prevailing interest rates. Loan applications had to be approved by the Department of the Environment or the Scottish Development Department, and, in this way, the central government exerted considerable control over the Corporations. Following Howard's principle, the 1946 New Towns Act specified that the New Town Development Corporations should eventually be transferred to the local authorities. However, as the New Towns were socially and financially so successful, there was great reluctance on the part of the New Town Development Corporations to transfer the New Towns to the local authorities. As an interim measure, the 1959 New Towns Act set up a New Town Commission, an independent body within the Treasury, for all the New Towns. This measure lasted until the 1980s, when the English New Towns were sold, either partially to private concerns and/or by transfer to the local authorities. The Scottish New Towns delayed the longest but were also transferred to the local authorities in a gradual programme ending in 1996, along with the completion of the work of the New Towns Commission (figure 6.1).

Common characteristics of first-generation New Towns

Between 1946 and 1950, 14 New Towns, the so-called first-generation New Towns, were designated. Eight New Towns – Bracknell, Crawley, Basildon, Hemel Hempstead, Stevenage, Harlow, Hatfield and Welwyn Garden City – were established in a ring around London, as a major part of the attempt to relieve congestion and pressure on housing in the central area, following the proposals in Abercrombie's 1944 Greater London Plan. Of the eight satellite town sites suggested in Abercrombie's Plan, only two, Stevenage and Harlow, were actually designated. The other six provisional New Towns were established to meet the special needs of areas of regional decline. Of these, Peterlee, Newton Aycliffe, Cwmbran and Glenrothes were established to provide housing and new industry for declining mining communities, while Corby was established specifically to provide housing for the growing local steelworks, i.e. to serve industrial growth. East Kilbride, proposed in the Clyde Valley Regional Plan, was established to provide alternative

employment and housing for overspill population from Glasgow. The fifteenth New Town, Cumbernauld, was the only New Town to be designated in the 1950s.

From the beginning, the early London New Towns differed from those in the provinces and in Scotland. Several were existing communities, like Hemel Hempstead and Welwyn Garden City, and therefore had less of an economic struggle than early New Towns in the English provinces and in Scotland. For example, Glenrothes was built to substitute a good urban community for a series of straggling mining villages where industrial life could be depleted at any moment. East Kilbride and Cumbernauld were built ostensibly to decentralise Glasgow's population, but actually to house its poor. London's goal was for decongested population but Scotland's goal, for its New Towns, was to correct social and urban disorders.

Urban form

The first-generation New Towns closely resembled each other in design with mutual characteristics. They were to be 'balanced' satellite towns, i.e. there should be a good balance between the size and structure of the population and the number and range of jobs available locally (*Self, 1972: 8*). This was to correct the defects of the two early Garden Cities, Letchworth and Welwyn, which remained dormitory towns for their first 30 years.

The similar features of the New Towns, both north and south, included moderate size, relatively low density and comprehensive development. The emphasis on open space which was so marked in the English towns was less marked in the Scottish New Towns, with the exception of Glenrothes, as the beautiful Scottish countryside was near at hand.

Each first-generation New Town had a population target of approximately 50,000 people, which allowed an acceptable town density with a convenient relationship of homes to work, the town centre and the countryside. The industrial areas and residential districts were placed in separate zones, surrounding a geographically central town centre. The residential districts were based on the concept of the neighbourhood unit (see chapter 5) centred on a primary school, a few shops, a pub and a community centre, and ranged in size from 3000 to 12,000 people. They were given a physical identity by main roads and mini-green belts separating one from the other (figure 6.2).

Harlow is an isolated example of a higher density first-generation New Town with an interesting variant on the neighbourhood unit (figure 6.3). Extensive

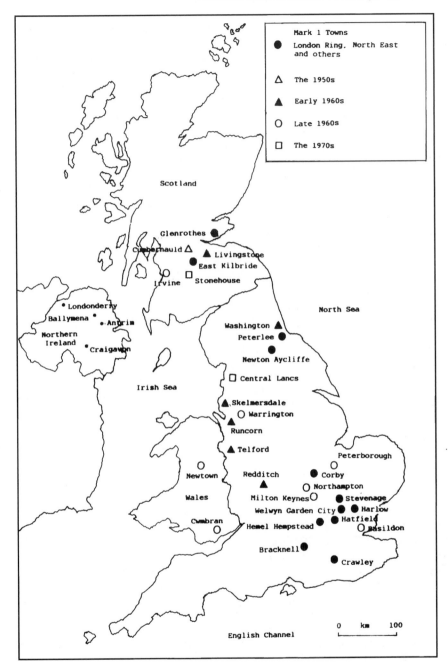

Figure 6.1   The distribution of New Towns in Britain (after Greed and Hancock)

landscape areas separate each planning unit in the hierarchy, neighbourhood, community and town centre. The town has four community areas, separated by mini-green belts; one community area is grouped around the main town centre, three others around major sub-centres. A community was composed of several neighbourhood units, each of about 5000–6000 people, with its own primary school and one or two shops. These units formed the community area round the sub-centre, which had shopping and community facilities for 17,000 to 25,000 people (*Gibberd, 1970*).

Stevenage, the first New Town designated under the

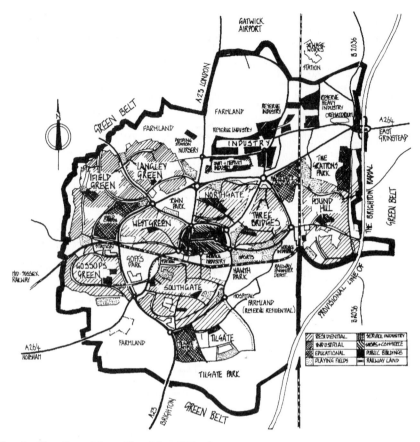

Figure 6.2   Crawley New Town Master Plan (after Gibberd)

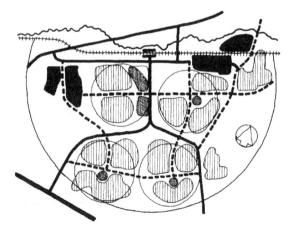

Figure 6.3   Harlow New Town Master Plan. Each circle is a community containing three neighbourhoods and a community centre. The industrial areas are in black and the pedestrian routes are shown by dotted lines. The plan is the classic prototype of a New Town plan (after Gibberd)

New Towns Act, had a master plan prepared by the Ministry of Town and Country Planning. Its nucleated form owes much to the plan of Welwyn Garden City by Louis de Soissons (*Gibberd, 1970*). Each has the similar arrangement of a large industrial estate alongside a railway with the town centre opposite it and the housing groups arranged as neighbourhoods, each with a subsidiary shopping centre and primary school in its centre. Stevenage, unlike Welwyn, used large areas of landscape to articulate the neighbourhoods and the road planning was considerably more advanced.

Housing

Housing in the first New Town was originally almost 100 percent public sector housing, where the overwhelming demand was for houses with gardens, which meant building homes at relatively low densities of 32 to 37 persons per hectare (13 to 15 persons per

Figure 6.4   Housing in Harlow New Town (by the author)

acre) or 10 to 12 houses per hectare (4 to 5 houses per acre). The result was mainly single-family houses with gardens. Such low density led to criticism, as it was considered wasteful of land and lacked architectural urban character. However, it also meant that, in the long term, the general standard of the first New Town housing was superior to that of any other local authority housing of the period (figure 6.4). Later densities were increased to 100 to 125 persons per hectare (40 to 50 persons per acre) and 35 to 38 houses per hectare (14 to 15 houses per acre).

The first New Towns demonstrated distinct economic advantages over other housing development. At the time, housing development in buildings of two (or at the most four) storeys was less expensive to build than taller blocks of flats. The cheapest form of housing was surburban development, protected against suburban sprawl because of safeguards such as the green belt policy. The green belt policy restrained public housing authorities from developing housing more than it did the private housing sector, which could always leap-frog the green belt and build beyond, whereas the public housing authorities had to build within their municipal limits on expensive urban land. The green belt inadvertently helped to increase the economic desirability of a house in a New Town. With Harlow's higher densities, for example, it was possible to provide for a considerably greater number of people within a reasonable walking distance of the sub-centre, enabling the provision of better facilities

in the sub-centres than could be achieved, for instance, in Stevenage.

Employment

The first-generation New Towns aimed to be 'balanced', that is, communities in which people both live and work. This was difficult to achieve in practice. The early New Towns were subject to the same Board of Trade control for attracting industry that existed throughout the country, and initially, industrial development was hampered by the conflict between the need to relocate industries in Development Areas in, for example, north-east England and the need to encourage firms to move to New Towns. For several years, the Board of Trade would assist firms to move to Glasgow or Merseyside, but not to East Kilbride or other New Towns. Eventually, New Towns succeeded in attracting industry. Once industries were established, the New Towns grew so rapidly that it was difficult sometimes to build houses at an adequate rate, because adequate finance to develop houses was not available. By 1970, over 45 million square feet of factory space had been built in New Towns, with the main emphasis on light industry and manufacturing (*TCPA, 1971*). On the whole, the goal of a balanced community was achieved.

Traffic planning

The advent of the Motor Age had a profound effect on most aspects of the planning of New Towns. The early

Figure 6.5   Landscape features in Crawley New Town (by the author)

New Towns (under the guidance of the Ministry of Transport) failed to provide for the increase of car ownership and its use, and at the same time failed to provide adequate public transport. On the other hand, there were some important developments in traffic design in housing areas, particularly in vehicle and pedestrian segregation and in the provision of good pedestrian routes.

Early housing schemes provided parking for only one car for every ten families. The problem of through motor traffic stimulated the development of designs on Radburn principles, whereby housing is placed around dead-end roads (cul-de-sacs), and through traffic is channelled to by-pass the housing areas. Very few traffic-conscious housing schemes were built prior to 1965, with exceptions as in Harlow, showing how long it took for the motor car to be accepted. Then when changes were required to be made in early housing areas, to incorporate the increased need for garages and parking, providing these facilities in a visually acceptable manner presented major difficulties.

Landscape features

The first-generation New Towns placed considerable emphasis on pleasant landscaping. Hemel Hempstead, Crawley and Glenrothes are particularly outstanding examples with good hard and soft landscaping in town centres and careful choice of shrubs and trees in housing areas (figure 6.5). True to Howard's Garden City scheme, all the first-generation New Towns had green belts and many incorporated mini-green belts surrounding neighbourhoods and town centres respectively within the town. Harlow is a classic example of the use of green belts.

Town centres

The planning of the town centres showed the need for a new approach to central area design. While Hemel Hempstead built a traditional 'High Street' shared by people and cars, Harlow's town centre was partially pedestrianised, yet allowed one road for motor traffic to enter into the shoppers' area (figure 6.6). (The road has since been closed.) Ironically, Stevenage, although the first designated New Town, suffered so many delays that it did not start its town centre until 1956. As a result, it benefited from experience elsewhere (including that of Rotterdam's traffic-free Lijnbaan), and was the first New Town with a completely pedestrianised central area and vehicle segregation. It remains a model town centre design.

There is no doubt that the first New Towns got off to a slow start and were bogged down in administrative preparation and paperwork. The initial lack of houses meant a shortage of accommodation for the labour force and there was typically a lack of provision of services, electricity, water and sewerage. Coming so soon after the Second World War, money was short and sometimes not available at all. The first New Towns were restricted in their policies, through lack of

Figure 6.6   Town Centre Market Square, Harlow (by the author)

funds and lack of investment policy integration between the various government departments. A number of local political battles and complicated bureaucratic approvals from central and local government also hindered progress. It was only after the first five years that the New Towns increased their pace of development. On the other hand, the heavy capital commitment of New Towns for roads, sewers and public utilities tempted Corporations to leave as much as possible of the commercial and industrial development to private enterprise, whilst the Corporations undertook all of the housing development. Later, the budgets of the New Town Corporations showed a year-to-year increase in profitability.

As to the social situation in the New Towns, in the beginning, it was believed that the incidence of neurosis was higher in the New Towns' population than in the country as a whole, and that the incidence of psychosis was definitely below the national average. It is true that the malady known as the 'New Town Blues' – depression occurring from loneliness – undoubtedly did exist and was one of the difficulties in building up a new community which only time overcame (*Young and Wilmott, 1957*).

The first group of New Towns also failed to affect the distribution of work and people in their regions. Those New Towns which were supposed to draw sufficient overcrowded population from London failed to achieve their objectives. There were several reasons for this. Some were too small; some grew too slowly to counter London's higher growth. Others were too near the heart of London to have any significant impact on

London; still others were designed to improve the lot of a static population and not to resist population growth. It was difficult for the first New Towns to increase their population as they were often frustrated by the inflexibility of a centralised plan based on rigidly segregated concentrations of different activities, or the central functions and communications could not be overloaded.

Due to numerous factors, the first New Towns failed to achieve their planned rate of growth through lack of sufficient initial finance and through management difficulties. For example, the Reith Committee had suggested a growth of 4000 people a year for Stevenage but it grew at only 2700 people a year, and its population reached only 57,000 in 21 years. The original intention for the first New Towns had been that the whole programme of decentralisation in London, which the New Towns were to help achieve, was to be completed by 1954. Initially, the first New Towns failed to keep work and homes in balance, thereby creating an economic and social lopsidedness where jobs, homes, social facilities and community buildings were provided and built at different rates.

One of the greatest deficiencies of the first-generation New Towns was the architectural poverty, created partly by continued wartime restrictions in the use of materials, as controls were not removed until 1955, coupled with the general lack of funds. The first New Towns also failed to anticipate the growth in car ownership and at the same time failed to promote adequate public transport.

problems of New towns.

Contributions of the first-generation New Towns

Statistically, the first-generation New Towns together with Cumbernauld had an impressive record of achievements:

'Fifteen towns almost built: a dozen more started. Nearly 175,000 new houses; hundreds of new industries in 35,000,000 sq ft of modern factory space; 350 new schools with 150,000 school places; 4,000,000 sq ft of office space; 100 new pubs, scores of churches and public buildings, several thousand acres of park, playing fields, and open space and a host of minor achievements too numerous to catalogue.' (*Schaffer, 1970: 257*)

Administratively, the independence of the New Town Development Corporations contributed generally to their success. Their success re-emphasised how individual corporations managed their tasks without central government interference.

In design terms, the pedestrian shopping precinct of Stevenage was an early pace-setter, and the centres of Crawley and Harlow have become equally renowned. The careful preservation of the old High Street at Crawley and the old village in Harlow are also fine instances of conservation and improvement incorporated with modern development. In fact, some aspects of advanced planning could be seen in every New Town and this marked them out from the average development experienced all too frequently in towns and cities of all sizes throughout the country.

Because the New Towns were viable and financially successful, many of them were considered for expansion to sizes far in excess of original proposals. On the other hand, of seven million new houses in Britain since the Second World War, only 175,000 were in New Towns. They did not stop peripheral urban expansion. They were not self-contained and did not prevent dormitory town living, because industry did not move out of existing towns and cities as readily as people did. They were not necessarily meeting directly the social need for which they were established, in that only a proportion of the residents were drawn from the crowded conurbations they were meant to relieve. Abercrombie's original proposal of 1.25 million people to be overspilled to New Towns and expanded towns was not fulfilled. The New Towns failed in this original goal, but succeeded in many other aspects. The fact that the first-generation New Towns proved a success administratively, socially and then financially, was underlined by almost universal support for more,

Figure 6.7   Housing, East Kilbride (by the author)

bigger and better New Towns. They were an overall success.

Statutory green belts

With the 1947 Town and Country Planning Act in place, statutory green belts could be applied elsewhere than around London. In 1955, the Minister of Housing and Local Government, Duncan Sandys, required other cities in Britain to submit green belt proposals. Circular 42/55 on green belts followed the Abercrombie principles for the planning of London (*MHLG, 1956*) and asked planning authorities outside London to establish clearly defined green belts with the objective of 'checking the unrestricted sprawl of the built-up areas and of safeguarding the surrounding countryside against further encroachment', with the further aims: (a) to check the further growth of large built-up areas; (b) to prevent neighbouring towns from merging into one another; and (c) to preserve the special character of a town (*Skinner, 1976: 8*).

Green belts were proposed for Manchester, Oxford and Cambridge, amongst other cities. Formal approval for these green belts was finally granted only in the 1960s and thus there was a considerable time-lag between the original 1938 Act for London and the final approval for towns outside London. By the 1960s, 18 green belts affecting half the population of England and Wales were still being formally defined and approved. Although an improvement over the 1950s, it was realised that the green belts could not be rigidly conceived and that the pressures for development were powerful. Hence the government issued a review of green belts (*MHLG, 1962a*) (figure 6.8). The permitted uses of the green belt included:

[handwritten margin note:] 175000 out of 7M.

[handwritten note at bottom:] populations moving to new towns were not from those 'overcrowded' cities envisaged.

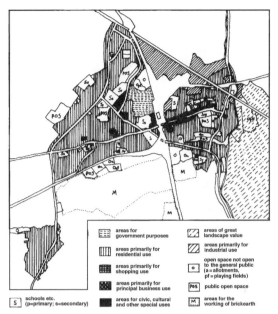

Figure 6.9 Planned expansion of county town (after Seeley)

Figure 6.8 Green belts in England and Wales in 1962 (after Elson)

1 Agriculture. The original use of green belts was for agricultural purposes. But land for use as a green belt around a metropolis may or may not be good agricultural land, and prohibition of land for other developments sometimes rendered the land idle. Thus the Scottish solution seemed more viable: land restricted from development must have some positive agriculture, amenity or recreation values.

2 Urban growth. If a green belt has little agriculture or amenity value, it still is likely to be used as a restriction against urban growth, and to regulate the urban growth pattern. In these cases, it should be intensively used for recreational purposes. By recognition of the restriction of urban growth as part of the use of a green belt, an additional weapon was provided to fight against the ever-present problem of the extension of local government boundaries.

Amenity was excluded originally as a green belt objective because of the weakness of the development control system in ensuring that standards of amenity could be maintained. From time to time, there were threats to take the green belt out of development control for use by developers to ease pressure for additional housing land throughout the 1970s and

1980s. The popular attitude has been that communities and local authorities must remain vigilant so the green belt can be maintained. In the popular mind, the principle of the green belt is the most sacred of planning principles, and has so far withstood the test of time.

Expanded towns: the 1952 Town Development Act

An Act complementary to the New Towns Act, entitled the Town Development Act 1952 (for Scotland, 1957), encouraged town development in county districts for the relief of congestion and overpopulation elsewhere and for related purposes. Although the Town Development Act was an additional instrument to the New Towns Act, to help relieve congestion in the big cities, it also became another tool for implementing regional and sub-regional policy for potential reception areas, and a useful tool for existing communities to revive themselves and become thriving once again.

The goals of the Town Development Act were similar to those of the New Towns Act: (1) to counteract (a) the trend for expanding industries to concentrate in the South East, (b) the higher rates of unemployment in regions outside London, and (c) the continued concentration of industry in inner London,

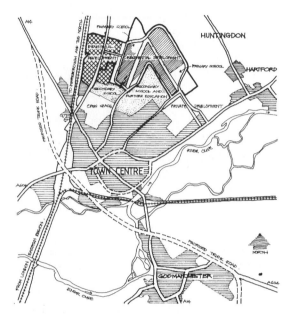

Figure 6.10 Town development (after LCC, 1960)

intermixing with housing and causing continued congestion; and (2) to implement (a) the spread of industries elsewhere than in the London region, and (b) the rehousing of people in existing communities expanded in the ring beyond the green belt.

The procedures of the Town Development Act were to enable receiving local authorities voluntarily to accept the overspill of people from the big cities and to give national help, in the form of a housing subsidy, and a 50 percent grant towards the cost of main sewerage and water works for the development. The authority exporting overspill population paid the importing authority for the necessary town expansion, and made an annual contribution towards each family rehoused in the importing town. In addition, government encouragement was given in the form of grants to help with the housing and services.

The actual development work was undertaken either by the town itself, or by the exporting city, or by the county council in whose county the town was situated (figure 6.10). The new tenants either came from the big city's housing list or were chosen from industrial selection schemes, in which case only the people who got jobs with the town's industry received a house.

Under the legislation, local governments were encouraged to deal with overspill by agreement amongst themselves. The aim of the Act was to be completely flexible. This was a quite different approach from that of setting up ad hoc development corporations for the New Towns. In practice, it was

Figure 6.11 Town Development Act schemes in progress, 1970 (after Self)

rather difficult to get all parties involved – the exporting big city authority, the small town importing authority, the county council – to work together. In fact, it required an unprecedented and, in the event, rare cooperation between the exporting authority, the reception authority, its county council, and among others the Board of Trade, which was responsible for encouraging industry to move. As a result only the most competent authorities were able to take advantage of these powers.

The London County Council and subsequently the Greater London Council were far and away the best organised of all the exporting authorities, and were involved in more than half the 78,000 dwellings provided under the Act and completed by 1970 (figure 6.11). But even so progress was slow, dependent as it was on the initiative coming from the receiving authority, a procedure scrupulously observed by the GLC and other exporting authorities.

Other conurbations were much slower to promote schemes under the Act and, in effect, its overall impact was fairly small. The most successful expansion schemes were those for the very small towns of 5000

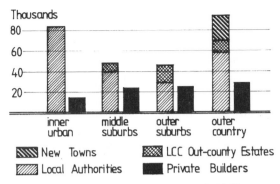

Figure 6.12   Housing in London (after LCC, 1960)

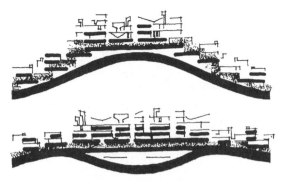

Figure 6.13   Cumbernauld's dilemma: hill-top or valley site for the town centre? The decision was made to put the centre on top of the hill (after LCC, 1961)

to 10,000 population and the more difficult schemes were those for towns of 30,000, 50,000 and 80,000 population, often meeting local opposition in accepting new people from overspill cities, whose way of life could be different from that of the receiving town.

The Town Development Act scheme always had one particular advantage over New Town schemes in terms of providing a good reception area for industrial employment. Having an existing industrial base encouraged new manufacturers to come, which in turn generated their own service employment, thereby using the excess labour growth not previously used in manufacturing. New and expanding industries were more easily placed in an existing industrial structure. Furthermore, existing community facilities helped prevent 'neurosis', or 'New Town Blues', which had been prevalent in the first-generation New Towns. It took the Town Development Act a long time to get going, and in the 1950s only single towns were expanded and those on a relatively modest scale, involving roads and renewal of town centres. In general, the 1950s were a period of consolidation.

Cumbernauld and Hook New Towns

Cumbernauld, created in 1956, was the only New Town to be created between 1951 and 1961. The 1946 Clyde Valley Regional Plan stressed the unique scale of the housing problem in the Glasgow area, where there were more people per room and less room per house than in any other part of Britain, and proposed to move out one-third of the City's population. East Kilbride, Glenrothes and Cumbernauld were part of the means for accommodating Glasgow's overspill population. Cumbernauld represented a significant departure from the first-generation New Towns. It differed in its residential areas, in its striking town centre surmounting a hill-top site (figure 6.13) and,

most dramatically, in its transport planning. The aims of Cumbernauld's master plan were to form a compact urban unit centred round the town centre, and to make adequate provision for vehicles and pedestrians (*Wilson, 1956*). Cumbernauld's great contribution was that it came to terms with the burgeoning increase in car ownership by providing a circulation system designed for full motorisation with a complete hierarchy of roads and a separate pedestrian network, on Radburn principles.

These aims were to be achieved with the abandonment of neighbourhood planning and by substituting high-density inner residential areas, which were not to have local centres of their own but to be oriented towards the town centre, by a system of footpaths connected to the compact town centre. Beyond the town centre were so-called 'villages', with their own local shopping and social centres.

The densities were high, with 45 percent of the population at 70 persons per net acre, 49 percent at 75 to 120 persons per net acre, and the remaining 6 percent of the population at 40 to 50 persons per net acre. This compares with Harlow's density of 30 to 50 persons per acre, which was high for its time. The high densities in Cumbernauld made it possible to group much of the town's population within half a mile of the town centre; they were also intended to help create a feeling of 'urbanity', a quality which many found lacking in earlier New Towns.

Fully integrated with the circulation system, for the first time, was the multi-level town centre designed as an architectural whole (figure 6.14). The town centre was conceived in a noble way, as a 'megastructure' of buildings with uses at different levels, with servicing and car parking beneath the shopping and pedestrian decks, an architectural attempt to recapture the cohesion and urbanity of historical towns, at least in

he corbusier influence more apparent in Cumbernauld N.T.

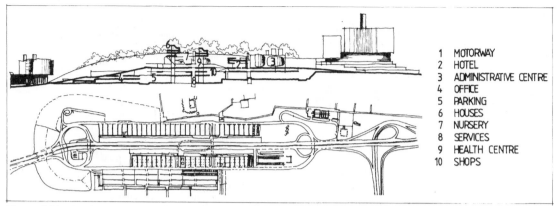

1	MOTORWAY
2	HOTEL
3	ADMINISTRATIVE CENTRE
4	OFFICE
5	PARKING
6	HOUSES
7	NURSERY
8	SERVICES
9	HEALTH CENTRE
10	SHOPS

Figure 6.14   Section and plan of Cumbernauld's town centre (after Civic Design Diploma, University of Edinburgh)

Figure 6.15   Aerial view of Cumbernauld's town centre and surrounding housing (by Cumbernauld Development Corporation. Reproduced by kind permission of North Lanarkshire Council)

its town centre because in its residential areas it was as suburban as the rest of the New Towns. It was accompanied by much admiration as well as criticism; its location was meant to imitate a hot Italian hill-top town, but in reality it was sited on a cold and exposed hill-top in Central Scotland (*Cumbernauld Development Corporation, 1960*).

In transport planning Cumbernauld differed most notably from the first-generation New Towns. In preparing the plan, it was assumed that eventually 70 percent of families would own a car, that 63 percent of cars would be used together at peak hours, and that 45 percent of the population would go to work by car, while 42 percent would travel to work by public

transport; 4000 people were expected to walk to work, and 20 percent to commute daily, mainly to Glasgow. These estimates demanded a radical approach to designing a road system. The result was a distinct hierarchy of roads, each designed to perform a particular function, and a maximum separation of foot and motor traffic with two distinct circulation systems.

Cumbernauld's town centre took years to complete on ever-smaller budgets, which negated the original grand concept (figure 6.15). By the time of the transfer of Cumbernauld to the local authority, the town centre stood as a forlorn, wind-swept monument to another confident age, needing major rehabilitation.

The road network proved over-lavish, and the remaining housing areas returned to the neigh-bourhood and village concepts with minor centres.

In 1959, the London County Council sought to resolve the difficulty of obtaining reception areas for themselves by promoting a New Town at Hook in Hampshire, being the only local authority who could have undertaken such a task without government aid. The proposals were published in the legendary 'Hook Book', which remains a much respected work of its kind on how to build a New Town (*LCC, 1961*). The Master Plan for Hook New Town is still an excellent guide to the New Town planning process, and many of its ideas were incorporated in the third-generation New Towns.

The town, 40 miles from London, was to grow in a linear form to contain an ultimate population of 100,000 people, to be connected to the South Wales motorway to the north and to the Exeter motorway to the south (figure 6.16). It was to be more urbane and coherent than the earlier New Towns – a town in a garden rather than a 'garden city' was required. The town was designed to absorb one car per household with the highest practicable degree of pedestrian and vehicular segregation (figure 6.17). The central area, three-quarters of a mile by a quarter of a mile, designed to be the town's main meeting place, was served but not dominated by the motor vehicle.

Particularly significant was the highly organised pedestrian level of the town centre, with well-defined pedestrian entries from the housing areas. Building on a deck over most of the central parking and service areas would avoid the isolation of the central area by a ring of car parks from the remainder of the town. The offices and public buildings were to be distributed along the length of the platform, but their parking requirements produced a dark underworld. As the central area was to be the main meeting place the neighbourhood unit idea was abandoned. The residential areas were envisaged as concentric rings increasing in density, height and concentration of building towards the centre (figure 6.18).

The proposal met well-organised opposition from Hampshire, particularly from those who did not want their lush countryside urbanised. The scheme was seen not to be financially viable and it eventually foundered. Nevertheless, this failure led to the LCC finalising working arrangements under the Town Development Act with nearby Basingstoke and Andover. Ten years later, some of the major aspects of Hook reappeared in the Greater London satellite community of Thamesmead.

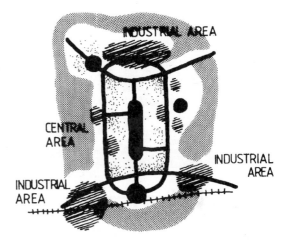

Figure 6.16 The Hook plan for a linear town has most residential areas concentrated around the centre and three dispersed industrial areas (after LCC, 1961)

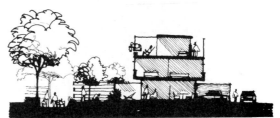

Figure 6.17 Hook: Stepped-section housing (after LCC, 1961)

Britain in the late 1950s

At first, the New Towns Act and the Town Development Act were thought to be a once-and-for-all job, but it became clear that the national population was growing, leading to an ever-increasing number of people to be housed. These two Acts became inadequate to solve the problem of housing the growing population. In the late 1950s and the early 1960s, the trend was for people to move from the centre of cities to the periphery, to lower density areas on first-class transport routes, while at the same time the small rural settlements declined. It became apparent that the aims for decentralisation and dispersal set by the 1947 Act and by the Abercrombie plans could never be met. The plans after the Second World War were too static, too inflexible, to meet the changing demands of technology.

The New Towns and Town Development programmes were successful and in themselves stand as a marvellous achievement. The first-generation New

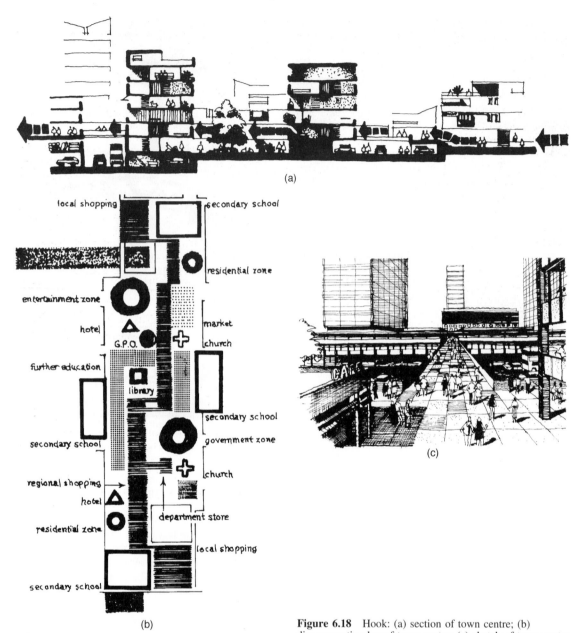

Figure 6.18 Hook: (a) section of town centre; (b) diagrammatic plan of town centre; (c) sketch of town centre

Towns and Cumbernauld followed Howard's original concept of a New Town of 60,000 people, but it gradually became clear that there was nothing sacrosanct about 60,000 people. There were economies of scale which justified New Towns going beyond this figure, and thus being able to offer more community facilities. Gradually after the slow experience of the 1950s, the New Towns Act and the Town Development Act were coupled to contribute to the formation of 'regional cities', where the smaller existing communities could be preserved within the existing framework. Thinking, in the late 1950s, led to a search for a regional framework, although in 1961 came a sudden reversal of government policy and a return to designation of the first-generation type of New Towns as a means of accommodating overspill population on a substantial scale and at some speed. Designations of New Towns included Skelmersdale

(d)

Figure 6.18 (continued) (d) sketch of town centre below pedestrian deck (after LCC, 1961)

and Runcorn for Merseyside; Dawley (later Telford) and Redditch for Birmingham; and Washington for Tyneside. The established London New Towns were invited to review the situation with a view to receiving additional growth. The New Town idea became fused into the concept of the 'City Region', with developing larger and larger New Towns.

It also became increasingly clear that although the aesthetics of physical planning demanded a fairly clear-cut definition of an individual city and of its boundaries, the isolated city was also largely a social myth, and more likely to be part of a group, hence the eventual development of regional cities. The search for a regional framework which would include both the New Town Act and the Town Development Act started a series of special studies focused on south-east England.

7 Regional cities and third-generation New Towns

Reorganisation of Greater London, 1957–65

The drawback to developing regional planning in Britain from a governmental position was the outdated structure of local governments in England, Wales and Scotland. The planning facts pointed to the need for fewer and more comprehensive planning units, the size of a city region, particularly in London. The Royal Commission on Greater London, 1957–60 (the Herbert Commission), proposed that the London County boundaries be stretched to include the physical and social entity of the London Region (*Herbert Report, 1960*), summarising that there were three important elements to urban and regional planning:

1 'the regional and historical object of town planning – the preservation and enhancement of local health amenity';
2 'the necessity of planning for Greater London as a whole' – this meant creating an authority which could act for Greater London;
3 'the function of holding the balance in terms of national policy between one region and another', which meant giving the Minister the power to consult with other Ministers on the level of a national plan.

Consequently, the Commission's main proposals were that there be a two-tier government for London Region to be called Greater London, consisting of a Greater London Council and individual boroughs, and that the directly elected council be the unit for local government performing functions which could only be better performed over a wider area of London. The Greater London borough should be the primary unit of local government, performing all local functions, with a range of population between 100,000 and 250,000.

The Greater London Council's original responsibilities included planning, traffic and main roads, refuse, fire and ambulance services. The boroughs' responsibilities were to include housing (with some Greater London Council exceptions), personal health, welfare and children's services, environmental health (but not refuse disposal), minor roads, libraries, education and certain planning functions. Following the Herbert Commission's proposals, the Conservative government produced its White Paper, which accepted a Greater London Council of members, elected on the basis of parliamentary constituencies, and the concept of 32 big new boroughs, each with a quarter of a million people (*MHLG, 1961*). The London Government Act 1963 created the Greater London Council (GLC) on 1 April, 1965, which became the basis for London's government from 1965 to 1986. The administrative area of the Greater London Council was defined as the London boroughs, the City and the Temples.

The allocation of responsibilities between the council and the boroughs did not proceed smoothly, with considerable argument over responsibilities for education and housing. In summary, the three main powers concerning planning, housing and traffic were shared between the GLC and the boroughs. The GLC was the strategic planning authority for Greater London as a whole, responsible for the preparation and periodic review of the development plan for the whole area, guiding the control of land use and overspill, while the borough councils dealt with individual planning applications. Both the GLC and the boroughs were to have the right to settle London's planning, but the exact division of powers between them was complex. Planning applications were made to the boroughs but certain classes of application, such as large shops, tall buildings and certain industrial and office development, had to be made to the GLC before decisions could be made. The GLC carried out a complete survey of the area, at the same time as submitting to the Minister the Greater London Development Plan (GLDP), along with the written statement, which dealt with general policy on the use of the land in Greater London, and included guidance as to the future road system.

The local boroughs, including the City, prepared local plans within the general framework of the Greater London Development Plan. These plans added to, and in some cases modified, the existing provisions relating to the borough areas. These plans, with their observations, were submitted by the GLC to the Minister. When the Minister had approved the plans, the GLDP and the local plan together constituted the development plan for each borough. The development plans for the boroughs included a summary of the main proposals contained in the GLDP.

The traffic problem in London was one of the main reasons for the formation of the Greater London Council, which became responsible for traffic management. The GLC had responsibility for those roads mainly carrying through traffic, known as metropolitan roads, and the boroughs were responsible for the others. The Act gave the GLC greater power over the boroughs to carry out the construction and maintenance of roads, while the GLC shared powers with the boroughs and the City regarding parking spaces on and off the streets.

Although housing was the responsibility of the boroughs, the GLC retained housing powers within Greater London to be exercised with the consent of the boroughs concerned, and kept sole power of building outside Greater London. There was widespread criticism of the removal of housing from the London County Council to the boroughs, which meant the break-up of the superb London County Council Housing Department into smaller units. The result was favourable for some boroughs but unfavourable for many others.

The Act also defined the borough councils to be the local education authorities for the outer London boroughs. The GLC set up the Inner London Education Authority (ILEA) as the central education authority, which lasted until its demise in 1988. In general, the London Government Act made the borough the authority for public health, sewerage, children's services, refuse collection and disposal, parks, and sanitary functions. However, the GLC was responsible for main sewerage and refuse disposal and the boroughs for smaller sewerage and the local collection of refuse. The GLC became responsible for the Greater

London 'London parks' and the boroughs for 'local parks'; the responsibility for London's port remained with the Port of London Authority.

The Greater London Development Plan and the London Transport Study

The Greater London Council became the strategic planning authority – a giant among local authorities in Britain, taking over an area of 600 square miles and nearly eight million people. Apart from Abercrombie's 1944 Greater London Plan, there had been no overall strategic plan for 20 years until the creation of the GLC in 1965, when discussions took place between the Ministry of Housing and Local Government, the GLC and the boroughs concerning the regulations of the development plan and the control of planning applications. Both the GLC and the boroughs were under obligation to consult each other and to make representations. The 1963 Act gave the Minister power to decide between the borough and the GLC in the event of disagreement. Needless to say, those planning applications which the boroughs had to refer to the GLC for either decisions or directions met delays, particularly as the GLC gradually extended the number of planning applications required to come to the council.

One of the GLC's functions was the production of the Greater London Development Plan (GLDP) and its written statement (*GLC, 1976a, 1976b*), which was not for a specified period of years but one stage in a continuing process, emphasising how much planning was to be done by the boroughs (figure 7.1). The development plan was also not so much a physical plan as a series of statements of view and policy on a number of different matters relating to each other. Some sections covered a wide range of topics, not necessarily related to one another. The three major subjects were land use, employment and housing. A complete land use survey of Outer London was carried out, while in Inner London the old London County Council material was used. The GLC also carried out one housing survey on the future life of dwellings and their capacity for improvement, and a second survey on current and future housing needs. A survey on employment in London was followed by the fourth and most controversial survey, the London Transport Study.

The most specialised part of the GLDP was the plan for the primary road system. The history of the planning of roads had been a long and highly specialised one in London. The LCC's original survey in 1961 covered the Greater London conurbation based

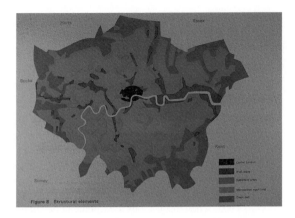

Figure 7.1   Greater London Council Development Plan (from GLC, 1976a)

on 50,000 household interviews, together with roadside interviews and traffic counts, published as Volume 1 of the *London Transport Study* (*LCC, 1964*).

The second stage forecast the travel patterns in London as they were likely to be in 1971, including an estimate of the number of vehicles using the road network, in Volume II of the *London Transport Study* (*GLC, 1966*). The third stage of the study evaluated a number of alternative transport plans, including the debatable and infamous 'motorway box', no longer a circular ring road (as in Abercrombie's 1943 London Plan) but a rectangular road system boxing in Inner London. The primary road network consisted of two further ring roads, with the outer ring road partly outside Greater London. The GLC made a commitment to the advanced transport plan, despite

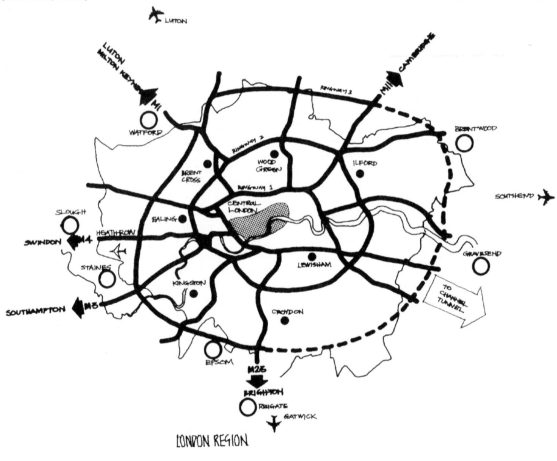

Figure 7.2   The motorway box (from GLC, 1976a)

considerable opposition to the motorway box (*GLC, 1967*) (figure 7.2).

The whole problem of public transport was left in doubt by the 1963 Act and it was the Labour government's Minister of Transport, Barbara Castle, who made changes in the GLC's responsibilities for public transport. The Conservative GLC in the White Paper *Transport in London* (*Department of Transport, 1968*) proposed a Transport Authority responsible for the running of public transport in London, under the management of the Greater London Council. Formalised in 1970, the authority's responsibilities included: (a) the Greater London Council as the transport planning authority with the duty of preparing and publishing transport plans; (b) the appointment of a London Transport Executive to run passenger transport services of buses and trains; (c) the establishment of a closer financial relationship with British Rail; and (d) becoming the highways authority for all principal roads and ultimately for trunk roads as well. The latter included some modifications in the arrangements for development control and strengthened the GLC's power in relation to on-street parking, installing traffic signals and imposing speed limits, augmented, for example, by including control over bus stops and routes. Sadly, these functions have still to be fully implemented in the 1990s.

The GLDP was to be approved in 1969, but the public inquiry concerning the plan lasted until 1972. Out of a record number of 21,000 objections to the development plan, 19,000 objections concerned motorways. Although parts of the motorway box had been built, further construction was eventually halted. The Layfield Report, summarising the results of the inquiry, led eventually to substantial changes in the development plan (*DOE, 1973b*). The Greater London Development Plan was not finally approved until 1976.

The 1964 Labour government, realising that the same reasoning which produced a two-tier government in London, with a strategic authority coupled with local authorities, could be applied to the rest of the nation and in particular to the seven conurbations, set up in 1966 the Redcliffe–Maud Commission for Local Government in England and Wales (*Redcliffe–Maud Report, 1969*) and the Wheatley Commission for Local Government in Scotland (Wheatley Report, 1969). The government thus unwittingly started the country on an almost ten-year search for the optimal local government for the conurbations and the towns, which continued until local government reorganisation in 1973. In planning terms, decision-making was stymied

and strategy shelved until the local government organisation was resolved. In the meantime, the Greater London Council pursued its independent government.

Planning in the 1960s: the regional city

The 1960s brought a complete reorientation of thinking and new legislation for the philosophy and practical machinery of planning. The old concepts changed to cope with the economic problems of the sprawling city, spreading throughout England and soon to occur in the central belt of Scotland. Through the National Economic Development Council, in 1965, nine economic planning regions were established in England, with Scotland divided into smaller regions. Administration of each region was placed in the control of two separate bodies: a Regional Economic Planning Council and a Regional Economic Planning Board. Scotland, Wales and Northern Ireland had their own planning councils (figure 7.3).

Figure 7.3 National and regional boundaries: planning regions (after Burke)

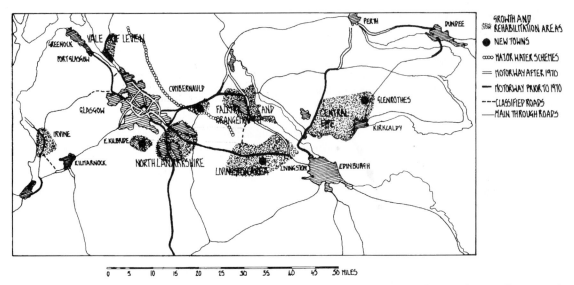

Figure 7.4   1963 Central Scotland White Paper – Programme for Development (after Scottish Development Department)

The Economic Planning Councils comprised co-opted citizens and civil servants from the main government departments concerned with regional planning. They had the function of advising on the needs and potentialities of their region and on the development of a long-term planning strategy, to plan the settling of the displaced and growing population, the expansion of industry and the demands of new and expanding towns. But the Economic Planning Councils had no executive role and were weak as instigators of regional planning. The boards had the function of preparing regional plans, and acting as departments for the councils, which were abolished by the Conservative government in 1979.

Post-war industrial location policies were two-fold; on the one hand, policies tried to reduce unemployment in areas of high unemployment, i.e. development areas; and on the other hand, policies tried to restrain widespread development in overdeveloped areas. The National Economic Development Council gradually realised that the poor distribution of employment throughout the regions had adverse economic effects on the national economy. As Britain went into heavier national debt, the economists turned to methods of revitalising the decaying industrial areas, and preventing immigration to the two prosperous overcongested industrial areas, the South East and the Midlands.

The search for a regional framework, which included the New Towns Act, the Town Development Act and the Economic Planning Regions, started a series of special studies focused on south-east England.

One of the first articulate reports was the 1963 White Paper entitled *London: Employment, Housing and Land*, which summarised the new thinking along regional lines (*MHLG, 1963*). The report acknowledged that it was no longer possible to think of a static London, and although urban growth should be restricted, total control of the growth was not so desirable, but rather effective control of the growth which was occurring anyway was important. The report suggested several policies, including (1) greater control over new office buildings; (2) dispersal of government offices outside London; (3) creation of office centres outside London; and (4) development for housing on those areas of least amenity value, as the London Green Belt was not so sacrosanct.

Two more regional White Papers appeared, one for north-east England (*Department of Industry, Trade and Regional Development, 1963*) and the other for Central Scotland (*Scottish Development Department, 1963*). The Central Scotland paper proposed supporting special growth areas to act as particular focal points for economic growth, such as the New Towns – the Livingston hinterland, Irvine New Town and the Grangemouth/Falkirk growth area (figure 7.4). Industrial location policy thus was changed from areas of high unemployment to favourable areas for development and redevelopment in order to help Britain's economy as a whole. The same attitude occurred in the White Paper for north-east England, covering Northumberland, Durham and the North Riding of Yorkshire. Here the goal was to diversify and strengthen the region's economic base with special growth zones in the Tyneside and Teeside areas. The programme included town centre development, clearance of derelict sites, roads, housing and urban development, industrial training facilities and financial assistance for the arts. These White Papers were the first attempts at comprehensive regional planning by central government.

The South East Study, 1961–81

The South East Study was the Ministry of Housing and Local Government's response to the need for a regional plan for the South East (*MHLG, 1964*). The regional plan examined the growth and movement of population in the South East, including overspill from London, and related growth and transport questions. It examined the need for a second generation of new and expanded towns which would provide both houses and work for Londoners, well away from London itself, and draw off some of the pressure on the capital.

The South East Study was one of the most powerful of the regional planning studies, partially because one-third of the nation lived within the review area. The problems of south-east England focused on strong population increase, strong employment growth, and the resultant large population overspill. The so-called 'drift to the South' was created not only by people coming in, but also by the natural increase of births and deaths. Between 1961 and 1981, there was an expected increase of three and a half million people, representing a 20 percent increase, two-thirds of which resulted from two and a half million excess births over deaths, and one million immigration from all over Britain. Coupled with the strong population increase was a tremendous growth in service employment, requiring offices in London and a strong industrial growth in Greater London. The results of the population increase and the employment growth produced a need to overspill and rehouse one and a quarter million people, 400,000 of whom were within Greater London, 600,000 were in the south-east and 250,000 more were immigrants. It was recognised that there was an acute land problem around London, where the population pressure requiring land for housing was restrained by the green belt. To accommodate the enormous rise in the population, the South East Study did not take the strong line of the 'Barlow Report Ban', but agreed that if this was the national trend the best idea was to go along with it, and not try, by artificial means, to stop people and industry from 'drifting' into the south-east areas (figure 7.5).

The broad strategy for the South East was based on planned growth, using overspill and planned expansion

 Counties losing population, 1951–61

Counties showing most rapid increase in population, 1951–61

Figure 7.5 Drift of population from the North and West to the South East (after Storm)

schemes to create conditions in which expansion could take place 'well clear' of London. The aim was to develop alternative centres of growth, for industrial and commercial growth as well as population growth. The South East Study concluded that the existing programmes for new towns and town expansion schemes were not big enough. New schemes were to provide for nearly one and a quarter million people.

The South East Study examined sites for more New Towns of 150,000 people each, requiring 8000 acres of land, and found that few sites in the South East were available. But there were quite a few existing towns which could accommodate large-scale expansion (of 50–100 percent growth in 15 years or 100 percent more people and 200 percent more cars). The towns chosen for expansion had to be economically

Table 7.1 Third-generation New Towns: three new cities proposed

1 Southampton/Portsmouth – expanded towns
2 Bletchley/North Bucks – New Town (became Milton Keynes)
3 Newbury – New Town
4 Six big expansions:
(a) Ashford
(b) Ipswich/Bury St Edmunds
(c) Northampton
(d) Peterborough
(e) Swindon
(f) Stansted
5 Twelve other schemes on a substantial scale
6 Expansion of first-generation London New Towns

Source: MHLG, 1964.

successful, big enough to provide sufficient employment, first-class shopping centres, with a variety of entertainment and well away from London. Thus the South East Study proposed a third generation of New Towns and expanded towns conceived on a scale never before conceptualised and located in areas which would be favourable to growth (table 7.1).

All the major proposals (except for Stansted) were the subject of detailed studies, and some designation areas were confirmed. All were to be developed jointly under the New Towns Act and the Town Development Act.

The planned expansion schemes were to cover one-third of the expected growth. The new towns, with some further expansion of the existing New Towns, were to accommodate half a million people from London. In addition, just under 400,000 people were to be housed in Town Development Schemes. The other two-thirds of the expected growth was to be implemented by the normal planning process. More land was allocated for development within the local planning authorities, that is, land for two million people. The implementation depended on the ingenuity of the local planning authorities by reviewing their development plans and raising densities. Land was not to be taken out of the green belt, which, if anything, was to be strengthened.

The New Towns Act and the Town Development Act united to help form 'regional cities' designed to be new centres of industrial expansion, and it was hoped that by linking more 'regional cities' to ports, new alternative outlets could be found for foreign trade.

Two examples of the proposed 'regional cities' were as follows:

1 The group of six expanding towns around the county town of Bury St Edmunds to have a total population of 200,000; with the expansion of Ipswich and other regional communities, the

'regional city' of the East Coast emerged.

2 The proposed development of Milton Keynes and Northampton, which with the expansion of Wellingborough and Bedford comprised a 'regional city' of over one million people.

Following another change of government in 1964 came a reversal of government policy and a return to designation of New Towns as a means of accommodating overspill population on a substantial scale and at some speed, although, by then, the breadth of concept and the scale of operation envisaged made the title 'New City' more apt. The 1964 government accepted the further extension of the New Town programme up to 1981, for the relief of London, Birmingham, Manchester and Liverpool, making a total commitment to 1981 of up to 1.8 million people in overspill, and proposed further third-generation New Towns. Growth studies were also prepared for Severnside, Humberside and Tayside.

Thus after two decades and more, projects undertaken under the 1946 New Towns Act and the 1952 Town Development Act 1952 coalesced. There was little distinction to be made between New Towns and the larger town expansion schemes. Many of the New Towns designated during the period 1967 to 1972 were expansions of existing towns, but these expansions were so massive as to create new city regions on a scale which dwarfed the post-war first-generation New Towns.

Strategy for the South East, 1967

The South East Economic Planning Council took a further look at London, and its 'Strategy for the South-East' reiterated the following points (*SEPC, 1967*):

1 London could not house any more people than were being housed at present. Better housing conditions were still needed and pressure must be taken off the centre.

2 The new estimate of housing shortage showed that one million people would have to move out of London by 1981. This was already being partially accomplished voluntarily, but the overspill programme must accomplish the rest in order to keep London's population static.

3 Employment pressure in London had to be reduced and therefore the 'strategy' advocated even stronger measures to move industry and offices out of London, including large government offices.

4 Within Greater London, new town-centre redevelopment should be linked to the communications systems.

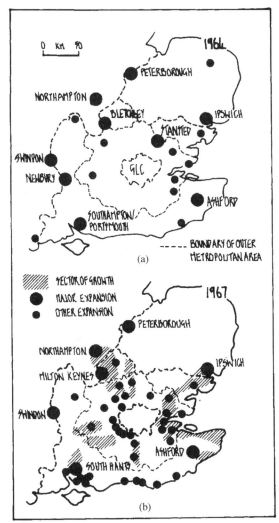

Figure 7.6 (a) South East Study, 1964; (b) Strategy for the South East, 1967 (after Clout and Wood)

The Strategy report recommended buffers of large areas of countryside between the growth sectors and to separate individual urban developments. These buffers of open countryside were titled 'country zones' and were no longer in the mechanical form of a green belt. Legislation would be needed to prevent development in these country zones. At the same time, the report approved the continuing existence of the Metropolitan Green Belt, but recommended that further open spaces should be part of the country zones. Regional recreation was also thought to have been neglected (figure 7.6).

Strong industrial growth in the South East should not be prohibited but moved to the major expansion areas. Offices were to be restricted and encouraged to move to the major expansion areas. The motorway

programme, already underway, was to be completed by 1975 to coordinate with the expansion areas. The Strategy report recommended an outer and an inner ring road for London by 1980, superseded by 'the Box' proposed by the GLC. The Strategy report ended with the need for a new Town and Country Planning Act, which followed two years later, in 1968. The report was, after all, a strategy and not a plan.

From the point of view of a national plan, the great objections to the South East Strategy report were that it arrogantly concentrated its thinking on the South East, treating the London region as an isolated region rather than as one of many other regions within the nation and as fitting into the national requirements. It tended to concentrate all investment in the one region. It was also heavily criticised for not looking at alternative strategies.

Third-generation New Towns

The third-generation post-1961 New Towns grew out of the South East Study and the Strategy for the South East, and attempted further to relieve congestion, yet they were conceived to be as large and economically viable as necessary so that they would act as counter-magnets to the centres from which they drew their population.

The affluent years of the late 1950s brought a massive rise in the standard of living and new levels of car ownership, increased leisure time and spending capital, enabling the creation of the third-generation New Town. The growth problem demanded new positive regional strategies. As the area of influence of a conurbation extended deep into its region, lost far beyond the traditional physical sphere, the New Towns were placed in areas of growth to provide incentive for the anticipated change, rather than in development areas, which had previously had large amounts of public capital poured into them with limited results. These New Town schemes were planned as multigrowth zones, and their strength as counter-magnets to existing urban areas was a product of their size.

After Cumbernauld in 1956, no more New Towns were designated until the designation of the eight third-generation New Towns between 1961 and 1966. Four were intended to help with accommodating overspill population from English cities: Skelmersdale and Runcorn from Merseyside; Redditch and Telford from the Midlands. Apart from the Welsh New Town, the other three New Towns represented the new thinking. Milton Keynes was the only green-field new city, as green-field sites were no longer available. Whereas the first-generation New Towns had been conceived in isolation from the surrounding economic area, Washington in the North East and Irvine and Livingston in Scotland were planned to help stimulate the economic development of their regions as growth points, and as part of a comprehensive regional programme for the central belt of Scotland in accordance with the regional plans. These latest New Towns broadened the New Town concept to include the construction of big New Towns based on substantial existing communities. The emphasis shifted from the designation for growth of a completely new area to the designation for expansion of an already large town to be a regional city and a counter-magnet to the great conurbations. Peterborough, Warrington, Northampton and, lastly, Central Lancashire New Town all fit into this category. The last New Towns were placed at greater distances from existing urban concentrations than the first New Towns, but with restrictions on the green belts.

The two most innovative of the third-generation New Towns were Runcorn and Milton Keynes, each exhibiting an opposing philosophy. Runcorn was planned around its mass transit system; Milton Keynes was planned for the automobile. Of the others, Skelmersdale was a mini-copy of Cumbernauld, while Redditch, Telford and Washington were straightforward in their planning. Table 7.2 lists the third-generation New Towns and expanded towns.

Peterborough, with an existing population of 83,000, was the first large centre chosen for major expansion in 1967 under the machinery of the New Towns Act. Despite objections to the quality and quantity of agricultural land to be taken up, Peterborough provided for an intake of 70,000 people plus an allowance for natural increase. Planned as four townships, these townships and the old town centre lay within a flexible grid of high-capacity primary roads, linking the townships, regional centres and industrial areas with each other and with the national trunk roads (*Bendixson, 1992*). The primary road structure, adapted to accommodate future growth, was based on a balance between public and private transport instead of an overadherence to one or other type of transport as at Washington, Milton Keynes, Runcorn and Skelmersdale.

The advantages of using established towns as a nucleus for large scale expansion included the existence of an experienced administrative organisation to work alongside a development corporation, public services and the presence of an established industrial base. Established towns could afford the opportunity to concentrate on the more vital house building programmes and urban renewal schemes in progress.

Table 7.2 Third-generation New Towns and expanded towns and their populations

		1960s	1981
	London:		
1967	Milton Keynes	40,000	250,000
	London expanded towns:		
1967	Peterborough	83,000	200,000
1968	Northampton	131,000	260,000
	North West (Manchester and Liverpool):		
1961	Skelmersdale (first-generation type)	13,000	70,000
1964	Runcorn (first-generation type)	12,000	90,000
1968	Warrington–Risley	127,000	209,000
1969	Central Lancashire (Leyland–Chorley)	250,000	500,000
	West Midlands (Birmingham overspill):		
1964	Redditch (first-generation type)	29,000	90,000
1968	Dawley–Wellington–Telford (large mark III type)	68,000	200,000
	North East:		
1964	Washington (first-generation)	20,000	70,000
	Scotland:		
1962	Livingston	2,000	100,000
1966	Irvine	35,000	120,000
	Stonehouse (abandoned 1976)		–
	Houston – expanded town	90,000	
	Total proposals	900,000	2,159,000

Successes: Runcorn and Milton Keynes

Two New Towns in particular, Runcorn and Milton Keynes, stood out from all the other third-generation New Towns, each demonstrating an excellent manifestation of exactly opposite policies. Runcorn's New Town Plan, one of the more controversial of the New Towns, was based on a public transport system. An original linear plan became a self-contained figure-of-eight when adapted to the topography of Runcorn (figure 7.7). The district centres are located along the public transport route; open space is in the loop of the figure-of-eight; and the population of the neighbourhoods is relatively low at 4000 people, and at a densities of 175 persons per hectare, to support the public transport. This physical structure was an attempt to find a planned balance between the use of the motor car and public transport. A spinal public transport route lined with communities means that most people

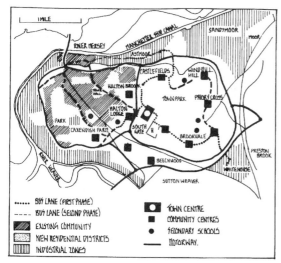

Figure 7.7   Runcorn Town Plan by Arthur Ling, 1964 (after Benevolo)

fenced off like a railway track. Complementary to the public transport system is a road network for private cars and lorries by expressways outside the residential area. The expressway system and the distributor road system is a partial one-way system, with left-hand turns only and loops around the shopping city.

Runcorn's plan for a reserved track for buses, its bus-way, was a breakthrough for New Town planning. From the start, the town was planned around this special rapid transit bus-way, and the route was planned with such concentration of population between the points needing to be served that there was a 50 percent saving in the length of the bus route as compared with the bus routes in towns of a similar size.

With the planning of the town in favour of public transport, the bus-ways connect the centres of the local and district centres, and the footpaths all lead to the bus-ways (figure 7.8). Likewise, the garages and parking spaces are placed further away from the houses than they might normally be in order to persuade people to take a bus. Factory car parks are placed further away than the easier clocking-on points of the bus stops. Even in the central shopping area the four major car parks are less easy to reach than the stops on the bus-way.

The plan for Runcorn ignored the old existing town centre of Halston and created a new town centre, which was upsetting to the shop owners at the time, but in terms of the new town it was the only way to make a viable town centre. The town centre building is an

are within five minutes (or 500 yards) of the express bus track, the maximum distance that anyone is expected to walk. Local centres occur at half-mile intervals to serve communities of 8000 people each.

The public transport system consists of single-deck buses operating on a separate rapid transit road reserved for buses, chosen as the most efficient and economic form of transport. The adopted system provides total separation of public transport from other road transport. The modified figure-of-eight, a single-carriageway two-lane road, only for buses, is

Figure 7.8   Runcorn: houses along pedestrian route leading to bus-way (by the author)

Figure 7.9   Runcorn Shopping Centre (from Runcorn New Town Development Corporation. Reproduced by kind permission of the Commission for New Towns)

'umbrella'-shaped structure, in an atmospherically controlled environment, with a 'shopping city' with 500,000 sq. ft. of shopping floor space, built on one level, and with four large car parks accessible from the expressway system and leading directly into the shopping malls (figure 7.9). Segregation of vehicles is by classes; private cars, service lorries and public transit are all vertically segregated. The local buses arrive on the special bus-way deck, and the shoppers are serviced by escalators.

The urban form of the 'shopping city' is a white megastructure with white convex roofs, cut through by a coloured red surface road, and pedestrian bridges to safeguard movements of people within the town centre. In the centre is a town square covered with a double storey height and a clerestory, giving natural lighting, pleasantly decorated with plants, telephones, with spots for shoppers and non-shoppers to stop and rest, taking a great deal of the labour out of shopping. Its atmosphere is a great improvement over the barrenness of the interior of Cumbernauld's town centre shopping area.

Apart from the attractiveness of the town centre, other reasons for Runcorn's 'shopping city' success were its organisational methods and its geographical location, between Liverpool and Manchester, very close to the network of the national motorway system, including the M56, the M6 and the M62. Its town centre became, in effect, a regional out-of-town shopping centre. With the organisational method adopted by Runcorn's Development Corporation, the shopping city was financed from private sources. Within six months, 90 percent of the shopping floor space was rented. Unlike other New Towns, where it took many years to get major companies into their shopping centres, Runcorn had a particularly dramatic success in attracting major companies into the new town. If it had depended on government finance, the construction of the shopping city would have been phased and geared to the actual development of the housing in the New Town, and spread over several years. Instead, the Development Corporation persuaded Grosvenor Estates to build a shopping precinct as a first phase, leaving room on an adjacent site to double its size in the future.

Runcorn's population was expected to rise to 70,000 by 1977, 90,000 by 1989, and 100,000 by the year 2000. The land-use components of the plan were unexceptional and followed normal New Town practice. The responsibility for building houses was divided between the New Town Corporation and private enterprise with an average net density of 165 persons per hectare. Education requirements remained the basic determinant of neighbourhood size. The standard two-form 'infant school', which required a catchment area of 4000 people, was adopted for its neighbourhood population, while secondary schools were grouped in campus sites, associated with community centres and linked to communities by rapid transport. The industry was exceptional, with 60 percent of all industrial workers working on industrial estates. In conclusion, Runcorn was a pace-setter with its public transport system and 'shopping city' town centre.

Figure 7.10   Runcorn housing designed by James Stirling, now demolished because people felt they were living in a washing machine (by the author)

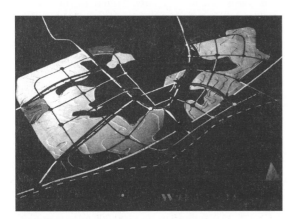

Figure 7.11   North Bucks City, 1958: Whaddon New Town (after E.K.S. Morris)

Milton Keynes was first envisaged in 1962 by Buckinghamshire County Council to accommodate overspill within the county, and from London, for 250,000 people ('North Bucks City', 1966), although there had been previous plans (*Morris EKS, 1960*) (figure 7.11). The Ministry proposed to accommodate one-quarter of a million people ('Northampton, Bedford and North Bucks Study', 1965). Then the 1967 Strategy for the South East included the concept in its proposal for a north-west corridor from London, the only third-generation New Town in the London area.

Milton Keynes Development Corporation was established in 1967. The consultants (Llewellyn-Davies, Weekes, Forestier-Walker and Bor) produced the Plan Report in 1970 for a New Town with an area of 21,900 acres, an existing population of about 40,000 and a planned intake of 150,000. The population was expected to be a quarter of a million by the end of the century. The aim of Milton Keynes was to cater for the 'new affluence' of the 1970s, assuming poverty was decreasing and average spending power doubling. The new town was to give the greatest possible freedom of choice in housing, shopping, education and flexibility in planning so that adaptation to new needs would be simpler.

The plan for Milton Keynes reflected social changes including (1) the availability of health services, (2) education available to vastly more people, (3) changes in housing policies away from local authority housing, (4) proposals to reinforce the better integration of personal services, particularly health and social services, (5) decreasing national poverty for most people, (6) real purchasing power of the average family doubling by the end of the century, (7) more families insisting on more education, recreational facilities and health care, and (8) use of better means of communications.

The central aim of the plan was to provide the greatest possible choice for the future inhabitants and to allow a wide variety in patterns of life. The plan emphasised especially (1) the desire to give maximum employment opportunities and to increase choice through a dispersed pattern of employment and social opportunities; (2) the need for a wide variety of

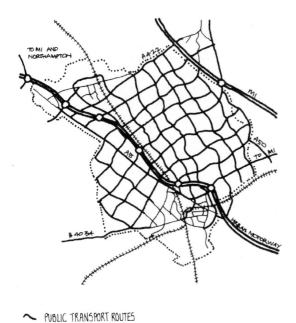

PUBLIC TRANSPORT ROUTES

Figure 7.12   Milton Keynes plan showing road grid and living sectors (after Llewellyn-Davies, Weekes, Forestier-Walker and Bor)

housing types to include owner-occupation and private housing, with a target of 50 percent in private housing; (3) meeting the demand for space because people on higher incomes will want more land and prefer net residential densities between 15 and 25 dwellings per hectare (6 to 10 dwellings per acre); (4) reinforcement of existing centres; and (5) an efficient transport system.

The particular aspects of Milton Keynes which stood out from other third-generation New Towns were its employment structure, its transport network, and its housing, leisure and educational facilities. The employment emphasis was on education, communications, technical and office occupations, on managerial and clerical rather than manufacturing, including the need to provide a wide variety of jobs, training and educational facilities.

The grid pattern of town roads is spaced at one-kilometre intervals (5/8 mile) (figure 7.12). Almost 160 kilometres (100 miles) of new main roads were built with no frontage access. Two-thirds of the roads are of two lanes in each direction with ground-level junctions controlled by traffic signals. The suggested alternative and more conventional answer of main roads further apart with multi-level junctions would have increased costs without significantly decreasing the journey time. The other one-third of the roads are

of one lane in each direction. The consequence of such a system was that the public transport was kept to a minimum. Housing, at lower densities than normal in New Towns, was aimed at attracting the managerial and professional classes. The recreation plan attempted to widen the variety of recreation offered by building three golf courses, a major indoor recreational centre and linked open spaces.

Aesthetic control was also quite different from that in other third-generation New Towns, as aesthetic control areas were designated. Maximum design control was required for specific areas such as the city centre, existing centres, all activity centres, existing villages, and city parks. Minimum design control areas included areas referred to as 'do-it-yourself' areas, where the minimum requirements cover only safety, sanitation and access.

Intermediate design areas encouraged good design from outside designers. The intention was to provide greater freedom to private developers and the private house owner. Untidy design areas included areas for junk yards and noisy sports. Milton Keynes also set itself to be a city of learning and succeeded beyond its wildest dreams as the home of the unique Open University and other colleges of further education. The town centre reflected a sophisticated, highly efficient centre, lacking human spaces.

Criticism of Milton Keynes has focused on the nature of the low-density housing, the over-elaborate road pattern, the poor public transport system and no articulated open space system. Milton Keynes has survived fairly well, though agricultural land was relied on for amenity and not parks. It was originally assumed that only 15 percent of the people would use public transport but in fact the proportion has been greater. Milton Keynes was ambitiously called the 'first new city in Great Britain', but the energy crisis of 1973–74 profoundly changed the context of many planning policies. Because of the increased cost of petrol, constraints on driving and constraints on ability to buy cars, new studies gave greater emphasis to local activities (figure 7.13).

The Milton Keynes 'new city' of 250,000 was suggested at a time when considerable growth in the South East was anticipated.

The development of the city region of one million or more people was the suggested characteristic of the 1970s. Abercrombie's 1944 Greater London Plan was based on a static concept: the idea that London would not grow. Instead, there was growth everywhere. Since 1961, the outer metropolitan belt of London had grown by 100,000 people every year. In the West Midlands, around Birmingham, there was growth of 600,000

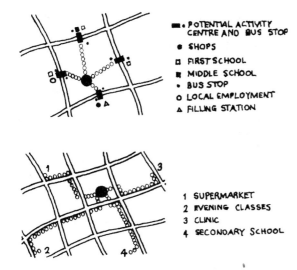

● POTENTIAL ACTIVITY
    CENTRE AND BUS STOP
● SHOPS
◻ FIRST SCHOOL
▪ MIDDLE SCHOOL
• BUS STOP
○ LOCAL EMPLOYMENT
▲ FILLING STATION

1 SUPERMARKET
2 EVENING CLASSES
3 CLINIC
4 SECONDARY SCHOOL

Figure 7.13   Organisation of local activities within the grid of Milton Keynes, showing magnification of one sector and the community services serving that sector (after Llewellyn-Davies, Weekes, Forestier-Walker and Bor)

Geographical spread

The third-generation New Towns had a wider geographical spread. Milton Keynes was the only New Town designated near London. In the North, Runcorn, Skelmersdale, Washington and Redditch were designated, in the hope that these northern towns would provide areas of economic growth, which could help to solve some of the other problems of their regions. Runcorn, for example, had a large allocation of heavy manufacturing industry, while Milton Keynes had none.

Plan form

Contrary to the first New Towns, the last New Towns had open-ended plans which allowed for expansion. Milton Keynes, for instance, was based on a grid pattern, with dispersed neighbourhood centres and amenities, suitable for extension. Redditch was laid out like a cluster of bananas, with three spines radiating from a centre, separated by green wedges. Any growth could be accommodated on the end of the spines. Warrington was built on a linear pattern that could be lengthened if necessary.

In line with the open-ended plans, most of the third-generation New Towns did not have a fixed upper limit to the population. The dispersal of land uses, coupled with a breakdown of industrial concentration, was an attempt to get a so-called richer urban mix of activity, building and land uses, as well as reduce the length of the journey to work patterns by distributing traffic peak periods over a number of different routes.

The third-generation New Towns display some disagreement in their approach to the hierarchy of social groups of neighbourhoods and communities and the allocation of community services at each level in the hierarchy. For example, in Milton Keynes, the distribution of social services was based on the assumption that greater mobility provided by higher universal car ownership would support greater dispersal of social services.

people in the years from 1961 to 1975. In East Anglia, there was a rate of population increase (over 13 percent) even slightly higher than that of the West Midlands. The East Midlands reflected the same pattern. In the North West, the space between Liverpool and Manchester was rapidly filling up. By 1973, however, the population forecasts had dropped. It became apparent that the purpose of planning and its future needed review.

Basic differences between third-generation and first-generation New Towns

Bigger population base

One of the most striking features of the third-generation New Towns was their size; in comparison with the Reith Committee's 'optimum' of 30,000–50,000 people the population base now became 100,000–250,000 people, whereas originally Hemel Hempstead had the biggest base population (20,000) of all the first-generation New Towns.

But size was not the only striking feature. Another feature was that four of the third-generation New Towns were based on substantial existing towns – not only because the best sites had already been taken up by existing towns, but also because the older towns were in need of rejuvenation and a share in the limited capital investment programme.

Land use

Residential density levels were reduced to between those of Cumbernauld and the first New Towns, between 30 and 75 persons per acre. As the English still do not choose to live in flats, the rising living standards provided a demand for space within and outside the dwelling. The density of housing was lowered to give higher standards of space around dwellings and to allow for play areas and parking.

In housing provision, the third-generation New

*) size of population
2) based on existing towns

community and accommodate minority groups (such as immigrant workers, or executive groups). Milton Keynes originally aimed for 50 percent private housing, while Skelmersdale expected to provide 89 percent public corporation housing and was prepared to provide factory and business accommodation and executive housing to attract firms. In Runcorn, for example, industrial densities decreased as well, from 50 to 30 workers per acre.

Design

Notably more experimental, the third-generation New Towns display considerably higher levels of design. Housing design is carefully detailed; shopping centres are dramatic in their expression, as seen in Runcorn and Milton Keynes, and neighbourhood/community centres reflect careful if safe taste, as in Washington New Town (figure 7.15).

Transport

The third-generation New Towns mostly allowed for one car to every five persons, and attempted to strike an economic balance between allowing complete freedom for the car on the one hand, and producing economically viable public transport on the other.

Figure 7.14 Milton Keynes poster (by Milton Keynes New Town Development Corporation. Reproduced by kind permission of the Commission for New Towns)

In Milton Keynes, the use of the motor car dictated dispersal and the geographical spread of population activities, with 60 kilometres of roadway. In Runcorn, a concentration of population was required to produce a viable public transport system, which attempted to be fast, clean, comfortable and frequent enough for people to prefer using public transport rather than the car, as certain sections of the community might never

Towns differed to quite an extent, but they aimed to control building in a way that would attract a balanced

Figure 7.15 Housing in Washington New Town (from Washington New Town Corporation. Reproduced by kind permission of the Commission for New Towns)

own cars and would therefore not be able adequately to make use of the facilities of a town based on universal car ownership. Hence in Runcorn, primary attention was given to an efficient bus service, operating on a separate roadway. Although there were different transport strategies, most of the third-generation New Towns continued the accepted policy of separating pedestrians and vehicles, particularly in their town centres.

Achievements of the New Town programme

Britain's New Towns have been globally admired as archetypal because they appear to possess a combination of the following admirable features:

1 The New Town was spatially separated from the parent city and built on land which had been acquired at a lower cost than that of land on the periphery of the built-up area of the city. The New Towns were in part a reaction against scattered ribbon development and so had designated areas which were compact in form, using less land per person than towns of similar sizes.
2 The New Town was comprehensively planned by a development agency, distinct from the local authority.
3 A large proportion of property in the New Town, especially public open space, remained in the ownership of a public body, dedicated to the growth of the New Town, although this approach changed with the termination of the New Town Development Corporations.
4 They intended to be, in accordance with the terms of the Reith Committee, 'self-contained and balanced communities for working and living'. The aim for self-containment was more like a wish than a goal as the Development Corporation could only make it possible, for example, by providing the environment and amenities which induced people to work in the towns and live there too.
5 The New Town Development Corporations proposed standards for facilities for the normal use of their inhabitants (per size of population) for shops, schools, hospitals, pubs, etc., which were outstanding and far superior to most standards which could be provided by local authorities in the larger conurbations. The Development Corporations accepted this responsibility as an aim, although there was nothing in the New Towns Act which required them to provide these facilities at such standards. However, problems did arise, as the provision of many kinds of local authority

facility was the responsibility of the county councils, and thus New Town development imposed a significant extra burden on the ratepayers, many of whom did not live in the New Town.

The overwhelming demand in all New Towns has been for houses with gardens. Development has therefore been at low densities and this has led to criticism that there is a lack of 'urban character', which was sometimes responded to by over-reactive megastructure town centre designs such as the 'shopping city' in Runcorn and the shopping mall in Milton Keynes.

The later New Towns offered their inhabitants a quality of home, social circumstances and physical environment unsurpassed by most urban areas throughout the country. The features which distinguished the last New Towns from other New Towns have been their ability to grapple with the challenge of the motor vehicle, the firm establishment of separating pedestrians from vehicular traffic, and the attempt to provide a satisfactory balance between private and public transport.

In financial terms, New Towns were viable as they matured, though the principal beneficiaries were not necessarily those the New Town idealists originally had in mind. For example, profits from the development corporations went to the Exchequer and the local authorities had little say in how the money was spent.

The last New Towns fulfilled a necessary function in taking large overspill populations from the congested cities and providing local employment for many of the people, proposing new development to stimulate economic activity and improving social infrastructure, acting as regional centres and making the area a more attractive place in which to work and live.

So much changed between the building of the first New Towns and the last New Towns – the increased level of car and television ownership, the appearance of supermarkets, increasing leisure habits and rising real incomes, all of which led to important changes in planning thought and practice. The last New Towns were planned at a time of economic boom to accommodate the rising living standards of the inhabitants. New Town policy would seem therefore to have been a success, because it was able to adapt to changes in the lifestyle of the majority of the people.

The New Town concept offered many administrative advantages. In particular, the assembly of land, comprehensive planning, provision of infrastructure, and the disposal to public and private bodies as part of an integrated programme was implemented effectively by the New Towns machinery for years. The New Town Corporations attempted to work in close partnership with local authorities (without constraints of local government boundaries or local politics). They provided expert staff which few local authorities could maintain.

However the great expense of the last New Towns led to some concern. The development at Milton Keynes cost more than £700 million, partly because of the high cost of roadway development. Even so, it was perhaps understandable in the South East to lay such an emphasis on car transport, while the provision of two car spaces per family at Washington in the North East was unnecessary, and the balanced public transport of Runcorn was more realistic. The lavish treatment of the New Towns only emphasised the problems in inner city areas and the need for urban renewal.

By 1970, Merseyside and Manchester had begun to arrest their economic decline and their future was more assured, but the position in the 'Cotton Belt', roughly the area between Manchester and Preston, was not assured. Central Lancashire new city was to provide a counter balance to the two conurbations to the south and in so doing provide a new focus and increased vitality in the area, the city combining the two prospects of creating a new regional centre for three-quarters of a million people and securing an economic base for renewal and expansion on a large scale.

Redevelopment and expansion were to half (128,000) of the projected growth, to be accommodated in 'green field' developments (*Matthew and Johnson-Marshall and Partners, 1967*). The other half of the projected growth was to take place in ten townships, which fitted into a proposed linear structure based on transport systems. The linear transport system was a masterly solution to a very complex problem, by superimposing a linear communications system capable of linking the structure into a single, clearly identifiable Regional City.

Perceptions began to change by the 1970s. Following the 'flight' of population and industrial development from the inner cities to New Towns, it was perceived that London received less urban aid than Milton Keynes! The question began to be asked whether New Towns were surviving at the expense of the old. When the projected population for London by 1981 was only 6 million, the view of the GLC changed from that of a need for the creation of New Towns for London overspill population to that of the

New Towns being competitors with London for scarce resources. The dispersal of whole communities and industries from the inner cities proved impossible to reverse and it began to be argued that if inner cities received the same sort of finance as did the New Towns, the chronic inner city problems could be resolved.

The last New Town to be designated was Stonehouse for Glasgow, which was cancelled in 1973. In the 1970s, the need for investment in city centres throughout the country had become paramount. The inner cities needed to be made as attractive as the New Towns, and thus support for the New Towns was switched to the inner city. By the end of the 1980s in England, New Town building was over, and it ended in Scotland in the 1990s.

The theoretical regional city: South Hampshire

In South Hampshire, a situation developed where additional population was being accommodated by piecemeal allocation of land for development on the outskirts of the towns and villages at each review of the various town maps. This created a series of congested towns and villages, spilling over haphazardly into the countryside. Within a decade or so, the possibility of planning coherent communities in an acceptable environment would have been irretrievably lost. Thus Hampshire County Council decided that the whole of southern Hampshire should be replanned, and commissioned Colin Buchanan to produce a comprehensive plan.

Buchanan's South Hampshire report, for the first time, assumed a theoretical approach and applied it to a definite region (*Buchanan and Partners, 1966*). Novel in its first attempt at analysis of urban structure, it represented an important milestone in planning perception. The theoretical approach aimed at providing maximum flexibility for the plan's implementation in an attempt to relieve the rigidity of planning applications and development control techniques, while planning expansion of one and a quarter million people in the Southampton–Portsmouth area. The report tested various alternative approaches, and finally proposed a course of action in novel terms. There was no definite 'master plan' or development plan at the conclusion. The goal of the report was to devise an urban structure which could respond to growth, change or evolution within the urban subsystems. For example, changes in the National Health functional subsystem implied a whole series of changes in the urban subsystem designed to accommodate it. A theoretical approach was adopted to discover the principles upon which the urban structure could be developed as one coherent integrated urban system.

Buchanan's theoretical approach adopted four concepts for the urban structure: (a) a functional subsystem based on a function, like education; (b) a nodal subsystem based on several functions and their catchment areas; (c) an urban subsystem or grouping of nodal subsystems, such as the neighbourhood; and (d) an urban system – the sum of the subsystems, such as a community or district. These four concepts were 'structured' in three ways: by either a radiating but centrally focused plan, by a linear plan, termed a directional grid, or by a grid structure. Such model structures provided maximum freedom of choice, each phase to function independently of growth elsewhere, and to provide change and renewal, versatility and growth capability.

The plan structures were tested. The centripetal structure plan was found to be very rigid. Any uneven growth immediately upset the catchment areas for the urban centres. There was a lack of flexibility within the transport network, the urban subsystems did not respond to change easily, and the slow growth pattern might easily change into a linear pattern before the completion of the development.

The traditional grid plan could support different categories of routes, but was not good under analysis. Centres were not really central and available to their catchment areas, while the grid could easily turn into a linear form. Public transport was difficult to provide in such a system. Freedom of interaction between each subsystem was more difficult than within the directional grid.

The traditional linear structure plan was renamed a directional grid structure because the main facilities occurred along the communication spines (figure 7.16). The directional grid structure was found to be very flexible, as not all areas for urban centres needed to be fixed. Public transport could be used to give a direction for growth, and there was great freedom of choice and communication along the spines of activity. Theoretically it could be highly adaptable to growth. In summary, without too much explanation of the analysis of the system (and this was a weakness in the study), the report adopted its preferred structure, the directional grid, particularly for the advantages to the transport and communication systems.

The report applied the proposed directional grid approach to one portion of the corridor (figure 7.17), proposing that growth would occur in different stages. In the first phase, the initial build-up of new development would occur at each end of the corridor,

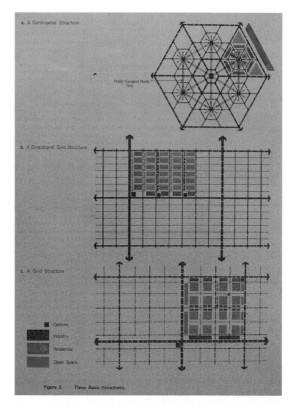

Figure 7.16 South Hampshire Plan Directional Grid (Reproduced by kind permission of Colin Buchanan and Partners)

with pressure on the existing Portsmouth–Southampton corridor. In the second phase, new centres located along the corridor would take pressure off Portsmouth and Southampton. And the third phase would adjust standards so that inside the old cities, standards would be the same as in the corridor city region.

For some, this approach was too unsophisticated and the jump from theoretical possibilities to the single choice alternative was too weakly supported. However, it was one of the first plans to promote an 'adaptive' approach to planning. The idea that various alternatives could become feasible over a period of time was new, and in that sense the South Hampshire study was epoch-making.

A special development agency would have been needed to handle the equivalent of ten conventional New Towns over a period of 30–40 years, within several existing cities and therefore highly sensitive areas. Most costs would be as economical in the corridor as elsewhere. Employment policy would have depended on the Greater London Council as the prime exporter of people and jobs. The cost of both public

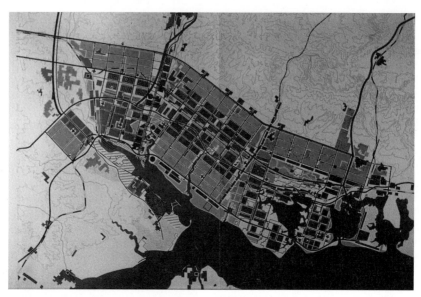

Figure 7.17   Preferred structure applied to South Hampshire (Reproduced by kind permission of Colin Buchanan and Partners)

and private transport was high because transport had not been adequately considered.

Strategic Plan for the South East, 1970

During the lengthy time spent discussing local government reorganisation during 1966–75, a voluntary committee, the South Hampshire Plan Technical Unit, implemented inter-county planning by first publishing a pilot study which reduced the aims of Buchanan's South Hampshire Report to four possibilities: a major new city between Southampton and Portsmouth; peripheral growth of the main cities; dispersed growth throughout the southern half of the area; or selective dispersal of growth for a number of key areas. Even these four possibilities showed excessive implementation costs and insufficient flexibility. The South Hampshire Draft Structure Plan contained very little of Buchanan's model plans for a corridor city region, although the draft plan was based on a linear form and accepted that the Southampton–Portsmouth corridor must be an area of rapid growth. Between 1966 and 1991, it was expected that the population would increase by 43 percent, that there would be three times the number of cars, twice as many people racing to the coast for leisure activities and twice the shopping turnover. However, the four 'possibilities' receded to the background, and eventually the post-local government reorganisation structure plan retreated to the concept of the growth of the existing centres of Portsmouth and Southampton,

and growth of six major urban areas.

By 1968, a South East Joint Planning Team commissioned by the South East Economic Planning Council, and the Standing Conference on London and South East Regional Planning, representing the local planning authorities, reported with recommendations on patterns of development for the South East, taking as a starting point the strategy proposals of the council but also taking into account the planning work of the standing conference with the object of providing a regional framework to guide local planning authorities and the government.

The 1970 Strategic Plan for the South East (SPSE) (*South East Joint Planning Team, 1970*) recommended a major new city, growing eventually to 200,000 people, set almost mid-way between Portsmouth and South-ampton; several new satellite towns of 50,000–100,000 people, some linked closely to the existing cities and towns, which would also grow a little; new major extensions of the existing cities and towns; and a series of new townships established near the motorway between Portsmouth and Southampton with jobs and shopping concentrated on at least two major east–west routes.

The method of accommodating London's overspill needs and the structuring of the south-east region was to propose a pattern of development for the 1980s and 1990s based on major sectors following the main radial communication routes out of London. These expansion areas, at a considerable distance from London, would serve as 'counter-magnets' to London (*Hall, 1963*)

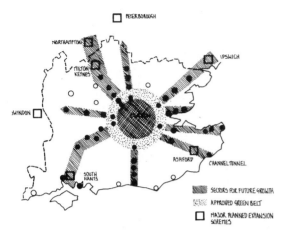

Figure 7.18 Diagrammatical presentation of the Strategy for the South East, 1970 (after South East Economic Planning Council)

(figure 7.18). The great value of the concept of the 'counter-magnets' was that it accepted the existing traffic routes and used them in a two-way flow rather than the single flow of commuters into London. Administratively within the sectors, the artificial separation between London and the Home Counties would have to disappear. These major expansion areas would also take London's overspill of 250,000–500,000 people plus a natural increase of another half a million people. The first three most important expansion areas were the Southampton/Portsmouth area, the Milton Keynes area plus the expansion of Northampton, Wellingborough and Bedford, and the Ipswich/Colchester area. Considerable population expansion would also have to take place in the Outer Metropolitan Area up to 1981.

The most telling conclusions from this second stage of evaluation were that the possibility of a major new city could clearly be implemented only by the creation of a New Town Corporation, which was anathema to the county council and not favoured by the government of the day. The possibility of satellite towns produced major infrastructure cost-phasing problems if several satellites were to be developed at once. The possibility of major extensions to existing cities was politically and publicly unglamorous, but had cost advantages. The possibility of New Towns was widely acclaimed but, with early construction of a second motorway, very expensive. The eventual plan proposals combined the best features of the possibilities of expanding existing cities and of creating small townships. The strategy concentrated development so as to minimise infrastructure costs, and comprised, in addition to the very large existing commitments, six new growth

sectors of 3,000–10,000 dwellings plus minor growth to the limits of existing installed infrastructure capacities elsewhere.

The 1970 Strategic Plan for the South East was also available to the Roskill Commission in its final stages of trying to resolve the development of Maplin Airport and Maplin City. The Roskill Commission finally recommended Cublington as the site for the new airport, which was later overturned by the then government in favour of Maplin.

In 1971, following the agreed Maplin airport decision, the government approved, in principle, the Strategic Plan for the South East (*South East Joint Planning Team, 1970*) and accepted the main limitations of the plan with the exception of making the Harlow/Bishops Stortford area a growth area. By 1971 south-east England had a regional plan with both central and local government committed to a new airport, new road and new rail links, the city of Maplin, the extension of a deep-water port, and EEC membership.

Some consider that the pioneering Strategic Plan for the South East (1970) represented a peak for regional planning in the UK, with the exception of continued regional planning in Scotland (*Glasson, 1992*). Thereafter regional planning declined in England and Wales, with the emphasis in the hierarchy of planning shifting downwards towards local planning, aided and abetted by the reorganisation of local government.

A new DoE monitoring unit was established to work in close cooperation with the South East Economic Planning Council and the standing conference. In its first report, *Strategic Planning in the South East* (*DoE, 1973b*), it already appeared that the population growth in the region was not reaching the expectation of the 1970 strategic plan and the major growth areas were experiencing smaller population growth than expected. Eventually, in 1976, the Secretary of State, after a change of government, deleted one growth sector west of Waterlooville and, although not deleting the proposal, raised doubts about a second at Horton Heath. The plan was eventually approved in 1977, nearly 13 years after its need was tacitly admitted in commissioning the Buchanan Study.

Summary

The 1960s and early 1970s were an exciting period for town planning (table 7.3). New cities were being proposed, and new towns were built, while dispersion and decentralisation policies gave many people new opportunities and a new way of life. But it was not to last. By the mid-1970s, statutory Structure Plans were

Table 7.3   Planning events, 1957–70

1957–60	1961	1962	1963	1964	1965	1966	1968	1970
Old development plan ——————————→				PAG Report	White Paper		T & CP Act	
				South East Study 1961–81		Strategy for the South East		Strategic Plan for the South East
	Third-generation New Towns					South Hampshire Study/Buchanan Study		Milton Keynes
Royal Commission Greater London 1957–60	London White Paper		Local Government Act		Greater London Council	——————————————————→		
						Royal Commissions on Local Government ———————→		

installed, and a revolutionary new idealistic plan, such as Buchanan's South Hampshire Report, was but a memory of an age based on principles and ideals. From then on, planning took the form of ad hoc policies, alternative strategies and specific local area objectives. The golden age of planning principles had come to an end.

Part III

Urban design and planning
policies

8 Urban design in the post-war period

Radical new techniques

In some cities, such as Coventry and Plymouth, the Blitz released the energies of architects and civic designers long before any direction from the Ministry of Town and Country Planning. The plans for the rebuilding of Plymouth, and particularly Coventry, were magnificent examples which dealt with the problems of reconstruction following bomb damage and problems associated with the need to impose a new conscious order on the course of urban development.

The prototype of urban design for reconstruction was Coventry, where medieval streets in the city centre and its cathedral were burned to the ground in the air raids of 14 November 1940. The enlightened council and equally enlightened first Architect's Department, under Donald Gibson, produced a radical new scheme of a pedestrianised shopping precinct protected by one of the first inner city ring roads (*Johnson-Marshall, 1966: 291–318*) (figure 8.1).

Being trained in the Beaux Arts tradition, Gibson aligned the pedestrian precinct on the only part of the cathedral to survive, the spire. Some have called this an architectural solecism since Gothic churches never closed symmetrical vistas (*Esher, 1981: 50*); nevertheless it gave an important visual focus. Further, the pedestrianised shopping area permitted two levels of shopping, with an innovative upper level shopping deck (figure 8.2). A brilliant part of the design scheme was the decision to place Basil Spence's new cathedral of 1962 at right angles to the ruin, thus both preserving the memory of the tragedy, yet forging ahead with the future. Coventry continued to expand its pedestrian city centre and this provided leadership to all the later reconstructed cities. In the 1990s, Coventry's councillors, architects and planners upgraded the 1950s buildings without destroying the design framework and added an essential escalator from the 1950s shopping precinct to a new West Orchards shopping complex.

Other consultant architects and planners produced beautiful plans such as Thomas Sharp's plan for Exeter Phoenix (1946), Sir Edwin Lutyens and Abercrombie's plan for Kingston upon Hull (1945) and Abercrombie and Plumstead's civic survey and plan for Edinburgh (1949). The Middlesbrough Survey and Plan 1946, directed by Max Lock, was a remarkable compilation of a vast array of survey information, exemplifying another type of consultant's report at this time. Many of these plans showed tremendous spirit and creativity.

The late 1940s through the 1960s was a prolific period for plan-making and civic design projects. Architects and civic designers were spurred on by the new Ministry of Town and Country Planning, set up in 1943 under the civic design leadership of Sir William Holford, who was responsible for the technical side of planning and brought into his team Thomas Sharp, Gordon Stephenson (a former apprentice of Le Corbusier), H. Myles Wright and John Dower, who were to figure prominently in the post-war reconstruction era. City centre planning was of utmost importance, particularly to those local authorities with vast blitzed areas. As an interim measure the 1944 Town and Country Planning Act, the so-called Blitz and Blight Act, provided funds for local authorities to acquire and redevelop blitzed areas. To help local authorities, Holford's Research and Technical Division produced many influential documents, collated into the historic *Advisory Handbook on the Redevelopment of Central Areas* (*MTCP, 1947b*), which explained the method that local authorities were to use: firstly, historical survey of the whole town; secondly, local and regional surveys; thirdly, decision-making on the main issues of land-use, housing and roads; fourthly,

Method .

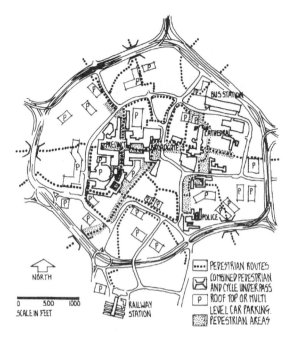

Figure 8.1   Plan of Coventry central area (after Tetlow and Goss)

uses are classified within one or other use class to determine whether permission is required for change of use. Use Classes Orders became statutory in 1955, and although altered from time to time have remained statutory definitions.

In addition, Holford's team devised radically new instruments to assess the amount and distribution of accommodation, which included:

1 Density of building accommodation, particularly for residential buildings
2 Sunlighting and daylighting indicators
3 The Floor Space Index

Having assessed the use, use zones, and density of accommodation, the street layout was considered and a sketched plan produced. The components of planning and building types, i.e. shopping, traffic, office blocks and open space, were individually discussed with examples of detailed schemes. This process was to be repeated for decades throughout Britain.

Holford was one of those rare architects who could communicate as excellently by the pen as by the brush, and thus the *Handbook* was exceptionally well written. The *Handbook* promoted the by then accepted principles of planning, which included decentralisation of population, planned dispersal of population and industry, strict zoning of land uses, and urban design schemes for city centres. The new techniques of the Ministry of Town and Country Planning have remained as tools of planning and urban design ever since.

detailed schemes; and finally, implementation and programming. To help with decision-making on the main issues, buildings were classified into building use groups and zones for planning purposes (*MTCP, 1947b: 23–30*) (table 8.1). Thus commenced the system of Use Classes Orders, in which all building

Figure 8.2   Coventry central area showing new pedestrian area on axis of spire of old cathedral (by the author)

Table 8.1   Zoning chart: Building Use Groups and Use Zones. Zones suitable for a Central Area are enclosed by a heavy line. P = primarily building uses of type opposite to which it appears; X = building uses not permissible in zone opposite to which it appears (after MTCP, 1947b)

Buildings use groups Index Type Letter	Zone 1 Residential	Zone 2 Business (shops)	Zone 3 Business (offices)	Zone 4 Business (wholesale warehouses)	Zone 5 Educational, recreational and public buildings	Zone 6 Light industrial	Zone 7 Industrial	Zone 8 Special industrial
A Dwelling houses	P	X	X	X	X	X	X	X
B Residential (other than dwelling houses)	P			X		X	X	X
C Schools and residential colleges		X	X	X	P	X	X	X
D Shops		P						
E Offices			P					
F Wholesale warehouses	X			P	X			
G Storage warehouses	X	X	X		X		P	
H Public buildings and places of assembly					P			
I Special places of assembly	X				X	P		
J Light industrial buildings	X			X				
K Industrial buildings	X	X	X		X	P		
L Special industrial buildings	X	X	X	X	X	X		P
M Other buildings								

Density zoning and residential density

Density zoning is a concept of physical control over the total amount of floor-area of new building which is permitted on a given site; it is a control over the intensity of building development and is closely related to size of population. On the one hand, it is a means of relating the future population of a town to the amount of land available for development or redevelopment and of controlling the rate at which such land is used. On the other hand, it is a rule of thumb which stipulates the desirable maximum amount of accommodation permitted to be built on sites within a particular area, and hence helps to set an approximate maximum limit to the number of people who can live or work there.

In residential developments, density can expressed in a number of ways (table 8.2):

persons
dwellings
habitable rooms
bed spaces
} per acre (originally) or hectare (later)

Residential density can be described as high density, implying blocks of flats, or low density, which implies houses with gardens. Low residential density occurs in suburban areas of expensive housing. Medium-density residential development, also in suburbia, outer city areas or New Towns, has been used for low-rise medium-density housing where land is fairly valuable and the journey to work or shop is kept as short as possible. The physical form of such areas comprises houses with gardens, or three-storey housing, or expensive low maisonette blocks.

High-density housing is now restricted to central areas, although the past history of post-war housing

Table 8.2 Residential density

Type of residential density	Type of dwelling	No. dwellings/acre	No. dwellings/hectare	Type of urban area
Low density	Houses with gardens	4–6 houses	10–15 houses	Suburban
Medium density	Terraced houses, three-storey housing maisonette blocks	10–16 dwellings (30 persons/acre)	24–38 dwellings (50–90 habitable rooms)	Suburban outer city area; New Town
High density	Flats	20 dwellings (100–150 persons/acre)	50 dwellings (250 habitable rooms/hectare)	Central area; outer city area

included many areas of high-density housing in the outer city areas, such as, for example, the 'dampies' in the Gorbals, Glasgow, tower blocks of high density, built immediately after the Second World War, torn down in the 1990s and replaced with three- and four-storey maisonette-type medium-density housing.

Daylighting and sunlighting controls

Minimum standards of sunlight and daylight were considered essential, following Gropius' original teaching. Adequate sunlight was to penetrate into the room of a house, not only in order to make the room more attractive to live in, but also to create additional warmth. The long shadow of dark satanic mills and houses of the Industrial Revolution hung over to ensure the requirement of the highest degree of sunlight and daylight. Sunlight was to reach all living rooms for a period of at least one hour for ten months of the year. If possible, sunlight was to reach the kitchen and bedroom in the morning and enter the living room in the afternoon. Elaborate sunlight indicator tests were instituted as well as permissible height indicators for daylighting (figures 8.3 and 8.4).

In the 1990s the excuse is made that, with greater technology, sunlighting standards are not so important, such that housing associations are allowed to build to a lower sunlighting standard than was permitted in the late 1950s. Daylighting and general sunlighting controls in the 1990s are set out in the Building Research Establishment guide: *Site Layout Planning for Daylight and Sunlight* (1991) which replaced the booklet *Sunlight and Daylight* (*DoE, 1971b*) and is approved by the Department of the Environment. The principle behind the 1990s guidelines for skylight is that the ground floor windows (and above) of a new building should have an adequate view of the sky. This is mathematically measurable to ensure that all obstructions are less than 25° above the horizon. This measure is more space consuming on an adversely sloping site than on a flat site. Nor should new development overshadow public open spaces and pedestrian routes throughout the whole day.

The guidelines for sunlight on buildings are given as percentages of probable sunlight hours. This is the long-term average of the number of hours during the year when sunlight reaches the ground (in London it is approximately 1500 hours per year). This basic sunlight guide applies to living rooms. In all cases sunlight

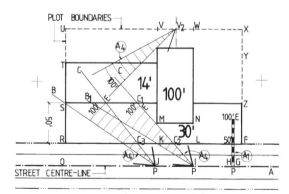

Figure 8.3 Daylighting control: architectural planners could test the amount of daylight on any surface by means of protractors; thus it was a brilliant simplification for general use of a complex scientific problem (after Johnson-Marshall)

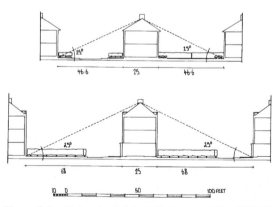

Figure 8.4 Obstruction of daylight diagrams (after MHLG)

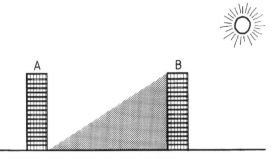

Figure 8.5 Skyscrapers must be widely spaced, otherwise the lower floors of building A, in the shadow of building B, will not receive any direct sunshine in winter (after LCC)

exposure is checked using diagrams in the BRE guide. The guide states that the advice is not mandatory, but it is likely to be used by planning authorities, particularly in solving disputes. In any case it complements the British Standard Code of Practice (BS8206) Part 2, with which architects have to comply.

Floor space index and plot ratio

For commercial development, the *Advisory Handbook on the Redevelopment of Central Areas* invented the floor space index: the ratio between the total area of the floors contained within a building (or buildings) and the area of the plot or other land area on which it stands. The floor space index was obtained by dividing the total area of all floors within the buildings by the area of land plus half the width of the adjoining streets (*MTCP, 1947b: 14–17*). Later the floor space index was abandoned in favour of the plot ratio index, although plot ratios are not formally part of the approved Local Plan, partially to provide flexibility and the ability to alter the ratios as needs require.

The plot ratio is the ratio between the total floor area on all floors within a commercial building and the area of the plot of land on which it stands, thus:

$$\text{Plot ratio} = \frac{\text{Total floor area}}{\text{Site area}}$$

Ratios are expressed as 2:1 or 3:1 (figure 8.6). One of the highest plot ratios occurred in the City of London, where the floor space index recommendation in the Holford Plan was 5:1 (*Holden and Holford, 1951*). A high plot ratio of 5:1 allowed a five-storey building covering the entire site, as happened in the City, or it permitted a 20-storey building using only a quarter of the site. By the 1960s in central London, the highest permitted plot ratio was 3:1, although exceptions did occur (*LCC, 1960*). In other cities or local towns, plot

ratio has not normally exceeded 3:1 (figures 8.7 and 8.8). The skyscrapers of New York, Chicago and Hong Kong are exceptional and can be based on ratios as high as 100:1.

Since the first *Advisory Handbook on the Redevelopment of Central Areas*, for over 50 years ministries have published handbooks and manuals on aspects of design in transport, residential areas, housing, etc. These handbooks unusually took on a god-given aura, especially when architects and planners were hungry for specifications for the 'New World' to be built after the Second World War. Later on, the Ministry Handbook became more the method by which the central government implemented its policies, particularly through the terms and guidance of housing manuals, but also through manuals on Roads and Services, House Design, Equipment of Houses, Tenders and Specifications, Multi-storey Housing, and Housing Procedure for England and Wales, and Scotland.

The first housing manual, for low-cost council housing, since the Tudor Walters report of 1918, was the *Design of Dwellings* report (*Dudley Report, 1944*), which advocated a maximum density of 120 persons per acre, lower than Abercrombie's standard of 135 persons per acre and lower than his maximum of 200 persons per acre. At this standard, community facilities and open space could be provided through the method known as 'mixed development', i.e. building some high-rise for couples, maisonettes and terraced houses for families, and low buildings for the elderly.

The next handbook on residential areas, *The Density of Residential Areas*, was written during Harold Macmillan's tenure as Minister of Housing and Local Government (*MHLG, 1952*). Clearly trying to increase the number of houses which could be built, it set out standards of densities corresponding to various combinations of house types and number of storeys in flats. The density was calculated by ensuring that terraced houses in one row did not rise above an imaginary line drawn at an angle of 25° from the foot of the adjoining row. The comparative layouts were heavily influenced by the Le Corbusier/Gropius type of slab blocks in rows marching across the site. The handbook also outlined 'mixed' developments, containing as high a proportion of houses as possible within given density standards. Mixed development became the goal for housing estates throughout the country in the 1950s and 1960s. Difficulties came when couples stayed in the high-rise after they had families or when so many families had to be housed that the majority had to be housed in high-rise maisonettes.

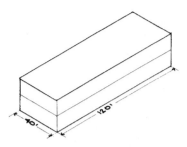

Plot ratio 2:1
100% site coverage
Permitted building area 9600 sq ft.

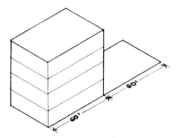

Plot ratio 2:1
50% site coverage
Permitted building area 9600 sq ft.

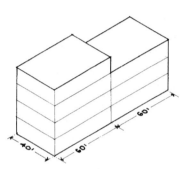

Plot ratio 3 1/2:1
100% site coverage
Permitted building area 16800 sq ft.

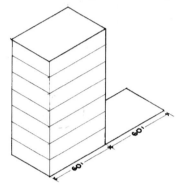

Plot ratio 3 1/2:1
50% site coverage
Permitted building area 16800 sq ft.

Figure 8.6   Diagram expressing plot ratio (after Burke)

In the next design step, the residential densities were related to the total land requirements for a neighbourhood and the quantitative relationship which needed to exist between the people and the space for each facility. Even the highest density shown in the handbook, of 60 persons per acre, was low compared with the reality. In the East End of London, densities of 150–250 persons per acre were normal (figure 8.9). Although tables were shown that reduced the amount of open space per family, by and large the density standards in the 1950s were still comfortable. The 1952 report concludes with the telling remark that the most significant aspect is the density at which dwellings are grouped together. It was also thought that residential density could be controlled through the Development Plan, which in fact did not happen.

Density control of commercial buildings is intended to relate the capacity of the new building, in terms of its working population, to the capacity of existing streets and parking places, and to prevent new buildings from denying daylight and air space to neighbouring buildings. Over-concentration of office development in central areas aggravates the problem of traffic congestion and parking. Since most developers are keen to get every last pound out of a commercial development, density controls of commercial development are absolutely essential. Density of workers per acre or hectare applies to industrial building and prevents over-concentration.

There are cases where a 'quid pro quo' deal is made with the developer. The developer gives the town a physical asset and the local council gives the developer more floor space. Such arrangements occurred with

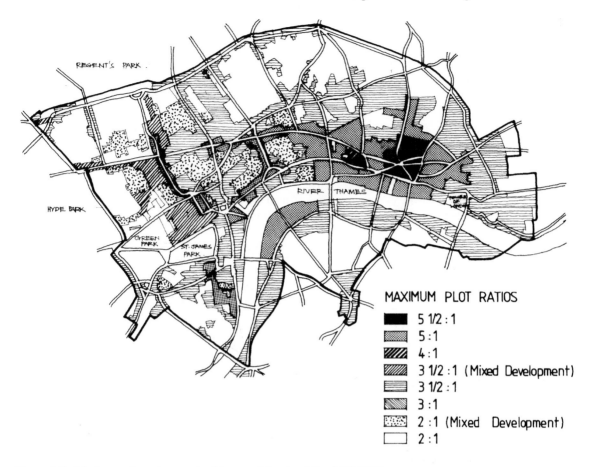

Figure 8.7   Maximum plot ratios permitted in central London (after LCC 1960)

great frequency in the 1970s in many town centre schemes. Generally the developer took more floor space than he gave back in public benefit, so it was not good practice. Straightforward plot ratios, which apply equally to everyone, are fairer.

Design handbooks and government manuals

Holford, being a clever architect himself, resisted the idea of a ministerial civic design guide to control design. In general, a design guide is 'a set of design principles and standards required by the local planning authority and applying to a wide area and not just a particular site' (*Llewellyn-Davies et al., 1976*).

It is said that when Patrick Abercrombie, who was not a skilful designer, questioned the lack of a civic design manual, Gordon Stephenson's reply was 'The architectural profession would give a hundred different views, all of which would tend to cramp and strait-jacket design and probably run counter to

some economic, or if you like, organic laws' (*Cherry and Leith, 1986*). Eventually, however, the Ministry bowed to local authority requests and published *Design in Town and Village*, by Thomas Sharp, Frederick Gibberd and William Holford (*MTCP, 1953*). But similar disagreements over design guides between the freedom-loving designer and the practical local authority planner have continued to the present.

Multi-storey blocks took over in the 1950s, and the maximum density of houses crept up to 38 houses per acre (90–100 persons per acre). Planning requirements such as community facilities and open space were more prominent. The handbooks warned that the higher the density, the greater the importance of providing open spaces, designed to be used by a lot of people. Garaging and car parking, barely mentioned before, became a major concern. Maisonettes and towers became acceptable, although the net maximum density was held to 38 houses per acre. High-density

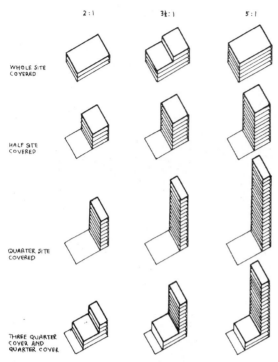

Figure 8.8 Plot ratios as allowed by the London County Council (after LCC, in Johnson-Marshall)

Figure 8.9 High-rise housing (after LCC)

mixed development with the orderly disposition of multi-storey slab blocks, which later became such a nightmare, were also recommended. Notwithstanding this, most of the proposals and suggested densities were still humane and carefully considered in the 1950s.

Roads

One of the most significant proposals concerning roads came from Sir Alker Tripp, who proposed a

clear definition of a hierarchy of roads, as Le Corbusier had done (*Tripp, 1942*). This hierarchy included arterials to form a national network, sub-arterials, which connected the national network with the towns, and local roads, which had limited access to the sub-arterials and none to the arterials. Tripp also proposed the concept of 'precincts', served by local roads and devoted to particular uses, protected from major traffic, which was kept to the periphery (figure 8.10).

The handbook *Design and Layout of Roads in Built-up Areas* remained the roads bible for over 20 years, until the roads handbooks of 1966 and 1968 (*Ministry of Transport, 1946, 1957, 1966, 1968*). It stressed a new road pattern which utilised the by-pass as an attractive alternative route for through traffic, particularly for towns of less than 250,000 people. The by-pass is still important, providing relief from heavy traffic and helping to preserve environmental quality in the town (figure 8.11).

For the larger town, the new road pattern promoted inner, intermediate and outer ring roads, pierced by radials, and 'sub-surface and elevated' roads providing traffic segregation by grade separation (figure 8.12). A few multi-level intersections were shown. The four main types of urban roads were specified as follows (*Ministry of Transport, 1966*):

1 Primary distributors: these roads form the primary network for the town as a whole. All longer-distance traffic movements to, from and within the town should be canalised on to the primary distributors.
2 District distributors: these roads distribute traffic within the residential, industrial and principal business districts of the town. They form the link between the primary network and the roads within environmental areas (i.e. areas free from extraneous traffic in which considerations of environment predominate over the use of vehicles).
3 Local distributors: these roads distribute traffic within environmental areas. They form the link between district distributors and access roads.
4 Access roads: these roads give direct access to buildings and land within environmental areas.

The inner ring road remained a prominent design feature for 50 years but has been replaced by radials and outer ring roads. The Roads Handbook did not stress pedestrianisation, although urban designers were advocating pedestrian precincts, thus showing the ideological gap between physical planners and the roads engineers (figure 8.13).

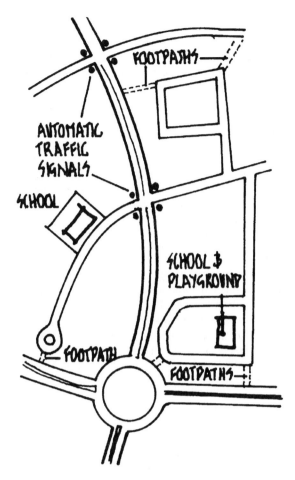

Figure 8.10 Tripp's traffic-free 'precinct' (after Tetlow and Goss)

Car parking standards can vary greatly from town to town, or from decade to decade depending on the strength of public opinion and/or developers' demands. They are some of the most controversial standards and are measured in terms of car space per square metre of gross floor area per type of commercial land. In housing, they can be measured as car spaces per dwelling, or per bed spaces, or in hotels, per bedroom. In public buildings, car spaces are measured in terms of seating capacity.

Planning, density and capacity standards

As well as zoning, density, sunlighting and daylighting yardsticks, the concept of planning and capacity standards was also invented. Planning standards are established as guides to control development when planning applications are to be processed. Most

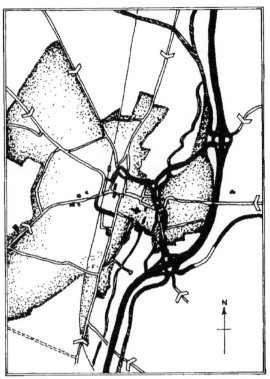

Figure 8.11 Proposed by-pass for Winchester (after Lee)

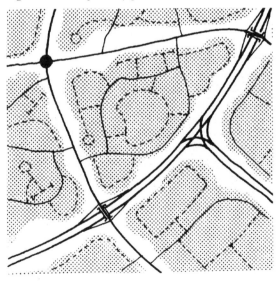

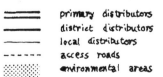
=== primary distributors
—— district distributors
— local distributors
----- access roads
∷∷∷ environmental areas

Figure 8.12 Urban form of roads (after Ministry of Transport, 1966)

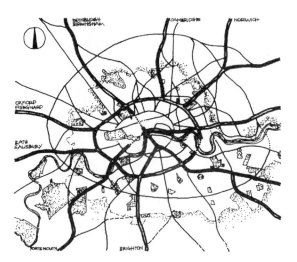

Figure 8.13 London roads network showing inner ring, radials and outer ring routes (after Gibberd)

planning standards have been in use for many years and apply throughout a district. They are revised from time to time and can be rigid or flexible depending on the councils or committees enforcing them at the time. All planning standards can be broken if the committee or official thinks the situation merits disregarding the standard.

Standards are meant to be universal. Many architects moan about planning standards, complaining mightily about the strait-jacket of planning controls. But planning standards are applied to support as high a quality of building as possible and to provide fairness, so that all applications are treated as nearly equally as possible. These are the underlying reasons for planning standards. For example, they enable the big developer to conform to the same rules as the little developer, or offer the single parent in a one-bedroom flat the same standard of sunlight and daylight as the mansion dweller; and offer the same school facilities to each child. Fairness and quality in the provision of the basic amenities of life prompts planning standards.

Standards can cover all aspects of planning, housing, schools, open space, etc., and proposals need to meet the relevant standards before a planning application is submitted. Failure to meet the required standards will, in most cases, result in refusal of permission, unless greater public gain can be achieved by the flexible rather than rigid use of the planning standard.

All physical development generates the need for physical services: for roads, water supply, sewerage, sewage disposal, power, lighting, telephones, etc. The density and capacity of these services have to be related to the demand in each area; and the demand is related to the density of development, which governs the number of persons living or working in the areas. It is possible to make a reasonably accurate estimate of 'demand' or what can be allowed with respect to all physical services. Water supply is a well-known factor. For example, developments can be perfectly reasonable except for the inadequacy of the existing water supply and therefore the whole scheme is dropped. The ability or capacity to provide or not provide the physical service for an area is very often a powerful 'hidden agenda' which can influence many more obvious issues.

Community standards refer to the standards of community facilities, such as schools, school playing fields, public open spaces and health clinics to be provided for all the people in the Local Plan (figure 8.14). In the euphoria and idealism of the 1950s and 1960s, planners and their plans indicated lavish standards for schools and schools playing fields, and tried very hard to compensate for the lack of adequate open space. Particularly schools and open space were united within the ideal of the neighbourhood unit. Health clinics were also to be liberally provided along with shopping facilities.

The most inspiring display of community standards can be found in the New Towns, particularly in the last to be built, like Milton Keynes and Irvine (table 8.3). In retrospect, these standards were Utopian, and could not be provided in the older or inner areas of the city. The contrast between the standards of the New Towns and those of the inner city residents became too great and contributed to the demise of the New Town policy.

The neighbourhood unit and the Radburn layout

Occasionally, Britain has borrowed American planning principles. One of the most influential of these was the neighbourhood unit principle; less influential was the Radburn layout principle, and the third principle, the parkway, was merely given lip-service. The influence of pre-Second World War American planners such as Lewis Mumford, Clarence Stein, Clarence Perry and Catherine Bauer was significant to the extent that their idea of the neighbourhood unit was put forward in the *Design of Dwellings* report (*Dudley Report, 1944*) and in 1945 the Ministry of Town and Country Planning proposed, but never published, a Residential Neighbourhood Manual (*Cherry and Leith, 1986*).

The neighbourhood unit, as a planning concept, first came to prominence in the USA in the 1920s. Based on

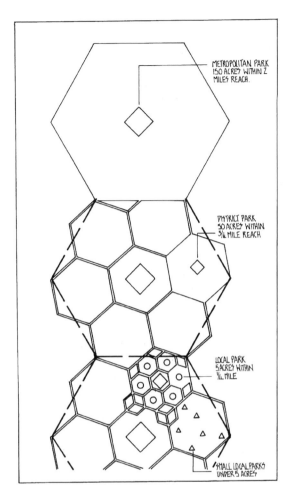

Figure 8.14   Standards of accessibility to public open space (after GLC)

Table 8.3   School support standards (after Irvine New Town, 1971)

Assuming:

1. Average occupancy = 3.5 people per dwelling
2. 0.6 Primary School children per dwelling
3. 0.35 Secondary School children per dwelling
4. One-sixth of all pupils are Roman Catholics

Given

5. 560 pupils per two-stream Primary School
6. 1500 pupils per Comprehensive School

Then

7. Population required to support one Primary School

$$= \frac{560}{0.6} = 933 \text{ dwellings at } 3.5 = 3265 \text{ people}$$

$$\text{plus} \quad \frac{933}{5} = 187 \text{ dwellings at } 3.5 = 655 \text{ RCs}$$

$$\text{Total} = 1120 \text{ dwellings at } 3.5 = 3920 \text{ people}$$

8. Number of Primary School residential units to support one Comprehensive School:

   4 Primary School residential units
   4 × 120 × 0.35 = 1568 pupils total
   5/6 non-dimensional = 1308 pupils
   1/6 RC   = 260 pupils

9. Population required to support one Comprehensive School

   $$= 4 \times 1120 = 4480 \text{ dwellings} = 15,680 \text{ people}$$

circulation. For example, the neighbourhood unit is the catchment area of the local primary school, depending on population density, within half a mile radius on foot. This dimension has served as a general theory, guiding planners in delineating and laying out housing schemes. Local shops in the American neighbourhood were placed on the edges of the neighbourhood within a quarter-mile of all houses (with an adjoining community centre). The British, when they adopted the neighbourhood principle, made two unfortunate alterations:

(1) they put the shops in the centre of the neighbourhood along with the community centre, thus importing unruly traffic inside the neighbourhood unit, when the aim was to keep traffic out of the neighbourhood (although Bor reverted to the American practice when designing the neighbourhood of Milton Keynes); and

(2) by using a two-stream primary school, they necessarily doubled the population, raising it to 10,000 people, way beyond the population originally intended.

some of Howard's ideas on self-contained residential units, it evolved mainly through the work of Clarence Perry into a formula for use in planning extensions to urban areas. Probably its most noted practical application, in the early stages at least, was the Radburn scheme in New Jersey, prepared by Clarence Stein and Henry Wright. Since then its use became widespread as a basis for planning residential areas and expanded towns, and in the immediate post-war New Towns. It was rejected in the plans for Cumbernauld and Skelmersdale New Towns but reincorporated into many of the smaller third-generation New Towns, like Washington.

The neighbourhood concept has two dimensions – technical and social. The first relates to two basic principles – the provision of all the facilities needed daily by the residents within walking distance from the home, and the separation of vehicular from pedestrian

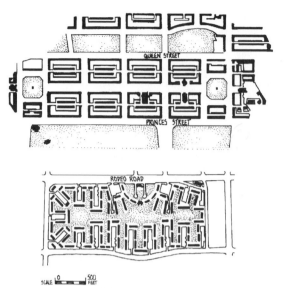

— BOROUGH BOUNDARIES
--- COMMUNITY BOUNDARIES
☐ SERIAL NUMBERS OF SUB-NEIGHBOURHOODS
(LINKED TO THEIR PARENT NEIGHBOURHOOD)
+++ BOUNDARIES (OTHER THAN NEIGHBOURHOOD)

Figure 8.15   Radburn layout: Baldwin Hills Village, California (below) at the same scale as the New Town of Edinburgh (above) (after Stein)

social

The second dimension refers to the claim that living in such 'units' would promote neighbourly relations and locally based activities, thus creating viable urban communities which would bring order and cohesion to expanding and fragmenting cities. Criticism, particularly of the second dimension, both on theoretical grounds and through social research, as being too 'deterministic', became increasingly voluble (*Bell and Tyrwhitt, 1972*).

The Radburn plan as demonstrated in Baldwin Hills Village (figure 8.15) was a physical form of a neighbourhood characterised by:

(1) residential area of superblock size;
(2) central green area;
(3) perimeter road keeping traffic to the edge;
(4) alternating access roads and pedestrian routes to the housing.

In 1951, the Festival of Britain took place mainly on London's South Bank. It was a popular event and, for town planners, an opportunity to show the public what planning could do for the people. The Festival of Britain gave a tremendous fillip to modern architecture, even though all the buildings were temporary with the exception of the Festival Concert Hall, designed by Sir Robert Matthew and Leslie Martin. The festival proved that modern architecture could be popular. The planners' exhibition was located in the East End of London, at Lansbury Neighbourhood Centre (*Johnson-Marshall, 1966*). Lansbury was one

BOROUGHS AND COMMUNITIES
COMMUNITY BOUNDARIES   ----
BOROUGH BOUNDARIES   —
COMMUNITY NUMBERS   63
EXISTING COMPREHENSIVE
DEVELOPMENT AREAS
PROPOSED COMPREHENSIVE
DEVELOPMENT AREAS
EXTENSIONS EXISTING C.R.A.S.
EXISTING AND PROPOSED
SUPPLEMENTARY TOWN
MAP AREAS

Figure 8.16   Analysis of existing neighbourhoods in the East End of London by the author, showing community boundaries and sub-neighbourhoods (after LCC, 1960)

of 12 neighbourhoods in a comprehensive development area of 2000 acres planned for an ultimate population of 100,000 (compared with a pre-war population of 217,000) and developed by the London County Council as part of the Stepney–Poplar reconstruction area as proposed in Abercrombie's County of London Plan 1943 (*Bor, 1978*) (figure 8.17). In Lansbury, visitors were invited to follow a route through a 'town planning pavilion' where the principles of planning were laid out, and then were invited to walk through Lansbury's pedestrianised shopping precinct and neighbourhood to see the new buildings and to see how reconstruction could be implemented in the surrounding blitzed areas.

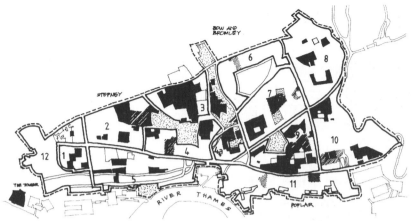

Figure 8.17 Stepney–Poplar reconstruction area showing 12 neighbourhoods (after Johnson-Marshall)

Figure 8.18 Lansbury shopping precinct (by the author)

Lansbury neighbourhood survives as one of the more humane expressions of town planning, in particular there have been no management problems with the 1951 Lansbury housing. Various house types (two- and three-storey houses, semi-detached and in terraces, four-storey maisonettes and three- and six-storey flats), mostly in streets and squares, were all tried to see which were the most popular. However, the densities were lower than the 136 persons per acre, which then had to be made up by higher densities elsewhere.

Another pace-setting feature was the Lansbury shopping precinct, the first post-war pedestrian shopping precinct to be built in the form of a shopping street opening into a market square (figure 8.18). Although its architectural design by Frederick Gibberd now looks dated, partly due to restrictions on materials, its planning function has remained highly successful (figure 8.19). A clock tower (closed to forestall suicides) contributes well to the three-dimensional design. The transport planning aspects were less successful. Although the local access road system was rationalised, the main traffic road, which was meant to be transformed into a walkway with traffic transferred to the periphery of the neighbourhood, still bisects the neighbourhood with heavy lorries. Provision of more open space was one of the other major goals of the post-war planners, as the

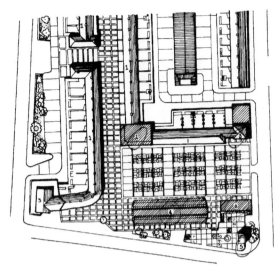

Figure 8.19 Plan of Lansbury market showing the types of space provided. Key: 1 shops; 2 store; 3 public house; 4 covered market; 5 clock tower; 6 public lavatory (after Gibberd)

East End was almost totally deficient in open space. This aspect was only partly successful. Overall, Lansbury neighbourhood was highly influential in planning neighbourhoods throughout Britain.

The neighbourhood unit was used extensively by all local authorities and New Towns throughout the 1950s and 1960s (*Mumford, 1954; Tetlow and Goss, 1976*). Based as it was on a population size of 5000 to 10,000 people, it ceased to make sense when automobile ownership increased, making the scale of population insufficient as a basis for an economic service unit (*Bell and Tyrwhitt, 1972*). Sociological studies repeatedly showed that it was too large ever to function in terms of 'neighbouring' (*Willis, 1972*). Greater accessibility through high car ownership and the desire for greater choice of facilities and services eventually diminished the powerful hold that the neighbourhood unit concept held over most plans. By the 1970s, other concepts of either smaller population units, (planned unit developments–PUDs) (*Burchell, 1972*) or the non-place realm (*Webber, 1964*) took the place of the concept of the neighbourhood unit.

Comprehensive Development Areas

The 20 years following the Second World War saw urban design policy concentrated upon reconstruction and redevelopment, which meant massive tearing down of old buildings, and substituting whole areas of new buildings. Efforts were concentrated on rebuilding war damage, adding hospitals, schools and other deficient services, or on redeveloping slum clearance housing.

Physical plans promoted urban redevelopment in Birmingham, Bristol, Coventry, Canterbury, Exeter, Plymouth, Brandon and Stepney–Poplar. The wartime spirit to rebuild anew was the philosophy behind concern about 'bad layout' and 'obsolescent development', to be removed in post-war reconstruction through the planning tool of Comprehensive Development Areas (CDAs) as provided by the 1947 Town and Country Planning Act, which were areas the local planning authority redeveloped as a whole. The main emphasis was on the renewal of slum housing and slum industry. The local planning authority designated the area and carried out the development either itself, for example as in Coventry, or in conjunction with private developers, as in the office developments in the City of London. Urban redevelopment funds were concentrated mainly on new building in CDAs, New Towns and city outskirts until 1954 by law, and through the 1960s in practice, because of scarce building resources, a housing shortage and an expanding and shifting population. Indeed, CDAs lingered on in some cities well into the 1970s.

Although massive redevelopment became anathema to later generations, the redevelopment areas, in comparison to the slums which existed before, were thought by many to be a major improvement, and were welcomed at the time (*Johnson-Marshall, 1966*). Many design lessons were learned from the redevelopment schemes, such as:

1 The need for a definite focal point in an area, as a Town Hall Square, a tall building or, for example, the replacement for the cathedral in Coventry.
2 Pedestrianisation of the town centre: Coventry developed a large-scale pedestrian precinct, while Plymouth and Exeter had small areas devoted exclusively to pedestrians. Walkways, covered by canopy, full arcades or covered footpaths, gave shelter and unity within the pedestrian area. Less successful was Coventry's experiment with upper-level walkways, which pedestrians found onerous. Many cities tried upper-level walkways well into the 1980s, when they became limited to indoor spaces and serviced by moving staircases. Only in this manner are upper-level walkways acceptable to the public (figure 8.20).
3 The disposition of important shops in a redevelopment area was carefully planned so that commercial values were spread, visual interests

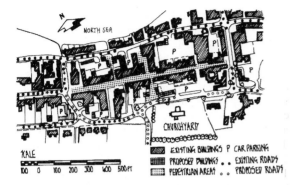

Figure 8.20 North Berwick: scheme for separating pedestrian and vehicular access to the High Street (after Tetlow and Goss)

created and peak pedestrian traffic spread over a large area. Rear access to shops was another innovation.
4 The emergence of the principle of separation of pedestrian and vehicle traffic resulted in an inner ring road which separated through traffic from local traffic and removed through traffic from the town centre.

In residential areas, positive lessons from post-war schemes included:

1 the need to create a total environment at each stage of the development, in which open space standards related to the housing, as, for example, the need for children to have well-sited playgrounds, and
2 the understanding that areas had different social characteristics, and needed different treatment.

Houses for the masses: local authority houses

In the 1950s and 1960s, the slum problem remained in the Midlands and North West England, with subsidiary zones in London and Tyneside, although towns differed greatly in the extent of their slum problem. For example, in Stoke-on-Trent, one house in seven was a slum; in Liverpool, two in five houses were slums in 1955. The problem of slums and the rate of clearance through redevelopment had little correlation. Some authorities with only a few slums cleared them quickly, while others such as Birmingham had to struggle for years.

The 'Housing Conditions Survey, England and Wales, 1967' found 1.8 million unfit slum dwellings: of these, 1.1 million dwellings were to be rebuilt in future redevelopment areas, 700,000 needed repair while 113,000 dwellings adjoined redevelopment areas

and would need help within 20 years (*MHLG, 1967*). The total national housing stock was between 12 and 13 million, but the survey found nearly one-quarter of the national housing stock (four million dwellings) lacked one amenity and nearly three million did not have an internal W.C.

The legislation referred to houses 'unfit for human habitation', which were defective in one or more aspects, according to a 12-point list which included:

(1) Repair
(2) Stability
(3) Freedom from damp
(4) Internal arrangement
(5) Natural lighting
(6) Ventilation
(7) Water supply
(8) Drainage conveniences
(9) Sanitary conveniences
(10) Facilities for food preparation
(11) Disposal of waste water
(12) Heating

The list reflected the century-old concern with health and sanitation. There was no mention of beauty, decent room arrangements, south-facing living rooms, or any architectural quality controls, the lack of which was to be so criticised in later decades. The 12-point list was consistent with the evolutionary approach based on health and sanitation. Design or architectural quality control was to evolve only much later, but meanwhile the health and sanitation approach was politically the most popular. At that time, between 60,000 and 70,000 houses were demolished or closed annually in England and Wales alone. Most of the larger towns and cities could point to areas of temporary devastation. Socially these figures represented the enforced movement of between 170,000 and 190,000 people each year (*Cherry, 1972*).

Thus, because of the continuous slum problem following the Second World War, public housing was built on an unprecedented scale with a drive and enthusiasm which originally was wholeheartedly endorsed by politicians, architects, planners and official engineers, based on social ideals that finally there could be sufficient good housing for all the people. Coupled with this social ideal of low-cost housing for the masses was the architectural vision of high-rise tower blocks whose high density would allow quantities of families to be housed. When the dilapidation, the suicides and other problems started occurring, the dream turned into disaster. Blame was placed immediately on architects, but the poor planner also took the rap for the ultimate disaster of high-rise housing. In fact, the politicians were primarily responsible, as they wanted the votes which came with the low-cost housing. The high-rise tragedy began in the 1950s and ended in the 1970s but some local authorities, having to pay off the cost invested in these buildings, continued to be burdened well into the 1990s and rehabilitated housing where possible.

During the Second World War, over 3.5 million houses had been damaged in addition to the 200,000 destroyed; and another three-quarters of a million houses were needed owing to the post-war marriage and consequent baby boom, bringing the total needed to almost four and a half million dwellings (including the 1.8 million unfit dwellings). The politicians quickly realised that there were a lot of votes available if families could be housed, and so each successive government pressed for more and more housing, achieving higher targets. Macmillan, when Housing Minister, insisted that 300,000 houses be built in 1953 alone. Moreover, the politicians kept raising the

housing targets, knowing that this brought a healthy voting base. Theirs was a quantitative point of view and the politicians must carry most of the responsibility for the high-rise towers that so many people came to dislike.

The architects, on the other hand, looked at the situation from a design point of view. For many years, Le Corbusier and Gropius had been heroes of the architectural profession with their similar vision that high-rise housing was the major method of housing people in the modern city. The younger generation of architects in the 1950s recognised four or five contemporary masters – Le Corbusier, Mies van der Rohe, Frank Lloyd Wright, Alvar Aalto and Walter Gropius – and particularly tried to follow the precepts of these masters. Although Le Corbusier's City for Three Million People with skyscrapers in a great park inspired British architects before the Second World War, hardly any opportunities presented themselves for such high-rise building until after the war. Many

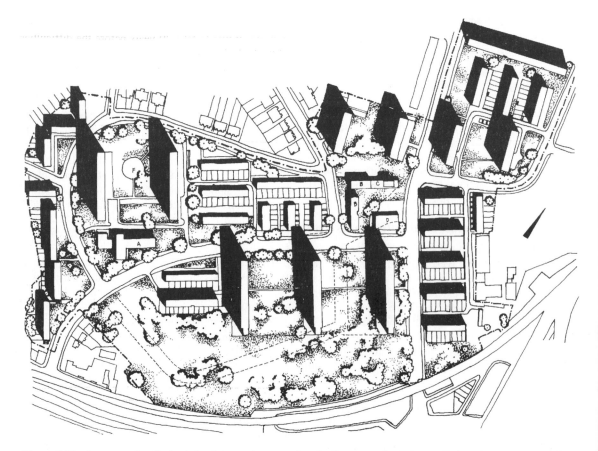

Figure 8.21 Layout study of mixed development incorporating the Department's recommendations for open space (after Department of Health for Scotland)

Figure 8.22   Industrialised housing in Runcorn New Town (by the author)

British architects during the Second World War dreamed of creating Huxley's Brave New World in Le Corbusian terms, and when the politicians offered the opportunity, they welcomed it. Architects truly love building towers, as it allows them to make their mark on the city landscape. They were also committed to the social ideals of mass housing as advocated by Gropius, and idealistically thought that high-rise housing was the best way to achieve this.

The idealist planners had housing lists of thousands, and as high-rise prefabricated system building allowed them to build 20,000 houses per year, they were resolving a major need. Besides, at that time, people wanted new houses with hot water and decent kitchens. It is difficult to remember that families were thrilled to move out of their damp, 'unfit for habitation' houses in London's East End into new housing, no matter that it was high-rise.

Then the sociologists did not know what they know now. The main prestigious examples of high-rise housing were found amongst the rich, where it has always been popular. Many families live in fabulous high-rise flats on Park Avenue in New York, at densities of over 300 persons per acre, and pay millions of dollars to do so. For the well-off, high-rise living provides security, clean air, anonymity and a space in the city centre. Even Le Corbusier was deceived by the success of the tower for the bourgeoisie. Montreal's Habitat, designed by Moshe Safdie in the Le Corbusian manner, with large gardens in the air, is a fine way of life. But translated for poorer

people, the assets disappear and then it becomes poor housing. It was to take 20 years before the difficulties of the high-rise became apparent, and then when it did, the housing disaster became one of the major excuses for trimming the planning process.

Another reason for building the new housing in high-rise buildings was the new technology of systems building which provided the means for cheap and rapid high-rise building. After the removal of wartime building, controls in 1954, new methods and materials appeared. Concrete panels, which easily stain in the English rain and hardly ever dry out, were used in a brutalising fashion, led by the Architectural Association gurus, Alison and Peter Smithson. This desire to follow Le Corbusier slavishly even in respect of an unsuitable material did the modern architecture movement a great deal of harm in the public eye. The failure of the shuttering of the concrete, leaving a rough surface and thus a brutal effect, turned the public away from so-called modern architecture in general and the International Style in particular. The architects should have followed the more humane Gropius style, in masonry, steel and glass materials more suited to the English climate. Systems building might have been more successful if the material used had been mostly anodised aluminium or pressed steel panels, which were not to appear until the 1970s.

Systems building mainly appealed to the builder because it was fast. The prefabricated systems allowed many flats to be built at once, which was extremely profitable for the builders. Furthermore, high buildings were encouraged as greater economies of scale were effected at greater heights. The engineers equally loved the high-rise tower blocks. It was cheaper to service dozens of families in one block; there were fewer roads to build and drainage was cheaper. In Europe, prefabrication had also led to systems building. Through the National Building Agency, the 1964 government encouraged local authorities to use European systems of building. By 1966, the National Building Agency concentrated on housing schemes on large contracts. In fact the run of buildings in Britain were smaller than in Europe and housing standards became lower. By 1968 systems builders were operating at less than full capacity, and plants were closing down, but not before Livingston New Town in Scotland and Thamesmead in London had produced large neighbourhoods of systems buildings. By the mid-1970s, numerous building failures resulted from an inability to master the new techniques required in systems building, costing local authorities hundreds of millions of pounds.

In the 1960s, the Ministry of Housing and Local Government produced batches of Planning Bulletins (Nos. 1–7), which were good, and Design Bulletins (Nos. 1–12), which were cold, officious and somewhat inhumane, including the *Housing Cost Yardstick*, Design Bulletin 7 (1963) and *Dimensions and Components of Housing*, Design Bulletin 8 (1963). Ergonomics, the science of the use of space by the human being, was detailed in Design Bulletin 6: *Space in the Home* (1963). All the families described were standard nuclear families. The most progressive report was *Homes for Today and Tomorrow (Parker–Morris Report, 1961)* which, unlike previous reports, advocated standards for all new houses, private as well as public. The Parker–Morris Report was the pace-setter for the 1960s, noting the vastly different trends which existed since the last major housing report, the 1944 Dudley Report, and raising housing standards to a new high, becoming mandatory in 1967 for New Towns and in 1969 for local government authorities. Principally, the standards recommended bigger houses, a family-type kitchen and some heating in every room, with good heating in principal rooms. However, by the time Parker–Morris standards became mandatory for local authorities, the 1969 Housing Act had been passed, recommending rehabilitation of existing housing stock rather than building high-rise housing, and new lower densities of 70 to 100 rooms per acre were required for new local authority housing.

Some of the Planning Bulletins were more helpful, giving general policy and allowing more individual scope, while other Planning Bulletins were more rigid.

Planning Bulletin No. 2, *Residential Areas: Higher Densities (MHLG, 1962c)*, continued to advocate higher-density housing to provide for six million new houses in 1980, with much of this new development to take place in 'mixed development' schemes, including flats, maisonettes, houses and garages.

For example, in London, there followed many housing redevelopment schemes, produced by the Housing Division of the London County Council, under the leadership of Sir Robert Matthew and Sir Leslie Martin. These schemes illustrated two approaches: the high-density approach and the mixed development approach (*Esher, 1981: 106–110*). The most successful high-density housing project was Churchill Gardens, Pimlico, designed by architects Powell and Moya, at the incredibly high density of 200 persons per acre in the hard mechanical system of Gropius and his density diagrams.

Some of the best mixed development schemes were the two Alton Estates at Roehampton (figure 8.23). The Roehampton site was blessed with undulating land and peppered with mature trees of the gardens of the demolished Victoria villas. It thus began with mature vegetation to soften any brusqueness perceived from the bare concrete. The soft approach was found in the lower-density housing project of Alton East, built at a density of 100 persons per acre and designed in the Swedish style with four-storey maisonettes and terraced housing set amongst old trees. But the hard density approach of Le Corbusier and Gropius won out in the struggle and the later Alton West epitomised Le Corbusier's vision transplanted to an English garden. Many families were placed in slab blocks with balcony access, striding across the meadow. Although the environment is beautiful, it could not overcome the disliked open balcony access and the stained brutal concrete, even if surrounded by monkey puzzle trees and thick rhododendron bushes. After that, throughout the 1950s, the great development housing projects – Loughborough, Brandon, Pepys, Bermondsey, Deptford – marched across London in the hard Le Corbusian tower block/slab block system.

When Le Corbusian principles were copied elsewhere in Britain, the mature parkland did not emerge, and densities were quite often raised to 200 persons per acre, a standard which Abercrombie, decades earlier, found unacceptable. The towers became bulky high-rise slabs. Birmingham built over 420 such tower blocks, while Manchester and Glasgow similarly built many such high-rise blocks. Nevertheless the government's Housing Manuals and Circulars continued to supply grants for the building of high-rise housing, at a rate three times that payable on

1969 — Start of recommending rehabilitation not NEW High rise.

Figure 8.23   Flats at Alton Estate, Roehampton (by the author): (a) old people's housing with high-rise housing in park; (b) maisonettes in slab blocks on 'pilotis'

a house. It was inevitable that local authorities would build high-rise housing even though a high-rise flat could cost twice as much as a two-storey house.

Glasgow has been the largest local authority landlord in Britain with 165,000 council houses, or 57 percent of the city's total housing stock (figure 8.24). Glasgow was so keen to build housing that it built on the cheaper peripheral land, but saved costs by not initially providing any community facilities, as at Easterhouse, which has nearly 13,000 houses and more than 40,000 people settled on the periphery of Glasgow

without community facilities. Castlemilk, built in 1965, contains 20-storey high blocks, housing nearly 5000 people, but most of the community facilities were not provided until decades later. Castlemilk Estate has been prone to vandalism, crime and mugging, but Community Action programmes in the 1980s have helped to rehabilitate the area.

The architects of the 1960s expanded their Le Corbusian dreams into continuous structures, labelled 'megastructures' (*Banham, 1976*). They were to be total environments encompassing all city activity and

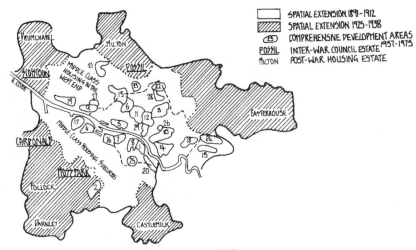

Figure 8.24   Housing estates in Glasgow (after Donnison and Middleton)

Figure 8.25   Park Hill, Sheffield: (a) housing; (b) Park Hill's 'street in the air' (by the author)

ideologically identified with space capsules and floating satellite towns in space. The megastructure included community facilities and streets as well as housing. One of the most innovative and famous of such megastructure schemes was Park Hill, Sheffield (figure 8.25). All the inhabitants from a part of inner-city Sheffield were rehoused in the same area, necessitating a high density of 200 persons per acre, and consequently requiring a megastructure. The maisonettes were arranged in single continuous blocks, using the so-called scissors arrangement, such that all entrances were on one floor, with bedrooms either on the floor above or on the one below. Every third floor was an entrance floor, facing onto an enlarged corridor which became a 'street in the air'. The blocks, four storeys at one end and 14 storeys at the other, were linked by these 'streets in the air', wide enough for the milkman and his electric cart to pass by. It was hoped that these 'streets in the air' would become hives of social interaction (figure 8.25). Indeed, when the BBC filmed Park Hill, the scheme was immensely popular (*Morris, E.K.S., 1961*). Sadly the 'streets in the air' eventually became excellent 'get-away' exits for petty burglars and vandals, such that Park Hill became more like the prison, Parkhurst. It was disappointing for the planners and architects, who truly believed that here was the solution to mass housing.

Another attempt at creative development in the 1960s appeared as high-density low-rise building schemes. The resulting buildings and car parking were so cramped on the site that the open space virtually disappeared and the hidden access routes were again prone to muggers and vandals. Still, the high-density low-rise developments were a great deal better than the worst tower blocks on the peripheral estates.

One of the few successful 'mixed development' housing estates was Byker, in Newcastle (figure 8.26). Built to a high density in 1968, and designed by Ralph Erskine, its British-trained architect employed Scandinavian methods. All the 2000 families were rehoused on the same site, and each family was invited to express its requirements. The result was a forest of terraced houses in amongst trees and shrubs, protected from an adjoining motorway by the famous wall, a continuous slab megastructure, faceless on the motorway side but full of individualised flat balconies, walkways and window openings on the other side, providing immense variety. Byker resembles a veritable Hanging Gardens of Babylon. The residents have loved it and it is still successful.

By 1970, systems building was no longer cheaper than rehabilitation; land in the inner cities was too costly to develop and the cost of the high-rise flats was too high, most of the worst housing had been cleared and the social problems of clearance and high-rise were too onerous. Central government no longer subsidised high-rise buildings and unit cost controls were introduced by the Ministry. The effect of the housing cost yardstick, the device to control unit costs, was to make high-rise developments uneconomic, and so the high-rise movement finally came to an end, yet cities were left with large stocks of high-rise buildings which were expensive to maintain and socially undesirable.

Social and physical problems of high-rise housing

The change in government attitude also resulted from the many social problems arising from the mass high-rise housing, which were more acute than the physical ones, focusing on mothers and children. As places to live, the high-rise flats with their tiny or non-existent balconies were psychologically and physically inhibiting to children; accident-prone children fell from windows and terraces, and lifts and staircases become dangerous places. Mothers become desperate and unhappy in the isolated and lonely flats; some even went so far as to commit suicide by jumping from the towers. They also missed the helping hand of the extended family. Other mothers were fearful of being raped, with violence on their persons and other crimes committed in the lonely corridors. All the residents feared the crime and vandalism.

The Ronan Point tower block disaster in 1968

(a)

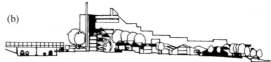
(b)

Figure 8.26 Byker, Newcastle: (a) housing (by the author); (b) section showing wall of housing (after *Architect's Journal*, 1976)

where, after a gas explosion, flats collapsed one on top of the other, killing five persons and injuring 17 others, brought home to the public that the structural defects of some of the tower blocks were dangerous to the point of fatalities. The Ronan Point disaster revealed the weakness of the technology, coupled with poor building supervision and industrial organisation. After Ronan Point, there was a return to normal and/or traditional building methods. The public antipathy to the high-rise tower blocks became so great that by 1979 the first block of unlettable flats was demolished in Birkenhead. Other local authorities followed suit. However, for most local authorities their investment in the tower blocks, for which they were still paying, was too great to consider demolition as an option. Instead they had to consider rehabilitation in new design forms, better management (such as improving the quality of lifts and installing concierges at the entrances) and increased maintenance.

Much of the wartime thinking by the famous planners was brilliantly creative. Pedestrianisation, precinctal planning, separation of vehicle and pedestrian and protection from the elements were amongst the planning tenets that are still in practice half a century later. The high-rise housing was admittedly a major mistake, but in contrast to the many planning successes has received too much

"Wave bye bye to Gran"

Figure 8.27   McCrae cartoon (source untraceable).

publicity. In the 1940s and 1950s, urban design was careful and sensitive, even with restrictions on building materials. By the 1960s, planners seemed to be hoodwinked by developers, with urban design becoming brutish and domineering. For the most part, however, Britain's post-war period of planning principles and practice was considered by many to be exemplary.

9 Urban redevelopment, urban renewal and urban conservation

Urban redevelopment in London

Comprehensive Development Areas (CDAs) were required immediately to rebuild blitzed areas. Originally goals were based on the idealism of creating a new world, but this idealism disappeared in the hands of councils and developers, when they created partnerships to build CDAs, which became destructive of the old patterns of life. Coupled with the council–developer partnership, the CDA technique was universally applied to British cities throughout the 1960s and early 1970s.

In London, many redevelopment schemes were prepared. Holford developed a new setting for St Paul's, throwing out earlier classical solutions, and instead adopting an asymmetrical plan which retained the small glimpses of the west front of St Paul's as one climbed Ludgate Hill. He set back the new buildings, creating a square, with its own tower block, obliquely aligned on the twin cupolas of the west front, which design was competent and left St Paul's in the dominant position (figure 9.1). But then the scheme was built in dull developer's architecture, which the public, and later Prince Charles, could not accept.

At the same time as the London County Council was building housing in the hard high-density fashion, private developers in the 1950s and early 1960s were promoting high office blocks, which a 1963 White Paper continued to allow, on the basis that any government control over the building of offices in central London would be impracticable. Wilson's government, after 1964, introduced throughout the country the need to obtain an Office Development Permit (ODP) before undertaking any major commercial development in designated areas, similar to the Board of Trade Industrial Certificates, which controlled the location of offices, for the purpose of removing service industry from London. However, the developers took advantage of the open system.

One of the best and largest mixed land-use London redevelopments was Golden Lane, Route 11 and the Barbican in the City of London, built on one of the largest bombed sites. Although many projects were carried out in the City, the Barbican project is perhaps the most celebrated. The City councillors stipulated that the LCC planners produce a model for the business sector lining Route 11 and that 35 acres between this business zone and Golden Lane be reserved for high-density middle-class housing in order to bring back residents to the City. Cripplegate ward, which had had 14,000 residents in 1851 and only 48 in 1951, would be back to 7000 people (*Esher, 1981*). The two zones, business and residential, closely interlocked and laid out on a single axis, emerged (after ten years of argument) quite different in character, but derived from the work of Le Corbusier. The 35-acre high-density middle-class housing of Golden Lane was borrowed from the great residential squares of La Ville Radieuse, with three triangular 43-storey towers that would become the tallest flats in Europe (with much criticised unliveable interior kitchens), and two great squares of maisonette housing (figure 9.2).

The adjoining Barbican area was built on an upper-level deck system, with massive car parking underneath (figure 9.3). The main pedestrian spaces, the Barbican Concert Hall and a school, were built as well as conserving a Wren church and parts of the old Roman Wall. There are great courts and a crescent, general public buildings, pools and terraces, all provided on as grand a scale as Nash's Carlton House Terrace; such a development has not been repeated since (*Esher, 1981*).

The building of the Barbican took years. The LCC's

Figure 9.1 Paternoster Square and west elevation of St Paul's (after LCC 1960)

model was produced in 1954 and the first glass tower opened in 1960. The residential areas took longer, with unorthodox eccentric detailing of the buildings. The Barbican Concert Hall, after many years, is useful but still difficult to approach and needs to be made user-friendly. On the other hand, the flats and maisonettes are successfully inhabited by senior executives in the City. The Barbican scheme was heavily influenced by Le Corbusier's scheme for St Dié, and is probably the best designed example of 'towers on a podium' in Britain.

In the residential section of the Barbican, the deck system is justified by the massive stacking of cars below the main pedestrian spaces. The effect is hard and severe to the point of oppressiveness. Immense sculptured towers stand uncompromisingly on the elevated pavement, but it has brought people back to living in the centre.

The LCC architect–planners, Arthur Ling, who had worked with Walter Gropius and Maxwell Fry, and Percy Johnson-Marshall, were leading advocates of vertical segregation of pedestrians onto decks and walkways; and the business zone surrounding Route

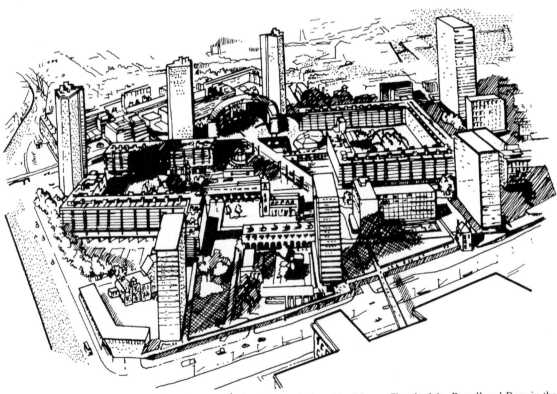

Figure 9.2 The Barbican, London, showing the residential area designed by Messrs Chamberlain, Powell and Bon; in the foreground are three of the office towers with a connected upper-level walkway system, designed by different architects (after Johnson-Marshall)

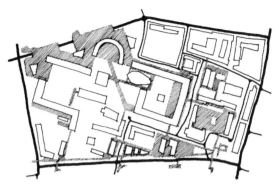

Figure 9.3 Barbican Plan showing upper-level decks in grey (after LCC, 1960)

11, later known as London Wall, was the perfect opportunity for such radical rethinking (*Johnson-Marshall, 1965: 191*).

The business zone surrounding London Wall became a mini-version of the centre of La Ville Radieuse. Six glass skyscrapers, clearly modelled after the Seagram Building and Lever House in New York City, were placed on an upper-level deck, bridging London Wall, and interconnected by walkway bridges (*Morris, E.K.S., 1957*). All main entrances to buildings, shops and restaurants were to be at the upper level, leaving the ground floor free for car parking and services (*LCC, 1960: 165–170*) (figure 9.4).

The radical upper-level deck system was possible because of the scale of post-war reconstruction. The intention, in the early 1960s, was to create a 30-mile 'pedway' network such that the deck would stretch all the way from the steps of St Paul's to Liverpool Street and from Golden Lane to the Tower (*Herbert, 1993: 444*). When the Greater London Council took over from the LCC, it adopted a strategic supervisory role over London's emerging upper-level circulation system, which was to unite the City with other great redevelopment areas such as Covent Garden, Trafalgar Square, Piccadilly and Shaftesbury Avenue (*Antoniou, 1968: 1038*). But the upper-level walkways created problems of policing and fire protection. Because the walkways were deserted, pedestrians shunned them. Only one lift and one moving staircase were provided and people generally used the traditional alleyways. The 30-mile network, with generous finance from the highways budget of the City and the GLC, remained the sole policy for pedestrian movement until the mid-1970s (*Herbert, 1993: 433–450*). But when towers and their podiums fell into disrepute, public sentiment turned back to rehabilitating the old lanes and medieval short-cuts. The rise of the conservationists' counter-revolution

Figure 9.4 London Wall and upper-level walkway (by the author)

and the concurrent listing of all the City's surviving Victorian buildings made the deck system concept unattainable as well as unwanted by the public (*Esher, 1981*). The planners retreated to a scheme of a minimum walkway network, using the old medieval alleyways, and the proposed upper-level system of walkways outside the Barbican and London Wall was quietly abandoned (*City of London, 1986*).

One of the most bitterly contested battles was over the redevelopment of the well-loved Covent Garden, when the vegetable and fruit market was relocated outside central London (1972). Covent Garden has two attractions: to the south-east the Inigo Jones piazza and church of the 1630s, the first piece of Renaissance planning in England, and to the north-west the little slum area of Seven Dials (1693), a Dickensian relic (see chapter 1).

The LCC plan (1968) proposed housing the indigenous population around the historic core of Covent Garden, together with the theatres, arcades, hotels, boutiques, bars and restaurants. The extension and improvement of the Royal Opera House was to be financed by a great conference centre (figure 9.5). The residential population would increase (from 2347 to 7000) as would space for hotels and entertainment, while office and warehousing floor-space would be reduced. Vehicular traffic of all sorts was placed underground, pedestrians radiating freely in all directions, and often under cover. The scale of the project, the destruction of the working-class dwellings, and the proposed annihilation of the character of Covent Garden brought a public outcry. The Covent

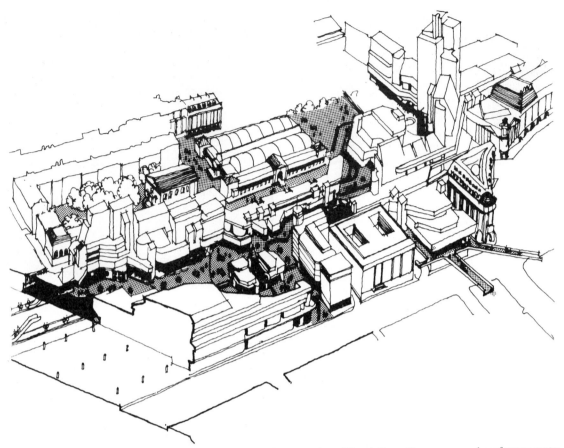

Figure 9.5 Covent Garden: proposed redevelopment showing extension of Royal Opera House, proposed conference centre and pedestrianised area (after LCC)

Garden Community Association became the focal point of 'advocacy planners' fighting for the local working-class point of view. Even the original leader of the LCC/GLC team, Brian Anson, deserted the GLC and went over to defend the side of the inhabitants (*Anson, 1981*).

The new London government gave the new GLC compulsory powers to act on its own without the two London Boroughs of Westminster and Camden. The Covent Garden Committee, chaired by the well-known then Lady Dartmouth, resigned. This further row caused the right-wing aesthetes and the middle-of-the-road conservationists to join forces with the left-wing Covent Garden Community Association. Sadly the planners had become the public enemy for all.

After the 1971 Public Inquiry into the 1968 scheme, the Secretary of State listed the great majority of its buildings and decreed that conservation was to be the central object of the operation and that 'full public participation' was to be the planning technique. From

1974 onwards, Covent Garden saw the first 'exercise in public participation' and one of the most successful because of the high motivation of the participating parties, a cross-section of an inner-London community, tenement tenants, theatre managers, publicans, craftsmen, property owners and shopkeepers and conservationists at large. It was the first major classless fight over the planners' concept of redevelopment.

In the emergent plan (*Keep the Elephants out of the Garden*, September 1976), the CGCA still fought the GLC, wanting to preserve their local housing, despite the deficiencies in schooling and open space. The GLC's Covent Garden Committee could not give up the tourist asset it would have in the rejuvenated market buildings. The piazza was going to be one of the most entertaining areas in Europe, whether the locals liked it or not.

The final plan (1978) was a compromise. In the 1970s, the characteristic community of Covent Garden

Figure 9.6   The charm of Covent Garden that attracts the tourists (after Tibbalds)

was traditional working-class, although it had started in the 1630s as aristocratic, moving to a literary and dramatic character, but always with a working-class sector. The local inhabitants retained some low-rent housing, but were effectively overrun by the entertainment and tourist industries. Despite the listing of 250 buildings, developers moved into Covent Garden. By defeating the GLC's proposals to sweep the area clean for office development, the Covent Garden Association preserved the historic character, but unwittingly paved the way for gentrification and the tourist industry. Covent Garden became a highly popular tourist spot. But the success side of the battle was that the tourist and entertainment activity had to take place within the old market buildings. Covent Garden became a conservation area of outstanding status, and is now a major attraction in tourist London (*Anson, 1987*) (figure 9.6).

Traffic architecture

Coupled with the Le Corbusian concept of 'tower and podium' was the Buchanan concept of traffic architecture. By 1962, the number of cars had reached 10 million and was projected to reach 30–40 million by the year 2010. Using these projections, Buchanan's report, *Traffic in Towns*, took a middle position between the two extremes of demolition and preser-

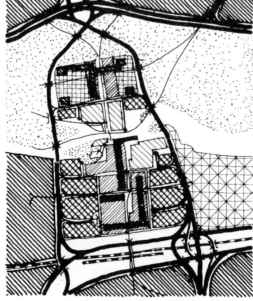

Proposed shops	▨
Existing shops	◪
Industry	⊠
Residential	▧
Offices	■
Car park	▨
Open space	▦
First floor deck	▦
Primary distributor	▬
Local distributor	▭
Pedestrian routes	▭

Figure 9.7   Newbury Town Centre Scheme showing optimum improved primary network and internal circulation (after Buchanan)

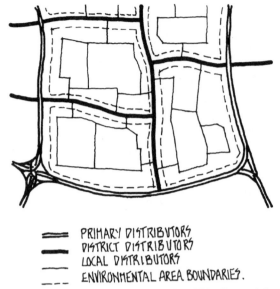

PRIMARY DISTRIBUTORS
DISTRICT DISTRIBUTORS
LOCAL DISTRIBUTORS
ENVIRONMENTAL AREA BOUNDARIES.

Figure 9.8   The Principle of Hierarchy of Distributors (after Buchanan)

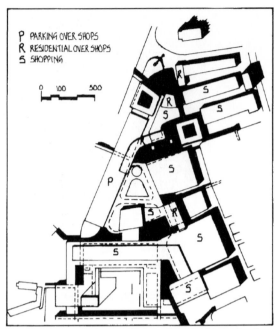

P PARKING OVER SHOPS
R RESIDENTIAL OVER SHOPS
S SHOPPING

0   100   500

Figure 9.9   Eldon Square, Newcastle, showing pedestrian deck (after Burns)

vation, and advocated so-called 'environmental areas'. An environmental area is defined as an area having no extraneous traffic and within which considerations of environment predominate over the use of vehicles (*Buchanan Report, 1963*). The Buchanan Report expressed the relationship between accessibility, environment and cost in the form of a 'law': 'in any environmental area, if a certain standard of environment is adhered to, the level of accessibility that can be obtained depends on the amount of money that can be spent on physical alternatives' (*Bruton, 1975: 217*).

The report outlines a technique which allows the three variables – environment, accessibility and cost – to be measured so that different road networks can be compared and the most efficient arrangement chosen. The report takes Newbury, Leeds and a central area of London as case studies. In Newbury, three alternative town centre schemes are put forward: one shows limited improvements, another improved primary networks, and a third a totally accessible network. The report showed that to accommodate even one-third of these cars would mean the demolition of the entire central area of a small town, such as Newbury (figure 9.7), or one-half of the physical fabric of the inner core of a major city like Leeds. Buchanan later justified his approach by saying that his brief did not include public transport and therefore he was not allowed to consider public transport (*Morris, E.K.S., 1975*).

Buchanan did raise the awareness of the need to categorise roads by their functions in the 'Principle of

a Hierarchy of Distributors' (figure 9.8). The consequences of his highly influential report were that every city planning office and developer proposed ring roads, multi-level spaghetti junctions, towers and podiums, pedestrian-decked traffic architecture, and environmental areas.

Cities, like Newcastle, followed London's example and produced similar city centre schemes, tearing down and rebuilding on a massive scale. Eldon Square shopping mall with office blocks was surrounded by a massive inner ring motorway, which ignored the river and the existing urban fabric (*Burns, 1967*). The shops and pedestrians remain at ground level on one side, and then are lifted, by slow ramps and steps, to a new ground level on top of the vehicles parked below. This enabled the pedestrians to cross the roads surrounding the redevelopment area by bridges, without having to change level. The scheme secures the segregation of pedestrians and vehicles in the vertical plane, and provides for easy servicing to the shops and car parking at the road level but egress by pedestrians onto the shopping deck (figure 9.9).

The Newcastle Eldon Square scheme was typical of 1960s town centre redevelopment (figures 9.10 and 9.11). Liverpool and Sheffield likewise produced equally monumental schemes, although both kept their extensive public transport networks (*Bor, 1972*). Liverpool's City Centre Plan had many outstanding

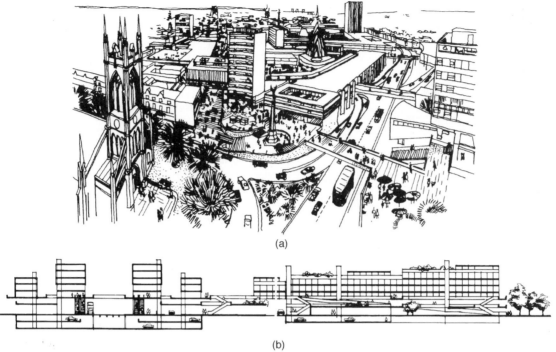

(a)

(b)

Figure 9.10   Eldon Square, Newcastle: (a) central shopping area; (b) section showing underground parking and upper level pedestrian areas (after Burns)

Figure 9.11   Eldon Square, Newcastle, pedestrian deck (after Burns)

features to it, particularly its grouping of new communities along existing rail routes (*Bor and Shankland, 1965*) (figure 9.12). But very often land was cleared and then funds were not available, preventing redevelopment, and, as in Liverpool,

leaving vast empty holes in the city centre for decades (figure 9.13). The new civic buildings that the plan proposed were not built.

One successful aspect of Liverpool's redevelopment was the eventual preservation of Albert Docks,

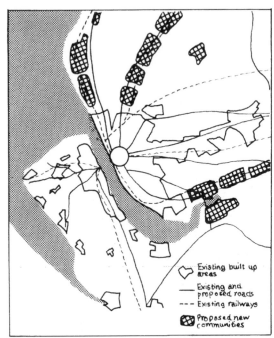

Figure 9.12   Liverpool urban areas (after Bor)

Figure 9.13   Liverpool: city centre redevelopment (after Evans)

prompted by local preservation societies and leading architects, R. Gardner-Medwin and Sir Peter Shepheard (figure 9.14). The Albert Docks now house the Tate Gallery outpost in the North.

Smaller towns were next attacked by the developers, and much of the urban fabric was destroyed and replaced by soulless enclosed shopping malls which had no identity with the town in which they were situated.

The rape of Bath and other English cities

The tragedy of Bath was that parts of it were bombed during the Second World War, and in the fervour to rebuild and commercially expand, many of the lesser Georgian buildings were destroyed to provide commercial buildings and modern hotels, whose ugliness created an outcry. Statutory listing of buildings protected nearly 2000 buildings of Grade I and Grade II quality. However, in the 1950s and 1960s, there was still a Grade III category, of which Bath had some 1000 examples, mostly artisan buildings. These buildings the Bath City Council consistently destroyed (*Ferguson, 1973*). When even more destruction was proposed in a scheme to tunnel a major road under Bath (*Buchanan and Partners, 1965*), public opinion decided that enough was enough and that the whole core of Bath should be designated a conservation area with government funding to keep it that way (*MHLG, 1968*). Sadly, almost a third of Georgian Bath had already been destroyed, unlike sleepy Edinburgh, whose peripheral geographical position had luckily placed it beyond the tentacles of rapacious developers.

Other historic English cities suffered a similar fate (*Amery and Cruickshank, 1975*). Bristol is a sad example, having lost hundreds of eighteenth and nineteenth century buildings for which permission to demolish was readily given. Even squares, like Brunswick Square, which was reprieved at the last moment by the Secretary of State against the advice of his Inspector, were left to crumble by themselves, even without the help of the demolition men. In Bristol's Clifton conservation area were Georgian buildings which survived bomb damage and two Public Inquiries but could not survive what was termed 'calculated neglect' (*Amery and Cruickshank, 1975: 44*). Bristol's prosperity as a booming regional centre for government and national organisations put pressure on for more office blocks, multi-storey car parks and roads, such that the old character of central Bristol was destroyed. Property developers and big companies were aided by the University and Bristol Royal Infirmary (*Punter, 1990a*).

The central area of Leeds suffered from a ring road, while Manchester had a ring road, with at least 10 CDAs within its ring road. Arndale Centre, consisting

Figure 9.14   The rehabilitation of Albert Docks (after Evans)

of shops, offices, market hall and bus station, linked up with other redevelopment areas. Cardiff centre was redeveloped, as was Chesterfield, whose Chairman of the Planning Committee said 'the Labour Group intend to implement the policy empowered by the Council and will brook no interference' (*Amery and Cruikshank, 1975: 58*).

Huddersfield epitomised the redeveloped town. Its central area was defined by a wide ring road and inside the ring road 50 percent of the commercial space was rebuilt. The redevelopment was accomplished by using CDA machinery and through so-called council–developer partnerships. The intention was to leave very little inside the ring road that was built before 1965. One of the factors which stopped this massive redevelopment of the centre of cities was the 1973/74 slump in the stock market and the sudden rise of the price of oil. From then on, these massive projects were less and less financially viable.

Urban redevelopment replaced by urban renewal   *Greater integration.*

Once the scars of the Second World War had been covered over or removed, the public started demanding greater integration of building into the rest of the city fabric. Redevelopment or clearance destroyed too many old familiar sights, too many old habits, losing the sense of continuity. CDAs were seen as too destructive of the old pattern of life (figure 9.16). The yearning for totally new buildings gave way to a yearning for integration with the old fabric of the city. The public desired a balance between preserving some of the old existing development and the new development, which redevelopment could not do.

Often new development would be insulated from the old by a belt of land, cleared of all buildings as well as people. A new development next to a blighted area soon became tarnished, but, originally, isolation was thought

Figure 9.15   Bath before and after redevelopment (from *Architectural Review*, 1973b. Reproduced by kind permission)

to be better than integration. The patching-up of old buildings was then not satisfactory and led to financial losses and problems. But the sensible rehabilitation of older, but not outworn, properties began to be pursued in almost all towns. On the other hand, there were negative repercussions from the financial point of view, as combining all the private interests in redevelopment areas was slower and more difficult than the rehabilitation. Substantial changes in the environment normally required large-scale land ownership and this in turn led to large-scale monotonous physical results.

Redevelopment encouraged a dullness in architectural character, a monotony and sameness.

By the late 1960s, halting the problems caused by inner area decline and redevelopment was effected by adopting the process of urban renewal, by which a large area of a town slowly renewed itself and thereby gradually changed its character to fit in with the needs of contemporary society. It included the radical changes of redevelopment as well as the status quo of preservation and rehabilitation, an amalgam of all the processes which acted on a town.

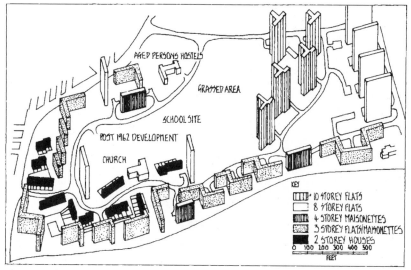

Figure 9.16 Leeds comprehensive redevelopment area (after Gibson and Langstaff)

The concept of urban renewal still required a comprehensive approach. Improving the whole physical fabric of urban life embraced (1) redevelopment, (2) rehabilitation, (3) improvement and (4) conservation. Redevelopment meant tearing down old buildings and substituting new ones, for the old buildings were worn out by age, blight and/or a change of use; or in residential areas were slums, had bad structural conditions, bad layout, poor maintenance, pollution by smoke and dirt, and/or poor environment; and in both areas were affected by traffic congestion. Rehabilitation meant restoring and repairing old buildings to such an extent that their lifetime was increased by perhaps 30 years (figure 9.17). The interiors of the buildings could be totally gutted. Improvement meant the short-term (30-year) rehabilitation of obsolescent buildings which could not be demolished. Conservation meant conserving the urban fabric as it was, restoring the buildings and adapting the uses of the buildings to the conserved physical fabric. Both the exterior and the interior were conserved exactly as they were originally built. But the real halt to total redevelopment came not from the adoption of urban renewal, but from the counter-revolutionary movement of the conservationists.

The conservation movement and development of the conservation concept

The conservation movement began in the late nineteenth century, with the first legislation for the protection of ancient monuments, the Ancient

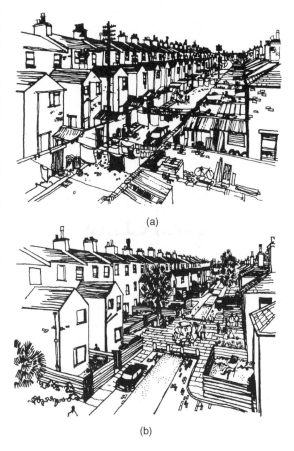

(a)

(b)

Figure 9.17 Newcastle Rye Hill rehabilitation (after Tetlow and Goss)

Figure 9.18   Pedestrianised urban space (after Cullen)

Monuments Act 1882. It had been preceded by the setting up of the first national voluntary body, the Society for the Protection of Ancient Buildings, founded by the Arts and Crafts Movement architect/designer William Morris in 1877, mainly to protect churches from over-restoration. At first it operated with the cooperation of the private owners, but since 1913 subsequent Acts have had compulsory powers to prevent damage or destruction of monuments. The actual listing of individual historic monuments has been in existence since the Royal Commission on Historical Monuments (England) was set up in 1908 to provide a detailed inventory of counties, covering all monuments and buildings of importance dated up to 1714.

The response to the Second World War and its devastation was a growing realisation that historic buildings needed to be protected, and the statutory listing of all historic buildings was introduced. The Historic Buildings and Ancient Monuments Act of 1953 protected 12,000 monuments in Britain, of which 800 were under the Department of the Environment. This Act also established three Historic Buildings Councils (for England, Wales and Scotland) to advise the Secretary of State; to make grants for the preservation of historic buildings; and to make grants for their acquisition by the local authorities and the National Trust.

The listing of selected historic buildings was first sanctioned by the Town and Country Planning Act 1944, in response not only to the Second World War but also to the slowness of the Royal Commission on Historical Monuments in assembling its inventory. Later Planning Acts from 1947 to 1990 refer in the same terms to lists of buildings of 'special architectural or historic interest'. Buildings suitable for inclusion on the list are recommended by investigators of historic buildings in the Department of the Environment as a consequence of country-wide surveys. It took over 20 years to produce the first list, completed in 1968, which included 125,000 buildings in England, 40,000 in Scotland and 5000 in Wales.

Three important publications captured the public's attention in the late 1950s and early 1960s. In the first two, appropriately titled *Outrage* (*Nairn, 1955*) and *Counter Attack* (*Nairn, 1957*), Gordon Cullen's brilliant sketches showed the destruction of the charm not only of individual buildings but also of groups of buildings, whole villages and town centres. A third publication, *Townscape* (*Cullen, 1961*), analysed the townscape qualities to be preserved, and how to do it (figure 9.18). The revised version, *The Concise Townscape*, still serves as a handbook on conservation of historic towns (*Cullen, 1971*). Gordon Cullen's concept of townscape exactly complemented the conservationists' desires. Cullen argued for the art of relationship, in which all the elements to the making of an environment – buildings, trees, nature, water, traffic, advertisements – are woven together in such a way that drama is released and beauty created. According to Cullen, this could not be achieved by scientific research or by technical prowess but must be understood by vision.

Cullen discovered three elements in the art of townscape: (1) serial vision, which occurs when one walks from the end of the plan to another as a series of revelations in juxtaposition; (2) a sense of place and how we react to the position of our body in the environment as, for example possession, occupied territory, enclaves, enclosures, precincts, focal points, change of level, and vistas; and (3) content of the fabric of towns as in details, texture, scale, style, character and personality. His message was brilliantly presented in wonderfully appealing sketches, which the general public could easily understand. Cullen had tremendous influence on the Civic Trust, which in turn influenced thousands of amenity societies to produce the Townscape movement. Townscape theory was regularly promoted during the 1960s by the *Architectural Review*, for which both Cullen and Nairn wrote, and also by Thomas Sharp (*Sharp, 1948, 1968*).

However, still in the 1950s and the 1960s, the Modern Movement's great desire to bring Britain up to date created a town planning consensus of redevelopment combined with limited preservation. For example, although Edinburgh University's Development Plan of 1949, which promoted the demolition of George Square, was opposed by the National Trust for Scotland, the Cockburn Association, the Saltire Society and the Scottish Georgian Society, these amenity societies, even in 1955–58, still accepted the principle of comprehensive redevelopment, dropping their objections instantly on planning grounds.

Listed buildings

Ancient monuments have been scheduled and protected since 1908, and listed buildings since 1944. The basis of this listing and scheduling has been amalgamated in the Planning (Listed Buildings and Conservation Areas) Act 1990 and the Town and Country Planning (Scotland) Act 1972.

With a listed building, the presumption is in favour of preservation. It is an offence to demolish or alter a listed building unless 'listed building consent' has been obtained. This is different from breaking planning permission, where an offence arises only after the enforcement procedure has been imposed. The legislation also provides a deterrent against deliberate neglect. Listing provides guidance to local authorities in carrying out their planning functions, such as redevelopment, where local authorities have to take into account listed buildings in the area. Grants are available under the Housing Acts.

Buildings are listed in England and Wales according to certain criteria, based on age and merit; they include (1) all buildings built before 1700 which survive in anything like their original condition; (2) most buildings of 1700 to 1840, though some selection is necessary; (3) between 1840 and 1914, only buildings of definite quality and character, the selection tending to be the principal works of the principal architects or industrial buildings; (4) between 1914 and 1939, selected buildings of high quality; and (5) after 1939, a few outstanding buildings, although more and more post-war buildings are being recognised as important. There are about 40 post-1940 listed buildings, some of which are examples of the Modern Movement.

The criteria for Scotland are different in that listed buildings include (1) all buildings erected prior to 1840 which are of any quality even if plain, and survive in anything like their original form; (2) buildings erected between 1840 and 1914 of definite quality and character either individually or as part of a group; (3) buildings erected between 1914 and 1945 if they are good examples of the works of an important architect, or of a particular style whether it be traditional, progressive or international modern; and (4) after 1945 buildings of outstanding quality over 30 years old, with a high degree of selection practised.

By 1990, age and merit were joined by new criteria, including (1) the principal works of better-known architects; (2) technological innovations or virtuosity, cast or wrought iron, prefabrication, early use of concrete; (3) distinctive regional variations in design and use of materials; and (4) association with well-known persons or events, as the special value of particular building types, for either architectural or planning reasons, or as illustrating social and economic history, for example industrial buildings, both urban and rural; railway and other transport buildings; schools, hospitals, theatres, civic buildings, markets, exchanges, charitable institutions, prisons and public memorials.

The categorisation of listed buildings (table 9.1) in England and Wales differs from that in Scotland. In England there were originally four grades of listed buildings distinguished by Roman numerals, Grades I, II*, II, and III, but in 1974 Grade III was abandoned and largely absorbed into the bottom half of Grade II

Table 9.1   1990 categories of listed buildings for England and Wales

Type	No. of buildings	Percentage	Examples
Grade I: Outstanding interest	5000	2	Hatfield House; Royal Crescent, Bath
Grade II*: Particularly important	20,000	9	Good eighteenth-century; prominent but not first-rank Victorian Town Halls; Peter Jones Department Store, London
Grade II: Special interest	375,000+	80	Standard timber-framed cottages; most industrial monuments; street furniture (lamp posts and telephone boxes)

as it was found that psychologically little attention was paid to Grade III, which grading gave the impression of a building not worth preserving.

The great majority of historic buildings are Grade II, and many are listed because they possess what is officially referred to as 'group value' – i.e. they provide pleasing compositions and townscape or may act as appropriate settings for finer buildings. Important examples of town planning are also listed. Churches are included, though they used to be excluded. (Anglican churches are listed A, B, C.) A revised listing in 1984, ordered by Michael Heseltine, added 200,000 structures to the then list of 400,000, making a total of over 600,000 structures. Scotland has always had fewer categories, based on letters – A, B and C(s).

The Historic Buildings Councils were replaced by English Heritage for England and Wales and by Historic Scotland for Scotland. Each advises the Secretary of State, particularly with regard to grants, and the acquisition and purchase of valuable buildings. Each puts forward proposals and watches over the use and condition of historic buildings in general.

Once a building is listed, listed building consent (LBC) is required for the demolition or alteration or extension of a listed building or buildings within its curtilage. LBC was introduced by the Town and Country Planning Act 1968 to replace the building preservation order.

The effect of LBC procedure, operated under Chapter II of the Planning (Listed Buildings and Conservation Areas) Act 1990, was to make it an offence to demolish, alter or extend a listed building in any manner which would 'affect its character as a building of special architectural or historic interest', without first obtaining listed building consent. The only major exemptions are for ecclesiastical buildings in use, ancient monuments and Crown buildings.

In England and Wales, there are distinct bodies whose views the local authorities must seek statutorily before the demolition of a listed building. In Scotland, the Architectural Heritage Society of Scotland and the Scottish Civic Trust are consulted fairly automatically but not statutorily. The local planning authority (LPA) makes the decision on the application, and written consent can be given by either the LPA or the Secretary of State.

If the LPA intends to grant consent, the intention goes to the Department of the Environment for consideration along with objections. English Heritage investigators can offer objections; the Minister can decide to 'call in' and override the LPA – either on the basis of written submissions but more likely on the basis of a Public Inquiry. The Minister's decision cannot be appealed against, but it can be challenged in the High Court as a point of law. There are, in addition, special procedures to deal with difficult situations.

The listing process has been very slow and also incomplete. If a building is threatened with demolition before it is listed in the next annual routine survey of an area, or has just been overlooked, the local authority, an amenity group or an individual can ask the DoE or the Scottish Office that the building be 'spot-listed' under a special procedure. The effect of this is to give the building immediate protection as if it were listed for a period of six months, during which the Secretary of State may include it in the statutory list, confirming the Building Preservation Notice. If there is no such confirmation, the building loses its protection and compensation may be payable. If buildings have been altered, etc., without consent, the local authority can either issue a listed building enforcement notice requiring rectification of the damage done or take the case to court. These notices used to be laughably weak, but now carry heavier fines.

Owing to the reluctance, over the decades, of local authorities and local councillors to preserve, pressure for conservation has come from the private amenity societies. Because of the vacuum created both by the lack of interest of various Secretaries of State, the blind-eye attitude of city councillors and the lack of local authority finance, the amenity societies became the self-appointed watchdogs of conservation.

Table 9.2 Types of buildings looked after by English amenity societies

Ancient buildings	1. Council for British Archaeology
	2. Ancient Monuments Society
Medieval, Tudor, Jacobean	3. Society for the Protection of Ancient Buildings
18th and early 19th century	4. Georgian group
Victorian and Edwardian	5. Victorian Society
Buildings from 1914 to the present	6. Twentieth Century Society
	7. Royal Commission on the Historical Monuments of England

Created in the climate of *Outrage*, the most important and powerful amenity society has been the Civic Trust, founded in 1955 by Duncan Sandys, Minister for Housing and Local Government, as a pressure group and as a coordinating body for the thousands of local amenity groups in England and Wales. The two Scottish national amenity societies are the Glasgow-based Scottish Civic Trust, which includes membership of many local amenity societies; and the Edinburgh-based Architectural Heritage Society of Scotland. Many local amenity societies do sterling work.

Local amenity societies voluntarily monitor planning applications for possible conservation programmes by commenting on applications 'for consent to alter or demolish listed buildings' (table 9.2). This semi-statutory watchdog job has been cheerfully, and sometimes passionately, fulfilled ever since.

The Conservation Area concept

By the late 1960s, the virtual completion of the redevelopment and rehousing programme, combined with the economic crises and the change in attitude against large-scale and high-rise buildings, gave greater power to the preservationists. Thus the Civic Amenities Act of 1967, passed at the instigation of Lord Sandys, and the Civic Trust, introduced the Conservation Area concept – a synthesis of 'conservation surgery' as advocated by Patrick Geddes, townscape as advocated by the *Architectural Review*, and group-listing, long advocated by the amenity societies. Ironically the Conservation Area could be considered the mirror-image of the Comprehensive Development Area.

The 1967 Civic Amenities Act gave statutory recognition for the first time to the area concept, by making it a duty of local planning authorities to determine which parts of their areas were areas of special architectural or historic interest, the character of which it was desirable to enhance or preserve, and to designate such areas as Conservation Areas. The criteria for the establishment of a Conservation Area are the number of buildings under preservation orders in the area, the character of the area, its historical background, the surrounding countryside (not only buildings but whole tracts of land being subject to listing), and the need for protection against adverse building developments. When a Conservation Area was designated, the Act required special attention to be paid in all planning decisions to the preservation or enhancement of its character and appearance.

The Conservation Area grew logically out of the established code for officially recognising and safeguarding buildings of special architectural or historic interest. But the logic was significantly modified. Unlike the 'listing' of historic buildings, decided by central government experts and put as a charge upon local authorities in exercising their planning and other functions, Conservation Areas were identified and established entirely by the local authorities themselves. Initially, whatever their choice, once designation was notified to the Minister/Secretary of State, he was duty-bound to support the designation when exercising his own functions (at appeal, Public Inquiry, etc.) in the area.

From 1968 onwards, the opportunity to designate Conservation Areas on as wide a front as they wished was open to all planning authorities. Yet the 1967 legislation did not require the LPA to actually pay for any conservation or rehabilitation. The 1967 Act simply gave the LPA the power to designate Conservation Areas. Financial aid did not occur until 1971/72 and then in the 1974 Town and Country Amenities Act.

The 1974 Town and Country Amenities Act extended the power of local authorities in dealing with Conservation Areas and the preservation of historic buildings, and brought the demolition of most buildings in Conservation Areas under control. The Department of the Environment was enabled to designate Conservation Areas if the local authority did not choose to do so. This amendment countered the sort of situation that occurred in Bath and Chesterfield, where the local authority did not declare obviously historic places as Conservation Areas because if it had, its own development plans would have been frustrated.

All trees in Conservation Areas became protected under a sweeping provision. Indeed development control became far more stringent in Conservation

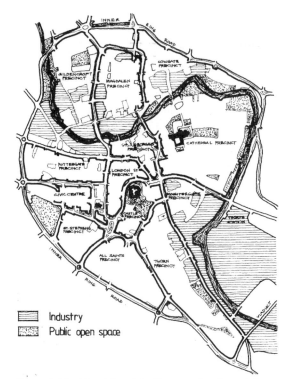

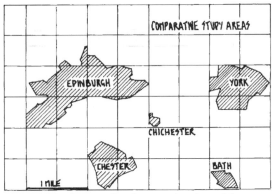

Figure 9.20 Comparative Conservation Areas (after Scottish Civic Trust)

Figure 9.19 Norwich and its Conservation Areas (after Gibberd)

Areas, because of the General Development Order. For example aerials are strictly controlled, and paintwork must follow area criteria. By 1990, there were over 5000 Conservation Areas in England and Wales.

Some early examples of conservation and the rehabilitation of historic towns highlighted the need for conservation and led the way. Particularly Norwich, York and Chichester were leaders in the conservation field.

In 1957, a decade before statutory Conservation Areas were established, Norwich City Council joined with the newly formed Civic Trust to show how the appearance of a given area in the city could be improved without major alterations or expense (figure 9.19). Magdalen Street was chosen, being the main street of a quarter of Norwich and combining historical associations and buildings of architectural character. With the help of consultant architect Misha Black, Magdalen Street was rehabilitated first, with an outline scheme on the basis of which all the traders on the street were invited to cooperate, with detailed proposals for approval and execution (*Civic Trust, 1959*).

The final project implemented: (1) repainting 66 properties in a coordinated scheme; (2) altering fascia boards over the shops, and lettering fascia boards; (3)

removing projecting names, signs and advertisements; (4) providing shops with new blinds and 16 shops with new curtaining to their upper windows; (5) restoring the astragals or glazing bars; (6) replacing six lamp standards by lanterns bracketed from the buildings; (7) designing two new bus shelters and replacing new bus stop signs; (8) redesigning and replacing eleven pairs of No Waiting and No Loading signs; (9) resiting overhead wires; and (10) removing some 40 other structures.

The Civic Trust's emphasis was on civic design in Conservation Areas through the detail of appropriate lettering, street lighting on the sides of the buildings, removal of street clutter and the reinstatement of carefully designed street furniture, carefully explained in Civic Trust Manuals (*Civic Trust, 1974*). Magdalen Street, Norwich, was an experimental pilot project in civic design in 1958–59 which was then imitated by many other schemes in England, Scotland and Wales. It demonstrated clearly the successful approach of the Civic Trust (figure 9.19).

Edinburgh favoured conservation because of its great architectural heritage and therefore many changes in Edinburgh came through public pressure. Unlike their English counterparts, most Edinburgh corporations were in favour of preserving the medieval town and thus serious efforts to conserve the High Street had gone on for almost 100 years. Between 1952 and 1969, conservation success centred in the Old Town, when the City Corporation, following Geddes' original example, completely restored the Canongate, the lower part of the High Street from buildings by the Tolbooth to Chessel's Court, with individual housing grants.

Conservation in the 1950s concerned individual buildings. For example, when developers proposed a 17-storey extension to the George Hotel in George

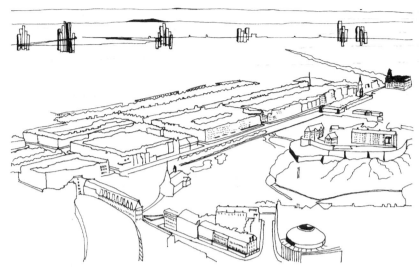

Figure 9.21   The impact of high buildings on Edinburgh showing high buildings as clusters of 'asparagus' away from the central area (after Morris, E.K.S., 1965)

Street a Public Inquiry successfully stopped this high block proposal in the middle of the Georgian New Town, and thus all subsequent high buildings.

Edinburgh, not presented with the commercial realities of the modern world, was left sleeping during the 1950s as the office-building boom was damaging the English cities. In the 1960s, pressure came to provide office spaces whose space standards were incompatible with either the city's medieval heritage or its Georgian and Victorian character. Office developers became the powerful bogeymen opposed to conservation and it was the big offices which caused some sections of parts of the later New Town to disappear.

The Princes Street Architectural Panel, appointed to safeguard Edinburgh's architectural heritage, reported in 1967, at which time most of Queen Street (mostly 'A' listed buildings) and George Street ('B' listed buildings) were still intact. The panel gave lip-service to the principles of the 1967 Civic Amenities Act but concluded that George Street, running parallel to Princes Street, was beyond recovery and could be redeveloped.

The east side of St Andrew's Square was the first to be redeveloped for large-scale insurance buildings. Then Princes Street became the target for multiple shops. Although the Princes Street Panel laid out limitations of height, plot ratio and materials for new developments, as suggested by Abercrombie, eventually it allowed most redevelopment proposals, whether they conformed or not. Since Abercrombie's 1944 plan suggested upper-level walkways on Princes

Street, provisional space for an elevated walkway at first-floor level was proposed so that all new buildings produced a canopy which could be converted to the upper-level walkway. Now the idea of an upper-level walkway has been dropped, the remaining Victorian buildings are appreciated architecturally, and the upper-level walkways will not be used. The panel report unfortunately prompted demolition elsewhere within the New Town for office development. However, the public outcry meant that no more listed buildings were demolished. Since the late 1960s, office developers have had to fit in with their Georgian neighbours, in respect to height, proportion, fenestration, etc.

A success story was the saving of St George's Church, in Charlotte Square, located in a pivotal position in Craig's New Town plan; the thought of its destruction or dereliction was appalling. The building was finally acquired by the Crown, deconsecrated, and converted as an annex for the Scottish Records Office. Thus the dome was saved, the dry rot removed and the grandeur of the urban design saved. The problem of the siting and height of office blocks prompted Edinburgh Corporation to engage Lord Holford to do a study on the siting of high buildings in Edinburgh. Lord Holford rejected high buildings in the central areas (*Holford & Associates, 1965*) which ultimately had the effect of forcing new office buildings elsewhere to Lothian Road and to the outer suburban South Gyle.

Amenity societies became the self-appointed conservation watchdogs of Edinburgh. Edinburgh's amenity societies were able to see the damage done to other cities, like Bath's wholesale redevelopment – which destroyed one-third of the city centre (*Fergusson, 1973*). Happily by 1995 UNESCO had inscribed Bath on the World Heritage List, with approximately 5000 listed buildings and a Conservation Area of 4730 acres.

Edinburgh adopted a far happier concept of urban renewal based on conservation and rehabilitation and some redevelopment. There was a 'sack' of Bath but not a sack of Edinburgh, and it is due as much to the amenity societies, street associations and local pressure groups that the developers were held at bay.

Summary

Redevelopment in the 1950s had been sensitive and careful, but by the 1960s the council–developer partnerships overruled the architect–planners and commerce became the dictator. With exceptions like the grandiose Barbican, many town centres were destroyed and replaced by unattractive shopping area towers on a podium, under which cars were stacked. The first great reaction of the public came in Covent Garden, which signalled the defeat of the old style of planning. The new theme of the late 1970s was that people were more important than architecture. The Brave New World was not to be any more. The concept of conservation was slow to be accepted and did not become really effective until the 1970s, when most outworn areas had been redeveloped, so there was less need for further redevelopment. Conservation then became more important than redevelopment.

One could say that after 1975 the combined architectural and town planning orthodoxy, 'The Conservation Movement', was firmly established and has enjoyed a near monopoly on policy and cautious comment in the architectural and town planning fields. The Modern Movement declined and post-Modernism adopted historicism as its *modus vivendi*. Yet the 1980s attempted to counter the Conservation Movement, which appeared to strangle industry and commerce, by organizing zones free of the Conservation Movement, i.e. Enterprise Zones and Simplified Planning Zones. Now in the 1990s, it appears that the preservation movement is as strong as ever, particularily as conservation has moved into the countryside.

Part IV

Planning Urban Design and the
Environment

10 The new planning framework, reorganisation, and planning theories

British life in the sixties

In 1947, Britain began a radically new system of town and country planning, when the 1947 Town and Country Planning Act nationalised the right to change the use of land, although the Act did not nationalise land itself. The Act required developers to obtain planning permission from the local planning authority before building operations or major changes of use could take place. If such developments did not conform to the development plan, they would probably not be approved. Where permission was refused by the local planning authority, the developer had the right to appeal to the Minister.

The system of land use planning changed remarkably little between 1947 and 1968. Amended by various orders and regulations to meet changing needs, the key features of development plans and development control survived virtually unchanged. In practice, the system worked fairly well but slowly. By the late 1950s, Britain was covered by plans prepared on a common basis, presented in a standard form, and approved by central government. Reviews did occur, though not usually at the required five-year intervals. The Public Inquiry that preceded the approval of plans, and the hearings for controversial planning applications, gave the public the opportunity to make formal objections, and in general there was a reasonable degree of usefulness and confidence in the system.

The changing circumstances of life in the 1960s exposed weaknesses in the 1947 planning system. It had been wrongly assumed that population and economic growth would occur slowly, and that the existing local authorities could cope with the rate and direction of change. Although the 'baby boom' of 1945–47 and the dropping birth rate between 1948 and 1954 (to 1930s levels) had been expected, few had reckoned on the continuous rise in the birth rate between 1954 and 1964. Population projections were continuously revised upwards and these forecasts in turn influenced other forecasts, such as trends in house building and the provision of public services. The rising prosperity which occurred in Britain after 1955 also expressed itself in an increase in car ownership. When most development plans were drawn, car ownership levels were barely above those of the 1930s, when only one family in ten had a car, but by 1966 half the families in Britain owned one car or more, and one garage per family became a standard in new housing.

The expanding urban population and the rise of mass motorisation created pressures for urban reconstruction and a further dispersal of the population which could not be organised at local government level. Higher car ownership permitted more people to seek homes in the outer suburbs and rural areas, or to visit the countryside at weekends. The resulting movement often crossed the city into the suburban fringe, while population from other areas moved into the urban regions. For example, the outer suburban ring of population around London grew to 800,000 people during the 1950s in the Home Counties. The vast majority of this number were not housed in the New Towns or expanded towns, but in private estates where employment was limited and commuting to work therefore became a necessity.

The resulting movement indicated the need for a changed emphasis in development plans, and the consideration of a wider range of topics (e.g.

recreation) over a wider area (e.g. regions, sub-regions). It also became clear that a financial appraisal was necessary if plans were to be realistic. The assumption that most urban development and redevelopment would be carried out by public agencies was mistaken; private enterprise undertook a far greater role than that foreseen in 1947. The period of change began with the Conservatives coming to power in 1951. They were heavily committed to reliance on the private sector and the balance of housing programmes shifted to 50 percent public and 50 percent private. Even after Labour returned to power in 1964, the proportion of housing remained 50 percent public and 50 percent private, with the result that local authorities in their development plans were left with powers that had too negative an emphasis when what was needed was a more positive approach.

Deficiencies of the 1947 planning system

It became evident that certain aspects of the 1947 development plan system were no longer adequate to meet the needs of the 1960s. From a procedural point of view, the system involved the Minister in immense local detail in plan appraisal, which should have been the responsibility of local government and not central government. This caused delays in approving and amending plans, and tended to obscure the major policy items that required decisions by the central government. The fact that plans looked forward uniformly over a 20-year period for every subject and for every part of the area resulted in many unrealistic solutions. In some cases, the plans appeared to make precise predictions where such precision was impossible, while in other cases, the plans were not able to show in adequate detail schemes for which such detail was required. In some areas and subjects, review was required more frequently than every five years, and in others, no review was necessary.

Members of the public were hardly involved in the preparation of the plans; their only opportunity to participate was to lodge formal objections after the plan had been prepared. This caused ill-feeling on the part of the public, and a reluctance on the part of the local authority to change the plan at a later stage. Although authorities were required to consult with neighbouring authorities, there was little emphasis on active collaboration to cope with shared problems, or on the need, in some cases, to see the authority's plan in the appropriate regional context.

In summary, the inadequacies of the 1947 Act were that development plans (1) quickly became out of date, and concentrated on irrelevant details which caused

delays; (2) failed to keep abreast of, and respond to, changes in society; (3) failed to relate land uses to traffic; (4) failed to take into account changing relationships between town and country; and (5) did not form an adequate basis for meaningful local planning or allow for public participation. The position was exacerbated by the boundaries of local planning authorities being too tightly drawn.

The architects of the 1947 Act believed that effective coordination of different plans could be achieved in three ways: by ad hoc regional advisory plans; by the monitoring and updating by the regional offices of the Ministry of Town and Country Planning; and by coordination by Whitehall itself. All regional plans were the work of ad hoc teams of central government officials and/or private consultants. With the regional plans of 1962–65, central government realised that no tradition of cooperation between local planning authorities had developed, and positive strategies were required.

It became clear that the machinery of planning required fundamental revision. In 1964, the then Minister of Housing and Local Government set up the Planning Advisory Group (PAG) to undertake a general review of the planning system and to consider remedies for the deficiencies of the system. In assessing the needs of the future, and in view of the great surge of physical development, the PAG Report enumerated the functions which a development plan system should perform (*MHLG, 1965a*). Its recommendations were substantially embodied in the 1967 White Paper and the subsequent Town and Country Planning Act 1968 for England and Wales (and 1969, for Scotland).

The new 1968 Act recognised two distinct levels of responsibility – the central responsibility of the Minister for policy and general standards, and the local responsibility of the local authority for detailed land-use allocation and environmental planning. The most important part of the 1968 Act related to the new form of development plans and the new procedures for planning inquiries and appeals. The new system of development plans consisted of (1) a 'structure' plan to deal with broad issues of strategy, submitted to the Minister for approval; and (2) a series of 'local' plans for particular parts of the area, dealing with detailed local matters which did not need ministerial approval.

The need for greater public participation was subsequently endorsed in the 1968 Town and Country Planning Act. The new approach to public participation outlined in the 1969 Skeffington Report, entitled *People and Planning*, enabled a greater involvement of the public in planning, by requiring the planning authority to submit a report on public participation with the plan and account for representations not accepted (*MHLG, 1969*). Consultations were to take place during the preparation of all plans.

The new planning framework and local government reorganisation

In England and Wales, all the provisions of the Town and Country Planning Acts, 1962 to 1968, were re-enacted in consolidated form in the 1971 Town and Country Planning Act, and in Scotland in the 1972 Town and Country Planning (Scotland) Act. These two Acts formed the statutory framework which lasted in England and Wales until 1990, with the 1972 Town and Country Planning (Scotland) Act lasting beyond. The 1968 and the 1971 Acts provided for a wide variety of plans, urban and county structure plans and local plans. It became apparent, at about the same time, that a new local government structure was required to create the new executive authorities with the political power to commission and implement such plans.

The pace of change quickened when the local government structure of London was reformed by the London Government Act, 1963, which established a two-tier system comprising the Greater London Council (GLC), formerly the LCC, and the 33 London boroughs. Although responsibilities overlapped, the work of authorities was broadly divided between strategic issues by the regional tier (GLC) and local issues by the lower tier (London borough councils).

The Royal Commission on Local Government in England (*Redcliffe-Maud Report, 1969*) and the Royal Commission for Local Government in Scotland (*Wheatley Report, 1969*) made recommendations for new authorities and boundaries. The Redcliffe-Maud Commission found weaknesses in the local government system because of (1) the divisions between town and country; (2) the division of responsibility within counties; (3) the small size of many authorities; (4) the relationship between local authorities and the public; and (5) the relationship between local authorities and the central government.

In response to these weaknesses, the Redcliffe-Maud Commission proposed that the greater part of England be divided into 58 single-tier authorities, which would be responsible for almost all executive action with regard to local government services. These unitary areas were to be city regions. Realising that there would be great difficulties in implementation if the population of a single-tier authority was over a million, the Redcliffe-Maud Report proposed a two-tier government similar to the organisation for Greater London for the three largest conurbations: (1) West Midlands/Birmingham, (2) Merseyside/Liverpool, and (3) Greater Manchester.

In these metropolitan authorities, the top tier was responsible for planning, transportation, water supply, sewerage, refuse disposal, police, fire and ambulance services. All other duties rested with 20 lower-tier metropolitan districts, the main duties of which were housing and education. These local councils were to express local opinion by making representations to the unitary authority.

Over and above the metropolitan authorities, the Redcliffe-Maud Commission recommended the establishment of eight provincial councils covering areas coinciding with those of the economic planning regions, consisting of people indirectly elected, that is, either elected by the unitary and metropolitan authorities or coopted, which, in the eyes of some, would have damaged their status and inhibited their activities. The provincial councils' main task would have been to create a broad strategic framework for the exercise of the main authorities' operational responsibilities. In the end they were not established.

The biggest issue which faced the commission was the choice between one-tier and two-tier local government, although the majority supported single-tier authorities. The Labour government's Local Government White Paper (1970) accepted the combination of the single-tier and two-tier concept and added two areas of metropolitan category – South Hampshire and West Yorkshire. Labour also proposed that education in the metropolitan areas should be an upper-tier and not a lower-tier function. With few exceptions, most of the planners giving evidence to the Redcliffe-Maud and Wheatley Commissions had a common theme, that the boundaries of the executive authorities should be based upon the areas of problems and solutions for which these authorities must plan. The difference between various proposals turned on whether to have a two-tier local government of regional and district authorities, or a simple single-tier local government system, a unitary system. In the end, the government established six metropolitan counties, taking away South Hampshire but adding Tyne and Wear and South Yorkshire. Thus the final list of metropolitan counties was Merseyside, Greater Manchester, West Midlands, Tyne and Wear, South Yorkshire and West Yorkshire, with a total of 35 metropolitan districts. Outside these areas were 39 counties and 296 districts. A two-tier system of eight counties and 37 districts was established in Wales, although Wales abolished parish councils and in their place set up statutory community councils, as did Scotland.

There was no difference in the planning powers of the metropolitan counties and the non-metropolitan counties: both were responsible for structure planning, for agreeing with the district councils a framework for local planning and for the determination of development control issues. England kept its parish councils (10,000 approximately), which had the right to be consulted on planning applications in their areas.

The Scottish Wheatley Report also recommended a two-tier structure consisting of seven regions and 37 districts making a total of 44 authorities (*Wheatley Report, 1969*). However, the three island areas (Orkney, Shetland, and Western Isles) remained unitary authorities as it was thought unnecessary to have a two-tier planning function in large remote areas which contained few people. The 1971 White Paper on the Reform of Local Government in Scotland made changes, and by 1975 the final result was nine regions, 53 districts and three islands areas (65 authorities, of which 49 were planning authorities).

Labour was committed to both the Redcliffe-Maud and Wheatley Commissions. The Conservatives wavered over the Wheatley Report while the problem of Scottish devolution was still to be decided, but eventually rejected the unitary system, and thus the Local Government Act 1972 established a two-tier system of counties/regions and districts which the government would demolish 15 years later in England and 24 years later in Scotland.

The election of the new authorities was coupled with the demise of the old authorities in 1975. There was a further 'shake-down' period lasting two to three years while new policies were formulated and new management structures developed. The change occurred over a ten-year period in total, which seemed an astonishingly long period for a country to reorganise its local government structure. As a consequence, fundamental planning policy decisions were postponed, leaving the country in difficulties concerning planning decisions for a decade. The stresses and strains during the reform period were considerable. Those areas which had established inter-authority relationships were able to shift over to the new structure plans relatively early. But in areas of intense rivalries, desperate problems forced a series of short advisory interim plans for the priority areas, rather than statutory structure plans, for the technical work required took longer than the ten-year interim period. Nevertheless in Scotland, there remained a clearer distinction of function between the region and the districts than was found in England and Wales.

National planning guidelines for Scotland

In Scotland, there was an additional plan, the National Planning Guidelines, which portrayed planning guidelines on Scottish national policy. The Scottish Office was forced to think of National Planning Guidelines when the oil and petrochemical industry boom started. The first National Planning Guideline in 1974, *Coastal Planning Guidelines*, concerned directing the oil industry into specific areas. Later guidelines concerned the aggregate industry, recreation, skiing, etc., and provided non-statutory guidance at the national level which nevertheless carried tremendous importance. The effectiveness of the Scottish Office and the relative accountability of the regions and districts to the Scottish Office and its promotion of the National Guidelines has meant that the system of guidelines has worked extremely well (*Prestwich and Taylor, 1990*). The Scottish National Planning Guidelines were a precursor to the Planning Policy Guidance Notes which were formulated in the 1990s for England and Wales, and the National Planning Policy Guidelines formulated for Scotland (see chapter 15).

Structure Plans and regional planning

Regional planning was a recent development within the field of planning, growing out of a need to understand and control development and growth at the strategic level. The theoretical basis is to be found in the subjects of geography and regional economics. The scale at which regional planning operates is between national and local levels, working as a link between the two. The boundaries of a region are, however, often very difficult to define, but generally fall into three categories: (1) political boundaries, (2) problem areas (such as the Highlands and Islands), and (3) geographical hinterlands of cities, which would account for most of the counties in England and regions in Scotland. Until 1973, advisory regional planning had been concerned with providing a more even distribution of wealth and resources throughout the region. This problem stemmed from the over-concentration of population, wealth and resources in South East England, with out-migration and under-investment in Scotland, the North East and West of England and South Wales. During the 1970s, regional planning developed into an integral part of the structure plan system.

A Structure Plan is designed for setting out strategic issues for the county's or (formerly) the regional planning authority's policy and general proposals for a

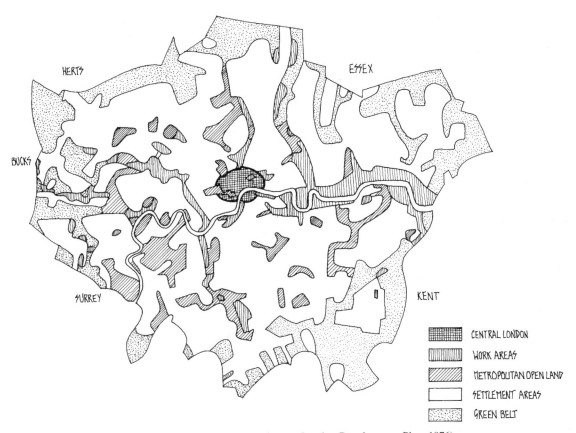

HERTS

ESSEX

BUCKS

SURREY

KENT

CENTRAL LONDON

WORK AREAS

METROPOLITAN OPEN LAND

SETTLEMENT AREAS

GREEN BELT

Figure 10.1   Structure Plan: structural elements (after Greater London Development Plan, 1976)

period broadly of five years ahead and more tentative proposals for the subsequent five years, capable of accommodating change. Structure Plans fulfil the following functions: (1) to state and justify to the public the authority's policies and general proposals for the strategic development and other uses of land (including measures for the improvement of the environment and the management of traffic) and thus provide guidance for development of issues of major importance; (2) to express national policies in terms of land-use planning, as they affect the area of the region; and (3) to provide a framework for Local Plans, which in turn provide the necessary further guidance for development control at the local level and guidance for decisions on single development issues of major importance to the region as a whole.

As the policies in the plan are confined to physical planning and the Minister approves only the physical policies within the plan, economic and social policies can be included only as part of a reasoned justification for the physical policies. The full content of the Structure Plan includes a Survey, a Key Diagram and a Written Statement. The survey report contains data and material which explains and supports the policies and proposals, including the selection of 'key issues'. Forecasts and financial resources for implementation are also included. The Key Diagram does not identify individual sites for development or delineate precise boundaries within which particular policies apply, as it only specifies policy and does not show Ordnance Survey boundaries. The Key Diagram is a locational index to the policies and proposals in the Written Statement (figure 10.1).

The Written Statement sets out the local planning authority's policy and general proposals for the development and other use of land as well as a reasoned justification for them. Authorities must indicate (1) any major alternatives they considered but rejected before favouring the policy and proposals in their submitted plan; (2) the extent to which the neighbouring authorities had regard to regional considerations; and (3) the resources likely to be available for carrying out the proposals of the Structure Plan. Only development control policies of strategic importance are included.

The interrelationship of policies as part of an integrated strategy should be emphasised.

Before approving a Structure Plan, the Minister (Secretary of State) could hold an Examination in Public into each Structure Plan or Structure Plan alteration, which provided the Secretary of State with any further information and advice he needed before making a decision. Since the Structure Plan is not site-specific, objections have to relate to general policies and proposals. The place for specific objections to particular proposals is the Local Plan Inquiry.

In time, the Structure Plan became more and more concerned with forecasting and studies to monitor policies to provide greater accuracy for long-term development practices (*Prestwich and Taylor, 1990*).

Typical issues contained in Structure Plans in the 1970s focused on a settlement strategy away from the green belt and suburban areas, towards urban regeneration and settling new housing in infill sites within the city. What was not foreseen were the economic pressures to switch to concentrating on industrial development in the 1980s. Pressure for shopping development outside central areas came at a rate many planners did not foresee. Not only shopping but more retail warehouses and superstores came as a surprise. Office development was restricted, particularly in historical areas. Some country parks were created and protection of the green belt remained an emotive and sacrosanct issue.

Most authorities tended towards a comprehensive approach to the preparation of the Structure Plan. They engaged in detailed surveys and subject reports, liaised with adjoining planning authorities on joint issues, and then prepared the draft plan and its examination in public and incorporated any central government modifications, which, altogether, became the final approved plan. Sometimes central government introduced substantial modifications but, in many cases, so afraid were the English authorities to produce any strong argument that the strategies resulted in mild proposals (*Prestwich and Taylor, 1990*). By the 1980s, most Structure Plans were producing pragmatic short-term solutions to key issues, such as allocating land for industry and housing, improving road networks but not public transport, and providing facilities for tourism (*Prestwich and Taylor, 1990*). At the time of the formulation of the Structure Plan there was economic expansion, and growth was expected to go on for ever, but later this growth did not happen. The economic planning aspect gradually took precedence over the physical planning aspect.

A major disappointment of the new development plan system was its lack of speed. By 1978, out of 89 expected Structure Plan submissions for England and Wales, only 23 had been approved. This occurred both because of lengthy examinations in public and because of excessive detail in the Structure Plan. Structure Plans were also meant to be revised or updated through a monitoring system, but authorities found this difficult and replaced the plans infrequently. The public also could not grasp the vague strategies.

Local Plans

By 1984, Local Plans played the major role in the development plan system. They provide the opportunity for the local planning authority to formulate its proposals for implementing the policy and general proposals of the Structure Plan within a time scale. Detailed Local Plans interpret and apply the proposals of the Structure Plan, and serve as a guide to developers and as a medium to coordinate public and private action. They enable interested parties to comment on specific proposals. A broad definition of a Local Plan is: 'The local planning field is concerned with the smallest system of land-use or settlement; and operates, for example, at the spatial scale of a village; a neighbourhood; an urban area ripe for comprehensive redevelopment; an industrial estate; and a precinct of special character or activity' (*RTPI, 1989*). A Local Plan guides development and changes in land use so that the physical environment can best serve the community (figure 10.2).

A Local Plan's most important functions are: 'to stimulate and encourage development where appropriate; to indicate land where there are opportunities for change; to give a clear locational reference to policies for the development or change of use of land, and to the authority's development proposals; to show how those who have an interest in the area, e.g. the authority, private owners, residents, commerce, industry, developers and investors, could contribute to the implementation of the plan; to apply national and regional policies; to show how policies and proposals for change in land use and activities fit together to form a coherent whole; and to provide an adequate basis for development control' (*Loew, 1979*).

Originally, the development plan system provided for three types of Local Plan: 'comprehensive', 'subject' and 'action area' plans:

1 Comprehensive plans apply to any part of a Structure Plan area, urban or rural, where the factors of local planning need to be studied and set out in a comprehensive way. A Local Plan covers a substantial area, such as the whole of a small town

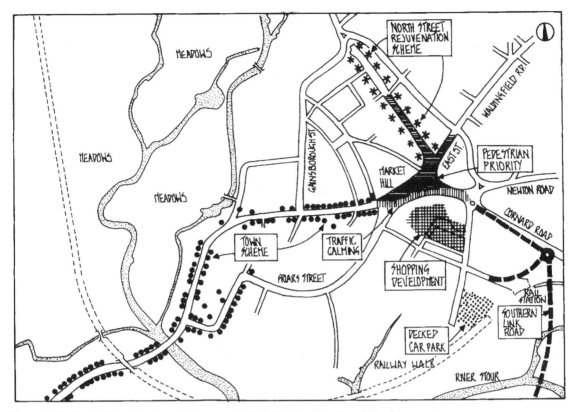

Figure 10.2   Local Plan objectives, Sudbury, south Suffolk (after Crouch and Ward)

or a sector of a larger one, and provides a link between the broad strategy of the Structure Plans and more specific proposals.

2 Subject plans enable detailed treatment to be given to particular aspects or issues and take the name of the subject or subjects they deal with. Limited in scope, subject plans may be prepared in some cases in advance of a comprehensive type of Local Plan, and in others where such a comprehensive plan is not needed. Subjects may cover a wide area and not only a specific district. Examples are land reclamation or recreation policy. Due to cost, few subject plans have been made.

3 Action area plans provided the means for local planning authorities to plan an area on comprehensive lines, for intensive change by development, redevelopment or improvement by public authorities or private enterprise, or a combination of these methods and agencies, and were designated in the Structure Plan. Action area plans were eventually discontinued.

A Local Plan consists of a 'proposals map' on an Ordnance Survey base, and a written statement together with any diagrams, illustrations and descriptive matter explaining and illustrating the proposals in the plan. The preparation of a Local Plan involves a thorough examination of conditions in neighbouring areas and the views of the public as with the Structure Plan. The proposals map should show the areas where policies will apply, and indicate the sites where future changes can be predicted with precision and confidence. In areas of intensive change, it is possible to predict a large amount of future change with accuracy, but in areas of piecemeal change, such as the suburbs, this may not be the case.

The written statement of the Local Plan gives the background to the plan and the reasoning behind it, and indicates the order in which interdependent proposals should be carried out. It should provide (1) objectives or alternative strategies; (2) a description of the relationships between the area and surrounding ones; (3) an explanation of likely alternative proposals; (4) an explanation of policies and proposals in the Local Plan; (5) an indication of the intended phasing and relationships between proposals; and (6) a description of the financial means of implementation (*Loew, 1979*).

Examples of the kinds of objectives or alternative strategies include (1) the redevelopment of the whole area in a rolling programme; (2) the redevelopment of the worst housing; (3) compulsory purchase and improvement of tenanted properties in bad condition or bad management; (4) building on the available sites and rehousing tenants from the worst conditions; and (5) using the available sites to provide public open space. The town planning aspects will relate to detailed land uses, other aspects such as criteria for development control, guidelines for design control, traffic and transport policies; programming of public investment and development and the related phasing of private development should also be included.

A diagnosis of the alternatives should produce a limited number of valid alternative solutions. These are put to the public and debated. A final choice of solutions is determined by the elected representatives and/or those who control the resources, as with the Structure Plan.

In normal cases, procedures for the adoption of the finalised Local Plan require copies of the Local Plan to be put forward for inspection by the public and a copy sent to the Minister or the Secretary of State. A period of time, not less than six weeks, is set for people to make objections and representations. A statement is sent to the Minister (Secretary of State) indicating what steps have been taken to take into account the public's views during the preparation of the plan.

Structure Plans and Local Plans: interrelationship difficulties

In general, Local Plans have been far more successful than Structure Plans. By 1984, comprehensive plans were the preferred type rather than small action area plans or subject plans as had been expected by the Planning Advisory Group. One of the major failings of the 1971 development plan system was that whereas certain powers were transferred to local authorities in the preparation of their Local Plans, other powers remained with central government, the major one being the control of financial resources through the allocation of grants, etc. This led to many compromises in local plans.

Structure Plans, as the coordinating document between national/regional policies and Local Plans, presented compromise policies. Because of the difficulties of relating two policy documents (Structure and Local Plans) and implementing them, the Conservative government in the 1980s gradually diminished the importance of the Structure Plan in England and Wales by transferring more power to the districts.

Theoretically, the 1971 planning system appeared, at least superficially, to be a great improvement over the old 1947 development plans in dealing with local problems. The 1972 system survived longer in Scotland, where the close relations between the Scottish Office and all the regions, the efficiency and high standard of the largest region, Strathclyde, and the relative promptness in implementing the system, contributed to its success.

Planning theories

With the expansion of planning methodology, planners from the 1960s onwards turned their attention to questions concerning theories of planning.

For many years, town planners were preoccupied with the Geddesian land-use planning process, specifically 'Survey, Analysis, Diagnosis and Plan' (*Geddes, 1915*). In the 1960s, with different complexities of possibilities, there developed other planning processes, with many followers and a variety of 'schools' of planning. Urban planning had its intellectual roots in architecture, urban design and engineering, and practitioners in these fields, used to problem-solving, did not feel the need for theories rationalising the activities of urban planning. With the introduction of social and natural scientists into the field, the desire for unifying theories of planning arose. Despite a good number of attempts, no single planning theory has been accepted by the planning professions. Instead several planning theories can be found which reflect the multidisciplinary variety of planners engaged in urban planning.

The theories can be divided broadly into decision theories and systems theories. Decision theories arise from the tradition of eighteenth and nineteenth century positivism, which promoted scientific methods and processes to be applied to human social systems. The nineteenth century Utopian experiments and model villages are in this tradition of seeking to improve the human condition through rational planning and the control of social institutions.

The contrasting approach to the decision theorists is the theorists of social operation, who developed the 'systems' approach and became more concerned with discovering how the system worked than with implementing decisions. Systems theory was a revolutionary counterbalance to decision theories by attempting to develop a totally comprehensive view of social systems and the operation of each independent secondary system within the system. Certain academic planners developed specialised views of system components and their operation.

The different types of planning 'schools of thought' include (*Catanese and Snyder, 1988: 43–53*):

A. Decision theories
   1 Rationalism
      (a) Traditional comprehensive planning – the Geddesian approach
      (b) Structure planning, a modification of the Geddesian approach which focuses on implementation
   2 Incrementalism
   3 Utopianism – urban design solutions
   4 Advocacy planning
   5 Public participation
   6 Ecological determinism

B. Systems theories
   1 General systems planning
   2 Other systems planning (cost–benefit analysis, linear programming, etc.)
      (a) Cost–benefit analysis
      (b) Planning balance sheet

Decision theories

It is no coincidence that Patrick Geddes, as a scientist, made the greatest contribution to philosophical planning thought in the nineteenth century by setting out a rational model of survey, analysis, diagnosis and plan in this tradition. British structure and local planning has continued in this theoretical mould of Rationalism. Geddesian disciples have continued to devote themselves to development, with concern for improving the quality of a plan's implementation as Rationalists. The Geddesian approach of survey, analysis, diagnosis and design was the sole approach in Britain. During the Second World War, the plans made for Plymouth, Coventry, London, Edinburgh, the Clyde Valley and Glasgow were all based on the Geddesian approach, which was formalised into legal action in the 1947 Town and Country Planning Act.

From 1947 onwards, all traditional plans were carried out on a survey, analysis, diagnosis approach, with varying levels of competency. The basis was a philosophical one, that after analysis and diagnosis, goals should be simply expressed. The Geddesian approach suited idealists and dedicated people to whom goals were all-important. The planners in the 1940s and 1950s, who were primarily architects, tended to be concerned with physical land-use action, separated from political decision-making and any kind of financial and administrative support. As a consequence of this philosophical attitude the emphasis on planning techniques was slight, particularly in relation to transport planning and fiscal budgets.

Geddesian planning was based on a nineteenth century attitude (inherited from the Beaux Arts tradition) that if the concepts of a plan were powerful enough the ideas would carry the plan through any administrative, social and financial difficulties, which, in fact, these traditional plans most often did. In their own way and in their time there were quite a few successful traditional plans and it is notable that Abercrombie's plan for Edinburgh, prepared in the traditional manner, is as good and significant as any of the plans which have since been prepared.

A variant on this rationalistic approach is popularly called 'muddling through' or more formally 'incrementalism', where a series of small incremental steps are taken into the future. It is an extremely politically acceptable approach in Britain, often adopted in Public Inquiries and planning appeals (*Faludi, 1973*).

Creative architects and urban designers often adopt Utopianism, and the Utopian Rationalists' approach, where broad, powerful ideas are proposed to catch the public's imagination and sweep through the proposed programme over all objectors. Ebenezer Howard, with his Garden City movement, was a Utopianist in this mould, as were Sir Raymond Unwin and Sir Patrick Abercrombie. Many of the successful post-war town planners were also of this tradition: architect–planners like Arthur Ling, who created Runcorn New Town; Hugh Wilson and Geoffrey Copcutt, who created Cumbernauld and Irvine New Towns; Walter Bor in Milton Keynes. Edmund Bacon attributes much of the success of Philadelphia's rejuvenation and planning programme to 'the power of a strong idea' and his projection of what modern Philadelphia could be like (*Bacon, 1979*). Most urban designers consider that the only lasting planning is that expressed in three dimensional form, expressing powerful ideas.

A third popular group of decision theorists, the 'advocacy planners', believed there should be no planning which was not committed to grass-roots values based in the actual area being planned. Advocacy planning had its greatest adherents in the multicultural United States, as it afforded minority groups the opportunity to express their goals and desires, which were often contrary to the goals of the ruling politicians. Its greatest proponent, Paul Davidoff, saw advocacy planning as a method of overcoming the disparity between rich and poor, black and white, men and women. The rise of advocacy planning was influenced by the social protest and political turbulence in the 1960s in the United States

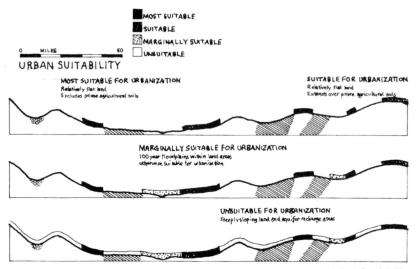

Figure 10.3   Comparison of suitability of land for urbanisation based on ecological standards (after McHarg)

(*Davidoff, 1965*). However, as American society became more pluralistic in the 1970s and 1980s, it became difficult for advocacy planners to know whom to serve (*Marris, 1987*). By the 1980s, some recognised that advocacy planning was too weak (*Hartman, 1984*) and that the shift away from physical planning may have weakened the potential of the advocacy movement, dependent as it is on local activities (*Krumholz and Forester, 1990; JAIP 60, 2: 1994 139–235*). They had moments of great political strength but when the political goal had been achieved, the advocacy planners tended to drop away from completing the rest of the planning process, whether official or non-official. In a curious way, advocacy planning, which stressed the frequently ignored views of minority groups, is a variant on physical Utopianism. In this case, the Utopianisms desired are the specific wishes of a particular group.

In Britain, against a background of 50 years of plans effected on a humanist basis, the interest in public participation in planning came late, presumably because the planners of the Geddesian school were, on the whole, self-effacing, idealistic and highly motivated. It was with statutory development planning, as part of the political system, that planners beholden to politicians and political committees expressed a political will in the objectives of the plan, and this in turn created a demand in the 1960s for greater public participation. This demand was recognised by the government in the Town and Country Planning Act 1968 and in the accepted proposals of the Skeffington Report (*MHLG, 1969*). After the Skeffington Report, councils were required

to report on the number of discussions held with the public over a plan or over development control and the public in turn were allowed to object to the Minister if there had not been sufficient public discussion. Throughout the 1970s and 1980s, the public participation mechanisms were continually refined. For many, the innumerable public associations and societies have succeeded in achieving many of their goals and can point to many examples of successes.

In the 1970s, the concept of physical planning expanded to include 'ecological determinism', which depends upon the correct ecological use of the land as the prime basis of planning, adopted through the efforts of Professor Ian McHarg (*McHarg, 1992*). Within this context, the planner is a catalyst suppressing his or her personal ego while attempting to bring forth and explain numerous planning options. The planner can offer scientific predictability about the consequences of different courses of action, help the community make its values explicit, and identify alternative, ecologically balanced solutions with their attendant costs and benefits. The land and all its processes set the parameters of the plan. An analytic orientation of both biophysical and social systems is rationalised in a non-biased apolitical perspective in McHarg's environmental planning.

Environmental planning requires an understanding of the complex relationship between the natural environment, economics and the man-made environment. It also implies a more cooperative and less selfish or egocentric approach to design and development (figure 10.3).

surely this s to regate our ability to modify natural parameters.

Systems theories

However, it was recognised that the traditional planning approach was too simple to handle the complexities of modern life, too remote from administrative and budgeting problems and finally did not or could not recognise what the public desired. As a reaction to the traditional Geddesian planning process, other planning processes developed.

The Structure/Local Plan system needed to be updated and phased actions in the plan needed to be constantly reviewed. Planning techniques became more important. Not only were techniques needed for survey and analysis but also for general objectives, evaluating the plan, monitoring and adapting it. The overall goal of structure planning was to be flexible and to set objectives in such broad terms that the plan could be easily adapted. This flexible approach meant the removal of the single total concept of the traditional plan. The planner became more of a technician on the one hand, and more of a political animal on the other hand, whereas in the former approach the planner was more of an idealist and remained outside the day-to-day arena of politics.

The 'systems approach' places its weight on efficient techniques to analyse the current urban system, forecast future changes and stimulate alternative futures. All activities and people are categorised into systems, subsystems and relationships, in an attempt to rationalise and bring the scientific method into the actual planning process (*McLoughlin, 1969; Chadwick, 1971*). The systems are based on human activities connected by flows of people, materials, energy and information. The physical framework for each system consists of buildings and their curtilages, open spaces, agricultural land and other adapted spaces, while the flows are accommodated by roads, railways, pipelines, wires and cables serving as communication channels (figure 10.4).

Based on the concept of the systems of human activities versus the systems of functional spaces, there has been a flow of theories on urban spatial structures which have stimulated new techniques. Gradually, planners separated those problems which are better solved on a systems basis, as in transport planning and regional planning, from those which are better solved on a decision basis, as in urban design.

British planners noted that, in America, after some 30 years of experience of the systems planning process, the widespread conclusion has been that the systems approach is helpful as a technique but any number of simulated alternative approaches may

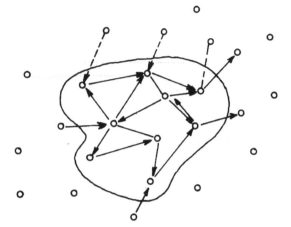

Figure 10.4   Systems diagram (after Chadwick)

confuse as much as help to eventually choose the right course of action. In the end no amount of mathematical techniques will help to express the kind of growth and change which is socially and financially desirable or fits the assumed social values. British planners benefiting from the American experience adopted a more humanistic approach, noting that the systems approach is not a total answer but must be complementary to the decision-making process, which can be made by other methods, but systems analysis led to work on urban land use and greatly stimulated the field of planning models research. In addition the new Structure and Local Plans which required monitoring and evaluation needed new techniques (*Bracken, 1981*).

Other technical approaches include cost–benefit analysis, and the 'planning balance sheet'. In cost–benefit analysis, for each alternative considered, the various costs and benefits are identified and enumerated and decisions made. Cost–benefit analysis has been helpful with problems such as the Victoria Underground line, the M25 and the siting of a third London airport. The 'planning balance sheet' is a method of overcoming some of the failings of cost–benefit analysis, by giving arithmetic values to social benefits and weighting these values as to planning costs (*Litchfield et al., 1975*). The planning balance sheet was one of the big steps forward in planning thought as it brought social benefits into the equation. The 'systems approach' is definitely helpful at the technical level of showing alternatives which are functionally based and related to specific spatial locations, and showing the consequences of certain policies.

The British planning system was established by

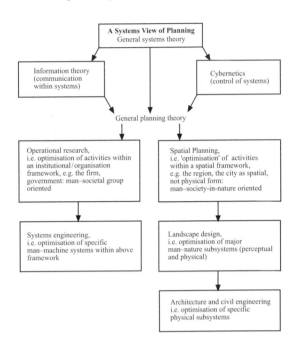

Figure 10.5   A conceptual systems basis for town and regional planning (after McLoughlin)

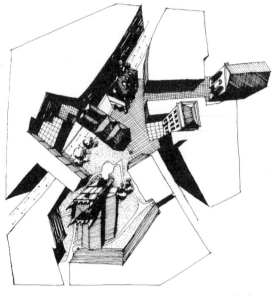

Figure 10.6   Creating urban spaces by the urban designer (after Cullen)

common consent over many years. The Second World War and the immediate post-war period made the concept of public interest even more acceptable and this has remained so. There have been many debates about planning, particularly in the Thatcher decade, but eventually the common consensus for planning has prevailed along with the traditional trust in public authority. The planners themselves have always promised individualism and socialism, town and country, past and future, preservation and change, which, some say, is promising people that they can have their cake and eat it, a very appealing doctrine (*Faludi, 1973: 58*). The big changes in thinking came later in the 1980s with the advent of Thatcherism but until then there was little self-consciousness, and little theorising.

The urban designer/physical planner

A further Utopian decision approach to town planning is that of the urban designer, who represents the middle ground between the town planner and the architect. Each has some claims in it, but neither fills it well, and it is better filled by the urban designer. The town planner regards land use as an allocation of resources problem, parcelling out land without much ability to handle the three-dimensional characteristics or the nature of the building that may be placed on it, with

the result that town planners can produce everyday stereotyped three-dimensional concepts but not necessarily highly imaginative solutions.

On the other hand, a good architect will try to relate his building to its immediate surroundings, but since he has no control over what happens off the site, the city is not necessarily improved. The architect will simply say that was not in his brief. Thus the urban designer helps relate the two approaches by giving design guidelines for buildings within the town planner's brief. The urban designer gives three-dimensional expression to the real institutional issues of the city, and relates individual buildings to the urban fabric. The kinds of decision-making area that the urban designer is responsible for are (1) preserving landmarks and a sense of historical continuity; (2) providing design guidelines without designing buildings; (3) designing for the neighbourhood; and (4) preserving the town centre and local centres (figure 10.6).

A Rationalist physical planner/urban designer is one who can interpret the socio-economic political contexts of the plan area and express them in physical planning objectives and form, which, in turn, is influenced by current aesthetic policies and reveals the historical background.

Summary

The new Planning Acts of 1968, 1971 and 1972 ensured the permanence of the planning system. They were followed by local government reorganisation in England and Wales and then Scotland, where new regions and districts were established which implemented the Structure and Local Plan systems.

With the new plans came new planning theories of how to order the process, dividing into decision theories and system theories, and including incrementalism, Utopianism, advocacy planning and ecological determinism on the one hand, and cost–benefit analysis and the planning balance sheet system on the other. The urban designer/physical planner continued to advocate the visual approach as predominant. In fact almost every thinking planner has new ideas and so no precise definitions exist. Many planners continue to think idealistically that their actions should be for the greatest good for the greatest number, and since the greatest good is indefinable, planners just keep striving.

11 Lessons from the seventies

The spread of the principle of conservation

The decade of the 1970s was beset by economic crises, political changes and uncertainty in planning. The reorganisation of local government, both in London and in the rest of the country, lasted from 1963 to 1975, a period of 12 years, during which time planning decisions were shelved or delayed. The new Structure and Local Plan system was meant to clarify planning issues and improve decision-making.

The national economic crises began when the oil-producing countries (the OPEC consortium) substantially raised their oil prices in 1973. The effect shocked the Western world, and not least Britain. The event heralded the end of the worldwide economic boom that had lasted since the Second World War, brought on the subsequent 1974 miners' strike and three-day week, increased inflation, and damaged Britain's economy; and the growth of the public sector and its demand for resources through taxation began to create problems for the central state. It is said that these events presaged the massive deregulation which dominated the Western world throughout the 1980s (*Batty, 1994: 9*). The Labour government's response throughout the 1970s was to allow a stop–go economy, which was not helpful to rational physical planning.

By the mid-1970s, Buchanan listed over a dozen urban problems which still existed 'despite 25 years of a planning and land use control system which foreigners maintained was the envy of the rest of the world, and yet was more rigorously applied than any nations outside of the communist countries' (*Buchanan, 1972: 258*). These urban problems included:

1 Shortage of housing accommodation
2 Inferior existing accommodation
3 Large unpleasant areas of towns
4 Lack of delightful architecture
5 Transport problems – rush hour congestion, overcrowded public transport, costly delays for the movement of freight
6 Environmental health problems
7 Inadequacies in social services
8 Defects in the economic base of towns leading to unemployment, boredom and outward drift of young people
9 Problems of maintaining law and order and of limiting vice and crime
10 Lack of leisure facilities
11 Physical ill-relationships, such as schools separated from houses; and social ill-relationships, such as the extended family separated from the nuclear family
12 Increasing racism and anti-religious actions
13 The difficulties of administering management, finance and planning of urban areas including securing councillors and staff of adequate calibre.

Buchanan listed as successes:

1 The reconstruction of the bombed cities
2 The New Towns
3 The broad containment of urban sprawl
4 The dispersal of industry to development areas
5 Some conservation of the architectural heritage
6 The provision of approximately sufficient accommodation to match the eight million increase in population.

The immediate problem of reconstructing the bombed cities had been completed. The establishment of the New Towns, the dispersal of some industry to needy development areas and the containment of urban sprawl had been successfully accomplished according to post-war goals. But major problems remained within existing cities: shortage of housing for the expanding number of households, large run-down areas, environmental problems, and a decline in public transport facilities. The greatest defect would be the poor economic base of towns, which would become the main issue of planning by the end of the 1970s.

Comprehensive redevelopment was the important physical planning principle of the late 1940s, 1950s and 1960s, but by 1975 had become an unacceptable concept, particularly when applied to slum clearance, city centre redevelopment or conservation areas such as Covent Garden. Instead, piecemeal redevelopment, small-scale change and conservation became the accepted policy. The small-scale approach allowed modest changes: human-scale architecture comprehensible to the ordinary man and woman; traffic management based on the environmental capacity of the existing street system; encouragement of the bus over the car; low-cost housing in cooperative ownership; local history preserved in historic buildings and streets; and public participation by the residents. The counter-argument to the small-scale approach was that it sacrificed wider goals for short-term local benefits, and did not solve the regional problem of imbalance of prosperity and employment, accommodation for increasing population, regional transport, energy, drainage and water supply.

Nevertheless, the concept of conservation took over, and not only in planning and architectural terms. Urban road projects were axed in favour of conservation. For example, the Westway part of London's motorway box destroyed many houses and left many others blighted in the lee of the viaduct. The Westway sparked off a public reaction against urban motorways, and after the Layfield Inquiry, the subsequent GLC dropped London's urban motorway programme (*Layfield Report, 1972*).

Between 1963 and 1965 London was reorganised; it then took four years for the Greater London Development Plan to be prepared (1969). The Public Inquiry lasted for two years, then another four years for a new GLDP to be produced, and two more years for a Public Inquiry, making a total of 13 years during which London was without an effective development plan (*GLC, 1976a,b*).

During the 25 years of post-war planning enormous changes occurred in towns and in the countryside. The public experienced massive and comprehensive environmental changes. In the opinion of some, it was inevitable that the pendulum would swing and that emphasis would be put less on change and more on continuity (*Nuttgens, 1989*). By the late 1970s public opinion returned to the town planning principle of building upon the past and not removing the past as was

done in the 1950s and 1960s. Public opinion enlarged its desire for architectural heritage to areas of environmental heritage, aided by the Town and County Planning Amenities Act 1974. The consensus centred on the total environment and the fusion of buildings and landscape. The major design movement of the 1970s became conservation of nature as well as resources, facilities, land and buildings. The concept of continuity appealed to the public, who felt isolated and powerless in the newly changing technological world.

Housing

Housing is the major physical component, the biggest user of urban land, and therefore any conservation policy had to start with housing. In the previous 25 years, a steady change of policy had occurred from redevelopment to housing renewal areas, which combined improvement of existing housing stock with redevelopment.

Under the 1968 Town and Country Planning Act, Comprehensive Development Areas for housing were transformed into smaller Action Areas and coupled with rehabilitation and improvement schemes in Local Plans. Action Areas were where intensive change (development, redevelopment, improvement) was likely to take place in the next ten years, and where action was required at an early date, later subsumed into the Local Plan, where the local authority made a broad strategy for:

1   a new traffic pattern
2   segregation of vehicles and pedestrians
3   areas designated for:
    (a)   redevelopment
    (b)   rehabilitation
    (c)   improvement
    (d)   conservation
4   a townscape guide
5   a guide for the coordination of public redevelopment interests and private ownership interests.

The 1969 Housing Act reflected the government's shift in emphasis from building New Towns or comprehensive redevelopment to investing in extending the life of the existing housing stock. This shift in emphasis arose from the inadequacies of the redevelopment programme, the cost of the New Town programme and the increasing need to limit the degree of disturbance of community patterns. Conservation was encouraged through Conservation Areas under the Civic Amenities Acts while rehabilitation of the housing stock was encouraged through discretionary and standard improvement grants applied through the new concepts of General Improvement Areas and Housing Action Areas.

Improvement grants and General Improvement Areas

The standard improvement grant programme, offered to the private owner to rehabilitate his own personal dwelling, was an immense success, helping thousands of individuals to improve their housing; it helped solve the problem of the thousands of odd pockets of housing too small for the local authority to rehabilitate, but causing blight without rehabilitation. Private owners were offered finance in three ways, by (1) discretionary improvement grant or (2) standard grant or (3) special grant. The discretionary improvement grant was made at the discretion of the council to improve a house, convert a house into one or more dwellings or convert a non-residential building into one or more dwellings, provided the result gave a useful life of 30 years. There was a minimum standard based on a list of 12 requirements, including heating, hot and cold water, bathroom provisions, insulation, etc. Unlike in the early 1960s, buildings of historic or architectural interest could also be converted by a discretionary improvement grant. The discretionary grant provided up to 50 percent of the total cost of the refurbishment and improvement of dwellings. Standard grants were available as of right to owners and provided for standard amenities for the first time, such as a bathroom, hot water, etc. Standard grants provided for 120,000 to 130,000 dwelling improvements a year throughout the 1960s. In the 1980s, the standard grants programme was so drastically reduced that it became ineffective, and by the 1990s, standard grants had become available only to owners in financial need. Special grants were and are for standard amenities for people in multiple dwellings, when there is no overspill housing available.

The 1969 Housing Act gave local authorities the power to declare General Improvement Areas (GIAs) within which owners were advised and financially helped to improve children's play spaces, and provide parking spaces, newly planted trees, traffic regulations and street furniture. A lot of voluntary action and cooperation had to occur between the citizen and the local authority, moving towards advocacy planning, although the planners were still in control. Three main groups participating in the rehabilitation programmes were (1) private owners, (2) local authorities (housing), (3) local authorities (planning) and (4) housing associations.

The Deeplish Study in Rochdale showed the feasibility and economic benefits of rehabilitation, which housing improvement methods, such as grants and housing associations, could resolve by retaining the fabric of the city (*MHLG, 1966*). On the other hand, many GIAs failed to generate any noticeable increase in home improvements. Many reasons for non-improvement were identified but not the chief one: that the administration of improvement grants was usually managed quite separately from that of environmental improvements, often in a mechanical way and by officers whose values were not necessarily consistent with those of the residents of the GIA (*DOE, 1978a*). The failure of administration should have been curable. The stated purposes of the GIAs were considered much too narrow, as they concentrated on physical aspects and tended to exclude social priorities. No attempt was made to estimate the cost of achieving the primary objective of changing a neighbourhood that people found discouraging into one that generated confidence (*Grove, 1979*).

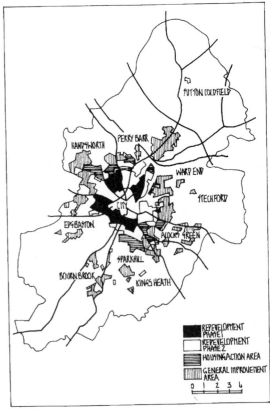

Figure 11.1   Birmingham: renewal areas, housing action areas and general improvement areas (after Gibson and Langstaff)

Ten years after the 1969 Housing Act created the concept of the General Improvement Area, well over 1000 neighbourhoods containing a total of more than 300,000 houses had benefited. But by 1979, few GIAs were declared and a procedure which at first appeared so promising in many different ways became ineffective. Although there were some good examples, there was not sufficient activity to have more than a marginal effect on rehousing in urban areas, and despite improvement in the quality of housing provided, overall conditions had actually deteriorated.

The government's White Paper *Better Homes – The Next Priorities* (*DoE, 1973a*) was followed by the 1974 Housing Act, which strove to overcome the deficiencies of the previous 1969 Housing Act by increasing the arrangements for renovation grants, by introducing repairs-only grants, by strengthening provision for compulsory improvement and by creating a package of stronger area-based improvement policies for Housing Action Areas, General Improvement Areas and Priority Neighbourhoods.

The General Improvement Area provided for voluntary improvement through increased renovation grants and local authority investment in environmental improvements. In the Priority Neighbourhood, the emphasis was on providing a holding operation until the appropriate improvement could be taken.

The Housing Action Area was aimed at alleviating the most acute stress by compulsory improvement. Local authorities designated areas of housing and social stress as Housing Action Areas with grants from 75 percent to 90 percent (for hardship areas). Funds were shifted from suburban and rural areas to inner areas. But the HAAs fared little better than the GIAs. Their impact was too small to make any difference.

Housing associations

Housing associations, gaining importance in the 1970s, originally sponsored co-ownership, when a building society lent two-thirds of the funds and the housing association the remaining third. They then turned to conversion and improvement of old houses, with a special improvement subsidy worth more than a discretionary improvement grant. Housing associations became a new tool for urban renewal.

The Housing Act of 1974 provided that the Housing Corporation in England and Wales could lend to any housing association for 'affordable housing'. These funds were channelled through the Department of the Environment and were therefore not at the behest of local authorities. By the late 1980s, the subsidy from the Housing Corporation to the housing associations

ranged from 75 to 90 percent. In the 1990s, the subsidy dropped back to 70 percent in some cases.

The Conservative government in the 1980s continually raised the annual budget of the Housing Corporation (and Scottish Homes for Scotland) and at the same time decreased the funds going to local authorities. The method of providing for mass housing changed from solely one of mass redevelopment in the 1950s to 1970s (organised by the housing and planning departments of the local authorities) to a variety of government programmes in the 1980s and 1990s. Residents could choose between local authority tenure, housing association tenure, right-to-buy council houses, homesteading or new housing.

As a result of these many developments, the face of urban Britain changed rapidly. Since 1964, the annual total of built dwellings, just above or below the 400,000 mark, represented an enormous physical change in the appearance of towns and cities as well as the redistribution of hundreds of thousands of people.

A new understanding of the causes of urban deprivation

The Inner Area Studies of Liverpool, Birmingham and Lambeth conducted in the mid-1970s presented a new diagnosis of urban malaise (*DoE, 1977d*). These studies suggested that certain false or inadequate premises had traditionally been invoked to explain the extent of the urban problem. Life cycles of poverty could not account for the totality of urban decay, nor could the physical and residential deterioration or the inadequacy of the scope and distribution of local government finance. These factors helped to describe the urban decay and might even be responsible for some aspects of the decay, but they could not be used to explain the real problems faced by the inner areas. It became increasingly obvious that the primary cause of the 'urban crisis' was the reduction in employment, together with the shrinkage of individual and community wealth.

In 1976, the Labour government carried out a complete review of inner city policy, drawing heavily from the Inner Area Studies of Liverpool, Birmingham and Lambeth and the West Central Scotland study relating to Glasgow, and published the White Paper *Policy for the Inner Cities* (*DoE, 1977e*). This review outlined the effects of the 1950s and 1960s programme of encouraging people and firms to move out of the inner areas, and analysed the problems as set out in table 11.1.

Since the Second World War, much was accomplished to improve the conditions of life in the

Table 11.1 Inner city problems

1. *Economic decline*: high unemployment/decayed industry
2. *Physical decay*: poor-quality housing/vacant sites
3. *Social disadvantages*: high concentration of poor people
4. *Ethnic minorities*: concentration together without adequate help
5. *Variations in condition*: Liverpool – unemployment; London, Glasgow – overcrowding

inner parts of the cities. But the main policy of relieving the congested inner areas created new problems. Between 1969 and 1975, the inner area of Manchester lost 20 percent of its population and Liverpool 40 percent, while Glasgow lost a staggering 60 percent. This decline was brought about by policies of (1) dispersal, (2) slum clearance rehousing, (3) road building, (4) commercial redevelopment, (5) removal of backstreet factories, (6) planning/zoning controls, (7) rationalisation of state industries, and (8) birth rate decline.

Dispersal of industry policy

The dispersal policy was based on the premise that new industry should be located in New Towns, or on the outskirts of existing cities. The policies of Abercrombie and the post-war decentralisation continued into the 1970s and had drastic repercussions on the inner areas. There was an assumption that people did not like workplaces in the same areas as their homes, but this was not always the case. Many people valued the way in which a factory or plant sustained a community, and the fact that they could walk or cycle to work.

With long-term structural change in industry and the importance placed on certain industries, those cities which previously were based on a single precise type of industry and its associated economic activities declined. The dock area of Bristol became derelict and in need of redevelopment, where once there had been a thriving industrial centre; in Leeds there were large areas of unused railway yards and warehouses. Furthermore, any industry left in the inner city areas in general was of the less desirable type not welcomed in New Towns or on suburban industrial estates.

Slum clearance rehousing

In the 1960s, many authorities carried out slum clearance but delayed redevelopment of the cleared sites, which were often left for many years; in this time the structure of the area declined or moved entirely and complete disintegration of the community occurred. Domestic, commercial and industrial property was acquired by compulsory purchase and prematurely demolished, when no plan for redevelopment was definite. It was noted that the appetite of local authorities for land historically outstrips their digestion. The sequence of over-ambitious proposals followed by spending cuts exacerbated this indigestion.

In inner Liverpool, for instance, over a tenth of the area selected for the Inner Area Study in 1975 was vacant, mainly cleared slum sites, reserved for schools, open spaces or highways, few of them likely to be built for many years and meanwhile strewn with rubble and refuse. Apart from these sites, the inner areas were typically without sufficient provision of open space, and no compensations appeared for the cramped and overcrowded conditions. It was not just the deterioration and decay of the actual buildings that was the problem: the inner areas where conditions were worst could not be isolated physically or socially from the adjacent districts. This often resulted in the development of 'twilight' zones, in an intermediate state of deterioration, as a result of contact, causing an outward spreading tendency, and this formed one of the strongest reasons for tackling the renewal of the urban cores before their problems spread beyond the possibilities of renewal.

The labels of slum and obsolescence were generally applied by planners and officials who were of a higher social income bracket than those living in the area, although the housing which they designated as obsolescent provided valuable homes, particularly in the case of multi-let dwellings, and even with a number of inconveniences, for those people who could not, for economic reasons, live elsewhere. The continued extent of slum dwellings constituted a considerable problem nonetheless.

Road building

The highways departments of local authorities used their statutory powers extensively throughout the 1950s and 1960s to clear paths for networks of new roads, several of which were subsequently cancelled. Many of these were built; but the cleared sites, together with the continued existence of proposed routes, allowed these plans to have a continuing blight impact on many areas.

Redevelopment

The inner city traditionally had a mix of domestic and commercial occupation. Houses, flats, offices and shops were combined as complete units. But many redevelopments excluded domestic accommodation and were designed as large blocks of office and shop space. This type of scheme was considered modern and efficient, but it formed pockets of inner areas which were unoccupied at night, adversely affecting adjoining neighbourhoods. Pressures for urban reconstruction, in the form of urban motorways or multi-storey car parks, created the possibility of a night-time desert and the traditional concept of an urban core as an area of functional diversity was threatened.

Removal of backstreet factories

The clearance of old property, together with redevelopment in the form of large schemes, removed the smaller premises used by backstreet factories. These businesses provided useful specialist services, and also a starting point for new enterprise. The demolished cheap factory space was replaced neither locally nor in the new suburban industrial estates. This removed an important foundation to the generation of the country's industrial base.

Planning/zoning controls

Diverse planning controls contributed to the decline of inner areas. Decisions delayed over controversial policies, or by appeals and public participation procedures, drove many developers to less controlled sites on virgin land. A further contributing factor to the number of dormant sites was the realisation that planning permission for a new building was easier to obtain for an ugly gap site than for an occupied one.

Rationalisation of state industries

Another cause of empty sites was the rationalisation of state industries. Much industrial land, notably former railway or Gas Board land, had lain dormant since the closure of lines, yards and works. For example, the British Railways Board was very slow in releasing surplus land for sale because of access difficulties along the lines, together with the fact that it was not under statutory obligation to act commercially, and incurred no direct penalty for neglecting pieces of ground. A similar story would be told about land formally owned by other statutory undertakers, especially the dock and gas concerns, together with, of course, the local authorities themselves.

Birth rate decline

The birth rate also fell, but the impact of this on the inner cities may not have been very great. There was already a voluntary exodus of families from central areas due to the declining environment and loss of job opportunities.

The Inner Urban Areas Act and planning policies

The 1978 Inner Urban Areas Act for England and Wales (and the Inner Urban Areas Act 1978 for Scotland), promoting the regeneration of the inner cities in partnership with the local authorities, placed great emphasis on employment creation in the older cores through various financial and physical policies. Government emphasis was now firmly towards (1) strengthening the economies of the inner areas and the prospects of their residents; (2) improving the physical fabric of the inner areas and making their environment more attractive; (3) alleviating social problems; and (4) securing a new balance between the inner areas and the rest of the city region in terms of population and jobs.

Local and central government were now required to be entrepreneurial in the attraction of industry and commerce. Local authorities were expected to stimulate investment by the private sector, and central government was to provide flexibility through Industrial Development Certificates, loans and grants. However, the 1978 Inner Urban Areas Act still placed heavy emphasis on the physical planning aspects of deprivation. Housing standards, the land issue, environmental and community deprivation were seen as the important aspects of the urban condition. Planning authorities sought to retain as much as was feasible of the existing urban fabric and favoured small-scale, incremental action such as conversion of premises, modernisation and rehabilitation. When appropriate, local authorities assisted in land acquisition and assembly.

Urban planning for the inner cities focused on five programmes, reflecting determined attempts to face up to the apparent demise of the inner areas of the major conurbations. These programmes consisted of (1) local authority partnerships; (2) central government partnerships; (3) participation by central government ad hoc agencies, such as the Department of Industry, the Manpower Services Commission, the National Enterprise Board and the various regional development agencies; (4) a strengthened role of the small firm in economic development; and (5) expansion of the private business sector, with programmes aimed at reinvigorating urban economic bases through a general reduction in public intervention and an expansion of the private sector, and special programmes for the proposed development of the inner areas.

Local government enterprises/partnerships

Local authorities concentrated their activities in four main areas:

1 Industrial development and rehabilitation
2 Improved local authority economic budgeting
3 Altering housing policies to help industrial expansion
4 General promotional services advertising the benefits of the relevant local authority.

Industrial development and rehabilitation: In the 1970s, a number of local authorities undertook their own industrial development plus industrial rehabilitation. In the case of industrial development, the authority acquired land and, where appropriate, derelict land grants were claimed for the restoration of the site. Sometimes the development itself was undertaken by the private sector with the authority receiving a capital payment of a ground rent geared to regular reviews. For example, advance factories were built as small, perhaps 1000–3000 sq. ft., simple one-storey buildings, with common servicing and access arrangements. Particularly, the small nursery unit was popular.

In the case of rehabilitation, the concept of an Industrial Improvement Area emerged in Rochdale in the mid-1970s (*DoE, 1979*). This concept was later embodied in the Inner Urban Areas Act (1978), as declared Industrial Improvement Areas within which councils were empowered to provide grants or loans for a wide variety of environmental and property improvements and for conversion costs involved in bringing buildings into industrial use.

Regional development grants, derelict land grants, inner city construction allocations, urban aid, EEC regional financial assistance, and other financial programmes all supported policies proposed for industrial improvement areas. Generally speaking, policies proposed for industrial improvement areas also included improvements to highways and access facilities, resurfacing, environmental improvements, construction, improvement or modification of buildings, acquisition and development of land, etc.

Improved local authority budgeting: Most local authorities elected to carry out budgetary processes and economic planning in a limited way, especially those authorities in the more deprived parts of urban Britain.

Housing policies related to industrial development areas: Local authorities adjusted their housing policies in order to help industrial development areas, and to provide accommodation for key workers. Local authorities and central government helped local councils provide more mortgages for all social groups, and encouraged housing associations to create a more flexible low-cost housing market.

Promotional activities advertising the relevant local authority: Local authorities greatly increased their promotional activities to highlight the advantages of their areas. Public relations/industrial development agencies were created to act as central agencies dealing with enquiries and to distribute relevant information relating to the locational, residential, cultural and commercial advantages of the city and town.

Central/local government partnership

The 1974–79 Labour government established central–local government partnerships. In 1978, the Inner Urban Areas Act provided the legislative framework within which both partnerships and the ostensibly less deprived inner areas, the so-called programme areas, operated. For all these areas, powers were granted to the relevant local authorities allowing them to provide loans for the acquisition of land and the carrying out of works on land, and both loans and grants for environmental improvements and the converting, improving or modifying of industrial or commercial buildings in Industrial Improvement Areas. In the partnership areas, additional powers were given such that appropriate district and county councils made interest-free loans for site preparation and infrastructure provision, and grants both for assisting in the payment of industrial and commercial rents and for relief from loan interest for smaller companies.

By 1978, seven partnership areas were initially selected: Liverpool, Birmingham and Lambeth (in part, because of their involvement with the Inner Area Studies), the London Docklands because of the scale of the problem, and Manchester/Salford, Newcastle/Gateshead and Hackney/Islington on account of the severe difficulties encountered in these localities. Fifteen other authorities in England were soon designated programme authorities and a further 19 administrations designated to which special attention was paid when urban aid grants were distributed.

The two partnerships which received more central government assistance than the others were Liverpool and Newcastle/Gateshead, which adopted additional employment subsidies and wider training programmes from the Manpower Services Commission, enhanced regional development grants and selective assistance,

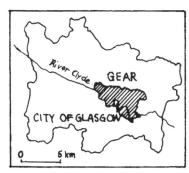

Figure 11.2   GEAR area in Glasgow (after Donnison and Middleton)

closer involvement with the National Enterprise Board, and wider promotional activities by the Department of Industry. The economic policies of the partnerships helped create jobs in the inner areas, or attempted to help the decline in employment, but also a wide range of educational, community, recreational and health services were adopted within the programmes.

The GEAR Partnership

In Scotland, the first and most important of the partnership projects was the Glasgow Eastern Area Renewal (GEAR) established in 1976, prior to the Inner Urban Areas Act, and undertaken under the aegis of a governing committee which included representatives from the two tiers of local government, from the Manpower Services Commission, the Housing Corporation, the Glasgow Area Health Board and the Scottish Development Agency (SDA), with a Scottish Office Minister as chairman. The overall coordinating management of the project was undertaken by the Scottish Development Agency (*Scottish Development Agency, 1978, 1979*).

The traditional east end of Glasgow, the GEAR area, had suffered from urban decay, industrial decline (particularly from metal manufacturing), rising unemployment, crime, poverty and other social disadvantages. It was made up of close communities, but the quality of life had declined and the people had started to lose faith in their society. It was said that the east end contained virtually the worst living conditions in a city which had already been shown to be among the worst in the country (*MacInally, 1981: 3*).

Within the GEAR area 2500 council houses were empty and needing to be demolished while 24,000–25,000 new houses were needed. Capital commitments of £156 million were made in the area in the period 1977–82, with a substantial proportion of this being spent in housing and industry, with the central objective of regenerating the economic base of the area (*Donnison and Middleton, 1987*). The GEAR Partnership renewal area was one of the most successful projects (figure 11.2).

In summary, central government increasingly allied itself with local authorities in order to attack urban problems. By providing additional funds, central government gained the central influence in decision-making, by-passing local authorities, and hence could impose its own ideas on appropriate administrative structures or effective industrial policies.

Central government ministries and agencies

Central government agencies, through their immense distribution of funds, indirectly made a considerable impact on town planning considerations. The most influential of the central government agencies were the Department of Industry, the National Enterprise Board, the Manpower Services Commission and the Scottish Development Agency.

The Department of Industry: By the end of the 1970s, the Department of Industry had provided more than £700 million per annum in assistance to industry, although only a small percentage of this investment was directly allocated to industry in the major conurbations. All the major inner areas were granted assisted area status except for London and Birmingham, and therefore participated in 50 percent grants from the Regional Development Fund. The long-term concern for regional growth through the decentralisation of industry from the inner areas probably did more damage to the inner areas than could be restored by the small inner area programme followed by the Department of Industry.

The National Enterprise Board: In the 1975 Industry Act, the newly created National Enterprise Board acted as an agent of central government, encouraging the efficient reorganisation of British industry, particularly through export-oriented, high-technology developments, by providing equity assistance. But since all NEB-supported enterprises had to achieve a 15–20 percent return on capital, few firms wanted National Enterprise Board assistance under such a hard rule. These penal financial duties were not imposed on those 'lame duck' companies, like Rolls-Royce and British Leyland, which the NEB took over from central government, which had previously rescued them from liquidation. By 1979, the National Enterprise Board had provided £1280 million to some 55 firms, of which £1170m was allocated to the very same 'lame ducks', with limited investment in the partnership and programme areas.

Manpower Services Commission: The Manpower Services Commission was established under the Employment and Training Act of 1973 to run employment and training services, which included improving training services, special employment benefits and job placement facilities.

The role of the small company: A concerted programme of action, aimed at encouraging the small to medium-sized company, involved policies designed to stimulate the expansion of existing companies and the creation of new ones. Particularly the smaller companies were encouraged to move into areas of industrial rehabilitation.

In summary, all these programmes were directed towards improving the economic conditions of cities.

Changes in the approach to planning

Ever since the strike of the OPEC oil countries in 1973, the miners' strike in Britain and the major economic crisis of the mid-1970s, British urban planners have enlarged their aim from regulating land uses to also promoting development and economic well-being. For most of the nineteenth and twentieth centuries, the concern with the determination of the physical environment and the need to ameliorate and improve physical conditions largely determined the nature of urban planning in Britain. The emphasis throughout the planning policies on the green belt, the development of New Towns and the large-scale construction of council housing was always on the physical outcome of a well-balanced community.

By the late 1970s, an intellectual transformation had occurred in the attitudes surrounding urban problems, away from the simplistic physical urban renewal assumptions adopted in the late 1960s and early 1970s towards a more economically oriented approach. The 1978 Inner Urban Areas Act under a Labour government began the new approach with its emphasis on stimulating economic growth by creating partnerships between government and the private sector and directly encouraging industrial and commercial development. Strategies were promoted with the aim of economically regenerating the inner areas, underpinned by the general consensus amongst urbanists that the primary cause of the so-called 'urban crisis' was economic. When the Conservatives came to power in 1979, few foresaw that they would remain in power for over a decade and a half and that they would totally transform the approach to town and country planning.

12 Changes in the Thatcher era

Planning policies: government action, 1980–83

Some say that it was in May 1979 with Margaret Thatcher's election that Britain parted company with the assumptions and beliefs on which the post-war political edifice had been built (*Hardy, 1991: 1021*). 'Thatcherism' provided the political context for town planning in the decade of the 1980s, embracing 'popular capitalism' in which working people were offered a stake in the property of the nation, either through share ownership in previously public corporations or through the transfer of council housing stock to sitting tenants. Thus the bias shifted from the public sector to the private sector, from the protective qualities of the state to individual enterprise.

Town planning shifted from being an intrinsically public sector activity to techniques within the private sector, for example

(1) regional economic planning councils were abolished;
(2) Enterprise Zones were created;
(3) Urban Development Corporations became powerful in their own right;
(4) most development control powers shifted to district council level.

Planning was not swept away, but it certainly changed. Planning became more pragmatic and more incremental, focusing on implementation and individual development initiatives. Some of the bureaucratic overlay was stripped away and localised initiatives were allowed to flourish. The Thatcherite commitment to breaking the hold of socialist local authorities was dominant. Thatcherism turned out to be a catalyst for the remaking of planning.

The new government initially accepted the policies begun by its predecessors. Then, in the 1980 Local Government Planning and Land Act (Scotland, 1981) it developed policies of its own, based as follows.

1 National policies for cities designed to stimulate the private sector, and to include private investment programmes. The stimulation of the private sector occurred through policies such as reduction in direct taxation and increased relief on corporation tax for smaller companies. In addition, the government encouraged the public sector to spend money in creating an infrastructure which allowed the private sector to prosper, such as providing improvements in transport facilities and additional investments in training facilities and environmental improvements.

2 Reductions in bureaucratic control. One of the areas in which the new Conservative government expended a great deal of time and thought concerned the delays in local planning and building regulations. Development controls needed to be more rapid, some planning controls needed to be relaxed, and planning activities needed to be more flexible. Throughout the 1980s, constant government circulars on speedier planning and reduced planning control were pursued starting with the first circular on Development Control Policy, with changes in the General Development Order (GDOs) specifying classes of 'permitted' development, followed by changes in the Use Classes Order (UCO) specifying groups of uses within which interchange is permissible. Statutory time requirements for decisions on planning applications were continually reduced, so that by 1981, 69 percent of all planning applications were decided within eight weeks. The introduction of Special Development Orders (SDO) for specific

locations or categories of development was also linked to architectural competitions in order to improve the quality of architectural performance either in Urban Development Corporation areas or in areas where planning applications had been called in.

3   New policies governing the physical development of the inner areas. These included:

(a)   Enterprise Zones, areas to stimulate widespread and commercial development with looser planning control and substantial tax concessions
(b)   Urban Development Corporations in designated areas where the government considered that the existing local authorities were unable to act effectively
(c)   Task Forces and City Action Teams
(d)   Estate Action and Housing Action Trusts
(e)   Garden Festivals
(f)   Urban Development Grants, Urban Regeneration Grants, City Grants
(g)   Derelict Land Grants for the reclamation of derelict land and buildings to create sites suitable for development and to provide landscaped open space.

The 1980 Local Government, Planning and Land Act greatly changed the balance of power in planning by centralising the following activities:

1   Transferring some planning functions from county to district
2   Expediting procedures for the making of Local Plans in England and Wales, allowing them to proceed in the absence of an approved Structure Plan
3   Empowering the Secretary of State to make a register of publicly owned land and to direct its disposal in England and Wales, or to force an auction which might force the local authority to use the land. The Land Registers described publicly owned land lying idle, which totalled 2000 sites and over 20,000 acres. To the government, it was a national scandal that so much inner city land lay idle, mostly in the public sector
4   Empowering the Secretary of State to set spending limits for individual local authorities
5   Creating new planning units. One of the characteristics of the 1980s was the plethora of ad hoc planning units created for particular purposes over and above the normal statutory unit, such as the Enterprise Zone, the Urban Development Corporation, etc.

6   Reducing all the main economic agencies, such as the Manpower Services Commission, in favour of private agencies and employment creation activities. The Youth Selective Service Scheme, which replaced the Manpower Services Commission, was restricted to assisted areas and inner city districts with high unemployment rates.

Also under the 1980 Act, the new government considered that the provision of additional owner-occupier housing and the retention of private rented accommodation was important to the regeneration of the inner areas. Wanting to create a better social mix, with policies which would respond to varied housing demands, it promoted policies such as:

(1)   relieving building societies of tax liabilities in inner areas on older properties;
(2)   providing government guarantees to cover mortgages on older properties;
(3)   encouraging the sale of council houses to tenants under the right-to-buy scheme;
(4)   providing broader powers for improvement areas which allowed a more flexible structure for the claiming of repair grants in areas other than just improvement areas;
(5)   allowing local authorities to guarantee mortgages in older areas; and
(6)   altering the Rent Act to allow for short-term tenancies which would not give tenants security of tenure.

Enterprise Zones

The 1980 Local Government, Planning and Land Act introduced the industrial planning concepts of the Enterprise Zone (EZ) based on the free port concept, in order to reduce the burden of regulation, as a response to the economic recession of the early 1980s. By 1995, 20 EZs had been established in England, three in Wales, three in Scotland and two in Northern Ireland, in areas of economic and physical decay, of about 500 acres in size. Designation orders agreed between the Department of the Environment and the relevant local authorities gave permission for the zone to last for ten years.

EZ schemes are prepared by authorities (district councils, London boroughs and development corporations), invited to do so by the Secretary of State. Within prescribed limits set by the Secretary of State, the authority is free to determine what planning concessions are to be offered and generally permission to develop is not needed. The local authorities keep control of transport and housing problems and

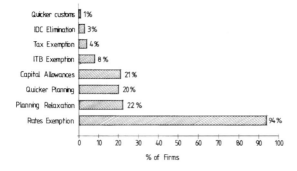

Figure 12.1   Percentage of firms regarding Enterprise Zone incentives as beneficial (after DoE, 1987)

supervise health, safety, fire and pollution control.

The financial attractions are amongst the most important elements of the Enterprise Zone, and include (figure 12.1):

(1)   exemption from development land tax;
(2)   exemption from all rates on industrial and commercial buildings for ten years;
(3)   100 percent capital allowance for corporation and income tax purposes for capital expenditure on commercial and industrial buildings;
(4)   no training levy from employers required from industrial training boards within the Enterprise Zones;
(5)   statistical information required by the government kept to a minimum, few forms/ applications being required; and
(6)   priority for certain customs formalities (i.e. importing and exporting outside the European Community without payment of customs charges).

There is also relaxation of planning controls, so that planning permission is not required for developments that broadly conform to the zoning specified. Reactions have been mixed as businessmen felt the zones merely offered another financial gimmick and the property sector considered that the financial incentives distorted the property market. For example, in Swansea, there were fears that the Enterprise Zone could undermine the viability of the city centre by drawing retail outlets away from the centre (one estimate has been £100 million a year from the centre) so Swansea local authority reduced the number of retail outlets. It is also thought that the Enterprise Zone does not help unemployment, as most of the new development and employment would have occurred in

any case (*PA Cambridge Economic Consultants, 1987*).

Urban Development Corporations

Following the creation of Enterprise Zones, Urban Development Areas were also established within the Local Government, Planning and Land Act 1980 under the planning authority of the Urban Development Corporation (UDC), which has been one of the most successful new vehicles of the 1980s in restoring areas of the inner city, such as Liverpool's Docklands; the most famous of all has been the London Docklands Development Corporation. Appointed, not elected, bodies were given wide powers to implement development programmes and to effect a speedy response to the problems of the cities.

For example, the substitution of a development corporation in London for the joint Docklands Committee transferred responsibility from local community leaders to a 'New Town'-type corporation. This decision was described as a reversal of the accepted policy of local committee and community involvement. The designation of the Urban Development Area is by statutory instrument, which simply requires parliamentary approval. This method, employed by the Conservative government, avoided the tedious method of designating New Towns (consultant's report, draft designation order, Public Inquiry and final designation), which could take up to two years. But it did give reign to the feeling that the Conservative government of the 1980s was planning by circular and by statute rather than by more democratic processes.

The UDCs are modelled on the New Towns, in that the UDCs have extra powers of compulsory purchase of land, and can take over the normal local authority's development control functions such as planning applications, tree preservation, conservation and listed building controls. The UDCs have had enormous freedom from local authority controls and planning and have had substantial amounts of money to spend. The new approach endorsed the wider concept of urban regeneration which aimed at integrating physical planning with other policies. These included the policies for dealing with the problems of deprived areas, stimulating economic activity in the inner cities, and encouraging environmental improvement through self-help action (table 12.1).

London Docklands Development Corporation

The scale of the east London docks problem had grown

Table 12.1   Urban Development Corporations, 1991

Black Country (West Midlands)
Bristol
Cardiff Bay
Central Manchester
Leeds
London Docklands
Merseyside
Sheffield
Teesside (Cleveland)
Trafford Park (Manchester)
Tyne and Wear (Newcastle)

with the closure of St Katharine's Dock, Wapping, in 1968 and the West India and Millwall Docks on the Isle of Dogs in January 1981. The local boroughs did not have adequate resources to tackle a project of this size within a reasonable time. The decline of jobs in east London continued. The Docklands Joint Committee was accused of repeated failures by the local authorities and other bodies to agree on a coherent common strategy and to attract investment in the early years of the port closures, thus frustrating any development of London's Docklands (*Docklands Joint Committee, 1976; Docklands Review Committee, 1980*). The select committee of Parliament, assessing the counter-argument, eventually accepted the government's view, in favour of a UDC. In this context, a nationally funded corporation became an efficient body to implement a scheme of this magnitude. Consequently, in 1981, the Docklands Joint Committee was abolished, and the new Development Corporation established.

The London Docklands Development Corporation (LDDC) acted like a New Town authority in redeveloping more than 5000 acres of land in London's docks, with responsibility for large areas of existing London boroughs like Newham, Tower Hamlets and Southwark. The corporation had wide-ranging powers compulsorily to acquire private land, finance land reclamation, and set up infrastructure and other environmental projects. The important difference between the New Town Development Corporations and Urban Development Corporations is that the former were not only the planning authority of the designated area with the statutory right to produce a development plan but were also the implementation authority for subsequent design and construction. The London Docklands Development Corporation was seen as an enabling authority charged with assembling sites through land purchase and sale as well as providing infrastructure renewal, including transportation systems, to provide incentives to maximise private

investment. Although the LDDC was charged with development control, it lacked the authority to prepare a conventional statutory development plan. This fact, combined with the designation of an Enterprise Zone with no formal planning controls and local rates exemption until 1992, 100 percent capital allowances on new construction, and no development land tax, created a recipe for visual anarchy and ad hoc development.

The LDDC was given title to all the public land. There was no grand master plan and most of the initial effort of the LDDC staff was devoted to selling the enterprise to potential investors in a highly sophisticated public relations and sales effort. The total area comprises 8.5 square miles with the largest office complex, Canary Wharf, located within the Isle of Dogs Enterprise Zone, an area of 12.5 million square feet of commercial space. The infrastructure programme constituted the principal contribution by the Urban Development Corporation. First came the light railway (figure 12.2) in 1987, an elevated, mostly single track, electric railway which runs from Tower Hill to the top of the Isle of Dogs. Next came a watered-down road-building programme. Private sources developed a small airport, also completed in 1987, which proved less than satisfactory as the short runway length prevented adequately sized aircraft using the airport, rendering it not commercially viable.

In 1981, the Docklands still retained almost 40,000 of its original inhabitants, who were displaced from their dock and industrial employment but continued to live in their council housing estates. Although over 30,000 housing units were completed between 1981 and 1984, 85 percent of these were privately developed upper-income housing – 'flagship' housing; the poor were largely ignored (*Docklands Consultative Committee, 1990*).

The Urban Development Corporations vary in their sensitivity to planning issues. The London Docklands Development Corporation began by paying little attention to planning principles and practice but gradually, after public outcries, the rise of community problems and impending financial difficulties, it paid increasing attention to planning matters and social concerns. As to conservation, success has been on an ad hoc basis, with many successfully conserved warehouses to the LDDC's credit. At first the LDDC was successful in attracting private investment, lured by the tax advantage of the Enterprise Zone. But in 1990 developers experienced a severe downturn in the rental market, which soon turned into a five-year recession, when the LDDC completed its task (chapter 15).

(a)   (b)

Figure 12.2   (a) Light railway, London Docklands; (b) Canary Wharf, London Docklands (attributed to the *London Docklands Development Corporation*. Untraceable)

The demise of the Greater London Council and the metropolitan county councils

By 1980, under a Conservative Greater London Council (GLC), practically all the strategic planners within the GLC had left, leaving mainly the civic design section. Under a subsequent Labour council (1980–81), an expanded review of the 1976 Greater London Development Plan (GLDP) took place to bring the plan up to date. In this period, the GLC was torn between the Conservatives, who wanted policy on an action and implementation basis, and Labour, which wanted policy as statements of principle, followed by action. In addition to these conflicts, the boroughs bitterly resented having to go through the GLC to reach central government, whether it was Labour or Conservative (*Lees, 1986*). On the other hand, the Home Counties actually worked with the GLC, as the Home Counties and South East England in general wanted the nation to pay for central London's decay, and perceived central London as a 'black hole'. The

political friction took on further tension when some politicians used the GLC as a national power base. In retaliation, the Conservative central government tried to control the GLC by reducing the rates and depriving the council of finance, yet the GLC managed to stay solvent. Rate-capping further limited the total amount the GLC was allowed to raise.

The atmosphere of tension between the GLC and central government increased with writs appearing from the boroughs. In court cases, the House of Lords stated that the GLC was required to fulfil its fiduciary duty to ratepayers, while central government was required to fulfil its duty to the taxpayers. The House of Lords also stated that it was no good doing strategic planning in a vacuum. As public transport was a top priority, London Transport was taken away from the GLC by central government. Central government then initiated a Paving Bill to abolish the GLC, and took powers not to accept the GLDP review. Consequently, the out-of-date 1976 version of the GLDP was the basis of decision (*Lees, 1986*).

Figure 12.3   Housing, London Docklands (attributed to the LDDC. Untraceable)

The decision to abolish the Greater London Council came with the White Paper *Streamlining the Cities*, in which it was stated that strategic planning was a passion of the 1960s, whereas in the 1980s there was a need for rationalisation of cities (*DoE, 1983*). Strategic planning was seen as a political activity to be eliminated. The Greater London Council was finally abolished in April 1986. Since then, London has been governed by an intricate network of bodies, including individual boroughs, joint groupings of the boroughs, various boards, advisory committees, regulatory authorities, central government quangos and privatised companies. The last vestige of the GLC, the Inner London Education Authority, became defunct on 1 April, 1990. In the opinion of some, none of the ad hoc combinations has been able to govern London better than the GLC, and in some ways the situation has become worse.

The function of the Greater London Council was replaced by the residual body, the Joint Planning Committee for Greater London, to (1) advise the boroughs and local planning authorities in Greater London on planning and development; (2) inform the Secretary of State of local authorities' views; and (3) inform local planning authorities in the vicinity of Greater London on the planning and development in Greater London.

Seen as a temporary body, the Joint Planning Committee was appointed by the Secretary of State for the Environment. It had no formal power to report to the Minister on strategic issues. The residual body became the 'dust bin' of all planning not carried out by the boroughs, and acted as residual authority for all the services that the boroughs could not handle. The residual body also sold Greater London Council assets, such as the GLC's famous County Council office buildings. In practice, the Joint Planning Committee for Greater London was a weak body unable adequately to look after the planning problems of one of the world's greatest cities, and many structural decisions were taken by the Department of the Environment. In 1993, the Joint Planning Committee for Greater London was replaced by the London Planning Advisory Committee (LPAC).

The demise of the Greater London Council was accompanied by the demise of the six metropolitan county councils, representing the remaining six conurbations in England. (Strathclyde Region embracing Glasgow remained.) The abolition of the Greater London Council and the metropolitan county councils was the most radical centrist change. Both were strategic planning authorities responsible for Structure Plans and their demise greatly affected plan-making in the conurbations. Together with the move to devolve planning and other powers from county to district, the abolition of the GLC and metropolitan county councils represented a trend back towards the 1947 concept of single-tier local planning authorities. Whilst this presents a guise of increased local autonomy (from county interference), it also made it easier for central government to rule.

Estate Action and Housing Action Trusts

Poor housing continued to be a problem. Despite mammoth efforts at slum clearance from the nineteenth century through the twentieth century, the slum housing problem remained. Although the number of dwellings lacking basic amenities dropped to 10 percent of the housing stock by 1981, or under one million dwellings, 12 percent of the total housing stock or 1,100,000 dwellings were unfit or needing repair (*1981 English Housing Condition Survey*) (*DoE, 1982*).

Most of the poor housing was pre-1919 stock but deterioration now appeared in the inter-war stock and in the public housing stock of the 1960s. The figures for Scotland and Wales were worse. Slum clearance had been the paramount policy in the late 1960s and 1970s with 90,000 houses demolished in 1969 and 54,000 houses demolished in 1974–75. But the policy in the 1980s shifted to improvement and in 1984/85 only 12,000 houses were demolished. The programmes of slum clearance and rehabilitation in Housing Action Areas and General Improvement Areas had not been able to keep pace with housing need.

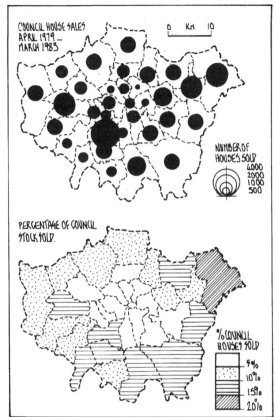

Figure 12.4   Council house sales in Greater London, 1979–83 (after Dennis)

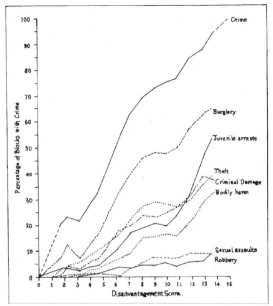

Figure 12.5   Trend lines for seven classes of crime in 729 blocks of flats in the Carter Street Police Division in Southwark. The average rate for blocks with scores of 13, 14 and 15 exceeded one crime per five dwellings (1980) (after Coleman)

The Conservatives' 1980 Housing Act tried to make the grant system more flexible so that financial resources would reach more people in financial need and more properties that needed improving. The effect of the 1980 Act was to produce a great rise in the number of repairs and renovations to private houses. The Housing Act of 1980 gave local authority tenants the right to buy their houses, whether or not their local authority wanted it. Special mortgages and discounts helped tenants to buy. The response was so popular that by 1986 over one million council and New Town dwellings had been sold in Britain. It had the effect of producing different types of ownership in every terrace or tower block, giving greater freedom of choice (Figure 12.4).

Following the riots in the Toxteth area of Liverpool in the summer of 1981, and the general consensus that something more had to be done, the urban development grant scheme was developed in 1982. The urban grant depended primarily on private sector funding to promote the economic and physical regeneration of inner urban areas. The ratio of private

to public money was approximately 4:1.

Not only did the slum housing problem remain but an overlapping problem of run-down council estates emerged. Many housing estates were in poor condition from the effects of being built with prefabricated reinforced concrete or not providing sufficient insulation or damp-proofing. While estates have been known to be in poor condition when only 20–30 years old, in some estates outright demolition of 15–20 blocks at a time has been the only solution. The related problems of poor materials, poor management, bad design, and violence and crime were highlighted by the extensive studies made by Professor Alice Coleman (*Coleman, 1985*). Professor Coleman found that total crime, burglary, juvenile arrests, theft and assault increased as design disadvantagement worsened. This was particularly true of those high-rise housing blocks with outside access balconies, upper-level walkways and unprotected lifts (figure 12.5).

Coleman's corrective measures included removing the upper-level walkways and providing private gardens to those tenants on the ground floor (figure 12.6). In response, the DoE established the Urban Housing Renewal Unit in 1985 to assist local authorities in developing a range of measures to cope with revitalising run-down estates.

The Conservative government, under the Housing

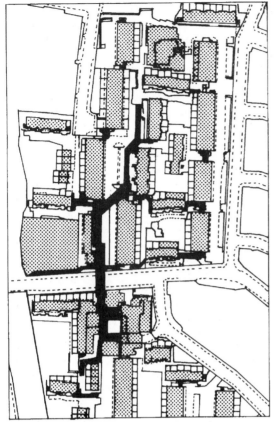

Figure 12.6 Mozart Estate, Westminster, London. Corrective measures involved the removal of the upper level walkway (shown in black) (after Coleman)

Act 1988, strove to find new ways of running existing council housing estates, since they had virtually abolished the ability of district councils to build new housing estates. The government created Housing Action Trusts (HATs) to take over council estates that had serious physical and social problems. After renovating the houses, the estates would be passed on to different forms of management and ownership including housing associations, tenant cooperatives and approved private landlords. HATs took on a large part of local authorities' housing stock as part of the dismantling of the public housing sector.

The Conservative government was particularly keen to get the administration and management out of the control of the local authorities into management trusts involving tenants or tenants' cooperatives. They also promoted the sale of portions or whole estates to developers and/or private trusts. To encourage developers to buy, the DoE initiated the process of 'enveloping' whereby the exterior fabric and its

surrounding area are renovated to dramatic effect. It is then hoped that the owners will tackle the further problems of rehabilitating the interior. Some success has been achieved by enveloping in Glasgow and Liverpool, for example.

At the same time, Conservative governments were bent on reducing public spending on local authority housing. From their point of view, the 1980s represented a success story in that they were able to bring expenditure down by more than 60 percent in the ten-year period by cutting subsidies, raising rents and restricting building. The local authorities were also able to gain £33 billion from the sale of 1.5 million council houses, and by the right-to-buy programme they expanded the owner-occupied sector from 55 percent of households in 1979 to nearly 70 percent by 1990 in England and Wales (*Cook, 1991*). At the beginning of the Thatcher era, there were 6.5 million council houses and 86,000 new ones were built in the one year. By the end there were about 5 million council houses in England and Wales and only 13,000 new ones being built in one year.

The consequences of this programme were many for the worst-off in society. Rising council rents meant that nearly two-thirds of the remaining tenants in England and Wales claimed housing benefit, paid by the Department of Social Security. The best-off have done well, remaining in the best stock of council housing. Naturally the city councils with large housing stock fought against government policy, but most authorities accepted the policy and raised rents.

By the 1989 Local Government and Housing Bill (England and Wales), the then Secretary of State for the Environment, Nicholas Ridley, announced that new council housing building was finished, bringing to an end over 100 years of direct government concern with slum housing. Thenceforth the public body offering new lower-cost housing was to be the Housing Corporation in England and Wales, and Scottish Homes in Scotland, quangos that channel government and private funds to non-profit-making housing associations for the purpose of providing low-income housing. Councils from then on would provide only for specialist needs, such as housing for old people in sheltered accommodation. After the 1989 Act, the government countered the big city and London Labour-controlled councils by 'rate-capping' the authorities and 'ring-fencing' housing accounts. Councils were prevented from subsidising rents by transferring money from ratepayers, or poll tax payers, after April 1990, forcing them to rely on rents and government income. Councils were allowed to spend only 25 percent of their receipts from council house sales, and the remaining 75 percent had to be placed towards paying off their debts and counted as a reduction in public borrowing. When a few housing authorities, mainly Conservative small town councils, produced a financial surplus, they began subsidising their rates from it. But the government retaliated by 'claiming back' surpluses and used the money for housing benefit claimed by poorer tenants.

The 1989 Act increased subsidies for the general improvement in the condition of the remaining council stock, by enabling councils to declare Housing Renewal Areas for refurbishment campaigns and by ending the old housing improvement grants and replacing them with a new set of means-tested grants for renovation.

Expansion of housing associations

In the early 1990s, the government greatly increased the funds available to housing associations, thus further removing the housing function from local authorities. Funding is administered by the Housing Corporation in England and Wales and Scottish Homes in Scotland. Since then, local authorities have joined forces with local housing associations to rehabilitate local authority housing. Glasgow also pioneered the homesteading idea, imported from the United States, where a family buys for almost nothing poor-quality housing in a deserted area provided they improve the housing aided by an improvement grant.

The housing associations' approach is proving far more popular than the previous large-scale redevelopments of the local authorities. Most housing association housing groups are small, therefore neighbourly; having higher design standards, their rents are very slightly higher than local authority housing rents. They have extended the choice of tenure types of housing.

The expansion of housing associations has been one of the success stories of recent government policy. The 1988 Housing Act allowed housing associations to secure private finance against a set percentage of funding from the Housing Corporation, enabling the number of houses provided by housing associations to increase from 14,000–15,000 units a year in the mid-1980s to more than 60,000 units in England and Wales in 1992/93, completed at a cost of £2.3 billion (*A J 10:11:93*). However, this is still nowhere near the actual need. The 1991 English House Condition Survey (*DoE, 1993a*) identified one in 14 houses as legally unfit for habitation and reported that £3 billion was needed to repair the worst housing.

The Conservative government's housing policy has been aimed at a tenure policy based on promoting owner-occupation, and has evolved through a series of specific initiatives by individual Ministers as they come and go. In fact the percentage of government money provided for the Housing Corporation in England and Wales fell from 75 percent in 1991/92 to 67 percent in 1993 and to 55 percent in 1995. Housing associations are expected to make up the difference through private finance. Scottish Homes, the Scottish version of the Housing Corporation, has fostered similar falls.

Rehabilitation of inner city housing, although a concern of the government, has difficulty succeeding within the financial parameters of the Housing Corporation. Before 1988, about 60 percent of housing associations' money was spent on rehabilitation. By 1993 this had fallen to 14 percent, even below the government's target of 18 percent. The rehabilitation of inner city housing remains a problem in an otherwise highly successful programme of housing associations.

The problem of mass housing continues. Every government has needed to provide subsidised housing as the private sector has not been able to provide low-cost housing since before the First World War. The quantity of housing required for the needy, for the homeless, for the elderly, remains high. The new multi-faceted approach of providing different tenures, different types of housing on small sites with tenant involvement, is clearly more popular than the mass housing schemes of the 1950s and 1960s. The approach has changed from a monolithic system to a pluralistic system but the numbers on the waiting lists remain. Successive governments have not yet been able to remove all waiting lists.

Politicians, architects and planners agree that bold architectural concepts on a grandiose scale should not be applied to housing. They can be applied to airports, museums or buildings of state, but not to housing. The era of high-rise, high-density housing has been supplanted by the era of low-rise, medium-density, popularly controlled local housing.

Garden festivals

Garden festivals became one of the more unique positive contributions of the Thatcher era. The idea came from Germany where garden festivals were held to overcome the scars of bombed sites. Unlike their British successors, the German festivals became permanent parks in mostly inner city areas. The British borrowed the idea but established that garden festivals should be temporary one-off reclamations of scarred sites.

Figure 12.7   Glasgow Garden Festival (by the author)

Although the garden festivals have altruistic goals, nevertheless these areas expand the limits of local authority planning control. Most garden festivals (Liverpool, Glasgow, Stoke-on-Trent) have been successful and appealing to the public but most local authorities have not been able to maintain them as open space, and after the festival is over the sites have been sold.

Urban regeneration

The budget of the urban programme had fallen from 1984. The concept of partnership changed from linking the various sections of government – central government departments, local and health authorities – to that of a partnership between the public and private sectors. Central government became impatient with the slow, cumbersome, sometimes obstructive and commercially insensitive aspects of local government and therefore developed new agencies which by-passed local authorities – most notably the UDCs, but also through urban development grants.

The private sector was brought into the inner city in two ways:

1 Derelict land grants, which were highly successful in attracting private house developers into 'brown field' sites to which they had previously shown an aversion. The 1988 Derelict Land Survey showed that despite reclamation of 14,000 hectares since

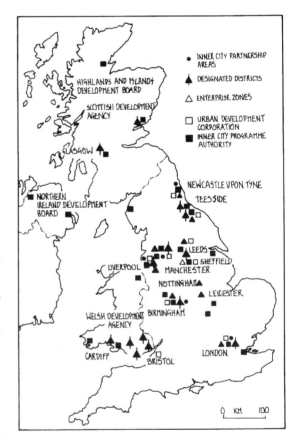

Figure 12.8   Enterprise Zones, Urban Development Corporation areas and Inner City Programmes (after Herington)

1982 and an overall decrease in the area of derelict land, large areas of land still required action and further steps were needed to force local authorities to bring vacant land into use. A total of 40,000 hectares was still derelict, half of which was contaminated.

2 Urban development grants, which were mostly embraced by local authorities with organisational talent in joint action as in Birmingham. There were some highly successful urban renewal schemes.

The switch to private sector involvement was the most significant development of the mid-1980s, helped by a combination of the frustration of central government, city authorities hating the lack of strategic planning, and the appearance of 'hard-left' authorities in Liverpool, Manchester and some of the London boroughs – which eventually precipitated the demise of the metropolitan county councils.

The Housing and Planning Act of 1986 introduced a further grant scheme, the 'urban regeneration grant', directed at large-scale schemes of 20 acres or more or the rehabilitation of buildings of 250,000 sq. ft. or more. In 1988, city grants replaced both the urban development grants and the urban regeneration grants and eliminated the local authority entirely in the development grant process. Eventually some Labour-controlled cities such as Newcastle, Glasgow, Sheffield and Birmingham, realising that the resistance of the early 1980s to the government's strategy had failed, made public–private partnerships with the private sector to encourage urban regeneration.

The government's *Action for Cities* concentrated urban regeneration on specific urban programme authorities revitalising run-down council estates. The urban programme and city grant areas include finance for landscaping derelict and vacant land, improvements to commercial buildings, walkways, parks and open spaces. The urban programme's intentions were good but the funds were inadequate. The 11 Urban Development Corporations have been far more successful in regenerating some of the worst areas of dereliction in the country. In many of the larger cities successful new commercial development replaced decline, e.g. in London's Docklands, Liverpool and Cardiff.

Green belts in the 1980s

The green belt idea changed in concept and became one of the instruments of regional policy – originally designed to control urban expansion, but increasingly thought of for scenic and recreational values. In the

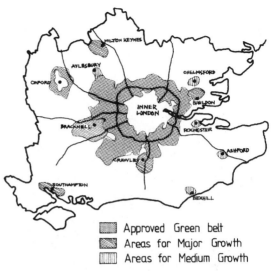

Figure 12.9 Green belts, growth and restraint areas in the South East, 1976 (after Elson)

South East Study (1964) amenity was made a major objective of green belts. The green belt around London was 850 square miles, and fairly steadily being extended. It had not served as a barrier to London commuters as the pioneers had hoped. The speeding-up of transport systems meant that many workers, often the more affluent, simply commuted across the belt. Plans increasingly showed bold attempts at using green belts, by expanding horticulture and forestry uses, by promoting outdoor recreation, by developing educational uses, and latterly for developments within hamlets or villages provided that they remained in character with the existing landscape.

The reorganisation of local government in the 1970s offered the opportunity to reconsider the position of green belts and the major towns. The inherited green belts consisted of 6930 square kilometres of approved green belt land of varying status. The 34 new Structure Plans contained proposals for new green belts and extensions to existing ones, totalling an additional 6270 square kilometres. If this had been approved, green belt coverage would have amounted to 13.8 percent of land in England and Wales. In the event, expansion of the green belt was limited to 10 percent (figure 12.10) (*Elson, 1986: 55–56, 74*).

The Department of the Environment issued two draft circulars, *Green Belts* (14/84) (*DoE, 1984a*) and *Land for Housing* (15/84) (*DoE, 1984b*), both implying a radical change in green belt policy, mainly of using green belt land for new housing. Developers, particularly, were anxious to build housing neighbourhoods and even New Towns within the green belt, and

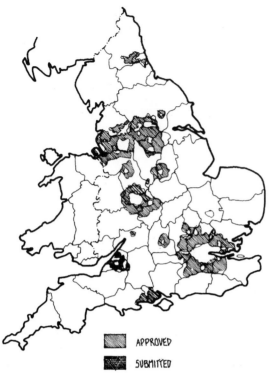

APPROVED

SUBMITTED

Figure 12.10   Green belts approved in Structure Plans, 1984 (after Elson)

Table 12.2   Green belts

	Acres
Approved Green belts in England, 1987:	
Tyne and Wear	200,000
Lancaster and Fylde Coast	5,750
York	50,000
South and West Yorkshire	800,000
Greater Manchester, Central Lancs, Merseyside, Wirral	750,000
Stoke-on-Trent	125,000
Nottingham, Derby	200,000
Burton/Swadlincote	2,000
West Midlands	650,000
Cambridge	26,500
Gloucester, Cheltenham	20,000
Oxford	100,000
London	1,200,000
Avon	150,000
SW Hampshire/SE Dorset	220,000
Total England	4,495,300
Green belts in Scotland, 1993:	
Aberdeen	58,475
Ayr/Prestwick	7,050
Falkirk/Grangemouth	8,636
Glasgow	296,526
Lothian/Edinburgh	36,077
Total Scotland	406,764

Source: PPG2 and the Scottish Office (from Cullingworth and Nadin, 1994, reproduced by kind permission of Routledge).

were encouraged by the Conservative government. Such was the widespread adverse reaction to the suggestions that the draft circulars on land and housing were withdrawn. By mid-1984, the government had agreed that green belts were sacrosanct, realising that green belt policy commanded even wider support in the 1980s than it did in the 1950s (*Cullingworth and Nadin, 1994: 122*).

Green belt policy became officially 'enshrined' in Planning Policy Guidance (PPG) Note 2 (1988). Green belts approved though Structure Plans cover approximately 4,500,000 acres (14 percent of England) in 15 separate green belts, varying in size from 1,200,000 acres around London to just 2000 acres at Burton-on-Trent. Green belts officially have five purposes (PPG2):

1 To check the unrestricted sprawl of large built-up areas
2 To safeguard the surrounding countryside from further encroachment
3 To prevent neighbouring towns from marrying into one another
4 To preserve the special character of historic towns
5 To assist in urban regeneration.

They are also meant to provide access to the countryside for the urban population. In terms of planning applications, there is a general presumption against inappropriate development within them. This still leaves a loophole for some development, i.e. if appropriate, and so the battle over the concept of the green belt continues. Scottish green belts continue to have a wider purpose than English ones, with a greater emphasis on providing for countryside recreation and institutional uses of various kinds and a greater emphasis on the environmental functions of the green belt (Scottish Circular: *Development in the Countryside and Green Belts*).

Simplified Planning Zones

The White Paper *Lifting the Burden* stipulated that there were still too many planning controls which constituted a burden, a deterrent to development and therefore to economic growth (*DoE, 1985*). It outlined further measures, with the aim of deregulation, to simplify the planning system by (1) proposing legislation for Simplified Planning Zones (SPZ), and

(2) further amending the General Development Order and the Use Classes Order. Although Enterprise Zones affected only small areas, their principle marked the beginning of the most important central intervention in development control since the 1946 New Towns Act, and their success prompted the government to increase the 'non-planning' areas by setting up Simplified Planning Zones.

Consequently the government created, under the Housing and Planning Act 1986, Simplified Planning Zone schemes for industry and commerce which were even freer of planning controls than Enterprise Zones or extended the type of freedoms allowed in an Enterprise Zone to other areas. A Simplified Planning Zone is an area for industry and commerce where planning permission is unconditional or subject to only a few conditions, lasting ten years. It is an attempt to provide freedom for industry to develop as needed. Planning control is pre-empted and the industrialist or developer is freer to do what he likes.

In practice, they have become areas where a particular form of development planning operates. SPZ schemes evolved in two forms: either a specific scheme for a desired development in detail, leaving all other development proposals to fall within normal development control; or a general scheme, as originally conceived, of broadly defined planning permission with only a few specific exceptions to the planning permission. Thus sub-zones within the SPZ may follow special conditions. Simplified planning zones are not allowed within a National Park, a Conservation Area, an Area of Outstanding Natural Beauty, an approved green belt, a Site of Special Scientific Interest, or as expressly excluded by the Secretary of State.

Relatively few SPZs have been designated – Corby, Derby and Nottingham in England – although more are in the pipeline. They have been wildly unpopular with local planning authorities, who viewed them as a means of evading their planning advice and policy. Scottish planning authorities, for example, steadfastly refused to adopt the concept of Simplified Planning Zones and only the three English ones exist.

Britain's first SPZ, Derby City Council's Sir Francis Ley Industrial Park, was successful in attracting private investment to help with Derby's economic regeneration, despite the fact that SPZs do not enjoy the rates and tax benefits of the Enterprise Zone. The SPZ allows business, general industry and storage or warehouse use. Sixteen smallish industrial units, ranging in size from 135 sq. m to 1200 sq. m, were built in the first year and sold freehold to investors. Although Derby hoped to attract investment from afar, the majority of the investors came from the local or the

sub-regional area. The zone has exhibited great flexibility and no disturbance to local residents and has vastly improved the physical appearance of the area (*Turner, 1990*).

There are no inducements to developers or firms to locate in a SPZ other than the advantage of streamlined planning processes, but most SPZs are in areas which also attract some form of grant. The greatest drawback to SPZs has been that in-coming firms are attracted away from other parts of the local or sub-regional area, giving little net benefit to the city region (*Arup, 1991*). For this reason many planners have conceded that SPZs are a redevelopment tool for special circumstances (*PPG5, 1992*).

Remaking the approach to planning: the new policy framework since the 1980s

The Conservative central government remade the approach to town and country planning by encouraging devices and techniques to develop land use for economic benefit (*Brindley et al., 1989*). It first established Enterprise Zones, then Urban Development Corporations, primarily set up to foster property investment. The most direct altering of the balance of power was the substitution of centrally appointed bodies for locally elected local planning authorities in the inner urban areas.

Central government did not relinquish any of its potential for direct control in an emergency over local planning, even though it retreated in its actual involvement at the local level in both plan-making and development control. It retained the ability to influence policy by restricting Structure Plans to physical policy-making. In any case, direct controls over planning were outweighed by central government's indirect control via legislation and circulars.

One of the major changes in the Thatcher era was to change the policy framework for town and country planning from the more straightforward reliance on the development plan, either as originally conceived as a single development plan or as conceived after the reorganisation of local government to the two-tier structure and Local Plan, to a variety of plan frameworks. Ever since, statutory planning policies are found in:

(1) structure plans;
(2) local plans (including subject plans); and
(3) planning schemes for Enterprise Zones, Simplified Planning Zones and Urban Development Areas.

The previous idea of having rigid land-use zones, i.e.

industrial, commercial and residential, changed to allow a greater mix of land uses. As industry became cleaner and more technological, there was less need to remove it from residential areas. Likewise commercial activities were allowed to stay, thus helping to reduce the journey to work of the many workers. The Use Classes Orders were amended time and time again in the 1980s to allow for a richer mix of land use.

The Conservative government also developed the habit of 'planning by circular'. From the 1980s onwards, the most common method of disseminating government policy and advice to planning authorities became the government circular. In the 20-year period between 1959 and 1979 there were 41 government circulars, or approximately two a year. In the ten-year period 1980–90, there were 89 or approximately nine per year, over four times the number previously. As these circulars were written by civil servants, emanating from the Department of the Environment, thus by-passing parliamentary procedure, there were protests against the seemingly undemocratic approach. Nevertheless the custom has continued.

The government circulars were originally augmented sometimes, then supplanted, by policy guidance notes, which began in the 1960s as planning bulletins, then in 1969 became development control policy notes. The eight original planning bulletins, dealing mainly with physical plan and design problems, were cancelled in 1983 even though much of the technical detail was still valid. By 1988, the 16 development control policy notes were supplanted by two types of policy guidance notes: planning policy guidance notes (PPGs) and mineral policy guidance notes (MPGs).

The intention of the revised system was to use the government circulars for advice on legislation and procedures and to use the policy guidance notes for actual development control guidance. In the first years, the planning policy guidance notes were concerned, for example, with General Policy and Principles (No. 1), Green Belts (2), Land for Housing (3), Simplified Planning Zones (5), Retail Development (6), Local Plans (12) and Archaeology and Planning (16). The mineral policy guidance notes were specifically concerned with detailed mineral matters.

Summary

It is a particular happenstance of British history that in the context of post-war politics, consensus in the support of town planning played a central role. There was and still is widespread agreement and general support for the practice of planning. Where the disagreement occurs is the extent – and it is this extent of planning which requires continual renegotiation between all parties (*Ambrose, 1986; Simmie, 1988*).

The end of the Second World War released an overwhelming sense of commitment to jointly build the city. The bottom line for post-war governments was a cast-iron commitment to economic management to secure growth and employment for all, and the construction and maintenance of a welfare state to guarantee basic material rights and to progress social equity. These two objectives enjoyed a broad measure of support across the political spectrum. Planning served as the physical arm of economic and social policy. From 1979 onwards many thought that the Thatcher decade was distinctly anti-planning but in fact this was not true, as the Conservatives maintained the planning status quo in many areas. At the start of the 1990s, the system of town and country planning remained recognisable and largely intact. Planning is here to stay, but its role and its needs are constantly reformulated.

13 The re-emergence of urban design in the late twentieth century

The retreat of urban design in the 1970s

With the continued economic strife throughout the 1970s, urban design projects faded away. Change in architectural and urban design terms was in the air but not yet accepted in the 1970s. It was a decade of elderly architects steadfastly building in 1960s Modernism, while young architects were attracted to the new High-Tech form and an inkling of Post-Modernism to come. Town planning was taken over by geographers, economists and social scientists, trained town planners who no longer thought in three-dimensional forms.

Urban design was left to be implemented by foreigners abroad. The Neo-Rationalists, like Manfredo Tafuri and Aldo Rossi, appeared in Italy (*Tafuri, 1976*); the Krier brothers, Leon and Robert from Luxembourg, both did projects for London which were not built (*Krier, R., 1973; Krier, L., 1974*). Bofill built in the French New Towns; Kevin Lynch, with the former Bauhaus member Georgy Kepes, produced a totally new perception of the city in his Image of the City in Boston, USA (*Lynch, 1960*). François Spoerry built picturesque designed marinas in the Mediterranean; Christopher Alexander produced his Pattern Language in California (*Alexander, 1966*) in the same year that Aldo Rossi wrote his *L'Architettura della Città* (*Rossi, 1966*) and Robert Venturi wrote his seminal work, *Complexity and Contradiction in Architecture* (*Venturi, 1966*), which was introduced to Britain in the 1970s. These new and different attitudes to urban design which emerged in the 1960s and 1970s were displayed in competitions and exhibitions throughout Europe. There was an Exhibition of Urbanism in Rome (1978) with participation by Nolle, Aldo Rossi, Giurgola, Venturi and Rauch, and two Britons, James Stirling and Colin Rowe (*Broadbent, 1990*).

In Paris, President Giscard d'Estaing and the then Mayor, Jacques Chirac, instituted a competition for the rebuilding of Les Halles. Both the president and his successor, François Mitterand, established an enormous programme for building architectural monuments in Paris, of which one of the first, the Musée d'Art Moderne, commonly known as the Beaubourg, was designed and built by an Englishman, Richard Rogers, in association with Piano. Barcelona, Spain, also embarked on a monumental rebuilding programme, employing some 50 architect–planners. The biggest competition and building programme of all was the rebuilding of Berlin, in which several Englishmen participated, including Rogers and Foster, but none of them succeeded (*Morris, E.K.S., 1994*).

British urban designers were hardly to be seen. There remained Gordon Cullen and Colin Rowe, although James Stirling made an attempt at an urban space in the Derby Civic Centre Competition, which was not built (figure 13.1). Concrete megastructures were still being built. The most significant were in council housing, particularly Neave Brown's Alexandra Road housing scheme for the London Borough of Camden, and Patrick Hodgkinson's Brunswick Centre in Bloomsbury (figure 13.2). Both were stepped housing terraces facing onto pedestrian ways in Camden and pedestrian and shopping precincts in Bloomsbury, respectively. Both schemes are reminiscent of Sant' Elia's high-rise sketches and both were, and still are, architecturally exciting. Later they were to be overrun by vandalism and other social problems such that local planners in the late 1970s judged them to be socially unacceptable and did not expand either of them.

High-Tech design appeared only in individual buildings such as Norman Foster's Willis Faber headquarters in Ipswich. Rather a return to Neo-

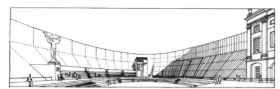

Figure 13.1 Civic Centre Competition, Derby, by James Stirling (after Cresswell and Grove)

Figure 13.2 Foundling Estate, Brunswick Centre, Bloomsbury, London (Untraceable)

Figure 13.3 Westminster Cathedral, London (from *Architectural Review, 1973a*, reproduced by kind permission)

Vernacular was favoured for public architecture in public spaces, whose popularity was probably a direct response to the public accusations of inhuman council housing architecture. The Neo-Vernacular approach consists of ideas and materials reminiscent of the village: for example, slated or tiled roofs, brick walls with nooks, weatherboarding, timber windows and doors. By the 1980s, Neo-Vernacular was considered a form of Post-Modernism which the developer and the local council could accept, knowing that the public would happily accept it. The Civic Centre for the London Borough of Hillingdon, designed by Robert Matthew and Johnson-Marshall in the 1970s, was the prototype. A Bauhaus plan with modern technology was enveloped in a shingle-style village architecture. Otherwise by the end of 1979, local authorities were beginning to blow up their high-rise housing blocks in favour of Post-Modernist designs.

Pedestrianised spaces and streets

British urban designers in the 1970s concentrated on making pedestrian streets, urban spaces and town centres. No longer able to afford the massive central area redevelopment schemes, or the equally large urban renewal schemes of the 1960s, British urban designers were forced to return to small-scale rehabilitation, humanising and making cities work with the buildings and spaces they already possess. When Prime Minister James Callaghan opened the new shopping centre of Milton Keynes in 1979, that was in celebration of a previous era. No more New Towns were to be built, and New Town Development Corporations were being disbanded.

In the constricted planning climate, pedestrianisation was one of the major methods that urban designers employed, resulting in some excellent pedestrian schemes and more importantly helping to renew civilised life in the town centres. Urban spaces and streets, walkways and public buildings were rehabilitated and incorporated into pedestrian schemes. In the design of the hard material urban spaces, British urban designers did well. For example, an excellent square was created in front of the Roman Catholic Westminster Cathedral adjoining Victoria Street, London (*Architectural Review, 1973a*) (figure 13.3).

The major British cities were not the leaders in urban design and their record was not impressive, with the exception of London and Leeds; whereas towns of 100,000 people did successfully pedestrianise their centres. For example, Rochdale, Greater Manchester, set aside £400,000 per annum for general environmental improvement. Yorkshire gave priority to pedestrian precincts in three town centres, costing just over half a million pounds in all (*Design Council, 1979*).

Figure 13.4 Hereford pedestrianisation (source untraceable)

The Leeds central area pedestrian precinct, one of the largest of its kind in Britain, was perhaps one of the best. Leeds was fortunate in its historical legacy of a compact shopping area, where pedestrianisation has been carried out since 1970, with careful treatment of ground surfaces, wall-to-wall paving and attention to the street furniture (*Leeds City Council, 1972*). In Leeds, 90 percent pedestrianisation of streets achieved the desired effect without the total irksome restrictiveness on cars and vans, which were allowed occasionally into the area, driving at 5 miles per hour, by deliberately having difficult surfaces.

Historic towns with an historic core, whose buildings are preserved and servicing restricted, are important to pedestrianise. Examples, like Chichester, are not comparable to the normal difficulties of pedestrianisation schemes (*MHLG, 1968a*). Chichester was well endowed with small medieval and eighteenth century urban spaces which the designers were able to integrate into a linked pathway–walkway open space system without harming the urban form. These areas easily adopted the design detail of street furniture, road surfaces and lighting, litter bins, seating, bollards, bus shelters, signs, trees and railings. Simple but delightful pedestrianised town centre examples were developed in Hereford (figure 13.4), Totnes (Devon), and Wakefield, Ossett and Pontefract (Yorkshire). Mostly humble examples, they exhibited the British desire to consolidate their urban design advantages in a highly civilised manner.

Urban design battles in the 1980s

In 1984, Britain entered into a genteel bloodbath over taste in urban design, started, most unlikely, by Prince Charles. The battle over taste was partly a battle over social goals but mostly over aesthetics. The aesthetic battle lines were multiple: Preservationists attacked Modernists; Modernists attacked Post-Modernists; the public attacked everyone except those who lived in the suburbs. The aesthetic war of styles had been rumbling ever since the mid-1970s but it really broke out with a vengeance with Princes Charles's Hampton Court speech in 1984 (*Prince of Wales, 1984*). Strangely enough, Prince Charles took it upon himself to be the catalyst of the aesthetic battle of taste. He began by attacking the arrogance of architects, planners and developers for imposing their taste on a long-suffering and silent public. The majority of the people, according to numerous polls, would prefer to live in traditional houses at a village scale and not in grandiose developments of the late twentieth century. The professionals, on the other hand, say they know best as they are trained in aesthetics, while the public is not.

Urban design projects tend to spark off a range of battles on multiple fronts – battles in front of planning committees, sparking off endless appeals and planning enquiries; battles in front of commissions, such as the Royal Fine Arts Commission, sparking off endless letters to the editors of all the major newspapers; battles in front of community groups, hastily put together to prevent the destruction of 'our neighbourhood' – 'not in my back yard' (NIMBYism). Architecture and urban design became the focus for an increasingly divided taste in society, because architecture and urban design are the most public of the arts. Everyone can see them. The one excellent result of this aesthetic battle is that architecture and urban design became public issues.

In the 1980s and 1990s, there were at least six major aesthetic movements: the Conservationists; the Classic Revivalists; the Modernists; Community Architects; the Post-Modernists; the High-Tech Modernists. The Conservationists believe in conservation, statutorily controlled by English Heritage, which embraces many aesthetic styles: Norman, Romanesque, Elizabethan, Jacobean, William and Mary, Queen Anne, Georgian, Victorian and, more recently, some modern buildings. The Conservationists have a wide spectrum of taste and are tolerant of almost every well-built style except the most recent, although English Heritage has listed for protection the first group of post-war buildings.

The Classic Revivalists, unlike the all-embracing Conservationists, maintain that the Georgian period is the only style of any aesthetic quality, and architects such as John Simpson build contemporary buildings clothed or costumed in a classic revival style (figure

Figure 13.5   London Bridge Scheme by John Simpson (attributed to Richard Sibley. Untraceable)

Figure 13.6   Prince Charles and Community Architecture (from *Architect's Journal*, reproduced by kind permission)

13.5). They do not copy, but the hope of the Classic Revivalists is to develop a late twentieth century classicism that is relevant to today's society. The Five Orders of architecture, on which classicism is based, give the architect ready-made pieces of architecture to put together to make his designs. The Orders give the designs their authority. Classicism demands the use of the Orders for their disciplined sense of scale and correct proportional relationships. The public, as demonstrated by builders' sales, would appear to endorse this narrow approach.

The third group are the Modernists, the followers of Le Corbusier's Radiant City plan for Paris' tower blocks, which were the philosophical inspiration for all the tower blocks built in the 1950s and early 1960s. The reality was different. Even into the 1980s and 1990s, there were later Modernists, such as Ahrends, Burton and Koralek, who still designed in the International Modern style, and won the first competition for the National Gallery, so the aesthetic was not dead.

Fourth are the proponents of Community Architecture, advocated by Prince Charles and the former RIBA President Rod Hackney (figure 13.6).

Community Architects rehabilitated local houses by tenant committees operating with the guidance of an architect. The aesthetic results of Community Architecture are heterogeneous, and less to do with aesthetics and more to do with the social goals of bringing a community together and helping them to improve their environment. A not-so-talented architect can produce a mundane result. The Community Architecture movement has not entered into the aesthetic battle, as its main purpose is to overcome the social ills of the inner city.

The Post-Modernists revolted against the Modernists' dictum of Mies van der Rohe, who said 'less is more'. Robert Venturi led the revolt by saying 'less is a bore', and proceeded to postulate that complexity in design more nearly indicated our current lifestyle. Venturi virtually created the Post-Modernist movement by publishing his thesis *Complexity and Contradiction in Architecture*, in which he argued that our pluralistic lifestyle required complex design answers (*Venturi, 1966*). Although written in the 1960s, it remains one of the most brilliantly argued and influential books on twentieth century architecture, advocating Pluralism, Eclectic Historicism, and Complexity in Decoration. This complexity was best exemplified by Pop Culture (*Venturi and Scott-Brown, 1972, 1984*). Although some Post-Modernists have not accepted the Pop Culture aspect but have leaned towards classical revival, most Post-Modernists have accepted complexity in decoration and historical derivation.

The sixth group are the High-Tech Modernists such as Richard Rogers, Norman Foster and Michael Hopkins, whose High-Tech design is the major British exposition of Modernism. The High-Ttech Modernists, who use polished steel and polished granite, which survive the British climate, have done well. A later

Figure 13.7 Lloyds Building, London, by Richard Rogers, architect (source untraceable)

development is to use high-quality plastic sheets. One of the best of the High-Tech Modernists, Richard Rogers, in 1978–86 designed the Lloyds Insurance Building, one of the great buildings of our time (figure 13.7). It is the immediate descendant and close in spirit to the clip-on, plug-in world of Archigram, with exposed engineering details and use of expensive materials (figure 13.8). High-Tech needs to be immaculately detailed to prevent failure of cladding materials and window gaskets. The Lloyds Building caught the excitement of the engineering process.

The public supported three groups: the Community Architects, the Classic Revivalists and the Conservationists. These three groups united against the Modernists, the Post-Modernists and the High-Tech Modernists.

The 'bêtes-noires' of Prince Charles

Prince Charles stirred the aesthetic battle with a few famous attacks on his 'bêtes-noires'. Firstly, he made the 'monstrous carbuncle' attack on the proposed addition to The National Gallery, London. Secondly, he attacked the 'glass stump' on the proposed Mies van der Rohe office block next to Mansion House, London; and thirdly, he spoke against the 'bore' on the redevelopment of Paternoster Square by St Paul's Cathedral.

The first battle: the carbuncle

At the 150th Royal Institute of British Architects' Anniversary Dinner in May 1984, Prince Charles called the proposed Modernist extension to the National Gallery 'a kind of vast municipal fire station, complete with the sort of tower that contained the siren … what is proposed is like a monstrous carbuncle on the face of a much-loved and elegant friend' – presumably because of the corner tower. The Prince apologised, but too late, for the Anti-Modernist campaign had started. Designed by the International-Style Modernists, Ahrends, Burton and Kovalek, the first proposal had been recommended by the Inspector, but this second design was refused planning permission by the Minister.

The planning process of directives from government agencies, ministerial pronouncements, architectural competitions, public inquiries and finally Prince Charles's opinions, brought planning and urban design into the public arena. In 1981, the government, through its Property Services Agency, which looked after the National Gallery, appointed advisers for the site over the heads of the trustees. The Conservative government insisted there be a commercial use (offices and shopping) to be combined with the extension of the Gallery – one-third gallery and two-thirds commerce. The Environment Minister, Michael Heseltine, sponsored a two-stage developer/architect competition and the planners were overruled. In 1982 seven schemes were short-listed. The public was invited to participate, but not to offer any opinions. In 1983, Ahrends, Burton and Kovalek were chosen as winners, but had to produce a third and a fourth design approved by the trustees. Two more government Environment Secretaries, and Westminster City Council Planning Committee, which was violently against the scheme, were overruled by government.

In 1984, a Public Inquiry showed the public distaste for mixing commerce and art. Prince Charles called the extension a carbuncle the week before the Inspector approved the scheme in his report to the Environment Minister. The trustees removed the scheme before the planners were able to give planning permission. After three years of notorious battle, the planners and the Inspector were overruled by three Ministers, the Prince

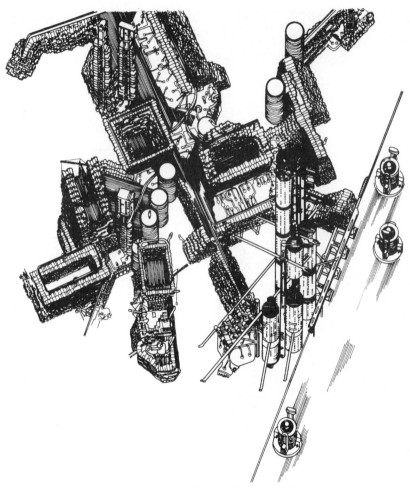

Figure 13.8   Plug-in City (axonometric) by Peter Cook (after *Archigram*, 1964)

and the private trustees. It was a Conservative central government decision. The Westminster planners and City Council Planning Committee were rendered impotent. In the end, the Post-Modernists, Venturi, Rauch and Scott-Brown, won the second round of competition entries and produced a design which satisfied the government and the public. The story had a happy ending.

Their extension is a quiet resolution of all the passion and fury. Venturi himself calls the extension a coda, an ending, and promised that the new addition would 'create harmony within the whole by combining contrast and analogy – that is, by combining some elements in the new building that are contrasting with, and others that are analogous to, elements of the old building.' Denise Scott-Brown stated that 'post modernism and classicism mesh' (*Venturi and Scott-Brown, 1992*). A brilliant and most ingenious solution,

Venturi's attached building carries Corinthian half-columns and pilasters (fake) to match the real Corinthian columns of the National Gallery and fake windows, which are at first at the same scale, increasing to the scale of the new building. The design is a pastiche of the Renaissance-style building in front, with a glass wall vernacular Modernism breathing out of the sides. It is a distinguished answer.

The second battle: the stump

Lord Palumbo wished to redevelop a site next to the Mansion House in the City of London by demolishing the existing Victorian buildings and replacing them with a posthumous Mies van der Rohe skyscraper about which Prince Charles said 'It would be a tragedy if the character and skyline of our capital city were to be further ruined and St Paul's dwarfed by yet another

Figure 13.9   National Gallery extension (Photo by Matt Worgo. Reproduced by kind permission of Venturi, Scott Brown and Associates, Inc.)

giant glass stump, better suited to downtown Chicago than the City of London.' Altogether, Palumbo spent 20 years amassing and purchasing the segments of the site and planned to give the nation its only example of one of the greatest twentieth century architects. This time the public did not necessarily agree with the Prince, as 32,000 people went to the public exhibition and, of the comments made, 75 percent were in favour of the scheme (figure 13.10).

Britain has hardly any buildings by the giants of the Modern Movement representing the twentieth century. No building by Le Corbusier exists and only one little church by Frank Lloyd Wright. There is no building by Mies van der Rohe, with only a couple of buildings by Walter Gropius. It is as if, architecturally speaking, Britain has kept its head in the sand, only lifting it to recognise, belatedly, a few late High-Tech Modernists like Richard Rogers, Norman Foster and Michael Hopkins. Where Palumbo went wrong was to suggest placing the buildings next to the Mansion House, a low-rise masterpiece. It was in the wrong context, and so the Minister was right to reject it, but then the design should have gone elsewhere. The Mies building was refused planning permission in 1985, shortly after Princes Charles had denigrated it.

With the Modernist solution rejected, Palumbo commissioned the architect, James Stirling, who produced a Post-Modernist solution for the office, shopping and restaurant development by keeping the same height and continuous window line of the

Victorian building, by using self-effacing materials which do not detract from the Mansion House, symbol of the power of the City of London, or its other neighbours, The Royal Exchange and the Bank of England. The final plan involved the demolition of more than an acre of the City's central conservation area, as well as eight listed buildings, including Number One Poultry and the Mappin and Webb Building (figure 13.11).

Although Stirling's Post-Modern style is heavy like a Mussolini mausoleum, Princes Charles described the design as looking like 'a 1930s wireless' and deplored the failure of the planning laws to protect areas around important monuments. Still, Stirling's fine example of Post-Modern architecture pleased many people. The scheme was opposed by the statutory body, English Heritage, which offered its own conservation project for the site. The Conservationists proposed to keep the existing Victorian Mappin and Webb Building, listed as only Grade II. This was not a sensible solution as the office space was antiquated, and the City of London must stay financially competitive with up-to-date office space. Another planning inquiry was held into this second scheme. The Inspector considered that there was 'exceptional reason' for acting against advice in government circulars, which all argue presumption in favour of conservation. Nicholas Ridley, the then Environment Secretary, gave the go-ahead for the office, shopping and restaurant development. The Environment Secretary's decision went against the

Figure 13.10   Proposed Mansion House Square (by Hellman in the *Architect's Journal*. Reproduced by kind permission)

Figure 13.11   Mansion House Square redevelopment (sketch by James Stirling) (from *Architect's Journal, 1988*. Reproduced by kind permission)

The third battle: the bore

Prince Charles's third intervention occurred in a Mansion House speech in December 1987. 'In the space of a mere 15 years in the 1960s and 1970s, in spite of all sorts of elaborate rules designed to protect that great view, your predecessors, as the planners, architects and developers of the City, wrecked the London skyline and desecrated the dome of St Paul's.'

After the Second World War, the City of London, having suffered extensive bombing, had two options:

(1) to rebuild the City as a major part of London's historic core, retaining the essentially medieval street pattern and the relatively small scale of building, leaving St Paul's and the remaining Wren spires to dominate the skyline; or
(2) alternatively, to rebuild the City with modern skyscrapers and efficient new road systems which would obliterate the past and make Britain a modern competitive country.

In the end there was a typically British muddle with some historic spots and lots of huge skyscrapers built on the medieval street pattern, just like the Wall Street section of New York.

Following Prince Charles's speech, Ove Arup's scheme won the competition for Paternoster Square and received planning permission in 1988. Arup's circular colonnade was reminiscent of Holford's first plan for St Paul's precinct (figure 13.12). The scheme emphasised human scale, mixed uses (not just offices), pedestrian movement, variety of individual buildings,

wishes of the City of London Planning Committee and was contrary to conservation policies.

The planning methodology employed in this most bitter planning dispute seen in the City for decades consisted of two Public Inquiries in four years, ignoring the advice of the Planning Committee, ignoring the advice of English Heritage, ignoring Princes Charles, and following the advice of the Inspector after the Public Inquiry, probably on the economic need to give the City office space. Save Britain's Heritage lost a further appeal to the High Court to stop demolition of the eight Victorian buildings. The judge considered that the case was exceptional and did not constitute any precedent for the determination of future applications to demolish listed buildings. Despite Stirling's death, the new building was opened in 1996.

Figure 13.12   Ove Arup's scheme for St Paul's (source untraceable)

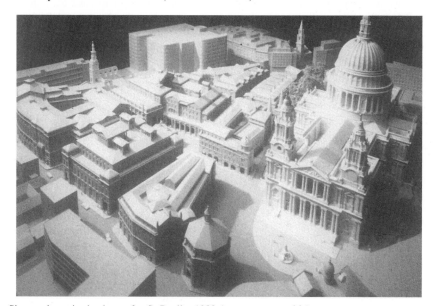

Figure 13.13   Simpson's revised scheme for St Paul's, 1989 (source untraceable)

deference to Wren's cathedral in preference to a great architectural statement, and a chance for contextually sensitive decoration.

The British developers for Paternoster Square, Mountleigh Estates, sold Paternoster Square to a Venezuelan consortium of developments which did not reappoint Arup Associates, despite their planning permission for the development of Paternoster Square. Instead the Prince's architectural choice, John Simpson, found a developer to head a consortium to develop Paternoster with Simpson and Leon Krier as master planners. As so many schemes were being rejected by the authorities on the mere rumour of the Prince's disapproval, to avoid such embarrassment developers of major projects increasingly requested the Prince's advance approval – so much so that it was observed by many that the Prince was 'rapidly emerging as the nation's Architect-In-Chief' (*Knevitt, 1985*).

Simpson's revised scheme in the Classic Revivalist style was of lesser density with its design theory formulated by Leon Krier and Dan Cruickshank (figure 13.13). The design was of the late eighteenth century in a series of loosely uniform elevations – English domestic (for smaller-scale uses) and French (for larger-scale uses), with arcades inspired by Inigo Jones. Simpson's plans incorporated (1) a new medieval street network as a natural extension of the surrounding area; (2) 'coherent public spaces'; (3) a hierarchy of design, i.e. individual buildings are only as important as their use demands; (4) reconciled masonry and brick elevations over structural frames within the building regulations (string courses and pilasters to cover up the expansion joints), and roofs of slate and lead; and (5) mini-temples to conceal ventilation equipment. Simpson used modern steel frames or reinforced concrete-framed structures with a classical skin of brick, stone and stucco. Such a concept is, of course, anathema to the Modernists. Major planning changes required the widening of the north/south street connecting the proposed square with the existing ceremonial space in front of St Paul's west elevation. This reorganisation led to the design of a new monumental building like a Roman market to close the north side of the proposed square. Subterranean roads were to service the ground floor shops and the crypt of the cathedral. Classical architecture was made relevant by being adapted to current needs, techniques and values.

The Venezuelan developers in turn sold again to a joint British–American partnership, which required substantial amendments to Simpson's original scheme and hired Terry Farrell in place of Leon Krier to work on planning issues. As of 1995, Paternoster Square had yet to start despite winning planning permission yet again in 1993. Farrell backed away from the decision to do the square all in Neo-Classical style. By 1996, it was clear that the Prince of Wales's vision of a classical redevelopment at Paternoster Square was unviable. No funders came forward because the classical scheme was incapable of being implemented as it was unsuited to modern requirements. London's most sensitive site, next to St Paul's, had become the centre of the urban design argument between Modernist and traditional architects. After eight years of argument and no progress, the City Corporation of London insisted on a more flexible design. The new Japanese developers, Mitsubishi, engaged Sir William Whitfield to produce a more open architectural scheme, not necessarily in the classical style and one with ample public space.

Architectural philosophies

The philosophical architectural wars in Britain continued into the 1990s. In the early 1980s, there seemed to be an acceptance of pluralism: Modernism, Post-Modernism and Classicism could exist side by side. But in the early 1990s, attitudes polarised owing to both Prince Charles's intransigent claims for Classicism and the architectural profession's determination to strike back with High-Tech Modernism. However, whatever one thinks of the content of the Prince of Wales's pronouncements on contemporary British architecture and planning, most design professionals (i.e. 78 percent of architects polled by the *Architects' Journal*) welcomed the higher profile that his crusade gave to urban design (*Punter, 1990b*). By the 1990s the best of the Modern Movement's approach was exhibited by British architects, unusually as Britain experimented so little with the Modern Movement in the 1930s or later in the 1970s and 1980s. The High-Tech Modernist Movement in Britain is as if Britain is only slowly awakening to what the rest of the Western world has been designing for the last 50 years. Led by Michael Hopkins, Norman Foster and Richard Rogers, High-Tech Modernism is the developed Modern Movement, evolving from the earlier struggles of the Modern Movement, allowing architectural pluralism, and diversity of cultures, ideas and philosophies coexisting, if not in discourse, at least in creative harmony. Clients are becoming better educated and the public now has the right to be heard. Thus architecture and planning should benefit from the Prince's debate in a holistic fashion rather than in the details. The specific design battles showed the public were interested in urban design and architectural interpretations.

Design guides and development control

In an effort to improve the quality of building design and townscape, the DoE and a number of local authorities issued 'good practice' design guidance. One of the first and still one of the best was the Essex Design Guide, although limited to the good design of residential areas (*Essex County Council, 1973*). The Essex Design Guide contained 'performance criteria which a development had to satisfy for approval; such as the layout; the amount of privacy between building, the accessibility of the car and the pedestrian; and some visual criteria which related to materials, proportion, fenestration', concluding with examples which were acceptable. Other counties and districts followed suit with some successful design guides, such as *Design Briefing in Towns* prepared for the Scottish Development Department (figures 13.14 to 13.17) (*Johnson-Marshall and Associates, 1978*).

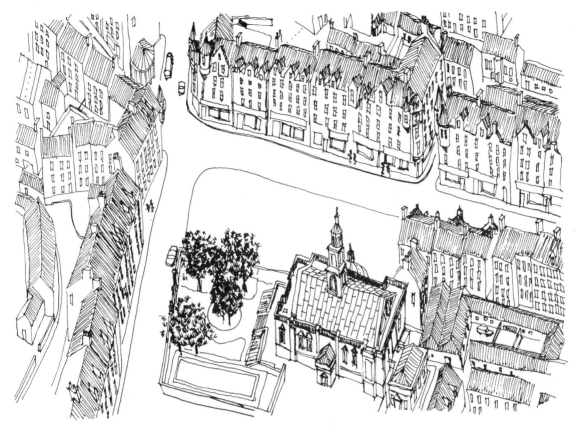

Figure 13.14   Urban space in Scottish town needing design guidance (after Johnson-Marshall)

Design guides, although favoured by most of the architectural and planning professions, were not always accepted by Environment Secretaries. The DoE itself entered into the design discussion, with an analysis of urban regeneration activity entitled *Improving Urban Areas* (figure 13.18) (*DoE, 1988*). Their good practice rules emphasised process rather than design:

1 Getting started, using imagination and commitment
2 Maintaining momentum, with a full-time project officer; maintenance funding; and establishing confidence
3 Providing critical choices
4 Establishing financial support from as wide a variety of sources as possible in the private–public partnership.

In November 1990, the Prince revealed his vision of Britain to the public on television and in an exhibition at the Victoria and Albert Museum, London. He called for ten principles to govern Urban Design, grouped thus (*Prince of Wales, 1989: 76–97*):

The Creation of a Friendly Environment
1 The Place – respect the land, the place
2 Hierarchy:
   (a) size of buildings in relation to their public importance
   (b) relative significance of the different elements which make up a building
3 Scale: 'Less might be a bore or more; too much is not enough'
   (a) relate to human proportions
   (b) relate to scale of buildings around them
4 Harmony: playing together of the parts – respect thy neighbour
5 Enclosure: one of the pleasures of architecture

Use of Sympathetic Construction Methods
6 Materials, incorporation of ornament
7 Decoration
8 Art

The Avoidance of Vulgar Signage and Clutter
9 Signs and light

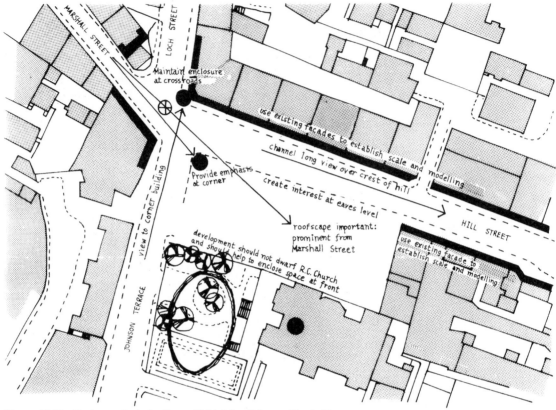

Figure 13.15   Design analysis for figure 13.14 (after Johnson-Marshall)

Involvement of Local People in Planning Decisions
10 Community participation.

Royal Town Planning Institute's ten commandments

The architectural profession hit back at the Prince's proposal but did not produce a set of principles (*Hutchinson, 1989*). Instead the Royal Town Planning Institute produced 'ten commandments', devised by the late Francis Tibbalds as follows (*Tibbalds, 1988*) (figure 13.19):

1 Thou shalt consider places before buildings. Need to concentrate on spaces – individual intricacy.
2 Thou shalt have the humility to learn from the past and respect thy context. Classical façades are a cop-out.
3 Thou shalt encourage the mixing of uses in towns (cities). Zoned segregation of uses has killed cities. Mixed uses make for a lively and safe environment.
4 Thou shalt design on a human scale/walking scale, landmark buildings excepted. Skyscrapers are all right if the street level is friendly. For example,

Lloyds Building at street level is appalling. Civic pieces of art.
5 Thou shalt encourage freedom to walk about.
6 Thou shalt cater for all sections of the community and consult with them; and reduce the impact of motor vehicles.
7 Thou shalt build legible environments. People should know where they are, where they are going, what the buildings are for. Landmarks and listed spaces.
8 Thou shalt build to last and adapt. Materials must be robust.
9 Thou shalt avoid change on too great a scale at the same time. Change is always painful but changes on a great scale are very painful. The comprehensive Development Areas of the 1950s and 1960s were painful. Need to redevelop smaller sites and/or break up larger sites into smaller units.
10 Thou shalt, with all the means available, promote intricacy, joy and visual delight in the built environment. No more anonymous megaliths – can be more full and enjoyable for ordinary people – good landscaping.

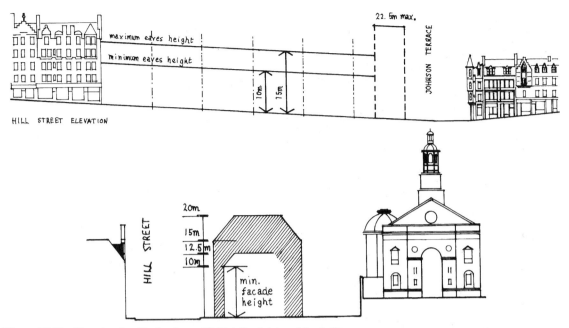

Figure 13.16 Elevational guide for figure 13.14 (after Johnson-Marshall)

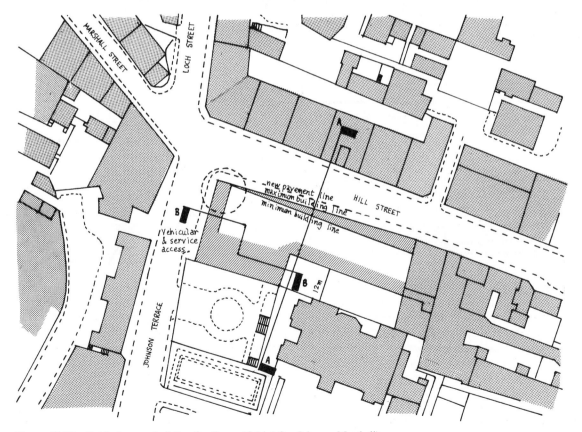

Figure 13.17 Guide for new building for figure 13.14 (after Johnson-Marshall)

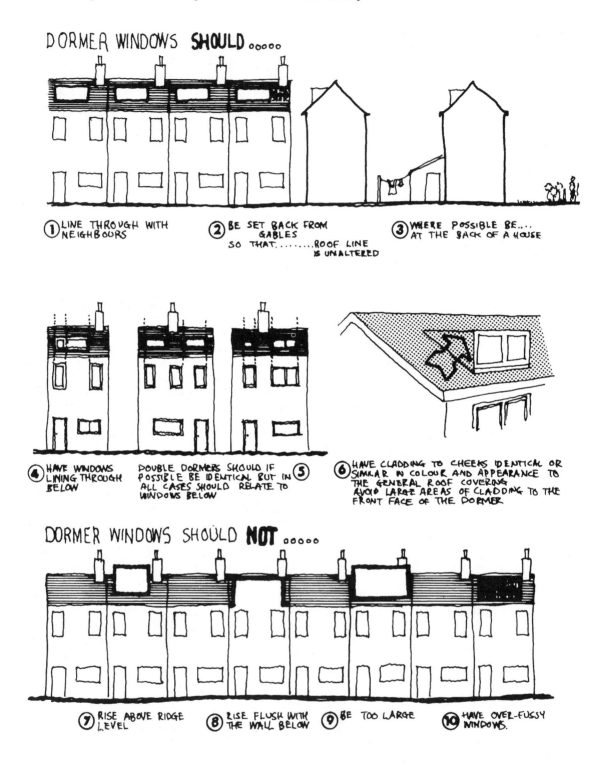

Figure 13.18　Design guidance for dormer window additions (after Department of the Environment)

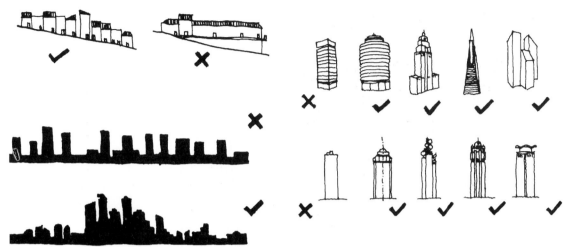

Figure 13.19   Tibbalds' check list of good design (after Tibbalds)

Tibbalds, in contrast to the Prince's emphasis on visual aspects, stressed the principles of mixed use, permeability and small-scale change (figure 13.20). On the other hand, the Prince of Wales was able to communicate clearly principles of design control to a vast public in his television films.

Despite the forthright quality of these 'commandments', the planning profession in Britain has had difficulty in supporting good urban design. In view of a world of rapid change and developing technology out of human scale, the planners, according to some, are a bit afraid of the public as well as being over-worked and under-resourced (*Knevitt, 1985*). The main responsibility for yesterday's aesthetic disasters lay with people who did not have ideals, such as developers who pushed for buildings far too big for their sites and employed third-rate architectural firms to design buildings, who had no sense of patronage with the developers; or planning authorities who let the plans through; or planning authorities who were frightened of developers and the government which abandoned vast areas, like the Docklands, to market forces for doctrinaire reasons.

The Prince's respect for place echoes the 'townscape' school with its emphasis upon the picturesque and its preoccupation with the visual experience to the denial of other aspects of urban life. This concept of hierarchy probably derives from the Prince's work with Leon Krier, and his concept of urban design purely as a visual art. Tibbalds' ten commandments preferred to emphasise the principles of mixed use, permeability and small-scale change, which Jane Jacobs put forward in *The Death and Life of Great American Cities* (*Jacobs, 1965; Punter, 1990b*).

Useful as these design codes are, design principles still have to be executed through the planning system of Local Plan, supplementary guidance and development briefs. The Prince of Wales contributed greatly by making the public aware of the importance of urban design and then negated some of that contribution by insisting on classical design. The planning profession, armed with Tibbalds' RTPI commandments, and the support of the Royal Fine Arts Commission and the Civic Trusts, can provide a more flexible urban design leadership, provided architect/urban designers, planners and developers are all trained in urban design.

In the early 1980s the Conservatives published a circular on development controls, policy and practice, setting the pattern for aesthetic controls throughout the decade. It proposed a checklist of areas where agreement could be reached including scale, density, height, areas, layout, landscape and materials.

By 1988, new planning policy guidelines had taken account of the changing political climate, including increasing public dislike of aesthetic controls and the possibility of awards of costs following Public Inquiries, which were awarded in several hundred cases. The planning inspectors, after the 'carbuncle' debacle, tended towards freedoms which, combined with the fear of costs, led some authorities to wash their hands of responsibility (*Hillman, 1990: 8*). Some areas still had strong controls, such as listed buildings, Conservation Areas, National Parks and Areas of Outstanding Natural Beauty.

Design guides became again more prominent in the 1990s. For example, planning applications for new development in the City of London need to conform to

Figure 13.20   The people-friendly design approach (after Tibbalds)

strict design guides prepared by Westminster City
Council, which include (1) vigorous conservation, (2)
no more high-rise buildings (they have to be built in
the Docklands) and (3) a maximum plot ratio of 5:1.
Planning permission was refused for a 108-metre tower
because, although the design was good, the height of
the tower would have overwhelmed the Church of All

Hallows and destroyed the views of St Paul's
Cathedral from Waterloo Bridge.

In 1990, the then Environment Secretary,
Christopher Patten, proposed devising design
guidelines and building codes on matters of taste, but
it took the next Environment Secretary, John Gummer,
actually to set up an urban design campaign to

encourage attention and a wider debate on urban design by promoting competition in case studies for a national exhibition in 1996 (*DoE, 1995*). Hopefully the urban design case studies should influence good design throughout the country.

Urban design examples

The two different schools of urban design strategy, the classic grand design (the Prince of Wales's School) and the organic small area design (the Tibbalds' School) (figure 13.20) turn up again and again. For example, in the competition for the new Conference Centre complex at Lothian Road, Edinburgh, only one entry was based on the notion of organic development; the other three entries, including the winning one by Terry Farrell and Co., were based on the grand design. The reasons given for the adoption of this approach include the single real-estate interest, the funding requirements to attract greater commercial and financial patronage, and Edinburgh District Council's desire to regain some of the City's past architectural and town planning glory (*Hornung, 1989*).

One of the greatest missed opportunities for urban design strategies was the London Docklands. In contrast to the classical design battles, the London Docklands Development Corporation Zone was developed with a great variety of contemporary architecture in Modernist, Post-Modernist and High-Tech styles. Canary Wharf, set in the Enterprise Zone section of the Urban Development Area, became the showpiece of the London Docklands. One of the biggest developments in Europe, built by Olympia Yorke, it is characterised by bulk and transatlantic character. The vast complex of offices and shops is dominated by the 850-ft office tower designed by Caser Pelli as the fourth tallest commercial building in Europe. The development is controversial for dramatically changing the famous views from Greenwich Park, and creating a mini-Manhattan skyline characterised by weighty neo-Edwardian and Art Deco-style office palazzi, surrounding a plaza twice the size of Trafalgar Square.

An urban design study (1982) was made for the LDDC by David Gosling with Edward Hollamby. The principal urban design approach was based on the so-called Greenwich Axis, between the view of Wren's Greenwich Hospital and Inigo Jones's Queen's Hall at the tip of the peninsula, Island Gardens and the same view from Canary Wharf. This invisible line was to provide the reference point for all the development on the Isle of Dogs (*Gosling, 1988*). The final plan adopted by the LDDC for development purposes was a pragmatic one, with little suggestion of any urban design. The only strong visual framework was the retention of the existing dock basis (*Moughtin, 1992*). The Docklands was a missed urban design opportunity.

In the City is the Broadgate development, a scheme in 14 phases of offices, shops and other commercial activities, an excellent example of city architecture (figure 13.21). The first four stages were by Ove Arup Associates and the later phases by Skidmore, Owings and Merrill, chosen for their unrivalled experience in

Figure 13.21   Broadgate, London (by the author)

putting up steel-framed buildings to very tight schedules. Broadgate is one of the better versions of urban design, great fun and people-friendly with its popular ice rink.

In the rest of Britain, urban regeneration schemes produce some of the most innovative urban design results. Glasgow has transformed many of its grim parts, and was recently European City of Culture. It has rebuilt the area around its cathedral, developed the shopping galleries of Princes Centre and revitalised the old Merchant City. Here the organic approach was adopted, revitalising the old buildings of the eighteenth and nineteenth century quarter, converting them into either middle-income housing or the Italian Centre of high-quality shops like Versace.

Other cities like Newcastle, Sheffield, Leeds, Hull and Swansea have urban design schemes in the pipeline (*Colquhoun, 1995*). Cardiff has produced the most controversial scheme, centred on the regeneration of the former docks and industrial land around Cardiff Bay. The scheme by Llewellyn-Davies depends on the construction of a barrage across the entrance to the bay to create a freshwater lake which was opposed by the nature conservationists concerned about the impact on marine life. The scheme includes 6000 new houses, the refurbishment of 2000 existing dwellings in the bay area, two million square feet of new office space, and industrial improvement policies for the existing industry (*Colquhoun, 1995*). The new public buildings include a Maritime Centre and the jewel, the new Welsh National Opera House. The scheme's proposals for a grandiose ceremonial mall, connecting the city centre to the waterfront, are matched by its support of a beautiful new State Opera House. The brilliant design by Saha Hadid was so controversial in its extremely beautiful and innovative flying form that Cardiff Bay Development Corporation applauded it, rejected it and accepted it several times over. If built, it should have the same breathtaking visual qualities as Sydney Opera House. The 'barrage' on which so much of the scheme depends had yet, by 1995, to be assured; it was supported by the Welsh Office as part of the grandiose scheme but less supported by Cardiff City Council (*Imrie and Thomas, 1993*).

Birmingham has taken the grand design approach to promoting city centre change, and created Centenary Square and Centenary Way with the International Convention Centre as the business tourism flagship project, in much the same manner as Edinburgh's Convention Centre scheme. Birmingham's inner ring road has been downgraded and a Victorian square has been designed as a major public space (figure 13.22) (*Colquhoun, 1995*).

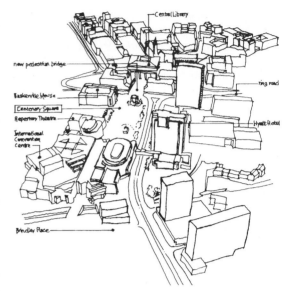

Figure 13.22 Centenary Square, Birmingham (after *Architect's Journal, 1992*)

Summary

Grand urban design strategy faded away in the 1970s as urban designers created pedestrianised spaces in town centres. In the 1980s several major urban design battles, initiated by Prince Charles, brought urban design once again to the public's attention. Based on the particular architectural styles being promoted, urban design strategy see-sawed between the organic approach pedestrianising spaces and vernacular architecture over the grand design approach shared (curiously) by the Classicists, the Post-Modernists and the High-Tech advocates.

Design guides took an increasingly important role as planners and the Environment Minister strove to give leadership in urban design. The debate gave rise to lists of urban design principles, again dependent on which philosophical camp the developers, planners or architects promoted. Thus the exercise of design and aesthetic control became a source of conflict between planners and architects which in the mid-1990s still continues (*Hubbard, 1994*). Confusion in architectural style also reigned. One can choose from Neo-Modernist, Neo-Classical, Neo-Vernacular, High-Tech or Post-Modernist styles. Depending upon one's point of view, the Prince of Wales either helped or hindered the progress of British architecture and urban design, but more importantly Prince Charles made architecture and urban design the subject of intense public interest by responding to the large building activity which is being generated in most British cities.

Many buildings and urban design projects flourished. London particularly became one vast building site – Canary Wharf, Broadgate, London Bridge City. The new developments were bigger and more sophisticated and, most importantly, more money was being spent on them. They replaced the commercial buildings of the 1960s and 1970s. Elsewhere urban regeneration schemes were a major factor in accomplishing urban design schemes. In the mid-1990s, many such schemes, as in Birmingham, and Cardiff, were well on their way to completion.

14 The countryside and the environment

The National Parks and Access to the Countryside Act, 1949

Early countryside policies focused primarily on the National Parks. Although Britain had a long history of voluntary bodies interested in rural green spaces, such as the Commons, Open Spaces and Footpaths Preservation Society and the separate Councils for the Protection of Rural England and Scotland, it did not have National Parks such as had been established in the nineteenth century in the United States, Canada, and later in Europe. The impetus for designating National Parks originated in the Town and Country Planning Act of 1931, and was followed by the Addison committee on the creation of National Parks, whose report (*Addison Report, 1931*) first put conservation, recreation and National Parks on the political agenda. Its recommendations were rejected. The 1930s were as discouraging for countryside conservation and access as they were for comprehensive land-use planning (chapter 3).

Britain was late in creating its National Parks and the present system came out of the new legislation after the Second World War. The Scott Committee on Land Utilisation in Rural Areas reported favourably on the establishment of National Parks (*Scott Report, 1942*) while the White Paper entitled *Control of Land Use* included the preservation of land in National Parks as one of its aims (*MTCP, 1944*).

Legislation was preceded by the John Dower Report, entitled *National Parks in England and Wales* (*MTCP, 1945*). Dower proposed a hybrid form of National Park, in which:

(1) the characteristic landscape beauty is preserved;
(2) access and facilities for public open-air enjoyment are amply provided;
(3) wildlife and buildings and places of architectural

and historic interest are suitably protected, while
(4) established farming is effectively maintained;
(5) rights of way are created and maintained; and
(6) long-distance routes are to be set up and managed.

The hybrid aspect was the retention of effective farming within the boundaries of a National Park. The definition of what could be termed effective was extremely loose and, as the farmers were the major landowners within a National Park, they had alternative and potentially conflicting aims. In addition, the government's statutory undertakers were free to develop the National Parks without having to seek planning permission.

Although the Dower Report saw a unity between nature conservation, landscape conservation, recreation and access to the countryside, the subsequent Hobhouse Committee on National Parks separated wildlife conservation, which resulted in the creation of a separate Nature Conservancy to establish nature reserves (*MTCP, 1947a*).

The National Parks and Access to the Countryside Act 1949 proposed National Parks, of which ten were designated between 1951 and 1957, covering an area of about 13,500 sq. km in England and Wales. The first long-distance route, the Pennine Way, was also established. Other long-distance routes and Areas of Outstanding Natural Beauty were designated after the parks had been established.

Areas of Outstanding Natural Beauty (AONBs) are areas where the landscape is of such beauty and quality as to be of national significance but which are not suitable for designation as National Parks because they do not have sufficient open country suitable for recreation. These areas have not, until recently, required special management as in the case of a National Park, but their beauty and contribution to the enjoyment of the countryside by the public needed to be protected. There are over 38 AONBs covering some 20,000 square kilometres, or over 13 percent of the total land area of England and Wales.

The responsibility for the English National Parks was given to the local authorities and not to the National Parks Commission as proposed in the Dower Report. The National Parks Commission was advisory in nature from 1949 until its incorporation into the Countryside Commission in 1968. Each park has its own planning committee or joint board but was under the control of its local County Council, except for the Peak District and the Lake District. When a park lay astride two local authorities, a joint planning board was to be set up, but in the end only two joint planning boards were established, one for the Peak District and another for the Lake District.

The English National Parks consist mostly of privately owned land, unlike National Parks in other nations, which are nationally owned. Ninety-nine percent of land in Britain is privately owned and the National Parks are no exception. The planning boards have proved to be little better than the special county council committees. Both local authorities and

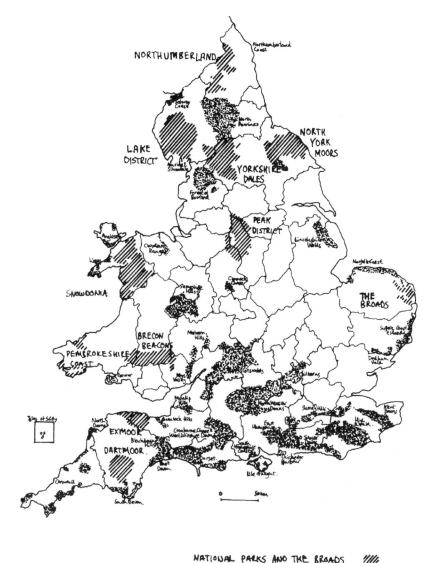

Figure 14.1   National Parks and Areas of Outstanding Natural Beauty (after PPG7)

planning boards have allowed a steady 'drip-drip' of development applications over the past 40 years, such that the National Parks have been saddled with more and more extraneous land uses. The English National Parks have also seen some destruction of much of the vernacular architecture within their boundaries in the 30–40 years since they were designated (*MacEwen and MacEwen, 1987*).

No National Parks were designated in Scotland, as Scotland did not accept the need for National Parks with its traditional attitude of the rights of clan members to have access to all of Scotland. Until 1995, there was no criminal trespass law in Scotland as in England and Wales, and traditionally the people of Scotland have enjoyed their land as a public right. Europeans now consider Scotland to contain some of the last wilderness areas of Europe, which has greatly altered the debate.

Two new National Parks were added to the original ten in England and Wales, in addition to the Norfolk Broads Authority (in 1988) and the New Forest, an ancient woodland. Conservationists hope that three further National Parks will be designated to protect other beautiful areas in England and Wales, such as the South Downs, the North Pennines and the Cambrian Mountains. The government, in the early 1990s, accepted that each of the English National Parks should have its own independent National Park authority, thus removing them from their county councils, which are often faced with conflicts of interest, e.g. their road-building programmes.

The Countryside Acts, 1967 and 1968

The White Paper *Leisure in the Countryside* promoted the concept that the National Parks were insufficient and that urban dwellers increasingly needed a hierarchy of parks in the countryside to serve their ever-expanding interests (*MHLG, 1966*). It proposed regional and country parks specifically for the town dweller to get out of the city without having to travel too far and be able to enjoy the countryside. Thus two more encompassing acts appeared. First came the Countryside (Scotland) Act 1967, and then the Countryside Act for England and Wales 1968, which imposed on every public body a duty to have regard to the desirability of conserving the natural beauty and amenity of the countryside.

Both the Scottish and the English Countryside Acts established Countryside Commissions, which took over the functions of the National Parks Commission. The Countryside (Scotland) Act 1967 came first because of its lack of National Parks, coupled with the increasing recreation pressures, particularly in areas like the Cairngorms and Glencoe, and provided for Country Parks of a maximum size of 400 hectares. The Countryside Commissions of England and Scotland provided for Country Parks, such that by 1990 there were over 250 Country Parks in Britain. The Countryside Commission also became responsible for Areas of Outstanding Natural Beauty. Areas of Great (or High) Landscape Value became a further designation used by local planning authorities in their development plans. Planning policy statements usually state that in these areas the design and siting of buildings is the subject of especially careful control, and where development would be harmful to amenities it is normally refused, but in many cases the areas still suffer, almost as much as if they were not designated, from the vagaries of design control.

The best of the British countryside is covered by National Parks, Areas of Outstanding Natural Beauty and/or Areas of Great Landscape Value. Their relative importance, in that order, is reflected in the amount of public money made available to local authorities for the improvement of each, and by the strictness of planning control, which varies correspondingly.

Altogether these areas make a formidable impression. But there is great danger that this may give a false sense of security: these areas may be better protected on paper than in reality. For instance all of them are liable to be subordinated to the national interest when threatened by major developments such as motorways, mining, power transmission and reservoirs. They are also still subject to minor developments like chalet-type houses built without regard to the local character of villages. Local planning authorities usually warn developers in written statements forming part of their development plans that in those areas high standards in both the siting and design of development are expected, and that planning consent will be refused for development which is harmful to amenities. Some local authorities more usefully issue guides to developers, e.g. in regard to the use of artificial stone as a building material in the Cotswolds' Area of Outstanding Natural Beauty.

Heritage coasts were highlighted by the Countryside Commission in its report *The Planning of the Coastline and Coastal Heritage* (*DoE, 1970*) which argued for the protection of Britain's coastline. Although the report requested yet another special commission to look after 'heritage coasts', the government rejected this and simply allowed the Countryside Commission to designate beautiful stretches of coastline as 'heritage coasts' and then asked the local authorities to incorporate appropriate policies in their Structure and

Local Plans after consultation with the Countryside Commission. About a third of the coastline of England and Wales is included in National Parks and AONBs. Scotland, with its national guidelines, was able to promote a National Guideline on Coastal Areas for the local authorities to follow after consultation with the Scottish Countryside Commission.

The Nature Conservancy and the Wildlife and Countryside Act, 1981

The Nature Conservancy protected nature for scientific purposes and provided research into animal, vegetable and mineral matters. Nature centres for the purpose of nature conservation are actually a bolder concept than the English interpretation of National Parks. Traditionally the English National Parks have not included special wildlife sanctuaries as in foreign National Parks, for the reason that the public needed complete access, although the need to protect wildlife has always been a primary aim of English National Parks. Thus it was felt necessary to set up National Nature Reserves and Sites of Special Scientific Interest. The Nature Conservancy (later renamed the Nature Conservancy Council) was also set up in 1949 at the same time as the National Parks Commission.

Unlike the National Parks Commission, which was not allowed to acquire land and therefore remained an advisory body (the county councils did not wish to give up power to the National Parks), the Nature Conservancy could acquire land and employ wardens and estate staff. It established National Nature Reserves (NNRs), while local authorities could establish Local Nature Reserves (LNRs) but not necessarily with any right of public access. Alternatively the Nature Conservancy entered into agreements with private landowners to establish a nature reserve. In these cases the owner continued to manage the land but on the advice of the Conservancy. Although it was the policy of the latter to allow as much access by the public as the site could bear, only 50 percent of Nature Reserves are open to the public.

The National Parks and Access to the Countryside Act 1949 also introduced the concept of Sites of Special Scientific Interest (SSSIs), important for their flora and fauna, geological or physiographical (landform) features. Sites of Special Scientific Interest are generally quite small in scale. The Nature Conservancy established and managed Nature Reserves, gave scientific advice and pursued research. During the decade of the 1980s, it became increasingly clear that many functions of the Countryside Commission overlapped with those of the Nature Conservancy. There developed a dispute between those who wished to save the countryside for nature and restrict public access, and those who wished public access increased and new facilities provided. Over the decade these disputes took different directions.

By the end of the 1970s, a gap had opened between the assumptions of the 1967 and 1968 Acts and the reality. The predicted growth in population had not occurred, and economic growth had waned. The rise in recreation demand upon the countryside had levelled off, but the growth in leisure time had occurred, partly from the enforced leisure of unemployment. Instead public concern over conservation grew to a huge extent, thus producing new conservation legislation, the Wildlife and Countryside Act 1981, which amongst other things required county planning authorities in National Park areas to identify, by map, areas of moor or heath where beauty was particularly important to preserve. Agricultural grants were modified.

The main dispute after 1981 came over who was to preserve the countryside, whether there should be permanent statutory controls on farming and forestry operations or whether the nation was to rely on the voluntary care of local farmers and landowners. Showing unusual political prescience, the voluntary method was chosen, as several years later Britain was deeply embroiled in agricultural battles within the European Union which were to totally change the situation.

Focusing attention on the countryside

Until the Industrial Revolution, Britain had slowly evolved towards a mature agricultural rural pattern, and the steady drift of labour from the countryside into the manufacturing towns meant an ever-increasing urban population which required an improved communication network, consolidated farmland and the operation of more intensive agricultural techniques.

These requirements transformed the countryside until, by the early twentieth century, Britain had a sophisticated communications network which extended into all the remote rural areas. By the beginning of the Second World War all but the most isolated farms and Highland crofts were part of commercial farming.

The constant depletion of Britain's forests throughout the centuries had created a serious timber shortage by the beginning of the twentieth century, so in 1919 the Forestry Commission was established and it has been planting trees ever since. But despite its work, by 1939 Britain was still only producing less than 4 percent of home timber consumption.

The Land Utilisation Survey, established in 1930, showed that for the first 40 years of the twentieth century, Britain had had a natural balance of arable farming in the lowlands, and grazing and forestry on higher ground. But then, both forestry and low-density suburban sprawl forged their way into the countryside and as a consequence good agricultural land began to be lost.

After the Second World War, increasing demands for food produced by a decreasing rural workforce encouraged larger and more intensive labour-saving agricultural techniques. Livestock also became intensively reared under indoor conditions and, in some cases, in factory units. Therefore the familiar traditional landscape gave way to larger-scale field patterns and larger agricultural buildings.

In the late 1980s, agricultural policy changed. A long period of sustained agricultural expansion based on land improvement and the replacement of labour by technology came abruptly to a halt due to the new European policies. The problem of food surpluses in the EC and the many ensuing political crises meant that Britain had to curb its food output, whilst enabling farm businesses to remain viable. The consequences of the EC-imposed quota squeeze forced many over-capitalised and/or heavily indebted farmers either into liquidation or into adopting alternative sources of income. Diversification has meant reducing the traditional farming operations and either selling land for development or forestry and/or offering a wider range of rural opportunities. Thus diversification has forced a wider mix of land uses, changes in the traditional landscape and the acceptance of a non-rural population, often commuter types, not connected with the land.

The rise of the continental European market and the dominance of the continental European farmers exacerbated the problems of farming, and less farmland is now needed. The decline in the need for agricultural produce reached such an extent that, in the late 1980s, the European Union and Britain initiated a programme where farmers were paid not to farm some of their land. Handsome grants are paid to farmers to 'set aside' land. The changing priorities of the Common Agricultural Programme (CAP) required an increasing amount of land to be 'set aside'. Farmers and landowners may be tempted eventually to give up set-aside grants in favour of small urban settlements, for the urban dwellers who want to live amongst rural surroundings. Some rural counties are under constant pressure for settlements of 25 houses here and 50 houses there, requiring a firm positive planning policy concerning the 'agro-urban' community.

Forestry, on the other hand, expanded, with the aid of generous government grants and tax concessions. Widespread planting took place, particularly concentrating in the private sector. Sections of the Forestry Commission were privatised by the Conservative government, but the increased scale of planting continued.

Changing policies in the countryside

Normal activity in the countryside became less and less important and farmers had to find alternative uses. This inevitably led to development and the need for development planning. At the same time a strong conservation lobby composed of amenity conservationists desired to retain the traditional farm landscape. The government encouraged alternative uses on the one hand, and yet provided grants, for example, for traditional farming such as conserving hedgerows throughout Britain.

The focus for agriculture in the 1990s is for diversification. But for many farmers there are many difficulties including severe financial strictures, a high proportion of tenancies (particularly in Scotland and Wales), environmental controls, restrictive planning policies (e.g. towards caravan sites and farm building conversions) and the lack of demand for recreational and tourist facilities away from prime routes. These factors limit the possibilities for change, particularly in the remoter areas and in most of the countryside with the exception of South East England. The many dilemmas have brought about the necessity for comprehensive rural planning in order to sort out the conflicting demands. In the hills, integration of farming, leisure needs and forestry activities helps to avert depopulation and provides a more prosperous and acceptable way of life for those who wish to remain in the upland areas of Britain. There agriculture had been under pressure in the last 20 years to open land for leisure activities, which farmers have been disinclined to do.

Problems exist for rural communities. Changing economies of scale in retailing, postal services and health care provision have caused a decline in services available to rural communities. Deregulation of bus services has not helped. Poor housing was more prevalent in rural areas, although rural housing associations have attempted to address this problem. Keeping affordable accommodation for the local population out of the hands of the more affluent commuter population has been another problem. The need to regenerate the rural economy in the face of agricultural unemployment has become another acute

THE EXTENT OF PROPOSED ESA IS
ILLUSTRATIVE.

EXISTING ESA

PROPOSED ESA

Figure 14.2   Existing and proposed Environmentally
Sensitive Areas (after PPG7)

need. The promotion of tourism and such leisure
activities as skiing has been encouraged by the locals
and has often raised the fury of the conservationists.

A new type of area designation, known as
Environmentally Sensitive Areas (ESAs), was created
by the Ministry of Agriculture as areas where the
wildlife and landscape are of special importance and
are particularly vulnerable to change arising from
agricultural intensification. Some are in National Parks
and AONBs. The main difference between ESAs and
other designated areas is that their special qualities are
protected through incentive payments to farmers for
the maintenance of traditional farming practices, and
hence ESAs are popular. Some 19 ESAs in England
and Wales were designated by 1990, covering 7900
square kilometres or 3.5 percent of all agricultural
land. Farmers may fulfil different functions in each
area: for example, restriction on fertiliser and pesticide
use may be combined with a requirement for hedges
and ditches to be managed.

Concern for the environment leading to a reappraisal of environmental policy

Contemporary town planning in Britain began with the
Public Health Act of 1848. Britain can boast of the

world's first national public pollution control agency:
the Alkali Inspectorate, established by the Alkali Act
of 1863 to control atmospheric emissions from the
caustic soda industry. Water pollution control followed
in the Rivers Pollution Prevention Act of 1876,
although it was virtually unenforceable.

It was not until the publication of the influential
World Conservation Strategy by the International
Union for the Conservation of Nature (IUCN, 1980)
that the British government began to recognise
formally the need for a wide-ranging national response
to global resource questions in order to achieve
sustainable global development. The World
Conservation Strategy advocated that conservation
should not be viewed as a constraint, but as a help to
development, in which case the objectives of
conservation and economic development become
equally important. However, progress towards a
revised national environmental framework for
development planning was slow.

The IUCN *World Conservation Strategy* was
followed by the report *The Conservation and
Development Programme for the UK*. The public
concern was at a level not foreseen in the 1970s. This
report, prepared jointly by government agencies and
the voluntary sector, identified the need for extensive
action in order to move towards a more resourceful and
sustainable Britain in line with the broad international
framework set out in the *World Conservation Strategy*.
Among the many recommendations was a proposal
that central government should revise the development
plan machinery to take account of global resource
issues, including energy questions. The report also
emphasised the adverse global effects of current
patterns of urban living and the need for better
resource management in cities, of particular relevance
to metropolitan planning. For longer-term
developments, *The Conservation and Development
Programme for the UK* advocated getting the balance
right between the forces of economic development and
the objectives of conservation.

Government policy during the 1980s emphasised
economic development and growth, with environmental concerns being secondary considerations. The
conceptual gulf between the two views was enormous,
particularly in relation to agricultural policies which
were now decided in Brussels. Both Whitehall and
Brussels needed to accept that financial and other
support given to agriculture should be made to work
for conservation rather than against it.

In 1983 the Secretary-General of the United Nations
asked Norway's Prime Minister, Mrs Brundtland, to
set up an independent commission to look at the

planet's rapidly growing population and how it was to meet its need. The Brundtland Commission published *Our Common Future* (1981) which set out an agenda for change focusing on three objectives:

(1) to re-examine the critical environment and development issues and to formulate realistic proposals for dealing with them;
(2) to propose new forms of international cooperation on the environment; and
(3) to raise the level of understanding of individuals, organisations and governments.

Our Common Future produced some core concepts including the famous definition of sustainable development (*Brundtland Commission, 1981: 43*):

'Sustainable development is development that meets the needs of the present without compromising the ability of future generations to meet their own needs.'

The objectives for sustainable development included:

(1) revising growth
(2) changing the quality of growth
(3) meeting essential needs for jobs, food, energy, water and sanitation
(4) conserving and enhancing the resource base
(5) reorienting technology and managing risk
(6) merging environment and economics in decision-making.

The Brundtland definition of sustainability gained widespread acceptance, but the proponents of sustainability fell into two broad groups. One group advocated economic growth, made much more environmentally sensitive, in order to raise living standards globally and break the links between poverty and economic degradation. The other group desired radical changes in economic organisation, producing much lower rates of growth or even zero or negative growth. The British government seemed to accept the principle of the need for a new era of economic growth and the integration of environment and development, and publicly rejected the philosophy of zero growth. However, it has, in fact, followed a pattern of 'low growth', thereby tacitly accepting the low-growth argument.

Growing public opposition to the economic approach was followed by a shift in government policy, marked by the publication of the White Paper *This Common Inheritance, Britain's Environmental Strategy* (*DoE, 1990b*) setting out proposals for future legislation and changes in government guidance. It reviewed the situation as of 1990, outlined the government's commitment to environmental

stewardship and the concept of sustainable development. The paper set out wide-ranging proposals indicating future government action, including a commitment to a review of the British planning system to ensure that it properly reflected the new environmental priorities.

After dealing with environmental standards and regulations common to Europe and internationally, particularly with regard to global warming and pollution controls, the White Paper focused on land use, countryside and wildlife. The 1990s planning system, in the government's words, is a 'slimmer, more flexible system, responsive to real strategic issues'. The paper proposed the following:

1 Central government responsibility for national and regional guidance through National Planning Policy Guidelines and Regional Guidelines. It proposed to issue National Planning Policy Guidelines on wildlife, pollution control, waste management and noise, and revised guidance on planning agreements.
2 Urban policies to encourage regeneration in the inner cities and the reuse of urban land.
3 A simplified development plan system.
4 Updating the Use Classes Orders that control development, in particular (a) seeing that local authorities exercise control over siting, design and external appearance of agricultural buildings, (b) protecting hedgerows, and (c) strengthening Tree Preservation Orders.

The White Paper stipulated that planning decisions strike a balance between the use of land for economic development and meeting local needs for green spaces. Many local authorities had been tempted by developers offering large sums for under-used playing fields. To stop this practice the government issued a Planning Policy Guidance Note on sport and recreation to make certain that local authorities addressed local needs for recreation and open space, protected valuable sites and identified suitable sites for additional provision, particularly in urban regeneration schemes; recreation land was also to be used for wider community uses.

As to transport, the government continued to rely on building by-passes as the most effective method of improving the urban environment by redirecting traffic and particularly heavy traffic to more suitable routes. Traffic management schemes were also to be promoted. But other than these proposals, *This Common Inheritance* is exceptionally weak on proposals for either improving public transport or making hard decisions about vehicular traffic.

The government advocated that environmental improvement should continue to be tackled through specific urban initiatives. In England and Wales these have sometimes taken the form of Groundwork Trusts. Like the urban fringe initiatives in Scotland, they bring together public agencies, private enterprise and voluntary effort to achieve a wide range of environmental improvements. The government supported the Groundwork Trusts' administrative expenses, but for their project funding they had to find finance from other sources. Twenty-eight Trusts exist, especially in the North of England, and the Groundwork Foundation hopes to expand the network to reach 50 Trusts by the mid-1990s.

In agriculture, the White Paper introduced general environmental policies that encouraged the development of organic farming, and introduced schemes to help farmers protect or improve the countryside through the Farmland Conservation Grant Scheme. The Farm Woodland Scheme hoped to achieve 33,000 hectares per year of traditional planting. The paper also advocated Community Forests, which are new forests on fringes of major towns for commercial forestry, improving the landscape, wildlife and recreation.

The government set up the Rural Development Commission to concentrate in rural areas of greatest 'need', to give advice and financial and technical help to rural enterprise. Twenty-seven Rural Development Areas existed by 1994, covering 35 percent of England. The Farm Diversification Grant Scheme helped with diversification for farm trails, landscape conservation and improvement, footpaths, and expansion of the Groundwork movement.

The paper made new provision for National Parks, Areas of Outstanding Natural Beauty and Environmentally Sensitive Areas, and promised to review the case for National Parks and other ways of managing Scotland's mountain areas, such as Natural Heritage Areas. But in terms of wildlife the White Paper did not propose much, as so much was already underway.

The legislative result of the White Paper was the Environmental Protection Act (EPA) of 1990, which brought together and improved upon the environmental controls contained in the Control of Pollution Act 1974 (now superseded) and the Water Act 1989, and also brought in new measures. The 1990 EPA was a framework within which can be placed new regulations as time goes on, which allows for flexibility and for the results of new research to be quickly incorporated. The EPA established two separate systems for pollution control:

1 Integrated Pollution Control (IPC), administered by Her Majesty's Inspectorate of Pollution (HMIP)
2 Air Pollution Control, (APC), run by the local authority environmental health department.

There has been some concern that these controls are coming into existence too fast for the ability of the British economy to absorb them. Integrated pollution control was introduced for new processes and large combustion plants in 1991. For other existing processes, integrated pollution control was introduced over a five-year period ending in 1996. At the same time, some 200 guidance papers for inspectors and industries were prepared on how to implement the legislation.

The Environmental Protection Act administers control of industrial pollution, but the control of pollution from domestic chimneys remains under the local authorities, which create smoke control zones (a great success), where only certain fuels may be burned. This kind of air pollution is controlled by the Clean Air Acts of 1956 and 1968, which also control the height of chimneys. Over 70 percent of Britain's emission of sulphur dioxide comes from power stations. Pressured by the EC Directive on Discharges from Large Combustion Plants, Britain agreed to cut emissions of sulphur in a phased programme over a 15-year period. International difficulties occurred as early as the 1950s, when the Scandinavian countries complained about the 'export' of Britain's production of sulphur dioxide and acid rain.

Some environmental issues relating to atmospheric pollution such as global warming are so large that they require proper international cooperation. In Montreal in 1987, the agreement to control substances which deplete the ozone layer was accepted. Unfortunately as the ozone layer worsened, tougher measures were introduced in 1990.

The 'consumer economy', producing a 'consumer boom' since the Second World War, has caused a tremendous increase in the volume of waste as goods are marketed in plastic packaging, drinks are sold in aluminium cans and plastic bottles, and items of all kinds are packaged in other less easily disposable materials. The concept of built-in obsolescence has led to an ever-increasing demand to replace disposable consumer goods with new disposable goods. Most of the waste disposed of in Britain is deposited in large holes in the ground, such as old quarries. But these can become dangerous as the substances break down, producing contaminating liquids or gas.

The disposal of waste was not seen as a problem until the 1970s, when the public became concerned over hazardous waste, leading to the Deposit of Poisonous Wastes Act in 1972, followed by the Control of Pollution Act in 1974. Unusually Britain, which trailed behind in all other aspects of environmental control, led the way in the world in terms of waste management.

The disposal of waste is dealt with at the strategic level and incorporated within the Structure Plan. In the Local Plan, specific sites are nominated for 'the disposal, storage or treatment of waste'. In the 1990 Town and Country Planning Act, local authorities may prepare subject plans on waste treatment. Since few local authorities wanted to do this, the waste local plan became compulsory in the later Planning and Compensation Act 1991. The EPA introduced a new extended system of waste management licences, i.e. a licence for each stage of the process rather than the final disposal. Licences are required for (1) the treatment of waste and (2) keeping or disposal of controlled waste on land or by mobile plant.

The Environmental Protection Act included a new duty on district councils to compile registers of contaminated land (subsequently cancelled). The government, on the basis of the 'polluter pays' principle, stated that those causing contamination and dereliction should pay for the cost of putting it right. However, in historic cases the government's Derelict Land Grant can provide funds. New priorities were urged.

The 1995 Environment Bill is the most important piece of environmental legislation since the Environmental Protection Act in 1990. Two new agencies have been created: the Environment Agency for England and Wales, and the Scottish Environment Protection Agency (SEPA), both of which replace the National Rivers Authority and Her Majesty's Inspectorate of Pollution. They also assume local authority responsibilities on waste. The Act contains new measures on minerals, Conservation Areas (including a number of changes to the National Parks system), air quality and contaminated land.

Sixteen new sections on contaminated land are added to the 1990 Environmental Protection Act, while the EPA land registers are repealed. As development is the principal means for cleaning up land, this means that contaminated land need only be restored to a safety level in keeping with its intended use, rather than restored to its original condition. A new principle has been inserted, that of 'suitable for use' rather than the 'polluter pays' principle. Thus under the 'suitable for use' principle, land is unlikely to be restored until it is needed, in which case the polluter may have disappeared and the public will have to pay for restoration.

The planning functions of the Wildlife and Countryside Act 1981 are extended to the National Parks authorities. Another clause promotes 'quiet enjoyment and understanding' in the National Parks, as against power-boating and off-road driving which, although not banned, are to be discouraged. Local authorities have greater powers to control air quality, with national standards on the most serious pollutants, the creation of Air Quality Management Areas and a 20-point action plan on transport. Likewise mineral operations are more carefully controlled.

The European Union and the environment

The European Union is a major and increasing source of British environmental protection law, and plays a role in Britain in the following ways:

1 Some EU legislation lays down rules and standards that are directly enforceable in Member States without any need for further implementation. In these cases, EU law is British law, but such instances are rare in the environmental field.

2 Other EU legislation is addressed to Member States and requires changes in British law or administrative practice. This is the most frequent situation with environmental legislation, particularly in the use of Directives (which are not directly effective within the Member States). In these cases, British law is not necessarily the same as EU law until the EU law has been implemented. It is the domestic British law, arising from the EU requirement, which is the law and must be applied in practice. Many times, EU law and British law will differ as EU law frequently consists of aims and goals rather than precise rules and allows some discretion for Member States in the implementation and in the timing.

3 The EU has an environmental policy and the general economic and environmental principles which underpin it have an important influence on British policy-making. It is in this context that there has been so much controversy between the wider European attitudes and some of the ingrained British ideas.

One of the most important EU Directives was the EEC Directive 85/337 on Environmental Assessment. Environmental Assessment (EA) is the name given to the whole process of gathering information about a project, its possible and probable effects and the analysis of the data obtained from all sources. For all projects the developer is responsible for preparing the whole Environmental Assessment.

Directive 85/337 required that certain major projects are subject to an Environmental Assessment before permission is granted for them. Accordingly, developers have to consider the environmental impact of their projects as part of the planning process. Environmental Assessment is now placed within British primary legislation, that of the Planning and Compensation Act 1991, which gives the government the power to draw on a number of project categories which seem to have fallen through the net (waste transfer stations, sludge incinerators, golf courses). In conclusion, EA is still experiencing teething problems. The government appears to be unenthusiastic about the benefits of EA, so although the government can expand the number of projects under EA, it probably will not.

The policy that 'the polluter pays' is unpopular with Britain, which contributes pollution to the air and sea but is not on the receiving end of any other polluter! Britain is now suffering many claims from European countries which have suffered UK pollution.

When the Directive was first formulated, UK legislators argued that the UK planning system already took into account all the environmental factors listed in the Directive and that there was no need for further controls. The other Europeans would not accept this. Nevertheless the UK placed the main environmental procedures within the Town and Country Planning System, implemented by Regulations: Town and Country Planning (Assessment of Environmental Effects) Regulations 1988 SI 1988/1199.

Therefore an Environmental Statement, which is the formal conclusion of an Environmental Assessment, forms part of the normal application for planning permission. With the exception of the Directive 85/337 on Environmental Impact Assessment, the EU has had little impact on the town and country planning system in Britain.

The countryside in the 1990s

The 1990s have brought unforeseen changes to the countryside and to the emphasis of planning efforts, particularly in the need for rural planning and the environmental controls required to ensure sustainable development. Indeed, the need for environmental planning is giving the planning profession a new lease of life and a new crusade, prompted by the ever-increasing environmental protection directives emanating from the European Union. From the continental point of view, Britain is considered 'the dirty man of Europe', resulting from the legacy of its early Industrial Revolution and its lethargy in rehabilitating the damaged areas. The changes in the countryside will be less dramatic but are also driven by European Union concerns and agricultural protectionism. As we approach the twenty-first century, there is plenty to accomplish in the planning world.

15 Transformations in planning into the twenty-first century

Conservative consolidation: the Town and Country Planning Acts, 1990

In 1990, the Conservative government produced three planning Acts, which together are defined as 'The Planning Acts' (T & CP Act S. 336(1)) for England and Wales, and which consolidated all previous planning Acts since 1971 (Town and Country Planning Act 1971, Local Government and Land Act 1980, and Housing and Planning Act 1986). The three Acts were the Town and Country Planning Act, 1990, the Planning (Listed Buildings and Conservation Areas) Act 1990, and the Planning (Hazardous Substances) Act 1990. Scotland, to its dismay, was left with the Town and Country Planning Act 1972. The Listed Buildings and Conservation Areas Act separated the policy for heritage from the mainstream planning Act. A Department of National Heritage was created in 1992, taking practically all of the historic conservation policy work from the Department of the Environment. Even with the consolidated 1990 Acts, the bulk of inner city policy and the environmental planning powers remained separate from the planning system. The Hazardous Substances Act covered those areas of health and safety risks in industrial planning, which had been left uncovered with the deregulation of the planning system's set of controls. A Planning (Consequential Provisions) Act 1990 dealt with legislative matters.

A further consolidating Act was the Planning and Compensation Act 1991, which gave legal authority for the new streamlined Structure Plans and district-wide Local Plans, and revised enforcement procedures and miscellaneous items. It restored the provisions of the plans in the determination of planning applications, and indicated a retreat from the Thatcherite philosophy contained in the 1985 White Paper *Lifting the Burden*

(*Ward, 1994: 221–222*). Development was stated to be 'plan-led' as much to give greater certainty to developers, and thereby help to reduce the number of planning appeals, as it was to reinforce planning policy.

Local government reform; unitary development plans

In an attempt to simplify the planning system further, local planning authorities were placed into a new unitary local government structure in Wales, under the Local Government (Wales) Act 1994, and a partial unitary system in England, under the Local Government Act 1992. Some counties retained their two-tier structure, while Scotland did not have its two-tier local government structure dismantled and replaced by a unitary system until April 1996.

For the metropolitan areas in England outside London, the metropolitan district council is both the local planning authority and the minerals planning authority. For the English 'shire' counties (non-metropolitan areas) which would not give up their ancient prerogatives, the function of planning is shared between the county council and the district council, with mineral planning resting in the county. The Conservatives tried hard in the late 1980s to replace the counties and districts with a unitary authority, but the constituents of the shire counties would not countenance it. Structure planning remained the function of county planning authorities with local planning and development control in the districts. The unitary authorities carry out both structure and local planning.

Likewise, an earlier attempt had been made to impose mandatory unitary development plans, replacing the existing Structure and Local Plans (*DoE, 1986*). The White Paper *The Future of*

Development Plans (*DoE, 1989b*) settled the matter. For each metropolitan district, the development plan became a unitary plan – a combination of Structure Plan (Part I) and Local Plan (Part II), coming into operation during 1988–90. Nevertheless considerable protest occurred and the government had to compromise (PPGs 12 and 15) and continue a mix of development plans. Developments therefore are based on various development plans, including the Structure Plan, the Local Plan, the unitary plan, the old-style development plan and special local plans specified in the 1991 Act (i.e. National Park local plans, minerals and waste local plans). The procedure for approval of a unitary plan is modelled on that for Local Plans, such that the approval of the Secretary of State is not required and there is no examination in public unless Part I of the unitary plan is 'called in' by the Secretary of State. The local authority must hold a public inquiry with objections to the plan, which the Secretary of State may modify and 'call in' for his approval.

The Use Classes Order (UCO) was revised again in 1987 to provide greater flexibility and greater mix of land uses by reducing to 16 classes of use the number of land use changes that required planning permission. Particularly, some traditional land and building use distinctions, such as that between 'high-tech' manufacturing and offices, had become so similar that the distinction was out of date. The ending of the distinction between light industrial and office use was the most important of the changes in the 1987 UCO (*Architect's Journal, 1987*). The General Development Order (GDO) was also revised in 1988, mainly introducing freedoms permitted previously. General permission which the GDO grants for a particular class of development can be withdrawn by a direction made by a local authority or the Secretary of State under Article 4 of the GDO. Subsequently various revisions were made (and continue to be made) via statutory instruments issued by the Secretary of State.

Special Development Orders (SDOs) apply to particular areas (Urban Development Corporations, National Parks) or particular types of development (oxide fuel processing plant at Sellafield, sites for nuclear waste disposal) (see chapter 12). The use of SDOs involves 'a high degree of central government involvement in local planning decisions' (*Cullingworth and Nadin, 1994: 83*).

Planning Policy Guidance Notes; Regional Planning Guidance Notes

Planning Policy Guidance Notes became the organ through which the government transmitted its policies

for England and Wales in the 1990s, as government circulars, Development Control Policy notes and other policy statements were mostly superseded by Planning Policy Guidance Notes. Circulars became confined to providing advice on procedures and legislation. Although PPGs are primarily directed at providing advice to local authorities, some PPGs are clearly more directed at the landowner and the developer. The Planning Policy Guidance Notes form one of two series of planning guides: the first on land use, planning and development control; the second on minerals guidance. The first Planning Policy Guidance (1988) was soon replaced in 1992 by PPG1 on General Policy and Principles, based on the Town and Country Planning Act 1990 and rewritten to reflect the changes introduced by the Planning and Compensation Act 1991 and development in policy stemming from the White Paper *This Common Inheritance* (*DoE, 1990b*). The General Policy and Principles PPG was probably the most important of all in that it provided the government's overall philosophy and laid out the essential aspects of the planning system. The aims were specifically noted as protecting and enhancing the environment in town and country, preserving the built and natural heritage, conserving the rural landscape, and maintaining green belts.

Following *This Common Inheritance*, the government insisted that policies must be consistent with sustainable development, in the sense that planning decisions should 'not deny future generations the best of today's environment'. PPG1 states that the planning system should be 'efficient, effective and simple in conception and operation', facilitating needed development and striking a balance between development and conservation. It should operate on the basis that development should be allowed, provided it fits in with the development plan and other material considerations. Further, the purpose of the planning system is to regulate the development and use of land in the public interest and not to protect the private interests of one individual against another.

PPG15, Planning and the Historic Environment, was the only PPG published jointly by the Secretary of State for the Environment and English Heritage. In practice it showed a more comprehensive view of the historic environment with gardens and other historic landscapes being included, and the proper maintenance of historic buildings on all economic (for example tourist) and environmental issues. The latest planning concepts, including sustainable development, the principle that 'the polluter pays', the environmental capacity for change and Environmental Impact Assessment were to be applied to the historic

Table 15.1 Planning Policy Guidance Notes (1995)

PPG 1   General Policy and Principles (1992)
PPG 2   Green Belts (1995)
PPG 3   Housing (1992)
PPG 4   Industrial and Commercial Development and Small Firms (1992)
PPG 5   Simplified Planning Zones (1992)
PPG 6   Town Centres and Retail Developments (1993)
PPG 7   The Countryside and the Rural Economy (1992)
PPG 8   Telecommunications (1992)
PPG 9   Nature Conservation (1994)
PPG 10   Strategic Guidance for the West Midlands (1988)
PPG 11   Strategic Guidance for Merseyside (1988)
PPG 12   Development Plans and Regional Planning Guidance (1994)
PPG 13   Transport (1994)
PPG 14   Development on Unstable Land (1990)
PPG 15   Planning and the Historic Environment (1994)
PPG 16   Archaeology and Planning (1990)
PPG 17   Sport and Recreation (1991)
PPG 18   Enforcing Planning Control (1992)
PPG 19   Outdoor Advertisement Control (1992)
PPG 20   Coastal Planning (1992)
PPG 21   Tourism (1992)
PPG 22   Renewable Energy (1993)
PPG 23   Planning and Pollution Control (1994)
PPG 24   Planning and Noise (1994)

Table 15.2 Mineral Policy Guidance Notes (1995)

MPG 1   General Considerations and the Development Plan System
MPG 2   Applications, Permissions and Conditions (1988)
MPG 3   Coal Mining and Colliery Spoil Disposal
MPG 4   The Review of Mineral Working Sites (1988)
MPG 5   Minerals Planning and the General Development Order (1988)
MPG 6   Guidelines for Aggregates Provisions in England (1994)
MPG 7   The Reclamation of Mineral Workings (1989)
MPG 8   Planning and Compensation Act 1991: Interim Development Order Permissions (1991)
MPG 9   Planning and Compensation Act 1991: Interim Development Order Permissions (1992)
MPG 10   Provisions of Raw Materials for the Cement Industry (1991)
MPG 11   The Control of Noise at Surface Mineral Workings (1993)
MPG 12   Treatment of Disused Mine Openings and Availability of Information in Mined Ground (1994)
MPG 13   Guidelines for Peat Provisions in England including the Place of Alternative Materials (1995)

Table 15.3 Regional Planning Guidance Notes (1995)

RPG 1   Strategic Guidance for Tyne and Wear (1989)
RPG 2   Strategic Guidance for West Yorkshire (1989)
RPG 3   Strategic Guidance for London (1989)
RPG 3   Supplementary Guidance for London on the Protection of Strategic Views (1991)
RPG 4   Strategic Guidance for Greater Manchester (1989)
RPG 5   Strategic Guidance for South Yorkshire (1989)
RPG 6   Regional Planning Guidance for East Anglia (1991)
RPG 7   Regional Planning Guidance for the Northern Region (1993)
RPG 8   Regional Planning Guidance for the East Midlands Region (1994)
RPG 9   Regional Planning Guidance for the South-East (1994)

environment. The presumption in favour of the preservation of listed buildings was retained, and the presumption in favour of the preservation of unlisted buildings which are helpful to the character or appearance of conservation areas has been added.

Subsequent Planning Policy Guidance Notes focus on land use, dealing with a wide range of planning subjects, as listed in table 15.1.

The other policy guidance notes are the Mineral Policy Guidance Notes (table 15.2), which provide a guide to the planning control of mineral workings and indicate the broad lines of policy on the planning problems raised by mineral workings, including minerals planning applications, permissions and conditions.

With the demise of the Greater London Council and the metropolitan councils and the switch to unitary development plans, the government began issuing regional guidance through the Planning Policy Guidance Notes, but so clearly were they regional policy that they came to be known as Regional Planning Guidance Notes (RPGs). The earlier PPG9, *Regional Guidance for the South-East*, published in 1988, became the regional planning guidance statement for the South East in the 1990s. Likewise PPG10, *Strategic Guidance for the West Midlands*, and PPG11, *Strategic Guidance for Merseyside*, became in the 1990s the Regional Planning Guidance Note for Merseyside and the West Midlands. These were followed by other strategic planning guidance notes, which became Regional Planning Guidance Notes. National policies are found in PPG12, Development Plans and Regional Planning Guidance, which superseded the earlier PPG9.

Regional Planning Guidance Notes are produced by the Department of the Environment for each region, and provide the necessary framework for the preparation of Structure Plans and Unitary Development Plans, which in turn provide the framework for Local Plans respectively in a kind of cascading process (*Hall, D., 1991*). Structure Plans are to be consistent with national and regional policy prepared by the Secretary of State through the Department of the Environment after consultation with joint planning boards such as SERPLAN, the joint Board for South East England. The 1992 reform introduced the requirement to have regard to environmental considerations: firstly, that the authorities should consider a broader range of environmental concerns and, secondly, that they assess the environmental impact of their proposals as a whole (*Policy Appraisal and the Environment*) (*DoE, 1991a*). The Conservative government brought in Regional Planning Guidance Notes as a way of simplifying the planning process and yet at the same time achieving a better focus on the key strategic issues.

Unlike previous regional plans, the RPG is advisory and was further weakened by the Planning and Compensation Act (1991), which allowed county councils to certify their own Structure Plans without, necessarily, total compliance with the RPG. The Regional Planning Guidance reports have to confine themselves to what can be advised through land-use planning powers, and warning is given in the Planning Policy Guidance Note setting out RPGs that non-land-use matters should not feature as plan policies or proposals and should instead be included in explanatory memoranda where they are relevant for full understanding.

Britain is the only European Union country with no regional government. For the 30 years prior to the Thatcher era, England and Wales had statutory regional planning and regional government. It was removed by the Conservative government, and the needs of regional planning are now being served by advisory Regional Planning Guidance Notes. Only in Scotland did regional government and hence regional planning survive until 1996.

Strategic planning for London

From 1888 to 1963, the London County Council managed the County of London, with the boroughs subordinated to it, gaining a long-standing reputation for efficiency and honesty. In 1963, with the creation of the Greater London Council, London doubled in extent; but the GLC had difficulties working with the new boroughs, and gradually the boroughs took the real control of local government. Thus a British pattern emerged of making piecemeal incremental adjustments that respected tradition, rather than grand schemes in the French manner (*Savitch, 1988*). After the Conservative government disbanded the giant Labour-controlled GLC in 1986, it substituted a new body, the London Planning Advisory Committee (LPAC), on the premise that only central government is powerful enough to force the London boroughs to work together through a commission directly responsible to the government (*Savitch, 1988*).

In the new development plan system, strategic planning guidance for London is issued by the Secretary of State, advised by LPAC. This guidance is combined with the Unitary Development Plans (UDPs) prepared by the boroughs, the unitary planning authorities. Thus *Strategic Planning Guidance for London* (RPG3) was prepared to assist London's 33 borough authorities in making interlinking unitary development plans which could form an ad hoc comprehensive plan (*DoE, 1989a*). *Strategic Planning Guidance for London* reversed many of the policies of the defunct Greater London Council. It emphasised strengthening (1) London's international competitiveness, (2) information technology, (3) developments such as the Channel Tunnel, and (4) helping the creation of the Single Market within the European Community in 1992. In all cases it stressed that opportunities should not be lost because of 'unnecessary planning restrictions' (*DoE, 1989a: 7*). Produced as an interim measure, it underlined the government's goals until the London Planning Advisory Committee was able to produce its own advisory strategy. The single market goal was postponed in the midst of the recession of 1992, but the other goals were incorporated into the LPAC's own *Strategic Trends and Policies* (*LPAC, 1992b*).

After its re-election in 1992, the Conservative government faced the need to integrate the management of London. Both Labour and Conservative parties agreed that the Greater London Development Plan (chapter 7) was too inflexible for today's rapid pace of change and both called for a small strategic Greater London Authority (*Morris, E.K.S., 1994*). The difference in concept between the two parties was that Labour's strategic authority would have statutory authority to plan the economic development and transport infrastructure, while the Conservatives, who would not relinquish any power to the Labour-controlled boroughs, desired only an advisory strategic London body, with the power to implement vested in the Department of the Environment. The Conservatives proposed a Cabinet sub-committee of ministers to coordinate policy for the capital and promote a modernisation programme designed 'to sustain into the next century London's special position as one of the world's great capital cities' (*LPAC, 1991b*).

Despite its liberal political structure compared with that, say, of France, the British government needed to produce a programme to keep London a first-class world city, and thus the LPAC produced its own strategic guidance in the LPAC's *London: World City* report (*LPAC, 1991b*) sponsored by the City of London, London Regional Transport, London

Docklands Development Corporation and Westminster City Council. The major issue was how to preserve London as a dominant world city, compared with Paris, New York, Tokyo and Frankfurt. A first-class world city was measured in terms of financial strength, infrastructure, the costs and quality of life. The criteria for financial strength, i.e. banking and financial centres, administrative headquarters and groups of think-tanks, were uppermost.

The consultants found that London was reasonably competitive in terms of wealth creation and the arts, but there were grave concerns about (1) the falling standard of public transport; (2) the lack of city-wide strategic planning; (3) the lack of sufficient low-income housing; (4) failure to accommodate new business in the East End of London; and (5) the lack of self-promotion, not only in business matters but also in terms of heritage/cultural assets.

Concerning public transport, the government spent £750 million on the London Underground in 1992, and will be adding the Jubilee Line extension, the Cross Rail and the additional rail link to Heathrow Airport from Paddington Station. It proposed to spend £750 million each year on infrastructure between 1992 and 2002, and £9 billion on updating commuter services for British Rail until privatisation plans intervened.

LPAC's policy supported the long-held concept, so beautifully detailed by Rasmussen, that London is a 'city of stable and secure residential neighbourhoods capable of sustained community development' (*Rasmussen, 1937*). While the LPAC advocated private rented accommodation, others considered that a programme of infill housing, of 'densification', was necessary (*Morris, E.K.S., 1994*). One-fifth of London's built-up areas was derelict and many houses stood empty on the poorer council estates. A programme of increasing housing densities could build houses for low rent or sale on these derelict sites, thus offering low-income families somewhere to live, and could save people having to commute from a dormitory suburb to a financial centre. The Docklands was a human disaster in promoting mainly offices, and not nearly enough homes and community facilities for the office workers and their families. The lack of shops, primary schools, clinics and community centres resulted in what has been described as a human desert (*Gosling, 1988*).

The large local authority housing estates were seen as a difficulty by the LPAC. In 1993, the government offered greater financial incentives to transfer local authority housing into their tenants' ownership. The problem still remained of rebuilding the inner city housing estates which had fallen into disrepair and disrepute. There will probably not be enough money for both housing rehabilitation and grand schemes such as those proposed for the Thames Embankment. It may come to a decision between maintaining London's place as a cultural and financial centre of Europe, which would benefit the whole country, and putting money into the housing and community needs of London's poorer boroughs, helping prevent housing estates deteriorating and becoming the ghetto of an underclass who then turn to drugs, violence and other social crimes.

Urban design proposals for improving London's culture and heritage areas

In the opinion of some, the main heritage characteristic of a city such as London is its polycentricity, with its cultural and heritage areas concentrated in selected districts, as islands of culture (*Ashworth and Tunbridge, 1990*). These specific clusters of historic cultural areas appeal to Londoners and tourists alike. London has five major tourist clusters which rank among the most popular in Britain with over a million visitors per year: (1) the South Kensington complex of the Science, Natural History and Victoria and Albert Museums; (2) the National Gallery and Trafalgar Square; (3) the Tate Gallery; (4) the British Museum; and (5) the Tower of London, Tower Bridge and *HMS Belfast*. Other tourist clusters exist in Westminster, the City and, on the outskirts, Greenwich and now the Docklands.

One enhancement proposal was for the enhancement of the River Thames. The LPAC report considered that the Unitary Development Plan of each borough, when strung together, would produce a River Thames strategy. In the opinion of some, London needs a River Thames *grand projet* for the twenty-first century, for the people of London and for the tourist (*Rogers and Fisher, 1992*). Sir Richard Rogers suggested the creation of a major park and pedestrian areas alongside the river, with the main road beneath the Embankment, bridges for pedestrians, the development of derelict sites, and a scheme for lighting the major buildings. Eventually the banks of the Thames would become a single linear park, interconnected by new pedestrian bridges. The movement corridor of such an Embankment Drive would be covered, making it a tunnel open onto the side of the river, with a terrace above the length of the river. The proposal would also reorganise Leicester Square and Trafalgar Square and create pedestrian links to the Embankment and the South Bank.

Through various urban design battles (chapter 13) London is revealing a reluctance to achieve grand urban schemes. This may be in the English tradition of preferring a democratic classicism in which the desire for individualism took precedence over the preference of kings and their master planners. Upon entering the new Europe, London is showing a passive sense of urbanity rather than any unified vision for the urban future (*Morris, E.K.S., 1994*).

The Conservatives pushed ahead with the Docklands but to many town planners it is a lesson in how not to redevelop the port and dock facilities of a capital city (*Gosling, 1988*). For example, the London Docklands Development Corporation developed new streets, roads, paths and office facilities at a fast pace, without much regard to local housing, shopping or community facilities. The dearth of these facilities, the isolation of the existing dwellings, the lack of a Docklands civic centre and the total disregard of any relationship to the rest of East London were all mistakes which will need to be expensively rectified.

South East England, the Channel Tunnel and the East Thames Corridor City

Previous governments had reviewed the strategy for the South East in 1976 (*South-East Joint Planning Team, 1976*) and in 1978 (*DoE, 1978b*), opting for changes of emphasis and adjustments to the 1970 *Strategic Plan for the South-East* (chapter 7). These previous reports stressed improving the environment and relaxing industrial controls for London, while noting that the problem of changes in household structure caused a greater demand for smaller homes. Over the period of Mrs Thatcher's government, plans were continually revised according to forecasts of great population growth versus small growth; acceptance and then rejection of Maplin Airport; rejection of the Channel Tunnel and then its completion; and proposals and counter-proposals for an East of London Corridor City. During the 1980s, regional planning in the South East reached an impasse. A new strategy for the South East was not to appear until 1989.

Figure 15.1   Thames Embankment pedestrianised linear path proposal (after Rogers and Fisher)

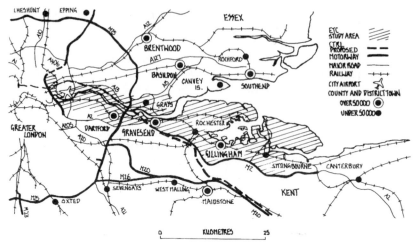

Figure 15.2   East Thames Corridor City (after DoE)

SERPLAN (South East Regional Planning Conference) published a *New Strategy* of planning objectives as well as a set of policies to guide the development of the south-east region into the twenty-first century (*SERPLAN, 1989*). The strategy concentrated on six main themes: (1) the importance of environmental conservation; (2) the maintenance of economic buoyancy; (3) the importance of the role of London; (4) changes within the south-east region; (5) the importance of harmonising land-use planning with other policies, such as transport; and (6) the relationship between the South East and other regions in the UK and Europe. A further SERPLAN report, *Shaping the South East Planning Strategy* (*SERPLAN, 1990*), coupled with the *Regional Planning Guidance for the South East* (*DoE, 1989c*), setting out government policy, updated the *New Strategy*. The result was incremental planning, mostly at the local level. Big bold schemes were not accepted, because they attracted too much political opposition. The exceptions were the Urban Development Corporation Areas in the 1980s and the East Thames Corridor City in the 1990s.

It is clear from RPG9 that the government had every intention of keeping regional planning policy under its control and away from the control of the regions themselves. This highly centralised approach was consistent with Conservative policy. The 1994 RPG emphasised coordinating land-use and transport planning policies to meet environmental objectives. It also promoted a balance of development between the west and east of the region, additional housing and the redevelopment and recycling of urban land, and an 'East Thames Corridor' City. The proposal included a new linear town east of London along 30 miles of the River Thames, as an urban regeneration scheme,

rehabilitating derelict sites and waste ground to meet some of the relentless demand for housing in South East England by relieving the pressure to take green belt land in the Home Counties as well as rehabilitating a run-down area; and as a way of shifting development east rather than west of London, while coordinating the possibilities of pan-European development offered by the Channel Tunnel. Other proposals for the East End of London were predicated on the need to shift development eastwards, away from expansion on green-field sites to the west of London (*Hall, 1994*).

In contrast to the New Towns programme, the East Thames Corridor City is to be developed as a series of development sites within a framework to be established by central government. Like the New Towns, it was assumed that the infrastructure, roads and new river crossings would be paid for by public subsidy. The East Thames Corridor would require a new motorway, the Thames Industrial Route (London to Tilbury), extension of the Underground line, a new rail terminus for the Channel Tunnel railway at Stratford, and a new east London river crossing; and extending the facilities of the City Airport. The housing, industrial developments, shopping centres and leisure complexes would be developed by private funds, coordinated by more than 20 local authorities. The concept was proposed in the form of an Urban Development Corporation. The Environment Minister pursued the concept in a determination to restrict development in the western Home Counties, but during Prime Minister Major's term the proposals for the East Thames Corridor were postponed. Of all the new settlement projects, the East Thames Corridor linear city is one of those that should take place to relieve the pressure on the west and restore a run-down area in the east.

Inner city regeneration: Urban Development Corporations and City Challenge

UDCs continued to be formed by the government to merge with sections of the city centre. Birmingham's International Convention Centre developed well on the fringe of its central area, while two mini-UDCs in central Manchester and Leeds also promoted parts of their central area (*Ward, 1994: 243*). The Urban Development Corporation area in Leeds emphasised the historical and cultural associations of its central area, its Victorian buildings, its Corn Exchange and retention of old façades in new developments. UDCs continued in the 1990s, in places such as Sheffield and Bristol.

The London Docklands Development Corporation began to wind down in 1994, as it was always intended it should, and by 1998 it will have totally de-designated the Corporation. LDDCs achievements since its beginning in 1981, and despite the economic upheavals, include (*Slavid, 1995*):

(1) £6.1 billion of private investment matching £1.7 billion of public investment;
(2) 240,000 m² of commercial and industrial floor space built;
(3) 18,700 new homes built;
(4) the derelict land reduced from nearly a half to one-eighth of the total;
(5) 101 km of roads;
(6) 29 km of railways;
(7) the city airport carrying over half a million passengers a year.

Other UDCs carried on, although the economic recession of the 1990s brought a long period of falling land values and lack of property demand. Thus the market-led regeneration strategies of the 1980s, which pushed UDCs, could not work in such economic conditions. Secondly, the government slowed down on deregulated planning as the isolation of the UDC was no longer necessary. The government could achieve all that it wished through other simpler means, such as, for example, City Challenge. Finally, the costs of UDCs were higher than the government expected. For example, £167m was required for the Cardiff Bay Barrage and £600m for the Docklands Highway (*Colenutt, 1993: 176*). For these reasons, the government switched to City Challenge as its major means of restoring the inner city.

Launched in 1991, City Challenge replaced the previous funding methods for deprived urban areas. Superseded after only two years by the Single Regeneration Budget, it was itself an amalgam of five previous grant programmes (see chapter 12): the Urban Programme, the Derelict Land Grant, City Action Team, Estate Action (Housing), and Housing Improvement Grants. Derelict Land Grants and Corporation funding remained separate.

When the City Challenge grants were first awarded, 17 authorities out of 57 urban minority areas that had been identified as areas of poor social and economic conditions were invited to make competitive bids for the funding. In 1991, 11 'pacemaker' authorities were then chosen to make detailed action plans starting in 1992 for completion in 1997 (*Stafford, 1995*). The

● = pacemakers   o = second-round winners

Pacemakers	Second-round winners	
1 Barnsley	12 Birmingham	22 Leicester
2 Bradford	13 Blackburn	23 Newham
3 Lewisham	14 Bolton	24 North Tyneside
4 Liverpool	15 Brent	25 Sandwell
5 Manchester	16 Derby	26 Sefton
6 Middlesborough	17 Hackney	27 Stockton-on-Tees
7 Newcastle	18 Hartlepool	28 Sunderland
8 Nottingham	19 Kensington &	29 Walsall
9 Tower Hamlets	Chelsea	30 Wigan
10 Wirral	20 Kirklees	
11 Wolverhampton	21 Lambeth	

Figure 15.3 City Challenge locations (after Stafford)

concept of local authorities, with the private sector and community groups, preparing an overall strategy for one or more of their inner city areas had been accepted. It was the idea that local authorities had to compete for the funding which was new.

Because of the great interest, a second competition occurred in 1992 with 54 bids, of which 20 were chosen, whose action plans started in April 1993, to be completed in 1998. City Challenge supported strategies helping urban areas to attract investment, stimulation of wealth creation, wider social provision and creation of environments which attract people to live and work there.

City Challenge brought mixed reviews. On the positive side, City Challenge was successful in working in partnerships, in the use of £33 billion of private investment which otherwise would not have been invested in inner city areas, and in the resolution of difficult sites, problems and situations. On the negative side, City Challenge emphasised small target areas for special treatment, brought forth no new money but just a rearrangement of existing budgets, and created budgetary problems (*Bailey et al., 1995*).

Inner city regeneration: Single Regeneration Budget and reviews of urban policy and housing

In more consolidations, the government in 1993 integrated more grant programmes into a Single Regeneration Budget for which bids were invited. Ten

integrated offices in England, combining the Departments of Trade and Industry, Employment, Environment, and Transport, were created for each office to issue an annual regeneration statement setting out the key priorities for regeneration and economic development in the Regions (*DoE, 1994; Bailey et al., 1995*). It is thought that the Single Regeneration Budget corrected several criticisms of urban policy, such as (1) integrating the many disparate grant programmes within a single budget; (2) providing a higher level of collaboration between four government departments; and (3) showing that central government was turning away from programmes seemingly designed to by-pass local authorities as it found that local authorities were important as enablers and coordinators of local bids (*Bailey et al., 1995: 69*).

The Review of Urban Policy by Robson *et al.* was one of the most comprehensive and detailed assessments of public policy ever undertaken (*DoE, 1994*). It consisted of quantitative studies of expenditure on all the various urban programmes in a sample of 123 local authority areas (including the 57 urban minority areas), qualitative surveys of residents and employees, and interviews with the residents of Greater Manchester, Merseyside, and Tyne and Wear. The conclusions are five (*DoE, 1994: XIV–XV*).

1 The importance of long-term collaborative partnerships
2 The need for local authorities to be given greater opportunities to play a larger role in such partnerships

Table 15.4   Urban expenditure 1988–89 to 1995–96 (£m) (from Bailey *et al.*, 1995. Reprinted by permission of UCL Press Ltd)

	88–89	89–90	90–91	91–92	92–93	93–94	94–95	95–96
Urban Programme	224	223	226	237	243	176	91	80
City Challenge	—	—	—	—	64	214	2144	214
City Grant	28	39	45	41	60	71	71	83
Derelict Land Grant	68	54	62	77	95	93	93	120
URA	—	—	—	—	—	2	2	2
UDCs and DLR	255	477	607	602	514	337	293	284
Task Forces	23	20	21	20	23	18	16	15
City Action Teams	—	4	8	8	4	3	1	1
Manchester Olympics	—	—	—	1	13	35	25	—
Other	—	—	—	—	—	3	8	1
CF extra receipts	—	−2	−4	−7	−2	—	—	—
Inner cities total	598	815	964	980	1014	952	813	800
New Towns Commission	−558	−463	−333	−371	−129	−117	−203	−254
ERDF	27	8	2	3	16	176	199	174
Total	67	360	633	611	901	1011	809	720

Source: Department of the Environment Annual Report 1993.

Note the dramatic shift in expenditure from New Towns to inner cities. Also note the increasing contribution of the European Regional Development Fund (ERDF).

3 The greater opportunities for local communities to participate in the partnerships
4 The need for greater coherent policies within government departments and the need for clear identification of strategic objectives
5 The need for the development of an urban budget administered at regional level.

The findings are mixed. Very large cities or the central areas of conurbations faced the most difficult futures and were shown to be an increasing proportion of the disadvantaged. In contrast, many of the smaller places and the peripheral districts within the conurbations showed relative economic and residential improvement over the 15 years of the Urban Policy Review period (*DoE, 1994: 32*). The final conclusion was that 'the cores of the big conurbations present deep and multi-faceted problems which appear not to have been deflected by policy intervention' (*DoE, 1994: 55*). There is still a great deal of rehabilitation and economic regeneration to be completed in the inner city.

By contrast, in the rest of England, the unexpected conclusion of the 1991 English House Condition Survey (*DoE, 1993a*) was that the conditions of housing in England improved with every indicator used in the survey including unfitness, amenities and disrepair. Only 1 percent of the housing stock lacks basic amenities whereas in 1986 the figure was 2.5 percent. Levels of disrepair fell in all tenures. Falling levels of disrepair and the provision of amenities previously lacking have led to a fall in unfitness from an estimated 1.66 million in 1986 to 1.5 million in 1991. It is in Scotland where the housing condition is still poor. More than 420,000 houses, or 20.8 percent of the total housing stock in Scotland, suffer from damp, serious condensation or mould (*Scott, 1995*). The 1993 survey showed that 94,000 occupied houses (or 4.6 percent)

were below the tolerable standard. When houses suffering from damp and condensation were included, the figures rose to 584,000 houses or 28.7 percent of the total.

Further, the 1995 White Paper on Housing for England and Wales, and a later White Paper for Scotland, extended the 'right to buy' scheme to all housing association tenants, as against just council house tenants, as part of a plan to create 1.5 million more home owners. The main condition was that tenant approval be given by ballot, as the Conservative government did not intend to enforce full-scale privatisation or takeover of council houses, but, in essence, the days of local authorities being the main providers of housing were over.

Science Parks and Business Parks

Structural changes within British industry have accelerated away from traditional industries to accommodating the expansion needs of high technology. Local authorities have assisted this expansion by creating 'Science Parks', High-Technology Industrial Parks and Business Parks.

The term Science Park originated in the United States as a result of developments near Stanford University, Palo Alto, California ('Silicon Valley') and the Massachusetts Institute of Technology in Cambridge, Massachusetts. A Science Park is a landscaped setting interspersed with high-quality industrial buildings at low densities. Some of the oldest British Science Parks are in north Cambridge and in New Towns. Science Parks and Business Parks, particularly in the New Towns, with their financial benefits, have been immensely successful in providing new employment. On the negative side, the parks exist on single-site areas, isolated from catering and shopping facilities, are often a considerable distance from any housing areas, and are often wasteful of land.

New settlements and town expansions

By 1991, there were over 200 planned private developments in the pipeline for England, Scotland and Wales (*Amos, 1991*). The argument in favour of the new villages is that they relieve the pressure on old villages and towns, preventing them from being destroyed by garish new housing estates. The Conservative government from 1991 onwards considered that 'new villages' were a good choice for housing development in rural areas. At the strategic level, the government included advice about such settlements in Regional Planning Guidance Notes, and

Figure 15.4 Cambridge Science Park (by the author)

Table 15.5   Chronology of urban policy measures in England, Wales and Scotland, 1977–94 (from Bailey *et al.*, 1995. Reprinted by permission of UCL Press Ltd)

Date	Department of the Environment	Department of Employment	Department of Trade and Industry	Scottish Office	Other
1977	3 Inner Area Studies				Home Office transfers inner cities functions to DoE
1978	Inner Urban Areas Act. 7 Partnership, 15 Programme and 19 Designated authorities				
1979				Clydebank EZ	
1980	London Docklands Development Corporation and Merseyside Development Corporation, 13 EZs				
1981	Land registers, Merseyside Task Force, Financial Institutions		Loan guarantee scheme for small businesses		
1982	Urban Development Grant, 1 more EZ				
1983		Youth Training Scheme			
1984	14 more EZs		New Assisted Areas. Revised Regional Development Grant		
1985	CATs set up in 5 estates, Estate Action	...Partnership...	...Areas wider remit for English Estates		
1986	Trafford Park UDC Stoke Garden Festival				
1987	4 more UDCs		8 more Task Forces		
1988	*Action for Cities* 2 more CATs 4 more UDCs City Grant More EZs British Urban Development launched Housing Action Trust			4 New Life Partnership Glasgow Garden Festival	Home Office announces Safer Cities Programme – 2 projects over 5 years
1989	*Progress on Cities* Bristol UDC	10 more Compacts	3 more Task Forces		
1990	*People in Cities* Gateshead Garden Festival	12 TECs launched		Glasgow European City of Culture	
1991	Round 1 of City Challenge Phoenix Initiative wound up	70 TECs launched		Scottish Enterprise set up with 13 LECs	
1992	Round 2 of City Challenge Private Finance Initiative. Birmingham and Plymouth UDCs UP reduced. Urban Partnership Found introduced. Urban Regeneration Agency announced Integrated Regional Offices				Ebbw Vale Garden Festival (Wales)
1993	Single regeneration budgets			Lanarkshire EZ. Progress in partnership review set up, etc.	
1994	English Partnership becomes operational. Bidding Guidance for SRB published. Bids for round 1 of SRB to be submitted by September. Assessing the Impact of Urban Policy published				

expected communities to make reasonable provision for new settlements.

Central government revised PPG3 on Housing to a new one which included a new settlements policy, giving additional limited support to new settlements and allowing proposals for them only if the following qualifications were achieved, thus greatly limiting the opportunities for new settlements:

1   No better alternative to expanding the towns or villages existed

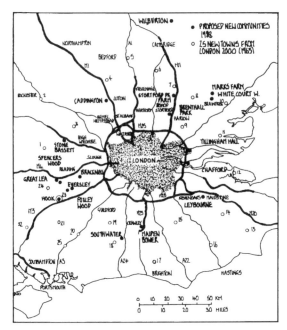

Figure 15.5 Proposed new communities in the South East as of 1988. Nearly 20 proposals for major privately developed new communities from different developers, among whom Consortium Developments is heavily represented. The map also shows the 25 proposed New Towns from the original *London 2000* (Hall, 1963) (after *London 2001*, Hall, 1989)

2 The local population and the local authority both desired it
3 The new settlement sat well with existing settlements
4 The new settlement positively improved the environment, cleaned up a redundant site or improved areas of poor landscape quality
5 The proposal was not in a green belt, National Park, Area of Outstanding Natural Beauty or Site of Special Scientific Interest.

Previously, in 1983, a group of ten large house-builders, Consortium Developments Ltd, had planned to develop self-contained communities, each including between 7000 and 15000 houses, in South East England. Consortium made the initial mistake of proposing five of its new settlements in the green belt, and so the planners originally had some success in defeating its proposals. But in the mid-1980s the then Environment Secretary, Nicholas Ridley, was persuaded that a major house-building drive in South East England would support economic growth.

Consortium's first major New Town proposal, Tillingham Hall, Essex, was rejected because it was to be sited in London's green belt. Stone Basset, Oxfordshire, was next to be turned down, although by that time Consortium Developments had already begun to reduce the scale of its proposals to 'small new county towns' (1988). Stone Basset was to be a little town, rather like the original size of Letchworth and Welwyn Garden City, placed in south Oxfordshire. Most of the workers would have had to commute to Oxford or London, thus negating one of the basic principles of New Town planning that your job is on your doorstep, dispensing with the long journey to work. There were to be some jobs in a Science Park and some service jobs. The houses would have been privately owned and highly priced, and the only low-cost housing would have been low-rent housing from housing associations, in place of council houses.

Another proposal of Consortium was Foxley Wood, which featured 4800 houses on 710 acres. Low-cost housing would account for 8 percent of the total housing and there were to be considerable community facilities. Many water park and leisure facilities complemented the scheme. Where it fell down was in the lack of employment facilities, and in its ecological impact on north-east Hampshire as the area contained a Site of Special Scientific Interest. It is an example of the future dilemma of housing versus countryside, as the Structure Plan for mid- and north-east Hampshire called for 63,000 new houses in the county by the year 2000, with a distribution of 10,000 houses for mid-Hampshire and approximately 15,000 new houses for north-east Hampshire. The county council, examining proposals for the Structure Plan, concluded that a new settlement was a better option for accommodating new housing than further expansion of existing towns and villages (*RTPI, 1989*). The DoE accepted this conclusion provided that significant countryside protection policies were also put in place, and that some low-cost housing and rental housing was provided as well as houses for sale. The Inspector at the subsequent planning local inquiry recommended refusal because of the loss of a significantly interesting ecological area. The Minister in 1990 likewise refused permission.

Consortium Developments tried at least four times to obtain planning permission to build a new village, Westmore, in the vicinity of Cambridge. Finally, in 1992 Consortium Developments disbanded, having spent nine years unsuccessfully trying to develop new settlements. Its proposed settlements were commuter settlements and did not show either social awareness or enough ecological sensitivity.

Consortium's mistakes included (1) proposing settlements in the green belt, which to the public is sacrosanct; (2) calling the new settlements New Towns; and (3) paying only lip service to environmental aspirations. The New Towns, the brilliant success that they are, are now viewed by some as urban, synonymous with industry and consequently unattractive. In marketing terms, new villages would have been a more palatable concept, harking back as they do to nostalgia, heritage, the country house and rural landscapes. New villages immediately reduce the scale of living while at the same time making the economies of scale more difficult.

In 1989, Cambridgeshire County Council also pursued the idea of four new townships. East Anglia is one of the most attractive areas for new settlements, where the economic growth in and around Cambridge has resulted in unacceptable housing pressure on the historic city of Cambridge, aided by the expansion of Stansted Airport as well as expanding science–technology industry. Cambridgeshire County Council recognised the housing need by calling for at least two new settlements in its Structure Plan, one to the north of Cambridge towards Ely, and one to the west.

Between 1989 and 1992 eight new privately promoted settlement proposals vied for different sites around Cambridge (Scotland Park, Alington, Highfield, Swansley Wood, Great Common Farm, Bovin Airfield, Hare Park, Belham Hill). None was the result of proactive planning policies. The then Environment Secretary, Michael Heseltine, turned down all eight proposals, despite the goal of the Cambridgeshire Structure Plan, which identified the need for at least one 3000-dwelling settlement coupled with a Business Park along the A45 (now A14) route.

One proposal which succeeded was a large new southern township for Peterborough for 5200 houses for 13,000 people on a 2000-acre site consisting of a number of abandoned brick and clay pits. The scheme has had greater success in achieving acceptance in that it concentrated on low-cost, as well as rentable, special needs and sheltered housing. It represents much more of a balanced community in its four residential neighbourhoods with schools, shops, community and leisure facilities. A 175-acre Business Park, hotel and leisure complex complement the housing. Receiving planning permission in 1993, it is the biggest private-sector development to be built in 30 years, as against Milton Keynes with its social housing of 25 years ago. In contrast to the other proposals, it hopes to provide 12,000 jobs. It is a complete turnaround for Peterborough Council, which was founded as a New Town for public-sector housing, to now give permission for a totally private-sector town expansion.

Scotland has had a number of proposals for new settlements, but little success. In 1992 Grampian Regional Council proposed building a new settlement of 3000 houses, but owing to the imminent revision of local government boundaries in 1996, its proposals were postponed. Other companies involved included Eagle Star, which in 1991 proposed a new market town, Micheldever in Hampshire, to exhibit sustainable development in practice, such as alternative energy heating schemes and close physical relationships of housing to local industry (*Eagle Star, 1991*). But as of 1995, it too had been postponed. Proposals have also been made in Norwich (1990); Chester (1990), South Yorkshire (1992) and many others.

The most publicised successful town expansion is Poundbury, an expansion of Dorchester proposed by Prince Charles. Leon Krier produced a master plan for a model community of 400 acres at Poundbury, Dorchester, incorporating Prince Charles's 'Ten Principles', and provided a layout and a development density code. Krier adapted Howard's Garden City language by designating four 'wards' of 100 acres each, separated by green buffer zones. Building uses were integrated; for example, flats were over shops and the suburban cul-de-sac was not acceptable. Detailed designs were drawn up by 25 architectural practices and builders according to either a vernacular or a neo-classical design code (Figure 15.6).

The layout was a phased development of 3000 houses with shops, some factory units, office space, shopping, and rugby and football grounds. Roads have been carefully designed to minimise traffic by (1) curving the streets to slow down traffic; (2) designing street corners which allow the traffic to turn freely while keeping a sense of street enclosure; and (3) controlling parking by placing cars in internal courtyards and providing parking spaces and garages attached to individual buildings. The urban village had executive houses alongside low-cost houses and industrial units, but these executive houses did not sell, and the land-use mix has been abandoned.

Krier has been philosophically opposed to the New Town building created in Britain in the last 50 years and wishes to reintroduce traditional European town qualities and nostalgia (*Cruickshank, 1991*). These qualities include:

(1) mixed uses dispersed throughout the town
(2) self-sufficiency with schools and shops within easy reach of each other
(3) public buildings in the centre of the town, and built to indicate their importance

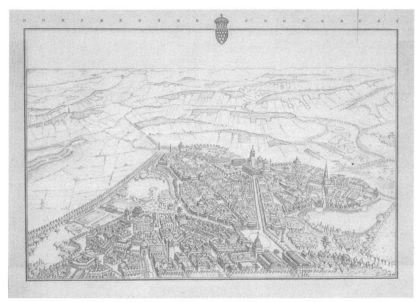

Figure 15.6   Poundbury Township, Dorset (from Krier, 1993. Reproduced by kind permission of the Academy Group Ltd)

(4) shopping focused on a market square and a High Street

(5) streets with continuous edges and gardens; this reconciles the ideal of the detached house with the urban terrace by connecting individual houses with a low wall to present a continuous frontage to the street

(6) courts and alleys leading off to create a hierarchy of urban spaces and network of routes

(7) the edge of the town of Dorchester defined by a green belt

(8) the scale of the town of Dorchester defined by the ten-minute walk to and from the centre; all points to be reached by a five-minute walk

(9) car parking to be incorporated within the fabric and not in multi-storey car parks.

Each ward of 100 acres would contain a High Street lined with shops at ground level with flats and offices above, a main square and smaller subsidiary squares, also given over to shopping and leisure and marked visually by the presence of the larger-scaled public buildings. Krier originally wanted houses mixed with workshops, light industry and office use, but that proved unmarketable and is no longer being promoted. Krier wanted the public buildings to be architectural statements and was unwilling to allow the supermarkets to be grandiose buildings.

Krier wanted museums, civic halls and theatres, but the Duchy of Cornwall only wanted to build buildings for sale. The Duchy is responsible for the infrastructure

and then sells individual sites and groups of sites to builders and developers. The original grand classical design was criticised as being alien and un-English. The revised scheme is more like an English village, to which the roads have to conform. The changing of the Department of Transport ideas of suburban roads, from being overly wide to small narrow lanes, may be Poundbury's greatest contribution.

The early 1990s property recession halted progress but when properties began their economic upturn in late 1993, the concept of new villages again became a possibility. The controversy in the government's policy centred on whether to build a new settlement on its own with a balanced community of jobs and homes, or to create more suburbs around existing centres. In either case, large chunks of agricultural or redundant industrial land would be swallowed up. The Rural White Paper (*DoE, 1995b*) backed new settlements in the countryside and liberalised development centres in villages and even arranged mixed communities by protecting social housing. The White Paper prepared a design code for the countryside, but mainly stressed the need for developing new patterns of work over buildings in the economic success of rural areas. Local economic initiatives further emphasised working in the countryside.

PPG12 (1992) required an element of affordable housing provision, with a common consensus of a 20 percent allocation. The need for high standards of layout, landscaping and design is also expressed as

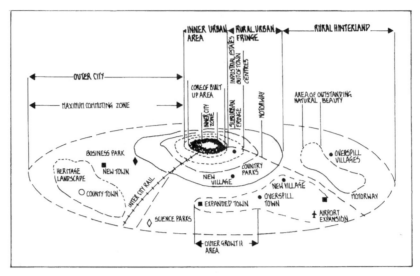

Figure 15.7   Effects of planning (after Herington)

well as the encouragement of walking, cycling and public transport. The local authorities are required to give developers guidance on the latter's contribution to the infrastructure and community facilities. The developers are expected to provide most of the infrastructure but there is no such outlay on community facilities. Compared with the vigorous New Towns programme pursued from 1946 to 1970, the government's current policy on new settlements is weak indeed. It is almost as if the New Towns proposals had never existed, as most of the new settlements proposals are acting as if the wheel has to be reinvented.

Urban design and town planning

The 1980s and the 1990s saw the rise and fall of Post-Modernism and the emergence of the Classicist architects. The High-Tech Modernists survived by building abroad and eventually triumphed over Post-Modernism. Some of the younger architects dabbled with the deconstructivist style, most notably in Daniel Libeskind's brilliant proposal for the extension to the Victoria and Albert Museum. But since the deconstructivist style relies on an overly affluent and extravagant economy, as found in Los Angeles, the recession of the 1990s mostly put paid to the deconstructivist style in Britain.

Contemporary approaches to urban design are divided between the classical approach of developing sites in the grand manner to attract commercial revenue, civic status and touristic success, but using Modernist or High-Tech Modernist buildings, and the approach of fragmented urban forms superimposed upon each other forming collages of current uses and using vernacular traditions (*Harvey, 1985: 66*). It is more than likely that both approaches will continue into the twenty-first century as different situations require different solutions and there is always the need for 'horses for courses'.

New Towns are making a comeback in the form of new settlements and green villages, particularly in South East England, where the population is house-hungry. In contrast to the government-sponsored last wave of New Towns in the 1960s and 1970s, these new settlements are privately conceived and built. The danger is that the New Town concept of a 'balanced community' (i.e. jobs in the town for the people living in the houses) will not materialise and that jobs will be located far away, thus turning the new villages into commuter dormitories.

Summary

Britain's 2000 years of town planning history have produced a wealth of superb town planning examples. Its relatively recent systems of planning legislation and development control are models for all the world to admire and for many countries to copy. Britain has succeeded in retaining its town planning heritage in a way that many other countries have not managed. This success has in turn given a relatively high quality of life to the majority of people. The effects of planning can be seen everywhere (figure 15.7).

British planning is also conceived in terms of policies that will advance the public interest, and moreover in determining the outcome of planning applications; sometimes the local authority will override local wishes because of concerns for broad policies on such matters as providing adequate land for new housing and safeguarding agricultural land (*Cullingworth, 1994: 163*). This is the magnificently humanist strength of British planning. In other countries like the United States, conflicts are resolved between parties over land use with the concern for individual property rights as paramount.

The processes of change have always provided a strong rationale for planning and the public has supported planning in the belief that the distributed consequences of these changes can be either mitigated or dealt with in an equitable and democratic manner (*Rydin, 1993: 371*). The idealistic planners have supported the proactive role of planners – that of improving society for the benefit of the greater number of people. For example, planning can increase the quality of community facilities and public transport, ensure access to recreational areas and areas of architectural beauty and protect the quality of local environments.

Since the promotion of the policy of *This Common Inheritance* (*DoE, 1990b*) and subsequent annual reports in 1991, 1992 and 1994), green issues and green ideas have achieved a widespread social appeal in a very short period. The new environmental strategy does appeal to the wider public and it is possible that planning will emphasise more environmental strategy. The current evidence of global environmental change is providing a magnificent opportunity for planners to take a proactive role. In addition the impact of the European Community in land-use planning in Britain is increasing, particularly in the field of environmental policies.

At the same time as being attracted to green issues and long-term environmental goals, planners are also dedicated to providing jobs, houses and facilities to all those who need them, thus opening up the supply of land for new housing, business and/or industry. The concept of sustainability, which provides for present needs for development, provided they do not compromise the ability to meet future needs, is an appealing challenge for planners (*Blowers, 1993*). Planners can help in ways such as lifting the burden of extensive unnecessary travelling, bringing jobs and houses closer together and providing more leisure and recreational activities.

The environmental vision offers planners in the twenty-first century a new lease of life, a new vision of planning. Planners can incorporate sustainability and greater social responsiveness than under the present system. The anti-planning sentiments of the 1980s have had their day. Recognition has been made of the continuing need for planning. We now need to build on a vision as equally important as the vision of the 1940s to herald a new golden age of environmental planning in the twenty-first century.

Appendix Planning progress in Great Britain – significant dates

1840–99	1842	Report on the Sanitary Conditions of the Labouring Population of Great Britain
	1848	Public Health Act
	1864	Octavia Hill begins her housing work
	1868	Artisans' and Labourers' Dwellings Act, Torrens Act
	1872	Public Health Act
	1875	Artisans' and Labourers' Dwellings Improvement Act, Cross Act
	1875	Public Health Act
1900–39	1900	Ebenezer Howard and Garden Cities
		Raymond Unwin and Garden Suburbs
		Patrick Geddes and Regional Planning
	1903	Letchworth Garden City Started
	1909	Housing, Town Planning Act (First Planning Act)
	1918	Tudor Walters Report on Housing
	1919	Housing and Town Planning Act
	1923	Housing Act
	1924	Welwyn Garden City started
	1925	Town Planning Act
	1930	Housing Act
	1932	Town & Country Planning Act
	1934	Depressed Areas Bill
	1935	Restriction of Ribbon Development Act
	1936	Housing Act
	1938	Green Belt (London and Home Counties) Act
	1939	Mars Plan for London
1940–49	1940–42	Barlow, Scott, Uthwatt Reports
	1940–41	Bombing of Coventry, London, Plymouth, followed by reconstruction plans
	1943	County of London Plan
	1943	Ministry of Town & Country Planning set up with Regional Offices, Research Organisations, etc.
	1944	Greater London Plan
	1944	Town & Country Planning Act (Reconstruction)
	1945	Distribution of Industry Act
	1946	New Towns Act
	1947	Town & Country Planning Act, with Circulars and Regulations
	1947	The Redevelopment of Central Areas Handbook, Ministry of Town & Country Planning

	1947	New Towns Programme started (Stevenage first post-war New Town)
	1948	Clyde Valley Plan; Tay Valley and South-East Scotland Plans
	1949	London County Council (LCC), Planning Organisation, Comprehensive Development Area (CDAs), Housing
	1949	National Parks and Access to the Countryside Act
1950–59	1951	LCC – Development Plan, Festival of Britain
	1952	Town Development Act
	1953	Historic Buildings and Ancient Monuments Act
	1956	Cumbernauld New Town started
	1956	Clean Air Act
	1957	Housing Act (Slum Clearance)
	1959	Greater London Commission on Local Government
1960–69	1962	Scotland – Lothians Regional Plan, Scottish Development Department, Central Belt Growth Areas etc.
	1963	London Government Act; Greater London Council
	1963	White Papers: North-East England; Central Scotland
	1965	Scottish Regional Plans: Borders, Highlands, Tay Valley
		Second-Generation New Towns – Runcorn, Skelmersdale, etc.
	1967	Civic Amenities Act
	1967	Planning Advisory Group (PAG) Report
	1967	Land Commission Act
	1967	Countryside (Scotland) Act
	1968	Countryside Act
	1968	Clean Air Act
	1968	Town & Country Planning Act
	1969	Town and Country Planning (Scotland) Act
	1968–70	Commissions on Local Government (Redcliffe-Maud and Wheatley)
	1969	Housing Act (General Improvement Areas)
1970–79	1970	Community Land Act
	1970	Development Plan Handbook
	1971	Town & Country Planning Act
	1972	Town & Country Planning (Scotland) Act
	1972	Local Government Act
	1973	Local Government (Scotland) Act
	1973	Protection of the Environment Bill
	1974	Town & Country Amenities Act
	1974	Control of Pollution Act
	1974	Housing Act (Housing Action Areas)
	1975	Community Land Act
	1978	Inner Urban Areas Act for England and Wales
		Inner Urban Areas Act (Scotland)
	1979	Ancient Monuments and Archaeological Areas Act
1980–89	1980	Local Government. Planning & Land Act – Enterprise Zones, Urban Development Corporations
	1980	National Heritage Act
	1981	Wildlife and Countryside Act
	1981	Mersey Development Corporation Programme begun
	1981	Minerals Act
	1981	London Docklands Development Programme begun
	1982	Derelict Land Act
	1983	National Heritage Act

	1983	Litter Act
	1985	New Towns & Urban Development Corporation Act
	1985	Mineral Workings Act
	1985	Local Government and Housing Act
	1985	Government White Paper: Lifting the Burden
		Simplified Planning Zones
	1986	Demise of Greater London Council and Metropolitan County Councils
	1986	Housing & Planning Act
	1987	South-East England in the 1990s: A Regional Statement
	1988	Town & Country Planning General Development Order (GDO)
	1988	Local Government Act
	1988	Housing Act
	1989	Strategic Guidance for London
1990 on	1990	Town and Country Planning Act
	1990	Planning (Listed Buildings and Conservation Areas) Act
	1990	Planning (Hazardous Substances) Act
	1990	White Paper: This Common Inheritance: Britain's Environmental Strategy
	1990	Environmental Protection Act
	1991	Planning and Compensation Act
	1991	National Heritage (Scotland) Act
	1991	Road Traffic Act
	1993	Leasehold Reform, Housing and Urban Development Act
	1995	Environment Act
	1996	Demise of Regions, Districts and New Towns in Scotland
		Unitary Authorities established in Scotland

Bibliography

Abercrombie, Patrick, 1933. *Town and Country Planning*. London, Thornton Butterworth.

Abercrombie, Patrick, 1945. *Greater London Plan 1944*. London, HMSO.

Abercrombie, P. and Forshaw, J.H., 1943. *County of London Plan*. London, Macmillan.

Abercrombie, P. and Jackson, H., 1948. *West Midlands Plan*. London, Ministry of Town and Country Planning.

Abercrombie, P. and Matthew, R., 1949. *Clyde Valley Regional Plan 1946*. Edinburgh, HMSO.

Abercrombie, P. and Plumstead, D., 1949. *A Civic Survey and Plan of Edinburgh*. Edinburgh, Oliver and Boyd.

Adams, Ian, 1978. *The Making of Urban Scotland*. London, Croom Helm.

Addams, Jane, 1910. *Twenty Years at Hull House*. New York, Macmillan.

Addams, Jane, 1965. *The Social Thought of Jane Addams*, edited by Christopher Larch, Indianapolis, Bobbs-Merrill.

Addison Report, 1930. *Report of the National Parks Committee*, Cmnd 3851. London, HMSO.

Aldous, Anthony, 1989. *Inner City Regeneration and Good Design*. London, HMSO – Royal Fine Arts Commission.

Aldous, Anthony, 1992a. *Inner City Regeneration and Good Design*. London, Royal Fine Arts Commission.

Aldous, Anthony, 1992b. *Urban Villages*. Foreword by HRH The Prince of Wales. London, The Urban Village Group, 5 Cleveland Place, London W.1.

Aldridge, M. Meryl, 1979. *The British New Towns: A Programme without a Policy*. London, Routledge and Kegan Paul.

Alexander, Christopher, 1966. *A Pattern Language*. Oxford, Oxford University Press.

Allaun, Frank, 1978. *No Place Like Home: Britain's Housing Tragedy*. London, Deutsch.

Ambrose, Peter, 1986. *Whatever Happened to Planning?* London, Methuen.

Amery, Colin and Cruickshank, Dan, 1975. *The Rape of Britain*. London, Paul Elek.

Amos, Christopher, 1991. Flexibility and variety – the key to new settlement policy. *Town and Country Planning*, February, 52–6.

Anson, Brian, 1981. *I'll Fight You for It – Behind the Struggle for Covent Garden*. London, Jonathan Cape.

Anson, Brian, 1987. The battle for Covent Garden. *Architect's Journal*, 22 July, 24–7.

Antoniou, J., 1968. Pedestrians in the City. *Official Architecture and Planning*, August, 1935–40. London.

Architect's Journal, 1976. Architect's account: housing at Byker by Ralph Erskine. *Architect's Journal*, 14 April, 732–4.

Architect's Journal, 1987. Planning Use Classes Order. *Architect's Journal*, 5 August, 57–8.

Architect's Journal, 1992. Making places, Centenary Square. *Architect's Journal*, 5 February.

Architect's Journal, 1988. Stirling in Context. *Architect's Journal*, 4 May, 24–9.

Architectural Review, 1973a. Vol. CLIII, Number 911, January.

Architectural Review, 1973b. Bath destroyed; Under Eros. Vol. CLIII, Number 915, 279–306.

Arup Economic Consultants, 1991. *Simplified Planning Zones: Progress and Procedures, DoE Planning Research Programme*. London, HMSO.

Ashworth, G.J. and Tunbridge, J.E., 1990. *The Tourist – Historic City*. London, Belhaven Press.

Ashworth, William, 1968. *The Genesis of Modern Town Planning*. London, Routledge.

Atkinson, Rob and Moon, Graham, 1994. *Urban Policy in Britain. The City, the State and the Market*. London, Macmillan.

Avril, Robert, 1969. *Man and the Environment: Crisis and the Strategy of Choice*. Harmondsworth, Penguin.

Bacon, Edmund, 1967. *Design of Cities*. London, Thames & Hudson, 173–201.
(1979. Reprinted.)

Bailey, Nicholas, Barker, A. and McDonald, K., 1995. *Partnership Agencies in British Urban Policy*. Lond, University College.

Banham, Reyner, 1976. *Megastructure: Urban Futures of the Recent Past*. London, Harper and Row.

Barlow Report, 1940. *Report of the Royal Commission on the Distribution of the Industrial Population*, Cmnd 6153. London, HMSO, 20, 86.

Barnett, Henrietta, 1918. *The Garden Suburb – Its Past and Plans*. Privately published, 198–207.

Batty, Michael, 1994. A chronicle of scientific planning. *American Planning Association Journal*, Winter, Vol. 60, No. 1, p. 9.

de la Bédoyère, Guy, 1992. *Roman Towns in Britain*. London, Batsford.

Bell, Colin and Bell, Rose, 1969. *City Fathers: The Early History of Town Planning in Britain*. London, Cresset Press.
(1972. Reprinted. London, Pelican.)

Bell, G. and Tyrwhitt, J. (eds), 1972. The neighbourhood concept, in *Human Identity in the Urban Environment*. London, Hutchinson, 231–40.

Bendixson, Terence, 1988. *The Peterborough Effect. Reshaping a City*. Peterborough Development Corporation.

Benevolo, Leonardo, 1970. *The Origins of Modern Town Planning*. London, Kegan and Paul, 39–54.

Benevolo, Leonardo, 1980. *The History of the City*. London, Scolar Press, 135–251.

Berdini, Paolo, 1983. *Walter Gropius*. Bologna, Zarichelli.

Berdini, Paolo, 1994. *Walter Gropius*, Spanish/English edition. Barcelona, Gustave Gili.

Beresford, M.W., 1967. *New Towns of the Middle Ages*. Guildford, Lutterworth Press.

Beveridge Report, 1942. *Social Insurance and Allied Services*, Cmnd 6404. London, HMSO.

Binney, Marcus, 1980. New life for Le Doux's masterpiece, The Saltworks at Arc-et-Serrans. *Country Life*, 10 July, 157–8.

Birmingham City Council, 1913. *Inquiry into Housing Conditions*. Birmingham.

Blake, Peter, 1960. *The Master Builders*. New York, Knopf.

Boardman, P., 1978. *The Worlds of Patrick Geddes: Biologist, Town Planner, Re-educator, Peace Warrior*. London, Routledge and Kegan Paul.

Bolsterli, Margaret J., 1977. *The Early Community at Bedford Park: Corporate Happiness in the First Garden Suburb*. London, Routledge and Kegan Paul. (Am. Edn, Columbus, Ohio University Press.)

Booth, C., 1886. *Life and Labour of the People* (17 vols). London, Williams and Norgate. (Booth's mammoth work is summarised in A. Friend and R.M. Elmon (eds), 1969, *Charles Booth*. London, Hutchinson.)

Booth, C. (ed.), 1892. *Life and Labour of the People in London. Vol. 1. East, Central and South London*. London, Macmillan.

Bor, Walter, 1972. *The Making of Cities*. London, Hill.

Bor, Walter, 1978. The Lansbury neighbourhood re-appraised. *The Planner*, January, Vol. 64, No. 1.

Bor, Walter, 1995. A meeting of minds. *Architect's Journal*, 2 March, 60–1.

Bor, Walter and Shankland, Graeme, 1965. *Liverpool City Centre Plans*. Liverpool City and County Borough of Liverpool.

Bracken, Ian, 1981. *Urban Planning Methods: Research and Policy Analysis*. London. Methuen.

Breheny, M., 1989. In search of survey–analysis–plan. *The Planner*, 2 June.

Briggs, Asa, 1963. *Victorian Cities*. London, Oldhams.
(1968. Harmondsworth, Pelican.)

Brindley, T., Rydin, Y. and Stoker, G., 1989. *Remaking Planning*. London, Unwin Hyman.

Bristol City Council, 1989. *Bristol Centre Draft Local Plan*. Bristol.

Broadbent, Geoffrey, 1990. *Emerging Concepts in Urban Space Design*. London, Van Nostrand Reinhold.

Brundtland Commission, 1981. *Our Common Future*. Oxford, Oxford University Press, 43.

Bruton, Michael, 1975. *Introduction to Transportation Planning, Built Environment*. London, Hutchinson.

Bruton, Michael and Nicholson, David, 1987. *Local Planning in Practice*. London, Hutchinson.

Buchanan Report, 1963. *Traffic in Towns*. A study of the long term problems of traffic in urban areas. Reports of the Steering Group and Working Group, Professor Colin Buchanan. London, HMSO.

Buchanan, Colin, 1972. *The State of Britain*. London, Faber & Faber.

Buchanan, Colin & Partners, 1965. *Bath, a Planning and Transport Study*. A report to the MHLG and

Bath City Council. London, Buchanan and Partners.

Buchanan, Colin & Partners, 1966. *The South Hampshire Study: Report and Feasibility of Major Urban Growth*, London, Buchanan and Partners.

Buckingham, J.S., 1849. *National Evils and Practical Remedies*. London.

Burchell, Robert, 1972. *Planning Unit Development. New Communities American Style, New Brunswick, New Jersey*. Rutgers University.

Burke, Gerald, 1971. *Towns in the Making*. London, Edward and Arnold, Ch. 7.
   (1977. Reprinted.)

Burke, Gerald, 1976. *Townscapes*. London, Pelican.

Burke, Gerald, 1980. *Town Planning and the Surveyor*. London, Estates Gazette.

Burnett, J., 1978. *A Social History of Housing 1815–1970*. Newton Abbott, David & Charles, 231.

Burns, J., 1908. Speech on Housing, Town Planning, etc. Bill. Commons Housing, Fourth Services, 186, 947–68.

Burns, Wilfred, 1963. *New Towns for Old, The Technique of Urban Renewal*. London, Leonard Hill.

Burns, Wilfred, 1967. *Newcastle – A Study in Replanning at Newcastle-upon-Tyne*. London, Leonard Hill.

Butt, J. (ed.), 1971. *Robert Owen: Prince of Cotton Spinners*. Newton Abbott, David & Charles.

Butt, J., Donnachie, I. and Hume, J.H., 1971. *Robert Owen of New Lanark (1771–1858), a Bi-Centennial Tribute*. Scotland, The Open University.

Cameron, G., 1980. *The Future of the British Conurbation: Policies and Prescriptions for Change*. London, Longman.

Caramel, Luciano, 1973. Futurist architecture. *Futurismo 1909–1919*. Exhibition of Italian Futurism, Royal Scottish Academy, 16 Dec. 1972–14 Jan. 1973. Edinburgh, Northern Arts and Scottish Arts Council.

Carson, Rachel, 1962. *Silent Spring*. London, Hamish Hamilton.
   (1965. Harmondsworth Penguin)

Carter, Howard, 1983. *An Introduction to Historical Geography*. London, Edward Arnold.

Catanese, Anthony and Snyder, James (eds), 1979. *Urban Planning*. New York, McGraw-Hill.
   (1988. Reprinted.)

Chadwick, Sir Edwin, 1833. *Report from the Select Committee on Public Walks*.

Chadwick, Sir Edwin, 1840. *Select Committees on the Health of Towns*.

Chadwick, Sir Edwin, 1842. *Report on the Sanitary Condition of the Labouring Population of Great Britain*.

Chadwick, Sir Edwin, 1842. *Report to the Poor Law Commission*.

Chadwick, Sir Edwin, 1844, 1845. *Reports of the Royal Commission on the State of Large Towns*.

Chadwick, Sir Edwin, Flinn, M.W. (ed.), 1965. *Report on the Sanitary Condition of the Labouring Population of Great Britain, 1842*. Edinburgh, Edinburgh University Press.

Chadwick, George, 1971. *A Systems View of Planning – Towards a Theory of the Urban and Regional Planning Process*. Oxford, Pergamon.

Checkoway, Barry, 1994. Paul Davidoff and advocacy planning in retrospect. *Journal of the American Institute of Planners*, Vol. 60, No. 2, 139–235.

Cherry, Gordon, 1970. *Town Planning in its Social Context*. London, Leonard Hill.

Cherry, Gordon, 1972. *Urban Change and Planning: A History of Urban Development in Britain since 1750*. Henley, Foulis, 20–31, 129, 133–5, 150.

Cherry, Gordon, 1974. *The Evolution of British Town Planning. A History of Town Planning in the United Kingdom during the 20th Century and of the Royal Town Planning Institute, 1914–78*. London, Leonard Hill.

Cherry, Gordon, 1988. *Cities and Plans, the Shaping of Urban Britain in the Nineteenth and Twentieth Centuries*. London, Edward Arnold.

Cherry, Gordon and Leith, Penny, 1986. *Holford: A Study in Architecture, Planning and Civic Design*. London, Mansell.

Choay, Françoise, 1969. *The Modern City: Planning in the 19th Century*. London, Studio Vista.

Church, A., 1988. Urban regeneration in London Docklands: a five year policy review. *Environment and Planning C: Government and Policy*, 6, 187–204.

City of London, 1986. *City of London Local Plan*. Corporation of London.

Civic Trust, 1959. *Magdalen Street, Norwich 1958–59, An Experiment in Civic Design*. London, Civic Trust.

Civic Trust, 1974. *Pride of Place: A Manual for Those Wishing to Improve their Surroundings*. London, Civic Trust.

Clout, Hugh and Wood, Peter (eds), 1986. *London: Problems of Change*. Harlow, Longman.

Coleman, Alice, 1985. *Utopia on Trial: Vision and Reality in Planned Housing*. London, Hilary Shipman.
   (1990. Second edition.)

Collins, G.R. and Collins, C.C., 1965. *Camillo Sitte and the Birth of Modern City Planning*. London, Phaidon Press.

(1986. Revised edition, Rizzoli International.)

Colquohoun, Ian, 1995. *Urban Regeneration, an International Perspective*. London, Batsford.

Commission of the European Communities, 1990. *Green Paper on the Environment*. Brussels: EEC.

Cooch, Chris, 1990. *Urban Renewal: Theory and Practice*. London, Macmillan Educational.

Cook, Peter, 1973. *Archigram*. New York. Praeger.

Cook, Stephen, 1991. Success story that moved the council housing goal posts. *The Guardian*, 5 November.

Cornforth, John, 1985a. Roman Camp, Norman Castle, Rochester, Kent. *Country Life*, 13 June, 1672–5.

Cornforth, John, 1985b. High Street rhythm, Rochester, Kent II. *Country Life*, 14 July, 28–32.

Cornforth, John, 1990. Changing city, City of London. *Country Life*, 13 December, 50–2.

Country Life, 1989. New Architecture Number Cover, 6 April.

da Costa Meyer, Esther, 1995. *The Work of Antonio Sant' Elia: Retreat into the Future*. New Haven, Yale University.

Creese, Walter, 1966a. *The Search for Environment: The Garden City Movement Before and After*. New Haven, Yale University Press, 255.

Creese, Walter, 1966b. The oasis at Bedford Park, in *The Search for Environment*. New Haven, Yale University Press, 87–107.

Creese, Walter, 1967. *The Legacy of Raymond Unwin: A Human Pattern for Planning*. Cambridge, Massachusetts Institute of Technology; contains collection of Unwin's writings.

Cresswell, R. and Grove, A.B., 1983. *City Landscapes: a Contribution to the Council of Europe's Campaign for Urban Renaissance*. London, Butterworth.

Crouch, M. and Ward, R., 1992. Managing town centres. *The Planner*, Vol. 78, No. 15, 16 March.

Cruickshank, Dan, 1991. Village vision. *Architect's Journal*, 16 October, 10–11.

Cullen, Gordon, 1961. *Townscape*. London, Architectural Press.

Cullen, Gordon, 1971. *The Concise Townscape*. London, Architectural Press.

Cullingworth, J.B., 1975. *Peacetime History Environmental Planning*, Vol. 3, *Reconstruction and Land Use Planning 1939–1947*. London, HMSO.

Cullingworth, J.B., 1988. *Town and Country Planning in Britain*. London, Allen and Unwin. Tenth Edition.

Cullingworth, J.B., 1994. Alternate planning systems. Is there anything to learn from abroad? *Journal of the American Institute of Planners*, Vol. 60, No. 2, Spring, 162–72.

Cullingworth, J.B. and Nadin, Vincent, 1994. *Town and Country Planning in Britain*. London, Routledge. Eleventh Edition.

Cumbernauld Development Corporation, 1960. *Report on the Central Area. Part One – Retail and Service Trade Provisions. Part Two – Public Use. Part Three – Design Written Statement*. Cumbernauld, Chief Architect and Planning Officers Department.

Curl, James Steven, 1976. Victorian garden village, Port Sunlight, Merseyside. *Country Life*, 16 December.

Curl, James Steven, 1983. Surrender to the motor car, Winchester under threat. *Country Life*, 13 October, 992–3.

Darley, Gillian, 1990. *Octavia Hill: A Life*. London, Constable.

Davidoff, Paul, 1965. Advocacy and pluralism in planning. *Journal of the American Institute of Planners*, Vol. 31, No. 4, 331–8.

Davis, Terence, 1973. *John Nash: The Prince Regent's Architect*. London, David & Charles.

Deakin, Derick (ed.), 1989. *Wythenshawe: The Story of a Garden City*. Chichester, Phillimore.

Dennis, Michael, 1988. *Court and Garden: From the French Hotel to the City of Modern Architecture*. Cambridge, Mass., MIT Press.

Department of Economic Affairs, 1965. *The North-West: A Regional Study*. London, HMSO.

Department of Economic Affairs and West Midlands, 1965. *The West Midlands: A Regional Study*. London, HMSO.

Department of the Environment, 1970. *The Planning of the Coastline and Coastal Heritage*. London, HMSO.

DoE, 1971a. *Site Layout for Planning for Daylight and Sunlight*. Building Research Establishment.

DoE, 1971b. *Sunlight and Daylight: Planning Criteria and Design of Buildings*. London, HMSO.

DoE, 1972. *Development Plan Manual*. London, HMSO.

DoE, 1973a. *Better Homes – The Next Priorities*. London, HMSO.

DoE, 1973b. *Strategic Planning in the South-East: A First Report of the Monitoring Group*. London, HMSO.

DoE, 1977a. *Unequal City: Final Report of the Birmingham Inner Area Study*. London, HMSO.

DoE, 1977b. *Inner London: Proposals for Dispersal and Balance: Final Report of the Lambeth Inner*

Area Study. London, HMSO.

DoE, 1977c. *Change or Decay: Final Report of the Liverpool Inner Area Study*. London, HMSO.

DoE, 1977d. *Inner Area Studies: Liverpool, Birmingham and Lambeth: Summaries of Consultants' Final Reports*. London, HMSO.

DoE, 1977e. *White Paper: Policy for the Inner Cities*, Cmnd. 6845. London, HMSO.

DoE, 1978a. *Research Notes: Environmental Improvement November 3/77. General Improvement Areas. Housing Improvement Groups*. London, DoE.

DoE, 1978b. *Strategic Plan for the South-East: Review Government Statement*. London, HMSO.

DoE, 1979. *Time for Industry: Evaluation of the Rochdale Industrial Improvement Area*. Tym and Partners, Franklin Stafford Partnership, Richard Bareti, Traffic and Transport Associates, Consultants. London, HMSO.

DoE, 1982. *1981 English Housing Conditions Survey*. London, HMSO.

DoE, 1983. *White Paper: Streamlining the Cities*. London, HMSO.

DoE, 1984a. *Green Belts Circular 14/84*. London, HMSO.

DoE, 1984b. *Land for Housing Circular 15/84*. London, HMSO.

DoE, 1984c. *Survey of Derelict Land in England 1982*. London, HMSO.

DoE, 1985. *White Paper: Lifting the Burden*, Cmnd 9571. London, HMSO.

DoE, 1986. *The Future of Development Plans*. London, HMSO.

DoE, 1987. *An Evaluation of the Enterprise Zone Experiment, Inner Cities Research Programme*. London, HMSO.

DoE, 1988. *Improving Urban Areas*. London, HMSO.

DoE, 1989a. *Strategic Planning Guidance for London*. London, HMSO.

DoE, 1989b. *White Paper: The Future of Development Plans*, Cmnd 569. London, HMSO.

DoE, 1989c. *Regional Planning Guidance for the South East*. London, HMSO.

DoE, 1990a. *Planning Policy Guidance: Regional Planning Guidances, Structure Plans and the Content of Development Plans*. London, HMSO.

DoE, 1990b. *White Paper: This Common Inheritance, Britain's Environmental Strategy*, Cmnd 1200. London, HMSO.

DoE, 1991a. *Policy Appraisal and the Environment*. London, HMSO.

DoE, 1991b. *City Challenge: Draft Guidance*. London, HMSO.

DoE, 1992a. *The Urban Regeneration Agency: a Consultation Paper*. London, HMSO.

DoE, 1992b. *Development Plan: a Good Practice Guide*. London, HMSO.

DoE, 1993a. *1991 English House Condition Survey*. London, HMSO.

DoE, 1993b. *The Effectiveness of Green Belts*. London, HMSO.

DoE, 1994. *Assessing the Impact of Urban Policy, Inner Cities Research Programme*. London, HMSO.

DoE, 1995a. *Quality in Town and Country. Urban Design Campaign*. London, HMSO.

DoE, 1995b. *Rural White Paper: Rural England: A Nation Committed to a Living Countryside*. Cmnd 3016. London, HMSO.

Department of Health for Scotland, 1958. *Housing Layout*. Edinburgh, HMSO. (1961. Reprinted.)

Department of Industry, Trade and Regional Development, 1963. *The North East: a Programme for Regional Development and Growth*, Cmnd 2206. London, HMSO.

Department of Transport, 1968. *Transport in London*. London, HMSO.

Department of Transport, 1990. *Roads in Urban Areas*. London, HMSO.

Design Council and the Royal Town Planning Institute, 1979. *Streets Ahead*. London, Design Council.

Docklands Consultative Committee, 1990. *The Docklands Experiment. A Critical Review of Eight Years of the London Docklands Development Corporation*. London, DCC.

Docklands Consultative Committee, 1992. *All that Glitters in not Gold: a Critical Assessment of Canary Wharf*. London, DCC.

Docklands Joint Committee, 1976. *London Docklands: A Strategic Plan: Draft for Public Consultation*. London, DJC.

Docklands Review Committee, 1980. *London Docklands – Past, Present and Future*. London, DRC.

Docklands Study Team, 1973. *Docklands: Redevelopment Proposals for East London, Main Report*. London, Travers, Morgan Planning Consultants.

Donnison, D. and Middleton, A., 1987. *Regenerating the Inner City – Glasgow Experience*. London, Routledge and Kegan Paul.

Donnison, D. and Soto, P., 1980. *The Good City: A Study of Urban Development and Policy in Britain*. London, Heinemann.

Dudley Report, 1944. *Design of Dwellings, Central Housing Advisory Committee, Ministry of Health.* London, HMSO.

Eagle Star, 1991. *Micheldever Station Market Town. A Town for Hampshire's Future.* Winchester, Eagle Star Estates.

Elson, Martin, 1986. *Green Belts, Conflict Mediation in the Urban Fringe.* London, Heinemann.

Enfield London Borough, 1971. 'The provision of public open space' by N.A. Stonard. London, Enfield London Borough.

Engels, F., 1971. *The Condition of the Working Class in England in 1844,* translated by W.O. Henderson and W.H. Chalmer. Oxford, Blackwell. Second Edition.

Esher, Lionel, 1981. *A Broken Wave – The Rebuilding of England 1940–1980.* Harmondsworth, Middx, Allen Lane.
  (1993. Harmondsworth, Penguin.)

Essex County Council, 1973. *A Design Guide for Residential Areas.* Chelmsford, Essex County Council.

European Commission, 1990. *Green Paper on the Urban Environment.* Brussels: EC Fourth Environmental Action Programme 1982–92.

Evans, E.S.P., 1981. *Planning Handbook.* Liverpool, Liverpool City Council.

Evenson, Norma, 1966. *Chandigarh.* Berkeley, University of California Press.

Faludi, Andreas, 1971. *A Reader in Planning Theory.* Oxford, Pergamon.

Faludi, Andreas, 1973. *Planning Theory.* Oxford, Pergamon.

Fergusson, Adam, 1973. *The Sack of Bath. A Record and an Indictment.* Salisbury, Compton Russell.

Fergusson, Adam and Mowl, Tim, 1989. *The Sack of Bath and After.* Bath, Bath Preservation Trust and Russell Publishing.

Fishman, R., 1977. *Urban Utopias in the Twentieth Century: Ebenezer Howard, Frank Lloyd Wright and Le Corbusier.* New York, Basic Books.

Gallion, A., 1950. *The Urban Pattern, City Planning and Design.* London, Van Nostrand.

Gallion, A. and Eisner, S., 1963. *The Urban Pattern, City Planning and Design* (reprinted). Princeton, Van Nostrand.

Garnier, Anthony, 1917. *Une Cité Industrielle: Étude pour la Construction des Villes.* Paris.
  (1988. Reprinted. Paris, Philippe Sers.)

Geddes, Patrick, 1904. *City Development: A Study of Parks, Gardens and Culture Institutes.* Edinburgh: Geddes & Co.

Geddes, Patrick, 1915. *Cities in Evolution: An Introduction to the Town Planning Movement and to the Study of Civics.* London, Williams and Norgate. Contains remarks about Sitte which are not in the 1949 edition.

Geddes, Patrick, 1916–22. Town Planning Reports in India: Lucknow, Madras, Patiala, etc.

Geddes, Patrick, 1917. *Town Planning in Lahore: A Report to the Municipal Council.* Lahore, Commercial Printing Works.

Geddes, Patrick, 1918. *Town Planning Towards City Development: a Report to the Durbar of Indore. Part I.* Indore.

Geddes, Patrick, 1922. *Town Planning in Patiala State and City. A Report to the Maharaja of Patiala.* Lucknow, Perry's Printing Press.

Geddes, Patrick, 1949. *Cities in Evolution,* edited by The Outlook Tower Association, Edinburgh, and The Association for Planning and Regional Reconstruction (editors: Arthur Geddes and Jacqueline Tyrwhitt). London, Williams and Norgate, 14–15.

Geddes, Patrick, 1965. *Urban Improvements: A Strategy for Urban Works. Part 2, Town Planning in Lahore.* Reprint of 1917 report. Government of Pakistan, Planning Commission, Physical Planning and Town Planning Section.

Geddes, Patrick, 1969. *Cities in Evolution, 1949* (Outlook Tower Association). Edinburgh, Edinburgh University Press.

Gibberd, Frederick, 1953. *Town Design.* London, Architectural Press.
  (1970. Reprinted.)

Gibberd, Frederick, 1980. *Harlow: The Story of a New Town.* London, Publications for Companies.

Gibson, M. and Langstaff, M., 1982. *An Introduction to Urban Renewal.* London, Hutchinson.

Giedion, Siegfried, 1954. *Walter Gropius.* New York, Dover.

Giedion, Siegfried, 1967. City planning as a human problem (pp. 430–9, 473–508); City planning in the 19th century (pp. 707–75); in *Space, Time and Architecture* by S. Giedion, Cambridge, Mass., Harvard University Press. Fourth Edition.

Ginsberg, L., 1955. Green belts in the Bible. *Journal of the Royal Town Planning Institute,* Vol. 1, 165.

Glass, Ruth (ed.), 1948. *The Social Background of a Plan, a Study of Middlesbrough.* London, Routledge and Kegan Paul.

Glasson, John, 1974. *An Introduction to Regional Planning.* London, University College.
  (1978. Second Edition.)
  (1992. Sixth impression.)

Golany, Gideon, 1976. *New Town Planning:*

Principles and Practice. New York, John Wiley & Sons.

Gosling, David, 1988. Urban forms and spaces: waterfront development. School of Architecture, Newcastle University. *Urban Futures*, Vol. 1, No. 1.

Greater London Council, 1966. *London Transport Study, Vol. II*. London GLC.

GLC, 1967. *London Transport Study, Vol. III*. London, GLC.

GLC, 1969a. *Greater London Development Plan, Statement*. London, GLC.

GLC, 1969b. *Tomorrow's London, a Background to the Greater London Development Plan*. London, GLC.

GLC, 1973. *Pedestrianised Streets, GLC Study Tour of Europe and America*. London, Department of Planning and Transport, GLC.

GLC, 1976a. *Greater London Development Plan. Notice of approval: written statement, proposal map, key diagram and urban landscape diagram*. London, GLC.

GLC, 1976b. *Greater London Development Plan, Report of Studies*. London, GLC.

GLC, 1976c. *Home Sweet Home: Housing Designed by the London County Council and Greater London Council Architects, 1888–1975*. London, GLC.

GLC, 1981. *Planning Policies for London Appraisal*. Report P124. London, GLC.

GLC, 1984a. *Alterations to the Greater London Development Plan: Explanations*. Memorandum. London, GLC.

GLC, 1984b. *Alterations to the Greater London Development Plan: Revised Plans Incorporating the Alterations*. London, GLC.

Greater London Regional Planning Committee, 1929. *First Report*. London, Knopp, Drewett.

GLRPC, 1931. *Interim Report on Open Spaces*. London, Knopp, Drewett.

GLRPC, 1933. *Second Report*. London, Knopp, Drewett.

Greed, Clara, 1993. *Introducing Town Planning*. Harlow, Longman Scientific and Technical, 67.

Grieve, Sir Robert, 1991. *Grieve on Geddes*. Edinburgh, Sir Patrick Geddes Memorial Trust, 16–21.

Gropius, Walter, 1935. *The New Architecture and the Bauhaus*. London, Faber & Faber.

Gropius, Walter, 1943. *Scope of Total Architecture*. New York, Harper and Bros.
    (1966. Reprinted. New York, Collier Books.)

Grove, J., 1979. The rise and fall of the GIA. *The Planner*, Vol. 65, No. 2, 35–7.

Hackney, Rod, 1988. *The Good, the Bad and the Ugly. Cities in Crisis*. London, Hutchinson.

Hall, David, 1991. Regional strategies. *Town and Country Planning*, May.

Hall, Peter, 1963. *London 2000*. London, Faber & Faber.
    (1971. Second Edition.)

Hall, Peter, 1973. *The Containment of Urban England*. London, George Allen and Unwin.
    (1977. Second Edition.)

Hall, Peter, 1974. *Urban and Regional Planning*. Harmondsworth, Penguin, 12.
    (1992. Second edition.)

Hall, Peter, 1980. *Great Planning Disasters*. London, Weidenfeld and Nicholson.

Hall, Peter, 1988. *Cities of Tomorrow. An Intellectual History of Urban Planning and Design in the Twentieth Century*. Oxford, Basil Blackwell, 68–71.

Hall, Peter, 1989. *London 2001*. London, Unwin Hyman.

Hall, Peter, 1991. A new strategy for the South East. *The Planner*, Vol. 77, No. 10, 22 March.

Hancock, John, 1980. *Urban Development and Planning*. Oxford, Basil Blackwell.

Hardy, Dennis, 1991a. *From Garden Cities to New Towns. Campaigning for Town and Country Planning, 1899–1946*. London, E. & F. Spon.

Hardy, Dennis, 1991b. *From New Town to Green Politics. Campaigning for Town and Country Planning, 1946–1990*. London, E. & F. Spon.

Harrison, J.F.C., 1969. *Robert Owen and the Owenites in Britain and America, 1946–1990*.

Hartman, Chester, 1984. *The Transformation of San Francisco, 1969–1984*. Ottawa: Rowman and Allanheld. London, E. & F. Spon.

Harvey, D., 1985. *Consciousness and the Urban Experience: Studies in the History and Theory of Capitalist Urbanization*. Oxford, Basil Blackwell.

Hellman, Louis, 1986. *Architecture for Beginners*. London, Unwin Paperbacks.

Herbert, Gilbert, 1959. *The Synthetic Vision of Walter Gropius*. Johannesburg, Witwatersrand University Press, 4.

Herbert, Michael, 1993. The City of London Walkway experiment. *Journal of the American Planning Association*, Vol. 59, No. 4, Autumn, 433–50.

Herbert Report, 1960. *The Royal Commission on Local Government in Greater London, 1957–60*, Cmnd 1164. London, HMSO.

Herington, J., 1989. *Planning Processes, an Introduction for Geographers*. Cambridge,

Cambridge University Press.

Hillman, J., 1990. *Planning for Beauty: The Case for Design Guide Lines*. Royal Fine Art Commission. London, HMSO.

Hiorns, F.R., 1956. *Town Building in History. An outline view of condition, influences, ideas and methods affecting 'planned' towns through five thousand years*. London, George Harrap.

Hobhouse Report, 1947. *Report of the National Parks Committee, England and Wales*. London, HMSO.

Holden, C.H. and Holford, W.G., 1951. *The City of London: A Record of Destruction and Survival with a Report of Reconstruction*. London, Architectural Press.

Holford, W.G., 1950. Introduction, *Town and Country Planning Textbook*, Association for Planning and Regional Reconstruction. London, Architectural Press, V.

Holford, Sir William & Associates, 1965. *High Buildings Report*. Edinburgh Corporation.

Home, R.H., 1982. *Inner City Regeneration*. London, E. & F. Spon.

Horne, R.K., 1982. *Inner City*. London, E. & F. Spon.

Hornung, B., 1989. *Scottish Planner* No. 8, April, Edinburgh.

Howard, Ebenezer, 1899. *Tomorrow: A Peaceful Path to Real Reform*. London, Swan Sonnenschein.

Howard, Ebenezer, 1902. *Garden Cities of Tomorrow*. London, Faber.

Howard, Ebenezer, 1974. *Garden Cities of Tomorrow*. Oxford, Alden & Mobray.

Howard, Ebenezer, 1976. Introduction by Lewis Mumford: *Garden Cities of Tomorrow*, edited by Frederick Osborn. London, Faber & Faber, paperback, 34.

Hubbard, Philip, 1994. Recognising design quality in development control. *Town and Country Planning*, November, 311–12.

Hutchinson, Max, 1989. *The Prince of Wales: Right and Wrong*. London, Faber & Faber.

Imrie, Rob and Thomas, Huw, 1993. *British Urban Policy and Urban Development Corporations*. London, Paul Chapman.

Irvine New Town Corporation, 1971. *Irvine New Town Plan*. Irvine, Irvine Development Corporation.

Isaacs, Reginald, 1991. *Walter Gropius, an Illustrated Biography of the Creator of the Bauhaus*. Boston, Little, Brown & Co.
(1983. German edition. Berlin, Gimbel.)

Ison, Walter, 1948. *The Georgian Buildings of Bath from 1700 to 1830*. London, Faber & Faber.

IUCN, 1980. *World Conservation Strategy*. International Union for the Conservation of Nature. Gland, Switzerland.

Jackson, F., 1985. *Sir Raymond Unwin: Architect, Planner and Visionary*. London, Zwemmer.

Jacobs, Jane, 1962. *The Death and Life of Great American Cities. The Failure of Town Planning*. London, Jonathan Cape.
(1965. Harmondsworth, Penguin.)

Jencks, Charles, 1988. *The Prince, the Architects and New Wave Monarchy*. London, Academy Editions.

Johnson-Marshall, Percy E.A., 1965. *Rebuilding Cities*. Edinburgh, Edinburgh University Press, 191, 291–318.

Johnson-Marshall, Percy & Associates, 1978. *Design Briefing in Towns, Report for the Urban Design Unit, Scottish Development Department*. Edinburgh, Scottish Development Department.

JURVE, 1986a. *An Evaluation of Industrial and Commercial Improvement Areas, Inner Cities Research Programme, DoE*. London, HMSO.

JURVE, 1986b. *Evaluation of Environmental Projects Funded under the Urban Programme*. DoE Inner Cities Research Programme. London, HMSO.

JURVE, 1988. *Improving Urban Areas: Case Studies of Good Practice in Urban Regeneration*. DoE. London, HMSO.

Keeble, Lewis, 1983. *Town Planning Made Plain*. London, Longman.

Kepes, Gyorgy, 1944. *Language of Vision*. Chicago, Chicago University Press.

Kitson, P.C., 1965. *The Making of Victorian England*. London, Methuen.

Knevitt, Charles, 1985. *Space on Earth*. London, Methuen.

Korn, Arthur, 1953. *History Builds the Town*. London, Lund Humphries.

Kostoff, Spiro, 1991. *The City Shaped: Urban Patterns and Meanings through History*. London, Thames and Hudson.

Kostoff, Spiro, 1992. *The City Assembled: the Elements of Urban Form through History*. London, Thames and Hudson.

Krier, L., 1974. Royal Mint Square housing. *Architectural Design*, 54 (7/8).

Krier, L., 1993. *Poundbury, Dorset, Architectural Design Profile No. 103*, 42–7.

Krier, R., 1973. *Urban Space*. London, Academy Editions.

Krumholz, Norman and Forester, John, 1990. *Making Equity Planning Work: Leadership in the Public Sector*. Philadelphia: Temple University Press.

Lawless, Paul, 1981. *Britain's Inner Cities. Problems and Policies*. London, Harper & Row.

(1988. Second Edition. London, Paul Chapman.)

Lawless, P. and Brown, F., 1986. *Urban Growth and Change in London*. London, Harper & Row.

Layfield Report, 1972. *Greater London Development Plan: Report of the Panel of Inquiry*, Vol. 1, December. London, HMSO.

Le Corbusier, 1929. *The City of Tomorrow and its Planning*, translated by Frederick Etchells from the eighth French edition of *Urbanism*.

(1947. Reprinted. London, Architectural Press.)

Le Corbusier, 1933. *La Ville Radieuse*.

(1964. Translated into English (*The Radiant City*. London, Faber & Faber.)

Le Corbusier, 1947a. *Concerning Town Planning*. London, Architectural Press.

Le Corbusier, 1947b. *When the Cathedrals were White*.

(1964. Translated from the French. New York, McGraw-Hill.)

Le Corbusier, 1953. *The Marseilles Block*. London, Harvill Press.

Le Corbusier, 1960. *Creation as a Patient Search*. New York, Praeger.

Le Corbusier, and Jeanneret, P. *Oeuvre Complète*:
1929. Vol. 1, 1910–1929. Zürich, W. Boesiger and O. Stonorov.
1934. Vol. 2, 1929–1934. Zürich, W. Boesiger.
1938. Vol. 3, 1934–1938. Zürich, Max Bill.
1946. Vol. 4, 1938–1946. Zürich, W. Boesiger.
1952. Vol. 5, 1946–1952. Zürich, W. Boesiger.
1957. Vol. 6, 1952–1957. Zürich, W. Boesiger.

Le Corbusier (Gans, Deborah), 1987. *'Chandigarh', The Le Corbusier Guide*. Princeton, Princeton Architectural Press; London, Architectural Press, 163–77.

Le Doux, Claude-Nicholas, 1804–46. *L'Architecture Considéré sous le Rapport de l'Art. des Moeurs et de la Législation*, Vols I–III. Paris.

Le Doux, Claude-Nicholas, 1971. *L'Oeuvre et les Réves de Ledoux*. Paris, Editions du Chêre.

Lee, Geoffrey, 1973. Threat to an ancient capital. *Country Life*, 27 September, 846–8.

Leeds City Council, 1972. *Leeds Pedestrian Streets*. Planning and Property Department, Leeds City Council.

Lees, Audrey, 1986. Seminar. Department of Urban Design and Regional Planning, University of Edinburgh.

Lindsay, Ian, 1948. *Georgian Edinburgh*. Edinburgh, Oliver and Boyd.

Ling, Arthur and Associates, 1967. *Runcorn New Town, Master Plan*. Runcorn Development Corporation.

Litchfield, Nathanial, Kettle, P. and Whithead, M., 1975. *Evaluation in the Planning Process*. Oxford, Pergamon.

Llewellyn-Davies, Weekes, Forestier-Walker and Bor, 1976. *Design Guidance Survey: Report on a Survey of Local Authority Guidance for Private Residential Development*. Department of the Environment and Housing Research Foundation. London, HMSO.

Lobel, Mary (ed.), 1990. *British Atlas of Historic Towns. The City of London, Prehistoric Times to c. 1520*. Oxford, Oxford University Press.

Lock, Max, 1946. *Middlesbrough Survey and Plan*. Middlesbrough County Borough.

Loew, Sebastian, 1979. Local Planning. London, Pembridge Press.

London County Council, 1960. *Administrative County of London Development Plan, First Review 1960, County Planning Report*. London, London County Council.

LCC, 1961. *The Planning of a New Town: Data and Design Based on a Study for a New Town of 100,000 at Hook, Hampshire*. London, London County Council.

(1969. Reprinted.)

LCC, 1964. *London Transport Study*, Vol. 1. London, London County Council.

London Planning Advisory Committee, 1988. *Strategic Planning Advice for London: Policies for the 1990's*. Romford, LPAC.

LPAC, 1990. *Strategic Trends and Policies, Annual Revision*. Romford, LPAC.

LPAC, 1991a. *Strategic Trends and Policies, Annual Revision*. Romford, LPAC.

LPAC, 1991b. *London: World City, Moving into the 21st Century*. London, HMSO.

LPAC, 1992. *Strategic Trends and Policies, Annual Review*. Romford, LPAC.

LPAC, 1994. *Advice on Strategic Planning Guidance for London*. Romford, LPAC.

Lutyens, Edwin and Abercrombie, Patrick, 1945. *A Plan for the City and County of Kingston upon Hull*. London, Brown.

Lynch, Kevin, 1960. *The Image of the City*. Cambridge, Mass., MIT Press.

McCallum, Ian, 1945. *Physical Planning. London*. London, Architectural Press, 100.

MacEwen, A. and MacEwen, M., 1987. *Green Prints for the Countryside. The Story of Britain's National Parks*. London, Routledge.

McHarg, Ian, 1969. *Design with Nature*. New York, Natural History Press.

(1992. Reprinted. New York, John Wiley & Sons.)

McHarg, Ian, 1978. Ecological planning: the planner as catalyst, in *Planning Theory in the 1980s*, eds Robert Burchell and George Sternlieb. New Jersey, Rutgers University, 13–17.

MacInally, T., 1981. *The Glasgow District Area Renewal Project*. PTRC Spring Meeting. Glasgow District Council, Bradford College.

McKay, Alexander, 1978. *Vitruvius, Architect and Engineer, Buildings and Building Techniques in Augustan Rome*. Bristol, Bristol Clerical Press.

McLoughlin, J.B., 1969. *Urban and Regional Planning, A Systems Approach*. London, Faber, 125.

McWilliam, Colin, 1975. *Scottish Townscape*. London, Collins.

McWilliam, Colin, 1984. *The Buildings of Scotland: Edinburgh*. Harmondsworth, Penguin.

Malt, Harold Lewis, 1970. *Furnishing the City*. New York, McGraw-Hill.

Mansley, R., 1972. *Areas of Need in Glasgow*. Second Review of the Development Plan. Glasgow, Corporation of Glasgow.

Marris, Peter, 1987. *Meaning and Action. Community Planning and Conceptions of Change*. London, Routledge and Kegan Paul.

Robert Matthew, Johnson-Marshall and Partners, 1967. *Central Lancashire New Town. A Study for a City*. Ministry of Housing and Local Government. London, HMSO.

Mellor, Helen, 1990. *Patrick Geddes: Social Evolutionist and City Planner*. London, Routledge.

Middleton, Michael, 1992. *Cities in Transition*. London, Michael Joseph.

Midlothian and West Lothian Planning Advisory Committee, 1966. *The Lothians Regional Survey and Plan*. Vol. I, *Economic and Social Aspects*, ed. J.J. Robertson. Vol. II, *Physical Planning Aspects*, by R. Mathew and P.E.A. Johnson-Marshall. Edinburgh, Scottish Development Department.

Miller, Mervyn, 1992. *Raymond Unwin: Garden Cities and Town Planning*. Leicester, Leicester University.

Miller, Mervyn and Gray, A. Stuart, 1992. *Hampstead Garden Suburb*. Chichester, Phillimore.

Ministry of Health. Circular 1305.

Ministry of Housing and Local Government, 1952. *The Density of Residential Areas*. London, HMSO.

MHLG, 1953. *Design in Town and Village*. London, HMSO.

MHLG, 1956. *Green Belts*, Circular 42/55. London, HMSO.

MHLG, 1958. *Flats and Houses*. London, HMSO.

MHLG, 1961. *White Paper*. London, HMSO.

MHLG, 1962a. *The Green Belt*. London, HMSO, 1–2.

MHLG, 1962b. *Town Centres: Approaches to Renewal*. London, HMSO.

MHLG, 1962c. *Residential Areas: Higher Densities*. London, HMSO.

MHLG, 1962–8. *Design Bulletins* (Nos 1–12); *Planning Bulletins* (Nos 1–7). London, HMSO.

MHLG, 1963. *London: Employment, Housing and Land*, Cmnd 1952. London, HMSO.

MHLG, 1964. *The South-East Study 1961–1981*. London, HMSO.

MHLG, 1965a. *The Future of Development Plans*. Report of Planning Advisory Group. London, HMSO.

MHLG, 1965b. *Northampton, Bedford and North Bucks Study*. London, HMSO.

MHLG, 1966a. *The Deeplish Study – Improvement Possibilities in an Area of Rochdale*. London, HMSO.

MHLG, 1966b. *White Paper: Leisure in the Countryside*, Cmnd 2928. London, HMSO.

MHLG, 1967. *Housing Conditions Survey, England and Wales, 1967*. London, HMSO.

MHLG, 1968. Four Studies in Conservation. London, HMSO:
Bath: A Study in Conservation, by Colin Buchanan and Partners.
Chichester: A Study in Conservation, by G.S. Burrows.
Chester: A Study in Conservation, by Donald Insall and Associates.
York: A Study in Conservation, by Viscount Esher.

MHLG, 1969. *People and Planning*. Skeffington Report. London, HMSO.

MHLG, 1970. *Development Plans. A Manual on Form and Content*. London, HMSO.

Ministry of Town and Country Planning, 1944. *White Paper: Control of Land Use*. London, HMSO.

MTCP, 1945. *National Parks in England and Wales*. Dower Report, Cmnd 6628. London, HMSO.

MTCP, 1947a. *Report of the National Parks Committee, England and Wales*. Hobhouse Committee. London, HMSO.

MTCP, 1947b. *Advisory Handbook on the Redevelopment of Central Areas*. London, HMSO.

MTCP, 1947c. *White Paper, Town and Country Planning, Explanations Memorandum*, 5.

MTCP, 1953. *Design in Town and Village*, by Thomas Sharp, Frederick Gibberd and William Holford. London, HMSO.

Ministry of Transport, 1946. *Design and Layout of Roads in Built-up Areas*. London, HMSO. (1957. Reprinted.)

MOT, 1966. *Roads in Urban Areas*. London, HMSO.

MOT, 1968. *Transport in London*. London, HMSO.

Moholy-Nagy, László, 1928. *The New Vision*. New York, George Wittenborn. (1947. Fourth revised edition.)

Moholy-Nagy, László, 1961. *Vision in Motion*. Chicago, Paul Theobald.

More, Sir Thomas, 1516. *Utopia*. (1965. Reprinted. Harmondsworth, Penguin.)

Morris, A.E.J., 1979. *History of Urban Form before the Industrial Revolution*. London, Longman, 92–156. (1994. Third edition.)

Morris, Eleanor Smith, 1957. Unpublished portfolio prepared for developers of London Wall. London, London County Council.

Morris, Eleanor Smith, 1960. Whaddon New Town master plan. *Architecture and Building*, Vol. 35, No. 6, June, 208–10.

Morris, Eleanor Smith, 1961. *The Growing City*. A series on Architecture and Town Planning for Sixth Formers. BBC Television for Schools. 30, 31 October, 6, 7 November, 13, 14 November, 20, 21 November.

Morris, Eleanor Smith, 1965a. The impact of high buildings in Edinburgh. *Edinburgh Architectural Association Year Book*, No. 9. Edinburgh, Edinburgh Pictorial.

Morris, Eleanor Smith, 1965b. *Comparative Urban Forms*. Civic Design Diploma Studio 1964–65. University of Edinburgh.

Morris, Eleanor Smith, 1975. Interview with Sir Colin Buchanan, Edinburgh.

Morris, Eleanor Smith, 1979. Pedestrian streets and spaces in Britain. Paper presented to the International Conference in Urban Design, Institute for Urban Design and University of Pennsylvania, 17–20 October. University of Pennsylvania, Philadelphia, Pa.

Morris, Eleanor Smith, 1986. An overview of planning for women from 1945–1975, in *New Communities, Did They Get It Right?*, ed. Marion Chalmers, Report of a Conference of the Women and Planning Standing Committee of the Royal Town Planning Institute (Scotland). Linlithgow, Edinburgh, RTPI.

Morris, Eleanor Smith, 1989a. The Carbuncle, the Stump and the Bore, Prince Charles' re-interpretation of urban design. Paper presented at Public Lecture, Department of Fine Art, University of Edinburgh, 27 April, Edinburgh.

Morris, Eleanor Smith, 1989b. The Bêtes-noires of Prince Charles. Paper presented to the 3rd AESOP Congress, 16–18 November, Tours, France.

Morris, Eleanor Smith, 1990. The Bêtes-noires of Prince Charles. Paper presented to the Institut für Stadtebau und Landes planning, Technischell Hochschule, 24 April, Aachen, Germany.

Morris, Eleanor Smith, 1991a. Urban design in Britain. Paper presented to College of Engineering, Division of Architecture, Temple University, and Department of City and Regional Planning, Graduate School of Fine Arts, University of Pennsylvania, Philadelphia, Pa.

Morris, Eleanor Smith, 1991b. Heritage, tourism and the people. Paper presented to the 5th AESOP Congress and 33rd ACSP Conference, 8–12 July, School of Planning, Oxford Polytechnic, Oxford.

Morris, Eleanor Smith, 1992. Heritage, tourism and the people. Paper presented to the 1992 Institute of British Geographers Conference, 7–10 January, Swansea.

Morris, Eleanor Smith, 1994. Heritage and culture – a capital for the New Europe, in *Building a New Heritage*, eds G. Ashworth and P. Larkham. London, Routledge, 229–59.

Morris, William, 1883. *Art and People*. London, Kelmscott Press.

Moughtin, Cliff, 1992. *Urban Design, Street and Square*. Oxford, Butterworth.

Mumford, Lewis, 1938. *The Culture of Cities, 'The Insensate Industrial Town'*. London, Secker and Warburg, 43–222. [Coketown: one of the most vivid descriptions of the horrors of the Industrial Town. *The Culture of Cities* contains a better version than *The City in History* (1961).]

Mumford, Lewis, 1954. The neighbourhood and the neighbourhood unit. *Town Planning Review*, January, 256–70.

Mumford, Lewis, 1955. *The Human Prospect 'Patrick Geddes'*. Carbondale, Illinois, Southern Illinois University Press, 99–115.

Mumford, Lewis, 1961. *The City in History, 'Paleotechnic Paradise, Coketown', Court Parade and Capital*. London, Secker and Warburg, 395–409, 446–82, 568–73.

Nairn, Ian, 1955. *Outrage* (a special number of the *Architectural Review*). *Architectural Review*, Vol. 117, 363–454.

Nairn, Ian, 1957. *Counter Attack, A Plan for Planning*. London, Architectural Press.

Naismith, Robert, 1989. *The Story of Scotland's Towns*. Edinburgh, John Donald, 28.

Nash, John., 1811. Plan for Marylebone Park.

Nash, John, 1812. Plan for Regent's Park.

Newham, London Borough, 1973. *Pedestrian Ways*. London, Newham Borough.

Newman, Oscar, 1973. *Defensible Space: People and Design in the Violent City*. London, Architectural Press.

Nuttgens, Patrick, 1989. *The Home Front – Housing the People 1840–1990*. London, BBC Books.

Olsen, Donald, 1964. *Town Planning in London, the Eighteenth and Nineteenth Centuries*. New Haven, Yale University Press.
(1982. Reprinted.)

Osborn, F.J., 1956. The Green Belt principle. *Town and Country Planning*, Vol. 24, 288–94.

Osborn, F.J. and Whittick, Arnold, 1977. *New Towns – Their Origins, Achievements and Progress*. London, International Textbook Co., 17.

Owen, Robert, 1817. *Report to the Committee for the Relief of the Manufacturing Poor*.

Owen, Robert, 1820. *Report to the County of Lanark*.
(1970. Harmondsworth, Penguin.)

Owen, Robert, 1972. *A New View of Society or Essays on the Formation of the Human Character* (1813–40), reprint. London, Macmillan.

P A Cambridge Economic Consultants, 1987. *An Evaluation of the Enterprise Zone Experiment*. DoE Inner Cities Research Programme. London, HMSO.

Parker-Morris Report, 1961. *Homes for Today and Tomorrow*. Central Housing Advisory Committee, Ministry of Housing and Local Government. London, HMSO.

Parliamentary Debates, 1908. Vol. 188, Col. 949, 12 May 1908. London, HMSO.

Pearce, David, 1989. *Conservation Today*. London, Routledge.

Pemberton, 1854. *The Happy Colony*.

Pendry, Richard, 1993. Dark forces fail to dim Sunlight's brilliant record. *Sunday Telegraph*, 28 February.

Perry, Clarence, 1929. *The Neighbourhood Unit: A Scheme of Arrangement for the Family–Life Community. Regional Plan of New York and its Environs*. New York, New York Regional Plan Association.

Perry, Clarence, 1933. *The Rebuilding of Blighted Areas: A Study of the Neighbourhood Unit in Replanning and Plot Assemblage*. New York, New York Regional Plan Association.

Pevsner, Nikolaus, 1957. *The Buildings of England: London*. Vol. I: *The Cities of London and Westminster*. London, Penguin.

(1993. Revised by Bridget Cherry.)

Pevsner, Nikolaus, 1958. *The Buildings of England: North Somerset and Bristol*. London, Penguin.
(1995. Reprinted.)

Planning Advisory Group Report, 1965. *The Future of Development Plans*. Ministry of Housing and Local Government. London, HMSO.

Port Sunlight Heritage Centre, 1990. *News Focus, Port Sunlight Heritage Centre*. New York, Harper Collins.

Powdrill, E.A., 1975. Vocabulary of land planning. *Estates Gazette*: 3–4.

Powell, K., 1984. The threat to Saltaire, road proposals for a West Yorkshire village. *Country Life*, 20 September.

Prestwich, R. and Taylor, P., 1990. *Introduction to Regional and Urban Policy in the United Kingdom*. London, Longman.

Prince of Wales, 1984. RIBA Gala speech, 150th anniversary of RIBA, Hampton Court, 30 May. See Charles Jencks, 1988, *The Prince, the Architects and New Wave Monarchy*, London, Academy Editions.

Prince of Wales, 1989. *A Vision of Britain: A Personal View of Architecture*. London, Doubleday.

Punter, John, 1990a. *Design Control in Bristol 1940–1990*. Bristol, Redcliffe Press.

Punter, John, 1990b. The Ten Commandments of architecture and urban design. *The Planner*, Vol. 76, No. 39, 10–14.

Purdom, C.B., 1925. *The Building of Satellite Towns: A Contribution to the Study of Town Development and Regional Planning*. London, J.M. Dent.
(1949. Reprinted.)

Rasmussen, Steen Eiler, 1937. *London, The Unique City*. London, Jonathan Cape, 67–69, 74.

Rasmussen, Steen Eiler, 1951. *Towns and Buildings*. *'A Tale of Two Cities'*. Liverpool, Liverpool University Press, 103–10.

Redcliffe-Maud Report, 1969. *Local Government Reform*. Report of the Royal Commission on Local Government in England, Cmnd 4039. London, HMSO.

Reith Reports, 1946. Reports of the New Town Committee. Chairman: Rt. Hon. Lord Reith of Stonehaven. Ministry of Town and Country Planning and Department of Health for Scotland: *Interim Report*, Cmnd 6759; *Second Interim Report*, Cmnd 6794; *Final Report*, Cmnd 6876. London, HMSO.

Rochdale Metropolitan Borough, 1977. *Industrial Obsolescence: The Rochdale Approach*. Rochdale Metropolitan Borough.

Rogers, R. and Fisher, M., 1992. *A New London*. London, Penguin.

Rosenau, Helen, 1959. *The Ideal City and its Architectural Evolution*. London, Routledge and Kegan Paul.
(1983. Reprinted.)

Rosenau, Helen, 1970. *Social Purpose in Architecture. Paris and London Compared, 1760–1800*. London, Studio Vista.

Rossi, Aldo, 1966. *L'Architettura della Citta*. Padua.

Rossi, Aldo, 1982. *The Architecture of the City*. Translated by Ghivado and Ackman. Cambridge, Mass., MIT Press.
(1989. Fifth edition.)

Royal Town Planning Institute, 1989. *Planning for Town and Country. Context and Achievement 1914–1989*. RTPI 75th Anniversary. London, Royal Town Planning Institute.

Ruskin, John, 1853. *The Stones of Venice*. Kent, George Allen.
(1886. Fourth Edition.)

Ruskin, John, 1960. *The Stones of Venice*, ed. J.G. Links. New York, Da Capo Press.

Savitch, H., 1988. *Post-Industrial Cities, Politics and Planning in New York, Paris and London*. Princeton, Princeton University Press.

Schaffer, Frank, 1970. *The New Town Story*. Introduction by Lord Silkin. London, MacGibbon Kee, 257.

Scott, David, 1995. Wholesale privatization may be out, but the days of councils being the main provider of housing are already over. *The Scotsman*, 28 June.

Scott Report, 1942. *Report of the Committee on Land Utilisation in Rural Areas*, Cmnd 6378. Ministry of Works and Planning. London, HMSO.

Scottish Civic Trust, 1972. *The Conservation of Georgian Edinburgh*, eds Sir Robert Matthew, John Reid and Maurice Lindsay. Edinburgh, Edinburgh University Press.

Scottish Development Agency, 1978. *The Future of GEAR: Key Issues and Possible Courses of Action*. Glasgow, GDA.

SDA, 1979. *GEAR Overall Proposals Working Documents*. Glasgow, SDA.

SDA, 1980. *GEAR Strategy and Programme*. Glasgow, SDA.

Scottish Development Department, 1963. *Central Scotland: A Programme for Development and Growth*, Cmnd 2188. Edinburgh, HMSO.

Scottish Office, 1961. *Scottish Planning Mission to the United States – Urban Renewal and Traffic*. Edinburgh, Scottish Development Department.

Seeley, I.H., 1968. *Planned Expansion of Country Towns*. London, G. Godwin.

Sekler, Eduard, 1956. *Wren and His Place in European Architecture*. New York, MacMillan.

Self, Peter, 1957. *Cities in Flood: The Problem of Urban Growth*. London, Faber & Faber.
(1961. Reprinted.)

Self, Peter, 1972. Introduction, in *New Towns: The British Experience*, ed. Hazel Evans. Town and Country Planning Association, Knight & Co.

SERPLAN (South East Regional Planning Conference), 1988. *Housing, Land Supply and Structure Plan Provision in the South-East*. London, SERPLAN.

SERPLAN, 1989. *A New Strategy for the South-East*. London, SERPLAN.

SERPLAN, 1990. *Shaping the South-East Planning Strategy*. London, SERPLAN.

SERPLAN, 1992a. *Housing, Land Supply and Structure Plan Provision in the South-East*. London, SERPLAN.

SERPLAN, 1992b. *SERPLAN: Thirty Years of Regional Planning 1962–1992*. London, SERPLAN.

Sert, Jose Luis, 1942. *Can Our Cities Survive? An ABC of urban problems, their analysis, their solutions based on the proposals formulated by CIAM*. Introduction by Siegfried Giedion. Texts by Le Corbusier, Newton, Maxwell Fry and others. Cambridge, Mass., Harvard University Press.

Sharp, Thomas, 1944. *Cathedral City: A Plan for Durham*. Durham, Architectural Press.

Sharp, Thomas, 1946a. *Exeter Phoenix: A Plan for Rebuilding*. Exeter, Architectural Press.

Sharp, Thomas, 1946b. *The Anatomy of the Village*. London, Penguin.

Sharp, Thomas, 1948. Oxford, Architectural Press.

Sharp, Thomas, 1968. *Town and Townscape*. London, John Murray.

Sheckley, Robert, 1978. *Futuropolis: Impossible Cities of Science Fiction and Fantasy*. New York, A & W Visual Library.

Simmie, James, 1988. *Planning at the Crossroads*. London, University College Press.

Simon, E.D. and Inman, J., 1935. *The Rebuilding of Manchester*. London, Longman and Green.

Sitte, Camillo, 1889. *The Art of Building Cities*. Vienna.
(1961. Reprinted. London, Phaidon Press.)

Skinner, David, 1976. *A Situation Report on Green Belts in Scotland*. Perth, Countryside Commission for Scotland, 7, 9, 14, 19.

Slavid, Ruth, 1995. LDDC prepares timetable for

winding itself down. *Architect's Journal*, 20 July.

South-East Economic Planning Council, 1967. *A Strategy for the South-East*. London, HMSO.

South-East Joint Planning Team, 1970. *Strategic Plan for the South-East*. London, HMSO.

South-East Joint Planning Team, 1976. *Development of the Strategic Plan for the South-East: Interim Report*. London, HMSO.

South Hampshire Plan Advisory Committee, 1972. *South Hampshire Structure Plan*. Hampshire County Council, Portsmouth City Council, Southampton City Council, September.

Spreigregen, Paul, 1965. *Urban Design: The Architecture of Town and Cities*. New York, McGraw-Hill.

Stafford, Frederick, 1995. Meeting the challenge. *Architect's Journal*, 22 June, 43–6.

Stein, Clarence, 1958. *Toward New Town for America*. Liverpool, Liverpool University Press.

Stewarton, M., 1981. *Houses Fit for Heroes: The Politics and Architecture of Early State Housing in Britain*. London, Heinemann.

Storm, Michael, 1965. *Urban Growth in Britain – The Changing World*. Oxford, Oxford University Press, 7.

Summerson, John, 1946. *Georgian London*. New York, Scribner.

Summerson, John, 1949a. *John Nash: Architect to King George IV*. London, Allen and Unwin.

Summerson, John, 1949b. *Heavenly Mansions, and Other Essays on Architecture*. London, Gesset Press, 219.

Summerson, John, 1966. *Inigo Jones*. London, Pelican.

Summerson, John, 1977. The beginnings of Regent's Park. *Journal, Society of Architectural Historians of Great Britain*, Vol. 20, 56–62.

Summerson, John, 1980. *The Life and Work of John Nash, Architect*. London, Allen and Unwin.

Tafuri, M., 1976. *Architecture and Utopia: Design and Capitalist Development*. Cambridge, Mass., MIT Press.

Tarn, J.E., 1980. Emergence of town planning in Britain, in *The Rise of Modern Urban Planning*, ed. Antony Sutcliffe, London, Mansell, 77, 89.

Tetlow, J. and Goss, A., 1976. *Homes, Towns and Traffic*. London, Faber & Faber, 38–47.

Thornley, A., 1991. *Urban Planning under Thatcherism*. London, Routledge.

Tibbalds, Francis, 1988. Urban design: Tibbalds offers the Prince his Ten Commandments. *The Planner*, Vol. 74, No. 12–1.

Tibbalds, Francis, 1992a. *Making People Friendly Towns: Improving the Public Environment in Towns and Cities*. London, Longman.

Tibbalds, Francis, 1992b. Mind the gap! A personalised view of the value of urban design in the late twentieth century. *The Planner*, Vol. 74, No. 311–15.

Tod, Ian and Wheeler, Michael, 1978. *Utopia*. New York, Harmony Books.

Town and Country Planning Association, 1971. Vol. 39, No. 1, January.

Townshend, T. and Kerrin, Christine, 1996. Administering a dose of restorative salts. *Planning Week*, Vol. 4, No. 37, 12 September.

Tripp, Sir Herbert Alker, 1942. *Town Planning and Road Traffic*. London, Edward Arnold. (1946. Reprinted.)

Tudor Walters Report, 1918. *The Report of the Committee on Building Construction in Connection with the Provision of Dwellings for the Working Classes in England and Wales, and Scotland*, Cmnd 9191. London, HMSO.

Turner, Ian, 1990. First SPZs success. *The Planner*, Vol. 76, No. 3, January.

Tyrwhitt, Jacqueline, 1945. Surveys for planning, in Association for Planning and Reconstruction, *Town and Country Planning Textbook*. London, Architectural Press, 146–78.

Tyrwhitt, Jacqueline, 1947. *Patrick Geddes in India*. London, Lund Humphries.

Tyrwhitt, Jacqueline and Waiden, W.L., 1949. *Basic Surveys for Planning*. The Architect and Building News. London.

Tyrwhitt, J., Sert, J.L. and Rogers, E.N. (eds), 1952. *The Heart of the City*. New York, Pelligrini and Cudahy.

Unilever, 1976. *Port Sunlight Village, Merseyside*. Unilever Services Co., Lever House.

University of Edinburgh, 1964. *Comparative Urban Spaces*. Civic Design Diploma Studio, University of Edinburgh.

Unwin, Raymond, 1909. *Town Planning in Practice: an Introduction to the Art of Designing Cities and Suburbs*. London, T. Fisher Unwin.

Unwin, Raymond, 1912. *Nothing Gained from Overcrowding: How the Garden City Type of Development may Benefit both Owner and Occupier*. London, P.S. King; London Garden Cities and Town Planning Association.

Uthwatt Report, 1941. *Interim Report of the Expert Committee on Compensation and Betterment*, Cmnd 6291. London, HMSO.

Venturi, Robert, 1966. *Complexity and Contradiction in Architecture*. New York, Museum of Modern Art.

(1977. Reprinted.)

Venturi, Robert and Scott-Brown, Denise, 1972. *Learning from Las Vegas*. Cambridge, Mass., MIT Press.

Venturi, Robert and Scott-Brown, Denise, 1984. *A View from the Campidoglio: Selected Essays 1953–1984*. New York, Harper & Row.

Venturi, Robert and Scott-Brown, Denise, 1992. Interviews, Philadelphia, Pa.

Vitruvius, 27 BC. *De Architectura*.

Vitruvius, 1914. *The Ten Books on Architecture*, translated by Morris Morgan. Cambridge, Mass., Harvard University Press.

 (1960. Reprinted. New York, Dover.)

Ward, Colin (ed.), 1973. *Vandalism*. London, Architectural Press.

Ward, Colin (ed.), 1993. *New Town Home Town*. London, Calouste Gulbenkian Foundation.

Ward, Stephen, 1994. *Planning and Urban Change*. London, Paul Chapman.

Webber, Melvin, 1964. The urban place and the non-place realm, in *Explorations into Urban Structure*, ed. Donald Foley. Philadelphia, University of Pennsylvania Press.

 (1968. Reprinted.)

Westminster City Council, 1974. *City of Westminster Development Plan, Leisure in Westminster*. December.

Wheatley Report, 1969. *Scotland: Local Government Reform. Report of the Royal Commission on Local Government in Scotland*, Cmnd 4150–1. Edinburgh, HMSO.

Wiebenson, Dora, 1969. *Tony Garnier: The Cité Industrielle*. London, Studio Vista.

Wiedenhoeft, Ronald, 1975. Planning for pedestrians. *The Planner*, Vol. 61, June, 228–31.

Wilkes, Lyall and Dodds, Gordon, 1964. *Tyneside Classical: the Newcastle of Grainger, Dobson and Clayton*. London, John Murray.

Willis, Margaret, 1972. Sociological aspects of urban structure, in *Human Identity in the Urban Environment*, eds G. Bell and J. Tyrwhitt. London, Hutchinson, 262–76.

Wilson, Hugh, 1956. *Cumbernauld Master Plan*. Cumbernauld Development Corporation.

Winchester City Council, 1983. Draft local plans. Winchester City Council.

Wolf, Peter M., 1968. *Eugene Hénard and the Beginning of Urbanism in Paris 1900–1914*. The Hague, International Federation of Housing and Planning.

Worskett, Roy, 1970. *The Character of Towns*. London, Architectural Press.

Wright, Michael, 1977. Conserving a wool town – Cirencester, Gloucestershire. *Country Life*, 21 July, 135.

Young, M. and Wilmott, P., 1957. *Family and Kinship in East London*. London, Routledge and Kegan Paul.

Youngson, A.J., 1966. *The Making of Classical Edinburgh 1750–1840*. Edinburgh, Edinburgh University Press.

Zucker, Paul, 1959. *Town and Square*. New York, Columbia University Press.

Index